A Brit's Guide
to
☀rlando
and
Walt Disney World

2005

★

Simon Ve

foulsham
LONDON • NEW YORK • TORONTO • SYDNEY

foulsham

The Publishing House, Bennetts Close, Cippenham, Berkshire, SL1 5AP, England

While every effort has been made to ensure the accuracy of all the information contained within this book, neither the author nor the publisher can be liable for any errors. In particular, since prices, times and any holiday or hotel details change on a regular basis, it is vital that each individual check relevant information for themselves.

ISBN 0-572-03037-1

Text copyright © 2005 Simon Veness

Series, format, logo and layout design copyright © 2005 W. Foulsham & Co. Ltd

A CIP record for this book is available from the British Library

Other books in this series:
A Brit's Guide to Las Vegas 2004–2005, Karen Marchbank, 0-572-02926-8
Choosing A Cruise, 6th edition, Simon Veness, 0-572-02946-2
A Brit's Guide to Disneyland Resort Paris 2004–2005, Simon Veness, 0-572-02949-7
A Brit's Guide to New York 2005, Karen Marchbank with Amanda Statham, 0-572-03033-9

SPECIAL THANKS

First and foremost to Susan Haass for her non-stop energy and support, plus her priceless researching and writing that now go into every edition.

Special thanks for this edition go to: Travel City Direct, The Walt Disney Company, Alamo Rent A Car, Virgin Holidays, Universal Orlando, Orlando Convention and Visitors Bureau, Kissimmee Convention and Visitors Bureau, Synergy and Anheuser-Busch Parks, The Royal Pacific Resort, The Sheraton Studio City Hotel, The Doubletree Club Lake Buena Vista, ResortQuest Orlando, The Reunion Resort, The Hard Rock Hotel, Disney's Pop Century Resort, The Portofino Bay Hotel, Renaissance Orlando Resort, Walt Disney World Swan and Dolphin Hotels, The Bahama Bay Resort.

My sincere thanks also go to all the hard-working people at Foulsham who help to bring my work to life every year, plus editor Caroline Radula-Scott.

Printed in Malaysia

Contents

8. Off The Beaten Track

(or, When You're All Theme-Parked Out). A taste of the real Florida: Winter Park, Aquatic Wonders Boat Tours, airboat rides and parasail, Cypress Glades Adventure Tours, balloon trips, Everglades and the Bahamas, Flying Tigers Warbird Restoration Museum and Warbird Adventures, Green Meadows Petting Farm, Osceola County Pioneer Museum, Reptile World Serpentarium, Disney and cruising, Seminole County, Florida Eco-Safaris, Disney's Wilderness Preserve. Beaches: St Pete's/Clearwater, Cocoa Beach and Daytona. Sports: golf, fishing, water sports, horse riding, spectator sports and Disney's Wide World of Sports Complex™, fitness centres, rodeo, motor sport.

9. Orlando by Night

(or, Burning the Candle at Both Ends). Downtown Disney, Cirque du Soleil, Disney's Boardwalk, Universal's CityWalk, Pointe*Orlando. Dinner shows: Disney shows, Arabian Nights, Pirate's Dinner Adventure, Medieval Times, Sleuth's Mystery Dinner Shows, WonderWorks: The Outta Control Magic Show, Dolly Parton's Dixie Stampede, Gator Safari by Night. Theatre, nightclubs, live music, bars.

10. Dining Out

((or, Man, These Portions Are Huge!). Full guide to local-style eating and drinking, rundown of the fast-food outlets, best family restaurants, American diners and speciality restaurants.

11. Shopping

(or, How to Send Your Credit Card into Meltdown). Your duty-free allowances, full guide to the main tourist shopping complexes, discount outlets, flea markets, malls, supermarkets and speciality shops.

12. Going Home

(or, Where Did the Last Two Weeks Go?). Avoiding last-minute snags, returning the car, full guide to Orlando International and Orlando Sanford Airports and their facilities for the journey home. Where next? (guide to Orlando's low-cost airlines).

13. Your Holiday Planner

Examples of how to plan for a 2-week holiday with a Disney 5-Day Hopper Plus Ticket. And the Theme Parks' Busy Day Guide.

Foreword

Welcome to the start of a brand new adventure in the most exciting holiday destination on earth; and welcome to an exciting new era in the development of the Brit's Guide series with the launch of our own website and a host of new services and opportunities on our 10th anniversary! This is where the fun really starts and you can begin preparing for a truly magical and memorable time.

Orlando has developed in astonishing fashion since Walter Elias Disney decided it suited his plans for a new style of theme park entertainment under the title Project X in 1966. And, although the master entertainer himself had some pretty detailed and creative ideas, even he might have been amazed at how central Florida has flowered ever since.

In simple terms, this is Entertainment Central – a region dedicated to ensuring people have the most wonderful and enchanting holiday possible. Nowhere else is your choice of attractions so broad and detailed, and things continue to change all the time. Of course, that means it can be confusing, vexing and tiring (especially the latter), but you have definitely made the right start by choosing us to provide the full inside track on how to get the very most out of your holiday.

*This 10th edition of Britain's best-selling guidebook continues to represent the most user-friendly and authoritative companion to all that lies in store, especially if used with our new website www.askdaisy.net/orlando, and our internet partners – the world's biggest information resource on all things Disney – www.wdwinfo.com. I believe we write and research with a tourist's eye for detail and value, including all the info you really need, not what the brochures want you to believe. We aim to give you a good idea of what to expect and how to plan and budget for it. Our exciting new online **Personalised Itinerary Planner** (see page 46) then goes a step further with the chance for us to tailor-make your own holiday campaign.*

The area also remains vigorously engaged in making things newer, bigger and better almost by the week. So here at the Brit's Guide, we are constantly looking to add new features and info according to the vast amount of feedback we receive. The website is a major step forward in this, but we have other extra sections this time, including the best FREE things to do and how to explore further afield using several of the low-cost airlines in Orlando. It is quite a challenge keeping up with it all, but I can't pretend it isn't also great fun (see pic!).

After more than 50 visits, Orlando has become quite a second home for me, so much so I now have a regular base there to be sure I stay in touch with it all. There is so much to do and see, I am determined to help you get the most out of your visit to central Florida. More significantly, you'll get the inside track on how to have the best holiday, at the best price and with the least fuss. Prepare to be amazed (and exhausted!) by what's in store, but don't say I didn't tell you so. Now, excuse me while I put my feet up for a while… have a nice day now.

Simon Veness

(email me at simonveness@yahoo.co.uk or visit www.askdaisy,net/orlando or www.wdwinfo.com)

1 Introduction
(or, *Welcome to the Holiday of a Lifetime*)

Welcome to the most exciting holiday experience in the world, bar none, guaranteed. This area of central Florida we call Orlando is a vast conglomeration of adventure rides, thrills, fun and fantasy the like of which exists nowhere else, and we are not talking just about the *Walt Disney World Resort in Florida* here.

First off, you need to be aware of the bewilderingly extensive and complex nature of this tourist wonderland. Disney remains the leading attraction in town, but there is a strong supporting cast, of which Universal Orlando and SeaWorld are outstanding examples.

There is something to suit all tastes and ages – young or old, families, couples or singles – but it exacts a high physical toll. You'll walk a lot, queue a lot and probably eat a lot. You will have a fabulous time, but you'll end up exhausted as well. It is not so much a holiday as an exercise in military planning.

Eight theme parks

In simple terms, there are now eight major theme parks that are generally reckoned to be essential holiday fare, and at least one of those will require 2 days to make you feel it has been well and truly done. Add on a day at one of the water parks, a trip to see some of the wildlife or other more 'natural' attractions, and the lure of the nearby Kennedy Space Center,

and you're talking of at least 12 days of pure adventure-mania. Then mix in the night-time attractions of *Downtown Disney*, Universal's CityWalk and a host of dinner shows, and you get an idea of the awesome scale of the entertainment on offer. Even with 2 weeks, something has to give – just make sure that it isn't your patience/pocket/sanity!

So, how do we innocents abroad, many of us making our first visit to the good ol' USA, get full value from what is still, without doubt, a truly magical holiday?

There is no guaranteed answer, but there are some pretty solid guidelines to steer you in the right direction and help avoid some of the more obvious pitfalls. Central to most of them is **planning**. At the back of this guide there is a useful 'calendar' to use as a ready reference guide. Don't be inflexible, but be aware of the time demands of the parks and allow a quiet day or two by the pool or at one of the smaller attractions to recover your strength. With so much on offer, it simply isn't possible to do it all, so try to ensure you get full value for what you do decide to do.

Also, be aware of the vast scale and complexity of this wonderland, and try to take in as much of the clever detail and breadth of imagination on offer, especially in the Disney parks.

Orlando

Orlando itself is a relatively small but bright young city which has been taken over to the immediate south-west by *Walt Disney World Resort in Florida*, to give it its full title, which opened with the *Magic Kingdom* Park in 1971 and has encouraged a massive tourist expansion ever since. New attractions are popping up all the time and it is easy to get carried away by the artificial (and highly commercial) fantasy of it all. However, there is still a genuine concern for the environment, and there are only a few areas where the development looks as if it is out of hand.

The tourist area generally known as Orlando actually consists of three counties. Orange County is the home of the city of Orlando, but much of Disney's fun and frolics are to be found in Osceola County, with Kissimmee its main town. Seminole County, home of Orlando Sanford Airport, is north of Orange County.

The local population tops the 1.8 million mark, of which some 244,000 are actively employed in the tourist business. But, in 2003, more than 40 million people made Orlando their holiday choice, spending in excess of $20 billion in the area.

Britain accounts for more than 40 per cent of all foreign visitors to Orlando, and in 2003 that was almost 1 million of us. Those figures represent a huge increase in the last ten years (even allowing for a dip after September 11), with the international airport seeing its traffic boom from 8 million passengers in 1983 to a massive 30 million just 17 years later. In addition, the Orlando area boasts more than 112,000 hotel rooms and 4,000-plus places to eat. And shopaholics have the choice of an amazing 250 shopping centres, including 30 malls. But let's give you a quick taste of the main attractions.

> **BRIT TIP:** The 10th anniversary edition of the *Brit's Guide* is now up to 312 pages – we started with only 180, indicating just how the area has grown since then.

Walt Disney World Resort in Florida

This is where the 'Magic' really starts – and the effect is vividly real. This vast resort actually consists of four distinct, separate theme parks, 20 speciality hotel resorts, a camping ground, two water parks, a sports complex, five 18-hole golf courses, four mini-golf courses and a huge shopping and entertainment complex (*Downtown Disney*). It covers 47 sq miles (122 sq km). The likes of Alton Towers and Thorpe Park would comfortably fit into its car parking space! Indeed, Alton Towers, Britain's biggest theme park, is 60 times smaller. Disney's most popular park, the *Magic Kingdom* Park, has a single-day record attendance in the region of 92,000 – most British parks peak at around 20,000. The Disney organisation does things with the most style, but the others have caught on fast and are rapidly creating new amenities.

Intriguingly, less than half of Disney's massive site has been developed, leaving plenty of room for new accommodation and attractions, while even the existing parks have potential for an extra ride or two, and there are several major projects on the drawing board. Disney maintains an extremely high level of customer service and is always looking at ways to refresh the existing attractions. Everyone who works for Disney is officially a Cast Member, not just staff, and they take that ethic to heart.

FLORIDA

How far from Orlando to . . .

Bradenton 130 miles/210km	Miami 220 miles/354km
Clearwater 110 miles/176km	Naples 230 miles/370km
Cocoa Beach 40 miles/64km	Sarasota 140 miles/225km
Daytona 60 miles/97km	Silver Springs 80 miles/129km
Fort Lauderdale . . 205 miles/330km	St Augustine 120 miles/193km
Fort Myers 190 miles/306km	St Petersburg 105 miles169km
Jacksonville 155 miles/250km	Tampa 75 miles/120km
Key West 375 miles/604km	Venice 160 miles/257km

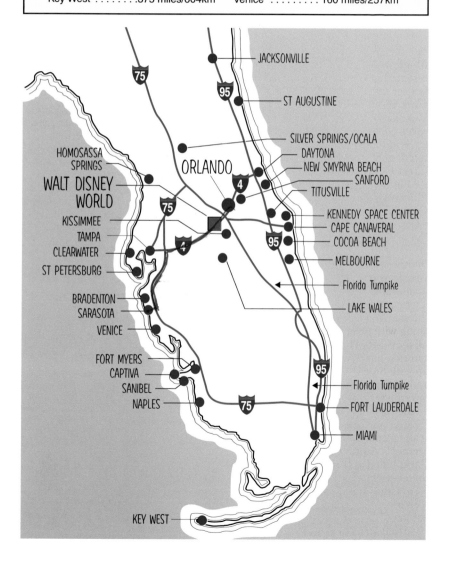

© Disney

Sleeping Beauty

Here's a quick rundown of what's on offer:

Magic Kingdom Park: this is the essential Disney, including the fantasy of their wonderful animated films, the adventures of the Wild West and Africa, the excitement of thrill rides like Space Mountain (a huge indoor roller-coaster), the fun of new attraction Stitch's Great Escape and the fabulous 3-D film amusement of Mickey's PhilharMagic.

Epcot: Disney's look at the world of tomorrow through the gates of Future World, plus a potted journey around our planet in World Showcase. More educational than adventurous, it still possesses some memorable rides, including Test Track and Universe of Energy, plus the amazing new Mission: SPACE, along with some superb dining.

Disney-MGM Studios: here you can ride the movies in style, meeting up with Star Wars™, the Muppets and Indiana Jones, and you can drop into the fearsome Tower of Terror or the thrilling Rock 'n Roller Coaster and learn how films are really made.

Disney's Animal Kingdom Theme Park: billed as 'a new species of theme park', this delivers another contrasting and hugely entertaining scenario. With realistic animal habitats, including a 100-acre (40.5-ha) safari savannah, captivating shows and several terrific rides, it offers a pleasant change of pace from the other parks.

Disney's Typhoon Lagoon Water Park: bring your cozzie and spend a lazy day splashing down water-slides and learning to surf in the world's biggest man-made lagoon.

Disney's Blizzard Beach Water Park: the big brother of all the water parks, this has a massive spread of rides and slides in a 'snowy' environment.

Downtown Disney: this incorporates *Pleasure Island*, Marketplace and the West Side with themed restaurants, a cinema multiplex, the *DisneyQuest* arcade of interactive games, Virgin Megastore and the world-famous Cirque du Soleil® company. New Year's Eve is the *Pleasure Island* theme, with eight nightclubs. The picture-perfect **Wedding Pavilion**, which appears in many brochures and offers marriage ceremonies in fairytale style, is another Disney feature.

The other parks

If you think Orlando is all about Disney, you will be pleasantly surprised at the huge range of other attractions on offer.

Universal Orlando is the other big resort development, with a choice of two theme parks, water park, wonderful entertainment district and three speciality hotels.

Water Mania

WATER MAN

Universal Studios: here you Ride The Movies as you encounter Jaws, the Men In Black and Back to the Future, the new Shrek 4-D show and stunning Revenge of the Mummy ride, plus Woody Woodpecker's KidZone and the amazing Terminator 2: 3-D Battle Across Time.

Islands of Adventure: new in 1999, Universal's second park is a superb blend of thrill rides, family attractions, shows and awesome, eye-catching design, with some of the most technologically advanced hardware in the world.

Wet 'n Wild: although on International Drive (I-Drive), this water park is Universal-owned and offers plenty of fun rides and slides.

SeaWorld: don't be put off thinking it's just another dolphin show, this is *the* place for the creatures of the deep, with killer whales being the main attraction, a bright, refreshing atmosphere (check out the new Waterfront district) and a pleasingly serious ecological approach, plus the 5-star thrill rides Journey to Atlantis and Kraken. SeaWorld also has an exclusive neighbour, **Discovery Cove**, which offers the chance to swim with dolphins, among other things.

Busch Gardens: the sister park to SeaWorld, here it's creatures of the land, with the highlights being the Rhino Rally ride, Myombe Reserve, a close-up look at the endangered central African highland gorillas, the Edge of Africa safari experience, and the new Haunted Lighthouse 3-D film show. A real treat, plus a number of brain-numbing roller-coasters and other rides.

More attractions include: **Kennedy Space Center:** the dramatically upgraded home of space exploration; **Silver Springs:** a close look at Florida's nature via jeep and boat safaris through real swampland, with a delightful, natural feel; **Fantasy of Flight:** an aviation

BRIT TIP: Be wary of travel agent pressure to buy too many tickets. You may well find you can't fit everything in, plus, for some attractions, you can often buy cheaper in Orlando, even from the tour operators' reps.

museum experience with the world's largest private collection of vintage aircraft, plus fighter-plane simulators; and **Cypress Gardens:** Florida's oldest 'theme park', reborn in 2004 with coasters and other rides as well as their wonderful gardens.

Disney tickets

Most people buy one of the multi-day passes which allows you to move between the theme parks on the same day and grants unlimited access to the monorails, buses and ferries (always get your hand stamped if you leave one park but intend to return). Make no mistake, you can't walk between the parks (except for a fairly long haul between *Epcot* and *Disney-*

BRIT TIP: Buy Disney Park Hopper and Park Hopper Plus tickets in advance, NOT at the park gates. You will save time AND money as there is a built-in advance purchase discount.

MGM Studios), and trying to do more than one in a day is seriously hard work. The choice of tickets is bewildering, so make sure you buy ONLY what you need.

All multi-day passes offer savings against buying **1-Day Tickets**, and

CHOOSING A TICKET

Ticket Type	*Park*	*Allowance*
1-Day Ticket	Any Disney park, Universal Orlando parks, SeaWorld or Busch Gardens; not available in advance	Access to one park ONLY for one day
4- or 5-Day Park Hopper	*Magic Kingdom Park, Epcot, Disney-MGM Studios, Disney's Animal Kingdom Theme Park*	Access for 4 or 5 days, with multiple parks on same day; valid until all days are used up
5-, 6- or 7-Day Park Hopper Plus	*Magic Kingdom Park, Epcot, Disney-MGM Studios, Disney's Animal Kingdom Theme Park*	Access for 5/6/7 days, with multiple same-day visits, plus 2/3/4 visits to any of *Disney's Blizzard Beach* and *Typhoon Lagoon* water parks, *Pleasure Island* and *Disney's Wide World of Sports Complex*™ (excluding special events)
Ultimate Park Hopper	All Disney parks; available with Disney resort stay only	Access to all parks, *Pleasure Island, DisneyQuest* and *Disney's Wide World of Sports Complex*™ for the length of stay, plus extras like 'kids eat free' at hotel. Price according to length of stay
10-Day World Ticket	All Disney parks; available only in advance in the UK	Access for 10 days to all parks, *Pleasure Island, DisneyQuest* and *Disney's Wide World of Sports Complex*™ (excluding special events), plus a free character breakfast. Expires 20 days after first use
Annual Pass	*Magic Kingdom Park, Epcot, Disney-MGM Studios, Disney's Animal Kingdom Theme Park;* includes numerous discounts for shops, restaurants and tours	Unlimited admission and free parking for 365 days after purchase date. If ordered online, you get a voucher which must be activated at a park. The 365 days start on the day you first activate the pass
Premium Annual Pass	All Disney parks; includes numerous discounts for shops, restaurants and tours	Unlimited admission and free parking for 365 days after purchase date; plus discounts on sports and recreation
2-Day 2-Park Ticket	Universal Studios, Islands of Adventure, CityWalk	Access to both parks, including both on same day, plus clubs of CityWalk
3-Day Ticket	Universal Studios, Islands of Adventure, CityWalk	Access to both parks, including both on same day, plus clubs of CityWalk
Universal Bonus Pass	Universal Studios, Islands of Adventure, CityWalk; available online only	Access to both parks, including both on same day, plus clubs of CityWalk, for five consecutive days from first use
4-Park FlexTicket	Universal Studios, Islands of Adventure, SeaWorld and Wet 'n Wild, plus CityWalk	Access to all four parks, with multiple parks on same day, for 14 days from first use, plus clubs of CityWalk
5-Park FlexTicket	Universal Studios, Islands of Adventure, SeaWorld, Wet 'n Wild, Busch Gardens.	Access to all five parks, with multiple parks on same day, for 14 days from first use, plus clubs of CityWalk
Adventure Passport	SeaWorld and Busch Gardens	Access to both parks for 21 consecutive days from first use

ORLANDO – MAIN ATTRACTIONS AND ROUTES

A   Magic Kingdom Park
B   Epcot
C   Disney-MGM Studios
D   Universal Orlando
E   SeaWorld Adventure Park
F   Busch Gardens
G   Kennedy Space Center
H   US Astronaut Hall of Fame
I   Cypress Gardens
J   Historic Bok Sanctuary
K   Silver Springs
L   Gatorland
M   Disney's Typhoon Lagoon Water Park

N   Disney's Blizzard Beach Water Park
O   Festival Bay
P   Water Mania
Q   Wet 'n Wild
R   Discovery Cove by SeaWorld
S   Holy Land Experience
T   Ripley's Believe It or Not
U   Hard Rock Vault/Titanic – The Exhibition
V   Orange County History Center
W   Downtown Disney area
X   Green Meadows Petting Farm
Y   Fantasy of Flight
Z   Disney's Animal Kingdom Park

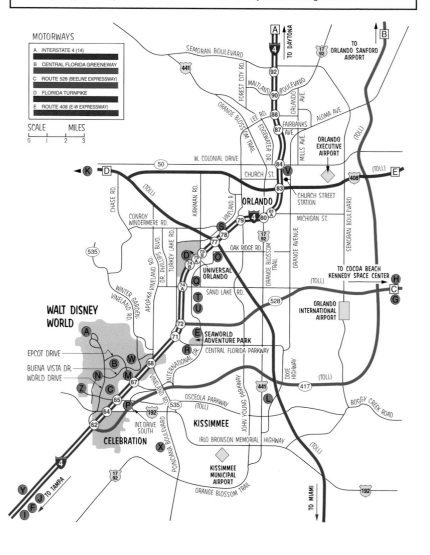

MOTORWAYS

A   INTERSTATE 4 (14)
B   CENTRAL FLORIDA GREENEWAY
C   ROUTE 528 (BEELINE EXPRESSWAY)
D   FLORIDA TURNPIKE
E   ROUTE 408 (E-W EXPRESSWAY)

SCALE   MILES
0   1   2   3

Downtown Orlando skyline

unused days never expire, so can be saved for the future. In the UK, you can buy the **5-, 6-** and **7-Day Park Hopper Plus** and **10-Day World Ticket** through tour operators, ticket brokers and Disney Stores.

In summer 2004, the **10-Day World Ticket** was possibly the best value at £189 for adults and £151 for children (3–9), as against its regular price of £259 and £208. Guests at Disney hotels can buy an **Ultimate Park Hopper** ticket for the length of their visit but, for stays longer than 2 weeks, it is worth considering the **Annual Pass** or **Premium Annual Pass** (check the Ticket Prices section on www.wdwinfo.com).

Other tickets

When it comes to Universal Orlando, SeaWorld and Busch Gardens, the choice is simpler. Again, you have **1-, 2-** and **3-Day Tickets** (in 2004, the 3-Day Ticket was extended to give 14 successive days' admission) while for CityWalk, Universal's answer to *Downtown Disney*, there is also a **CityWalk Party Pass** ($9.95 plus tax) or a **Party Pass with Movie** ($13), as the centre has a 20-screen cinema. Better value are the **Orlando FlexTickets**, which are valid for 14 days from first use. There is even a **Universal Bonus Pass** online at www.universalorlando.com for 5 consecutive days for the price of a 2-day ticket. A trip to the exclusive **Discovery Cove** includes a **free 10-Day Pass** for SeaWorld, too.

With price hikes every year, it is worth buying your tickets as soon as you book. However, **tour operators** can be above gate prices for the convenience of being able to book early and budget for your main costs, so I recommend shopping around: **Keith Prowse** (08701 232425, www.keithprowsetickets.com or see your travel agent) is the premium advance sales ticket outlet in the UK, with competitive prices AND early booking convenience, while they do several one-off tickets (notably a 2-day Gatorland ticket), excursions (to the likes of Kennedy Space Center and Clearwater) and 2-day trips further afield (Miami–Bahamas) plus an array of Orlando dining options. They also supply the actual tickets (as opposed to a voucher for exchange at a ticket booth), and are fully ABTA bonded for your security. Other worthwhile agencies with real tickets and ABTA bonding are **Theme Park Holidays** (www.themeparkholidays.com, 0870 240 2510), who also offers car hire and accommodation, **Attraction Tickets Direct** (0845 130 3876, www.attractionticketsdirect.com), who promises no credit card fees and free delivery in 7 days (plus car hire, dinners shows and Kennedy Space Center, as well as an online Florida Forum), and **Holiday Travel Essentials** (01444 231486, www.attractiontickets4less.com). There are numerous others, but these four all guarantee the right product, with the right service and

Summer Bay Resort

BRIT TIP: The humidity levels – up to 100% – and fierce daily rainstorms in summer take a lot of visitors by surprise, so carry a lightweight, rainproof jacket or buy a cheap plastic poncho locally.

the right level of local knowledge. (For more information on tickets see Chapters 5 and 6.)

A first word of warning: you don't want to try to do the main parks in one chunk. Apart from ending up with serious theme park indigestion, you'll probably also hit one of them on a busy day (check the Busy Day Guide on page 305). The *Magic Kingdom* Park and *Epcot* can be particularly exhausting (especially with children) and you'll need a quiet day afterwards.

The climate

The next question is when to go? Florida's weather does vary from bright but cool winter days in November, December and January, with the odd drizzly spell, to furiously hot and humid summers punctuated with tropical downpours.

The most pleasant option is to go in between the two extremes in spring or autumn. You will also avoid the worst of the crowds. However, as most families are governed by school holidays, July to September remain the popular months for British visitors, and so this guide contains advice on how to get one jump ahead of the high-season crush.

And now to business: it's big, brash and fun, but above all it's American and that means everything is well organised, with a tendency towards the raucous rather than the reserved. It's clean, well maintained

and anxious to please: Floridians generally are an affable bunch, but they take affability to new heights in the theme parks, where staff are almost painfully keen to make sure you 'have a nice day'.

Tipping

Close to every American's heart is the custom of tipping. With the exception of petrol pump attendants and fast-food restaurant servers, just about everyone who offers you any sort of service in hotels, bars, restaurants, buses, taxis, airports and other public amenities will expect a tip. In bars, restaurants and taxis, 15 per cent of the bill is the usual rate while porters will expect $1 per bag and chamber maids $1 a day per adult before they make up your room. As all service industry workers are taxed on the assumption of receiving 15% in tips, whether they do receive it or not, it's important not to forget those few extra dollars.

BRIT TIP:
Tipping Guide

Bill	Suggested Tip
$15	$2.25
$20	$3.00
$25	$3.75
$30	$4.50
$40	$6.00
$50	$7.50

Visa requirements

Holiday visitors to America do not need a visa providing they hold a valid British *machine-readable* passport showing they are a British citizen (ALL members of the family must have their own passport which does not expire for 90 days from the time of entry). Instead, all you do is fill in a green visa waiver form

Orlando timeline

Here's the full list of how the area has grown since Disney first opened its doors in Florida.

1971: MAGIC KINGDOM PARK (MK)

1973: Pirates of the Caribbean and Tom Sawyer Island (MK); Church Street Station; SEAWORLD (SW)

1974: Star Jets (now Astro Orbiter) (MK)

1975: Space Mountain and WEDway People Mover (now Tomorrowland Transit Authority) (MK); Central Florida Zoo

1976: River Country; Mystery Fun House (closed 2001)

1977: WET 'N WILD (WW)

1980: Big Thunder Mountain Railroad (MK)

1982: EPCOT (E)

1983: Journey into Imagination pavilion (now Imagination) (E); Medieval Times Dinner Tournament

1984: Morocco pavilion (E)

1986: The Living Seas (E)

1987: Fort Liberty

1988: Wonders of Life and Norway pavilion (E); Mickey's Birthdayland (now Mickey's Toontown Fair) (MK); Flying Tigers Warbird Restoration Museum; Arabian Nights Dinner Show

1989: DISNEY-MGM STUDIOS (MGM); Body Wars and Cranium Command (E); Typhoon Lagoon, Pleasure Island, Green Meadows Petting Farm

1990: Star Tours and Honey I Shrunk the Kids Movie Set Adventure (MGM); Mickey's Starland (replaced Mickey's Birthdayland) (MK); UNIVERSAL STUDIOS (U)

1991: Jim Henson's Muppet*Vision 3-D (MGM); SpectroMagic parade (MK); Terror On Church Street (closed 1999)

1992: Splash Mountain (MK); The Voyage of the Little Mermaid (MGM); Ripley's Believe It or Not!

1993: New production of Hall of Presidents (MK); Kumba in Busch Gardens (BG); A World of Orchids; Splendid China (closed 2003)

1994: Legend of the Lion King (E); Innoventions (E); Honey, I Shrunk the Audience (replaced Captain EO) (MGM); Food Rocks (replaced Kitchen Kabaret) (E), The Twilight Zone™ Tower of Terror (MGM); Planet Hollywood

1995: The Circle of Life (E); Extra TERRORestrial Alien Encounter (MK); Blizzard Beach; Disney's Wilderness Lodge; Fantasy of Flight

1996: Mickey's Toontown Fair (replaced Starland) (MK); Ellen's Energy Adventure (E); Disney's The Hunchback of Notre Dame (closed 2003)(MGM); Fantasia Gardens; Mini-Golf; Celebration; Boardwalk; Pirate's Dinner Adventure; Montu (BG)

1997: Downtown Disney West Side; Disney's Wide World of Sports Complex; Skull Kingdom; The Edge of Africa (BG)

1998: DISNEY'S ANIMAL KINGDOM THEME PARK (AK); Buzz Lightyear's Space Ranger Spin and Enchanted Tiki Room – Under New Management (MK); Fantasmic! (MGM); Journey to Atlantis (SW); DisneyQuest; Disney Cruise Line; The Pointe*Orlando, WonderWorks; Lake Buena Vista Factory Stores

1999: Sounds Dangerous starring Drew Carey and Rock 'n Roller Coaster starring Aerosmith (MGM); Kali River Rapids and Maharajah Jungle Trek (AK); Test Track (E); The Many Adventures of Winnie the Pooh (MK); Gwazi (BG); Cirque du Soleil®; ISLANDS OF ADVENTURE (IoA) and CityWalk; Titanic – The Exhibition

2000: Journey Into Your Imagination (now Journey Into Your Imagination with Figment) (E); Storm Force and Flying Unicorn (IoA); Kraken (SW); Discovery Cove; Guinness World Records Experience (now Hard Rock Vault); Orlando Premium Outlets

2001: Who Wants to Be A Millionaire – Play It! (MGM); The Magic Carpets of Aladdin (MK); Rhino Rally (BG); The Holy Land Experience; Disney's Animal Kingdom Lodge;

2002: Chester and Hester's DinoRama, TriceraTOP Spin and Primeval Whirl (AK); Men in Black – Alien Attack (U); The Scriptorium: Center for Biblical Antiquities (Holy Land Experience)

2003: Mission:SPACE (E); Goofy's Country Dancin' Jamboree and Mickey's PhilharMagic (replaced Legend of the Lion King) (MK); Jimmy Neutron's Nicktoon Blast and Shrek 4-D (U); Waterfront, Odyssea, Sharks Deep Dive (SW). R L Stine's Haunted Lighthouse (BG). Dolly Parton's Dixie Stampede; Festival Bay; Hard Rock Vault; Mall at Millennia; Disney's Pop Century Resort

2004: Wishes firework display and Stitch's Great Escape (MK); Revenge of The Mummy (U); Fusion and Mistify (SW); Cheetah Chase and KaTonga (BG); The Blast (WW); Disney's Saratoga Springs Resort & Spa

2005: Motors, Action! Stunt Show (MGM); Soarin' (E); Cinderellabration (MK)

The Cadillac Diner in Kissimmee

(usually given out on your flight or when you check in) and hand it in with your passport to the US immigration official who checks you through after landing.

However, British subjects AND those who do not have a *machine-readable* passport DO need a visa (£60), and should apply at least 2 months in advance to the US Embassy (see right).

Some travellers may NOT be eligible to enter under the visa waiver programme and will have to apply for a special restricted visa or they

BRIT TIP: The new US-VISIT immigration programme requires ALL visitors to give fingerprints and photo ID on arrival, which may slow things down a touch, but the process is pretty simple – first, left index finger then right index finger on their glass panel, then stand still for the camera.

may be refused entry. This applies to those who have been arrested in the past (even if the arrest did not result in a conviction), have a criminal record, (the Rehabilitation of Offenders Act does not apply to US visa law), or have a certain serious communicable illness, or have previously been refused admission into, or have been deported from, the US, or have previously overstayed on the visa waiver programme. (Minor traffic offences which did not result in an arrest and/or conviction do not count.)

In England, Scotland and Wales write to the Visa Office, US Embassy, 5 Upper Grosvenor Street, London W1A 2JB (0891 200 290). In Northern Ireland, write to US Consulate General, 3 Queens House, 14 Queen Street, Belfast BT1 6EQ. You can call 0906 8200 290 (60p per minute) for more detailed advice, or visit www.usembassy.org.uk.

What's new

In keeping with Orlando's tradition for providing an ever-changing profile of attractions, there is much that is new in this region of the Sunshine State.

Walt Disney World Resort in Florida® remains at the forefront with four of their latest attractions, another in the offing and a celebration to mark the 50th anniversary of *Disneyland Resort in California*, Walt's original park.

Manatees at Blue Spring

Mural at Kissimmee

In the *Magic Kingdom* Park, **Stitch's Great Escape** was brand new in autumn 2004, while the park is also introducing Cinderellabration, a show borrowed from *Tokyo Disneyland Park* as part of the 'Happiest Celebration on Earth' anniversary starting on 5 May, 2005. At *Epcot*, the blockbuster simulator ride Soarin' is coming from California, while *Disney-MGM Studios* is getting a version of the amazing **Lights! Motors! Action!**™ **Extreme Stunt Show** from *Disneyland® Resort Paris*. *Disney's Animal Kingdom Park* is opening its doors to **Lucky**, the incredible free-roaming audio-animatronic dinosaur.

For new accommodation, Disney can boast the *Saratoga Springs Resort & Spa*, which is expanding throughout 2005, as is the *Pop Century Resort*, with the completion of the second half of this huge budget-priced hotel.

Looking further ahead, *Disney's Animal Kingdom Park* is to unveil **Expedition Everest** in spring 2006 – a unique high-speed train adventure (both backwards and forwards) round the glaciers, canyons and caverns of a 200-ft (60-metre) high 'Everest' in search of the mythical Yeti.

Around the other parks, Universal Orlando opened **The Revenge of the Mummy** to dramatic effect in early summer 2004, while SeaWorld added **Fusion!**, a new water-ski show, and **Mistify**, an end-of-evening pyrotechnic extravaganza (in peak season). Busch Gardens has opened a magnificent new show, **KaTonga**, in the Moroccan Palace Theater and has a spectacular new **Stanleyville Coaster** in 2005, while **Cypress Gardens** is re-opening in late 2004 with a new line-up of coasters and other rides. The Kennedy Space Center has launched an all-new **Astronaut Training Experience**.

Elsewhere, two of the newest resort openings are equally spectacular – the **Reunion Resort** (including three golf courses), just south of Disney, and the nearby **Omni Orlando Resort** at Champions Gate (with an equally impressive golfing background). Both **airports** continue to expand and update their facilities (see Chapter 12) and, of course, we now have our very own website – **www.askdaisy.net/orlando** – to keep you fully up to date with everything to do with this holiday wonderland! Don't forget to check the UK Discussion Boards of partner site www.wdwinfo.com as well.

The Revenge of the Mummy

Central Florida festivals

Here are some major – and unusual – annual events that are worth keeping an eye out for in 2005 (and even planning your holiday around).

Blue Spring Manatee Festival, Jan 27–28 (www.dep.state.fl.us/parks/): this beautiful state park is home to the wonderful manatee, and special celebrations are staged around their seasonal migrations, with craft shows, park tours and interpretive programmes. In Orange City, it's worth seeing at any time of year. (Off Exit 118 on Interstate 4 or I-4.)

Florida State Fair, Feb 10–21 (www.floridastatefair.com): this 100-year-old (in 2004) fair just outside Tampa (right on I-4) draws almost half a million people to its mix of fairground rides, art, crafts, livestock and live entertainment and offers a huge variety of dance, contests and competitions. A real Florida showcase.

Silver Spurs Rodeo, Feb 20–22 and Oct 15–17 (www.silverspursrodeo.com): a twice-yearly celebration of an original American sport, this is held at the new Osceola Heritage Park in Kissimmee and features some top quality events, plus associated crafts and activities. (Just off the eastern end of Highway 192.)

Plant City Strawberry Festival, Mar 3–13 (www.flstrawberryfestival.com): one of the most unusual and fun events – a fully grown country fair based on the local produce, but with concerts, shows, exhibitions and parades, plus lots of activities for kids. One of Florida's great social events. (Off Exit 19 on I-4.)

Daytona Beach Bike Week, Mar 4–13 (www.daytonachamber.com/bwhome.html): a celebration of all things two-wheeled and mechanical, with races at Daytona Speedway, concerts, parades and street festivals.

Sidewalk Arts Festival, Mar 18–20 (www.wpsaf.org): Winter Park is home to one of America's most prestigious fine arts festivals, with three days of art, food, music and children's events, 9am–5pm.

Fun 'n Sun, Apr 12–18 (www.sun-n-fun.org): the annual aviation spectacular in Lakeland, with museums, vintage planes, aerobatics and much, much more. One of the biggest in the USA. (Off Exit 27 on I-4.)

Zellwood Corn Festival, May 28–30 (www.zellwoodcornfestival.com): another offbeat but fun offering, with the festival featuring corn-eating contests, carnival rides, live entertainment, games, arts and crafts. (25 miles/40km north-west of Orlando, take Route 436 to Route 411.)

Independence Day, July 4: a huge national holiday throughout the country, but watch out for big annual special events at Lake Eola (downtown Orlando), Lakefront Park (Kissimmee), Mount Dora and Winter Park, as well as the main theme parks.

Great Outdoor Festival, Nov 6–7 (www.floridakiss.com): right at the end of Kissimmee's annual 8-week Anglers' Challenge (a huge fishing festival on the local lakes that attracts devotees from all over the US) is this environmental celebration of family fun, races, live music and outdoor recreation exhibits, at Lakefront Park South on Lake Toho.

Plan your visit

The next few chapters will help you plan your days and tell you everything you need to know to make your holiday perfect. Draw up a rough itinerary and then fine tune it with our help here, our new website www.askdaisy.net/orlando, the UK Discussion Boards on www.wdwinfo.com and with your Personalised Itinerary Planner (see page 46).

Now read on and enjoy…

2 Planning and Practicalities

(or, How to Almost *Do It All and Live to Tell the Tale)*

There is one simple rule once you have decided Orlando is the place for you. Sit down and PLAN what you want to do very carefully. This is not the type of holiday you can take in a freewheeling, carefree 'make it up as you go along' manner. Frustration and exhaustion lie in wait for all those who do not have at least a basic plan of campaign.

First of all work out WHEN you want to go, then decide WHERE in the vast resort is the best place for you. Then consider WHAT sort of holiday you are looking for, WHO you want to entrust your holiday with and finally HOW MUCH you want to try to do.

> **BRIT TIP:** Thanksgiving is always the fourth Thursday in November; George Washington's birthday, or President's Day, is the third Monday in February. Try to avoid those weeks!

When to go

If you are looking to avoid the worst of the crowds, the best periods to choose are October to December (but not the week of Thanksgiving in November or between Christmas and New Year), early January up until 2 weeks before Easter (avoiding President's Day in February) and April (after Easter) to the end of May. Orlando gets down to some serious tourist business from Memorial Day (the last Monday in May, the official start of the summer season) to Labor Day (the first Monday in September and the last holiday of summer), peaking on July 4, a huge national holiday. The Easter holidays are similarly uncomfortable (although the weather is better), but easily the busiest is Christmas time, starting the week before December 25 and lasting until January 2. It is not unknown for some of the parks to close if their massive car parks have filled up by mid-morning.

The best combination of comfortable weather and smaller crowds is to be had in April (avoiding Easter) and October. However, few of the main attractions are affected by rain – although the roller-coasters and water rides will close if lightning threatens – and you will be one jump ahead if you have waterproofs, as the crowds noticeably thin out when it gets wet.

All the parks sell cheap, plastic ponchos (cheaper at Wal-Mart or other supermarkets). In the colder months, take a few lightweight but warm layers for early morning queues then, when it warms up later, leave them in the park lockers. When it gets too hot, you can take advantage of the air-conditioned attractions and restaurants (and drink LOTS of water).

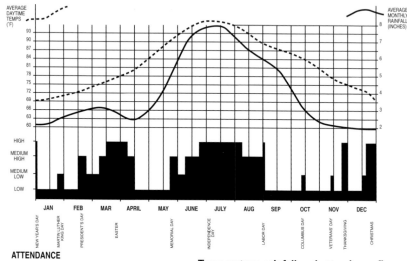

Temperature, rainfall and attendance figures

Where to stay

The choice of where to stay is equally important, especially if you have a family that demands swimming pools and games rooms.

> BRIT TIP: Having the use of a pool where you are staying is a major plus for relaxing at the end of a busy hot day.

Inevitably, there is a huge choice of accommodation areas and prices. As a guide, four main areas make up the greater Orlando tourist conglomeration:

Walt Disney World Resort in Florida: some of the most sophisticated, convenient and fun places to stay are to be found in Disney's great range of hotels. The same imagination that has gone into the creation of the theme parks has been at work on the likes of *Disney's Polynesian Resort* and *Disney's Animal Kingdom Lodge*. They all feature free, regular transport to the parks, your own resort ID card (so you can charge meals and souvenirs to your room, and have your purchases delivered to the hotel), free parking and the BIG bonus of the **Extra Magic Hour**. This allows Disney resort guests entry to one theme park each day a full HOUR before the official opening time, meaning you can do many of the main attractions before the majority have arrived. In summer 2004, Disney was also experimenting with running the extra hour in the *evenings* as well (in place of the old E-Nights), which would make a Disney stay even better value. Many resorts also have great kids' clubs and baby-sitting

Disney's All-Star Sports Resort

© Disney

services. The drawbacks here are that, with the exception of *Disney's All-Star Resorts* and the new *Pop Century Resort*, Disney hotels are among the most expensive, especially to eat in, and are a fair drive from Universal Orlando and most shopping centres. It makes a good 1-week holiday though.

Lake Buena Vista: a loosely defined area around the eastern fringes of *Walt Disney World Resort in Florida* and along Interstate 4 (I-4), this again features some upmarket hotels. It is also handy for all the Disney fun, with most hotels offering free transport to the parks, while there are excellent restaurants and shops. Still a bit pricey, but its proximity to I-4 makes it convenient for much of Orlando.

International Drive: this ribbon development, known as I-Drive, lies midway between Disney and downtown Orlando and is therefore an excellent central location. Running parallel to I-4, it is about 15–20 minutes drive from the main theme parks. It is also a well-developed tourist area in its own right, with some great shopping, restaurants and attractions like Wet 'n Wild, Ripley's Believe It Or Not, WonderWorks and Skull Kingdom. The downside is it does get congested and occasionally chaotic with tourist traffic in peak periods, so it's best to make an early start in the mornings. But it does represent good value for money and is one of the few areas with extensive pavements, making it easy to explore on foot. A sub-district off I-Drive is the Universal area of Kirkman Road and Major Boulevard, where new hotels are regularly being added.

Kissimmee: budget holiday-makers can be found in their greatest numbers along the tourist sprawl of Highway 192 (the Irlo Bronson Memorial Highway), an almost unbroken 12-mile (19-km) strip of hotels, motels, restaurants and

> **BRIT TIP:** Phase II of the BeautiVacation of Highway 192 is well underway, meaning serious roadworks from Route 535 to Hoagland Boulevard. Use (toll) Osceola Parkway to beat the traffic.

2

shops. It offers some of the best economy accommodation in the area and is handy for all Disney's attractions, although it is furthest away from Universal Orlando and downtown Orlando. A car is most advisable here, although the completion of the first phase of the BeautiVacation project, which has enhanced the heavily built-up stretch of 192 – from Route 535 as far west as Formosa Gardens – with pavements, landscaping, bus shelters, benches and water fountains, has made it a much better location for getting around on foot or by bus.

Split holidays

Florida has so much to offer that many people opt to split their holiday by having a week or two in Orlando as well as a week elsewhere, like the Gulf Coast, Miami or the Florida Keys. The Atlantic coast has some great beaches only an hour's drive to the east, the magnificent Florida Everglades are some 3–4

International Drive

hours to the south, and there are more wonderful beaches and pleasant coast roads to the west. Great shopping is to be found almost everywhere, while Orlando has some stunning golf courses along with plenty of opportunities to play or watch tennis, baseball and basketball, or go fishing, boating or canoeing.

The main tour companies offer a huge variety of packages, with some popular cruise-and-stay options.

If you can afford the time (and expense), the best option is to have 2 weeks in Orlando itself, then a week relaxing on one of Florida's many fabulous beaches. A 2-week, half-and-half split is a regular choice, but can make your time in Orlando rather hectic, unless your additional week is on the Atlantic coast at somewhere like Cocoa Beach. This resort, near to Cape Canaveral and the Kennedy Space Center, is only an hour from Orlando and gives you the chance to return to Disney for the day.

Several companies offer a highly worthwhile 10-day Orlando and 4-day coast split. Fly-drives obviously offer the greatest flexibility, but there is a lot to tempt you in just 2 weeks and you may find it better to book a 1-centre package that includes a car as well as your accommodation, so you can still travel around but avoid too much packing and unpacking.

Travel companies

There is serious competition for your hard-earned holiday money and the travel companies have been working hard to keep the cost of an Orlando holiday down, whether you fly-drive, book your own flights or take a package.

Shop around to get the best value for your holiday £, but make sure your package is booked with an ABTA agent for security should anything go wrong. At the last count, there were more than 70 tour operators offering holidays to Florida, and here is a rundown of the biggest and best:

Travel City Direct: the UK's largest independent direct-sell Florida specialist, with more than 150,000 customers a year, they offer a wide range of holidays at ultra-competitive prices (because you book direct), including fly-drives, 1- and 2-centre holidays, private pool villas and Caribbean cruises. New features include a dedicated (and well-written) Disney brochure and their own tie-up with Carnival Cruise Line for a range of tempting Caribbean cruise add-ons. A sharp reservations team (and improved online booking) has excellent local knowledge and can advise on where to stay, what to do and keep you up to date with what's new. They are continually looking at new ideas to add value.

Most flights year-round are now with their in-house branded airline (Gatwick and Manchester, eight flights a week in summer), using Air Atlanta Europe Boeing 747s and with one of the most generous seat pitches (32in/82cm of leg room) for a charter, plus free drinks, meals and headsets in all classes (unlike many). There is an economy cabin (the Sunshine Cabin), the Sunshine Upper Deck (no under-9s allowed, still economy-size seats but better service and meals, 30kg luggage allowance and priority check-in and disembarkation, from an extra £99) and Sunshine First (22 seats with a 50in/127cm pitch that recline almost flat, upgraded menus and individual video screens, 40kg luggage allowance, priority boarding and late check-in, all from £249 extra – the best value on any Florida flight, in my opinion).

You can also pre-book seats on most flights (for £20 return or £69 for a family of four). They have a double baggage allowance offer

2

(£15/person, or £99 for a family of four if buying pre-bookable seats too) allowing you to increase your limit from 20kg to 40kg (useful if you are shopping in Orlando). Other flights depart from six regional airports, including Belfast and Cardiff.

Travel City Direct has three dedicated arrivals centres and their own check-in for selected flights at Orlando Sanford Airport, as well as a user-friendly welcome centre at the Lake Buena Vista Factory Shops, open 7 days a week (plus one on I-Drive in peak season). Travel City Direct can be found on Teletext page 298, for direct bookings call 08709 505128 or visit www.travelcitydirect.com.

Airlines: Travel City Direct, plus Air Atlanta Europe, BA, Virgin, US Airways, Continental Airlines and charters.

Airport: Orlando Sanford (Travel City Direct, Air Atlanta Europe and charters), Orlando International (BA, US Airways, Virgin and Continental).

Virgin Holidays: the biggest overall operator to Florida and MCO (that's Orlando International in airport-speak), Virgin also has the biggest and most extensive brochure. They offer the largest variety of combinations with more than 200 properties to choose from, including Miami, the Keys, New York, Washington, Boston, the Bahamas, Mexico, nine Caribbean islands (including Cuba) and some tempting cruises, as well as the Florida coasts.

A strong selling point is Virgin's non-stop scheduled service to Orlando (from Manchester and up to 17 times a week from Gatwick in summer 2005, plus occasional flights with other carriers) with award-winning in-flight entertainment, free drinks, kids' packs, meals and games. They have a wide choice of accommodation in the different areas (including most Disney resorts), villas and are popular for fly-drives, flying into Orlando and out of Miami, and vice versa.

Flight upgrades to their Premium Economy (highly recommended; extra leg room and bigger seats from £150–225), Club Orlando (from Manchester only, with extra luxurious seats for £160 on top of the Premium Economy supplement) or the unequalled Upper Class service (from £850–1,025, with seats that recline fully, plus personal attention and service, use of the wonderful Virgin Atlantic Clubhouse in UK airports and a double car upgrade in Florida) are all available and the service throughout is impeccable.

You can pre-book seats free of charge (on 0871 222 0050) no more than 180 days before departure and even check in the evening before your flight at Gatwick. Virgin's unique Downtown Disney Check-In has also been re-introduced ($5/person in Economy, free in Premium Economy and Upper Class), exclusively allowing guests to check in the morning of departure freeing up the rest of the day to enjoy at leisure.

Orlando is also hugely popular as a wedding venue, and Virgin can provide wedding co-ordinators for ceremonies throughout Florida. Other bonuses include single-parent discounts, a top class service for passengers with disabilities, 'kids eat free' deals at selected hotels (and a free meal at the Hard Rock Café for all Orlando guests) and some excellent non-driver packages, plus a chartered bus from Orlando to Miami or Fort Lauderdale. Call 0871 222 1232 or visit www.virgin.com/holidays.

Airline: Virgin Atlantic.

Airport: Orlando International.

Thomson: another of the largest, mass-market operators, Thomson has an excellent reputation in Orlando, having a large team of reps and Service Centres on I-Drive, and offers six departure airports (including Birmingham, Cardiff,

The Travel City Direct jumbo

Newcastle and Glasgow). You can pre-book your seats (£17 adult, £7 child), while good in-flight entertainment and kids' packs are provided (with Britannia).

Thomson price packages well for the family market, with special children's fares (from £99 first child) and 'kids eat free' and 'extra value' hotels, while offering a decent selection of cruises, coastal resorts for 2- or even 3-centre holidays (including Miami and Key West) plus pre-bookable golf packages. An increased range of private villas (sleeping up to ten) is available as are wedding packages (from £519) at Cypress Grove, the Wyndham Palace or Wyndham Orlando hotels.

Flight upgrades cost £60 (for extra leg room) and £150 (£169 in summer 2005) or Premium service (with free drinks, wider seats, choice of meals, entertainment and priority boarding). Call 0870 550 2567 or book online at www.thomson.co.uk.

Airline: Britannia and other charters.

Airport: Orlando Sanford.

Airtours: also in the leading group who take more than 100,000 tourists to Orlando each year, Airtours flies from eight UK airports with good in-flight entertainment, children's fun packs and seat-back TVs (on selected flights). They offer an excellent Premiair Gold upgrade (extra leg room and baggage allowance, free bar, pre-selected menu, late UK check-in) for £179. Airtours has some novel 10- and 11-night packages (from Manchester

and Gatwick only) for a more flexible choice and offers a wide range of car hire options and upgrades. There is an Airtours service desk at the huge McDonald's on I-Drive and Sand Lake Road and Welcome Meetings are imaginatively held in Universal's CityWalk (with free parking), so you can hit the fun straight away.

Airtours offers some good 2-centre combos, including a week at a *Walt Disney World Resort in Florida* hotel and a week at a Universal resort, and the Gulf Coast. Private villa accommodation is now a feature, with good quality pool homes in Kissimmee and the Gulf Coast. Airtours also has a range of 'Drive and Stay' holidays, including new packages that combine a fly-drive with the first 3 or 4 nights at a Disney or Universal hotel.

Their flexible options approach puts the onus on you to select the exact package you want, which means if you can book early enough, you get the pick of Airtours' early booking offers, including 10,000 free child places, free pre-bookable seating, and free in-flight meals. Premiair Gold upgrades are available (£179), as are extra-leg-room seating (£70), 25kg luggage allowance (per person) and low deposit.

Or you can choose to go for a *Sundeal Holiday*, the no-frills option, with accommodation assigned on arrival, a 2½-hour latest check-in,

Disney Cruise Line

Kids have fun on Virgin flights

only 15kg luggage allowance and no optional upgrades or in-flight meal (it is £15 extra); and *Flight Only* (as Sundeal, but no accommodation and no in-flight meal unless you pre-book seating). For a brochure, call 0870 900 8639 or visit www.airtours.co.uk.

Airline: My Travel.
Airport: Orlando Sanford.

First Choice: a comprehensive programme to Florida from five UK airports (Gatwick, Manchester, East Midlands, Glasgow and Newcastle) using First Choice Airways. Summer 2005 sees the introduction of their new long-haul service which features personal seat-back entertainment, more leg room, wider seats and all meals included – plus premium cabin upgrades giving even more leg room, entertainment on demand and personal widescreen TV. Holidays are available throughout Orlando, the Gulf Coast and Cocoa Beach plus a dedicated programme to *Walt Disney World Resort in Florida*

featuring all on-site resort hotels, theme parks and entertainment. First Choice has a family-friendly touch offering hotels (mainly the 3- and 4-star variety) with themed Kidsuites and 'kids eat free' deals, plus villas and apartments.

There is a meet-and-greet service at Orlando Sanford Airport, plus a new service desk at the Holiday Inn Resort on I-Drive. Visit the website www.firstchoice.co.uk or request a brochure on 020 8880 8155.

Airline: First Choice Airways.
Airport: Orlando Sanford.

Other First Choice brands that also sell Florida are: **First Choice Disney** (0870 750 0001, www.firstchoice.co.uk) for all Disney Resort Hotels and extensive information on how to experience *Walt Disney World Resort in Florida;* **First Choice Villas** (0870 750 0001 www.firstchoice.co.uk) for a solely villa-based holiday; **Eclipse** (08705 010203, www.eclipsedirect.co.uk), a direct-sell operator with a standard range of accommodation, including holiday homes and some coast combinations; **Unijet** (08705 336 336, www.unijet.com) for a selection of self-catering options including Orlando holiday homes; and **Sunstart** (0870 243 0636, www.firstchoice.co.uk), the budget operator in the First Choice range, featuring mainly 2- and 3-star hotels.

British Airways Holidays: another company to benefit from its own direct, scheduled air service, BA

BRIT TIP: Beware the low baggage allowances, as there are some steep charges for any excess, especially on the return flight. An empty suitcase can weigh a good 5kg, and you will be tempted to buy a lot of souvenirs.

Doubletree Club Hotel

Holidays offers great flexibility with almost any duration and combination possible. Beach add-ons, 2 centres – both coasts and the Florida Keys – and an extensive selection of quality but great-value private homes are all on offer. BAH also flies to Miami and Tampa, opening up plenty of fly-drive and multi-centre possibilities.

However, you won't find them in most travel agents as they only do direct-sell, but their packages are all well tried and trusted. BA flights also come with the option to upgrade to the luxurious Club World (with fully flat beds) or World Traveller Plus (larger seats with more leg room), plus special kids' meals and seat-back TVs. Call 0870 243 3406 or browse their online brochure at www.baholidays.com.

Airline: British Airways.
Airport: Orlando International.

Thomas Cook: two choices are available under the famous Cook banner: a new mass-market Thomas Cook brochure and the more distinctive Thomas Cook Signature Holidays programme (see right). The straightforward Thomas Cook brand is a fairly standard choice, broken down into three value ranges – Extra, Standard and Economy – primarily using their own Thomas Cook charter airline (with optional upgrades available), which has replaced the old jmc brand. Extra leg room seats (for £30 each way), pre-bookable seating (at a small charge – call 0870 243 0416) and executive lounge facilities are all available at selected UK airports (for a charge). They also have one of the best punctuality records of all the charter airlines in recent years and their in-flight service is one of the best, from my observations. You can either book through their own High Street agencies, by phone (0870 111 1111), online at www.thomascook.com or via Thomas Cook TV (Sky Guide channel 648, ntl:home channel 857).

They offer some good wedding packages (from £1,379 per couple at a Disney location, to just £349 in Winter Park), 2-centre options and cruises.

Airline: Thomas Cook.
Airport: Orlando Sanford.

Thomas Cook Signature: now here's an operation to compete with the Virgins of this world – a more quality-conscious and selective offering using ONLY scheduled air services (although their prices are still pretty competitive). They tend to suit repeat visitors especially, and bonuses include early booking discounts, free night offers (stay 6 and get another free), 'kids eat free' and free room upgrades at many hotels. Their ticketing info and material is first class and there is a strong tailor-made element to the range of choice. And, as with many nowadays, Disney's Ultimate Park Hopper ticket now comes with a 'kids eat breakfast free' offer at the Disney resort where you're staying.

Their selection of holiday homes is particularly good (with some of the most upmarket properties in the area), and the twin-centre options include both coasts, Miami, the Keys, as well as the rest of the USA and the Caribbean. Call 0870 443 4453 or visit www.tcsignature.com.

Airlines: Virgin Atlantic, British Airways, American Airlines, Continental Airlines, United.
Airports: Orlando International, plus Miami and Tampa.

Kuoni: as with all their holidays, Kuoni offers the upmarket version of Orlando, with some of the best hotels, a strong Disney tie-up, a comprehensive wedding and honeymoon service and a Price Watch guarantee (money back if you find an identical holiday for less). They have a range of twin-centre options, including the Florida Keys, exclusive Boca Raton and Marco Island, the Caribbean and even New York and Las Vegas. The average price reflects the more exclusive nature of many of their packages (plus their flexible, tailor-made choice facility), but there are some big child reductions, 'kids eat free' hotels, and Kuoni use only scheduled airlines. Free airport–hotel transfers for non-drivers are provided, too. Call 0870 990 9905 or visit www.kuoni.co.uk.

Airlines: Virgin Atlantic, United (via Washington), Continental (via New York), American (via Miami) and British Airways.

Airport: Orlando International.

Funway Holidays: this is the sister company of America's largest tour operator and a leading specialist in holidays to the US, hence they offer a tailor-made service to match Orlando with any other option, providing total flexibility of choice from no less than 16 UK airports. Their private villas are a big feature of the Florida programme, but they also serve up some terrific-value deals, especially for children, if you book early, making them among the best prices for a family of four. They use only scheduled airlines (with an option to upgrade to Virgin's Premium Economy service from £175 each way).

A wide range of 2-centre choices include the Gulf Coast, Miami and the Keys and the Caribbean. Other bonuses include 'kids eat free' hotels, free kids' clubs, free hotel nights at certain times and free shuttles at selected hotels for non-drivers. Visit www.funwayholidays.co.uk or call 0870 220 0626 for a brochure.

Airlines: various scheduled, including Virgin Atlantic, British Airways and Continental.

Airport: Orlando International.

Style Holidays: one of the UK's top self-catering specialists (and a Thomas Cook-owned company), this company offers a huge selection of private-pool homes and hotel suites, with accommodation up to luxurious 5- and 6-bed varieties, as well as the usual range of hotel and *Walt Disney World Resort in Florida* options. All properties are in named, well-described situations and can be booked on an accommodation-only basis, leaving you free to sort out your flights. Their comprehensive brochure has an excellent range of Gulf Coast villas (all of which can be combined with Orlando), while they maintain a high standard of in-resort service. Transfers can be arranged for non-drivers (£15/person each way). For a brochure, call 0870 444 4474 or check out www.style-holidays.co.uk.

Airlines: Various charters.

Airport: Orlando Sanford.

Jetsave: Florida specialist Jetsave puts the accent on flexibility, with a wide range of choice. For accommodation, you have the full selection of hotels (especially the kid-friendly variety), resorts, apartments and holiday homes (or villas as we would call them), and simple, accurate star ratings are given for each property. Jetsave use Virgin Atlantic as their primary airline from Gatwick and Manchester so customers can fly any day and stay for any duration. Flight upgrades with Virgin are available, including Club Orlando, their unique Premium Economy Plus service from Manchester. Jetsave can also tailor-make a holiday in Florida with any combination of flights, accommodation and resorts, including self-drive itineraries and offer a wedding service for those wanting to get married in the Sunshine State. Visit www.jetsave.co.uk or call 0870 161 3402.

Airlines: Britannia, Virgin Atlantic, British Airways.

Airport: Orlando International.

A number of other travel companies worth checking out include: **Trailfinders** (the UK's largest independent travel company and highly recommended by several readers, call 020 7937 5400 or download their online brochures at

Clearwater Beach

www.trailfinders.com); **USAirtours** (tailor-made US itineraries, many with villas in Orlando; 0800 195 8660, www.usairtours.co.uk); **Travelbag** (0870 814 4440, www.travelbag.co.uk); **Transolar Holidays** (another US specialist, also great for attraction ticket offers on 0151 630 3737 or www.transolarholidays.com); **Premier Holidays** (more tailor-made choice, 0870 889 0850, www.premierholidays.co.uk); and **Ebookers** (the travel agent arm of Flightbookers, 0870 010 7000, www.ebookers.com).

For flight-only offers, try **Flight Centre** (0870 499 0040 or www.flightcentre.co.uk), **Airline Network** (0870 700 0514, www.airline-network.co.uk), **Dial A Flight** (0870 333 4488, www.dialaflight.com; also for villas, hotels and car hire) and the excellent **Cheap Flights** (an internet-only service, www.cheapflights.co.uk). A look at **Teletext** (page 222 on ITV, or www.teletextholidays.co.uk) often reveals special deals, as do www.expedia.co.uk, www.lastminute.com and www.opodo.co.uk. A new internet company, **Vacation Florida** (www.vacation-florida.co.uk, and partner website www.cheapestflights.co.uk, 0800 015 8030), offers the full range of flights, packages and car hire. You might also consider the well-designed

Disney specialists **Theme Park Holidays** (0870 240 2510, www.themeparkholidays.com) for more than just tickets, while **Holiday Travel Essentials** (0870 036 0060, www.usa-essentials.co.uk) also offers accommodation and car hire, in addition to tickets.

Watch out for two new direct flight operations in 2005, who both promise a variation on the low-cost/higher quality theme. First, Manchester-based Air Scandic will have a weekly flight from Manchester and Glasgow (on Thursdays) and Newcastle and Belfast (Sundays) to Orlando Sanford Airport, operated by **Pure Flights**, which will work like a scheduled service, i.e. for any length of stay, one-way and with booking even on the day of departure (or up to a year in advance). Some flights (using a Boeing 757) have a refuelling stop at Gander in Canada, making for a 10-hour-plus flight. Call 0870 777 0747 or look them up at www.pureflights.com. If you live in the Midlands, **BluArrow** may be the new airline for you, with plans for a notably more upmarket, quality-conscious yet value-for-money service from Birmingham to Orlando Sanford, Tampa and Fort Lauderdale five times a week. They promise the most comfortable economy seats to Florida (seven abreast and a generous 38in/97cm pitch on Boeing 767s), plus an even more spacious business class, with departures no earlier than midday and for any duration, not just 1 or 2 weeks. The whole experience is designed to be more enjoyable, with high levels of in-flight entertainment and service and, while it is not a low-cost operator, they aim to be highly cost-conscious for the quality. Their opening statement was: 'If you seek the lowest fare, you should look elsewhere. Our prime objective is to make you say "Wow!" every time you deal with us. Our prices will always be competitive against more famous brands, but the BluArrow service will make you want to come again.' Visit www.flyblu.com or call 0870 112 2767.

Finally, for those looking to book things themselves but wanting help with Disney accommodation, meal reservations, etc, the excellent **Dreams Unlimited Travel** service is the answer. Visit www.dreamsunlimitedtravel.com for the essential information on this no-cost service which can save time, money and hassle. Other Orlando hotels (with some serious discounts) feature on their DreamsRes online booking service plus a discount ticket agency, TicketRes.

What to see when

Once you arrive, the temptation is to head for the nearest theme park, then the next, and so on. Hold on! If there is such a thing as theme park indigestion, that's the best recipe for it. Some days at the parks are busier than others; it is simply not possible to cover more than one a day, and it may be inadvisable to attempt two of the main parks on successive days. So here's what you can do.

With the aid of the Holiday Planner on pages 303–5, make a note of all the attractions you want to see over the length of your stay.

The most sensible strategy is to plan around the eight 'must-see' parks – *Magic Kingdom* Park, *Epcot*, *Disney-MGM Studios*, *Disney's Animal Kingdom Theme Park*, Universal Studios, Islands of Adventure, SeaWorld and Busch Gardens. If you have only a week, consider dropping Busch Gardens (it's furthest away from Orlando and doesn't have quite the same magical appeal as the others) and concentrate on the Disney parks and Universal Studios, with SeaWorld as an extra if it fits into your plan. Space travel fans will be hard-pressed not to include the Kennedy Space Center, but it would probably bore young children.

As a basic rule, the *Magic Kingdom* Park is the biggest hit with children, and families often find it requires 2 days. The same can be said of *Epcot*, but there are fewer rides to amuse the younger ones and the emphasis is as much on education as entertainment, although it all has Disney's slick, easily digestible coating. Only the most fleet of foot, given the benefit of a relatively crowd-free period, will be able to negotiate *Epcot* in a day. *Disney's Animal Kingdom Theme Park* is also a little short on attractions for the youngest kids (unless they really love their animals, as mine do), but it still requires nearly a whole day.

Disney-MGM Studios is usually possible to do in a day (not forgetting the early evening Fantasmic! show), while SeaWorld occasionally needs rather longer and Universal Studios can be a 2-day park when at its busiest. Islands of Adventure will almost certainly keep everyone, except possibly under-5s, busy all day, too. Busch Gardens, extremely popular with British families, is another full-day affair,

Sunset over Clearwater

especially as it is a 75–90-minute drive away in Tampa to the southwest. However, an early start to the Kennedy Space Center (an hour's drive away on the east coast) will mean you can be back in your hotel swimming pool by teatime.

All the attractions are described in detail in Chapters 5–8, so it's best to try to get an idea of the time requirements of them all before you pick up your pencil.

Smaller attractions

Of the other, smaller-scale attractions, the nature park of Silver Springs is a full day out as it also involves a near 2-hour drive to get there, but everything else can be fitted around your Big Eight Itinerary. The water parks provide a good place to spend a relaxing afternoon, while Historic Bok Sanctuary is another quieter spot to while away half a day or so (NB: the wonderful park of Cypress Gardens closed in 2003, but was due to re-open in late 2004 with new attractions). There are also a number of smaller-scale attractions in Orlando which will probably keep the children amused for several hours (often after the major theme parks have closed).

Gatorland is a unique look at some of Florida's oldest inhabitants and is a good combination with a ride at Boggy Creek Airboats. Ripley's Believe It Or Not museum and WonderWorks interactive house of fun are both good family centres for several hours. Add in the terrific haunted house attraction, Skull Kingdom and the more old-fashioned lure of go-karts and other fairground-type rides at Fun Spot or Magical Midway (all on the I-Drive corridor), and you have a full day of alternative fun and frolics. Aviation fans must not miss a trip to Fantasy of Flight (further down I-4) or the

Flying Tigers Warbird Air Museum in Kissimmee for a novel experience.

DisneyQuest, another part of the *Downtown Disney* area, is a hugely imaginative interactive 'arcade' that guarantees up to half a day's fun (especially for older children). Each main area is also well served with creatively designed mini-golf courses that will absorb any excess energy for an hour or two.

Evenings

The evening entertainment harbours a similarly wide choice of extravagant fun-seeking. By far the best, and worth at least one evening each, are *Downtown Disney's Pleasure Island*, Universal's CityWalk and the Pointe*Orlando area. All will keep you busy until the early hours. Dinner shows provide a lot of fun – 2-hour cabarets based on themes like medieval knights, pirates, Arabian Nights and murder mysteries that all include a hearty meal. Rounding it up is the huge variety of nightclubs and bars, many offering live music.

What to do when

There are several general guidelines for avoiding the worst of the tourist hordes, even in high season. The vast majority of fun-seekers in town are American, who tend to arrive at weekends and head for the main theme parks first. That means Monday is generally a bad time to visit the *Magic Kingdom* Park and Tuesday is usually humming at *Epcot*.

The Extra Magic Hour, which allows Disney hotel guests early entry to one of the parks on a set day each week, also creates a greater build-up of crowds, so avoid the following parks on those days: Sunday, *Magic Kingdom* Park; Monday, *Disney's Animal Kingdom Theme Park*; Tuesday, *Disney-MGM Studios*; Wednesday, *Epcot*; Thursday,

Magic Kingdom Park; Friday, *Disney's Animal Kingdom;* Saturday, *Disney-MGM Studios. Disney's Animal Kingdom* is also the hardest to get round when it's crowded. *Disney's Blizzard Beach* and *Typhoon Lagoon* water parks hit high tide at the weekend, and Thursday and Friday in the summer.

At Universal Orlando, the picture is different as there are no early entry days and the weekends are usually busiest as the locals tend to visit then. This often means Monday is quietest at both Universal and Islands of Adventure, getting busier through the week, with the former being slightly more crowded.

If *Walt Disney World Resort in Florida* is humming in the early part of the week, that makes it a good time to visit SeaWorld, Busch Gardens, Silver Springs or the Kennedy Space Center. Avoid Wet 'n Wild and Water Mania at the weekends when the locals come out to play. The Busy Day Guide on page 305 shows you at a glance the busiest and quietest days at each park.

Making sure you get the most out of your days at the main theme parks is another art form, and there are a number of practical policies to pursue. The official opening times seldom vary from 9am but arriving early is highly advisable. Apart from the obvious advantage of being near the head of the queues (and you will encounter some SERIOUS queues, or lines as the Americans call them), the parks do sometimes open earlier than scheduled if the crowds build up quickly before the official hour.

So, you can get a step ahead of the masses by arriving at least 30 minutes before opening time, or an hour early during the main holiday periods. Apart from anything else, you will be better placed to park in the vast, wide open spaces of the public car parks and catch the tram to the main gates (anything up to half a mile away).

Once you've put yourself in pole position, don't waste time on the shops, scenery and other frippery which will lure the unprepared first-timer. Instead, head straight for some of the main rides and get a few big-time thrills under your belt before the main hordes arrive. You will quickly work out where the most popular attractions are as the majority of the other early birds will

BRIT TIP: If your hotel is not far away, take a break from the park for a couple of hours and return for a siesta or a swim. Have your hand stamped for re-entry when you leave (your car park ticket will be valid all day) and then return to enjoy the spectacular evening entertainment.

be flocking to them. Use Chapters 5 and 6 to help plan your individual park strategies.

You can also benefit from doing the opposite of what the masses do after the initial rush has subsided. Try not to have all your meals in the parks, too. While they still represent great value for money, eating out has become expensive here, I feel, and it can be $10/person for even a basic counter-service meal. Instead, having a good buffet breakfast at somewhere like the Ponderosa or Golden Corral means you won't need lunch and can save $$$s!

Pace yourself

Another word of warning: Disney's parks, notably the *Magic Kingdom* Park, stay open late during the main holiday periods, occasionally until 11pm, and that can be a long day for young children. Therefore, it is important to pace yourself,

A romantic outing in Old Town, Kissimmee

especially if you have been one of the first through the gates.

There are plenty of options to take time off for a drink or a sit-down somewhere air-conditioned, and you can benefit from the American propensity to take mealtimes seriously by avoiding lunchtime (12 noon–2pm) and dinnertime (5.30–7pm). So, after you've had a couple of hours of real adventure-mania, it pays to take an early lunch (ie before midday), plunge back into it all for another 3 hours or so, have another snack mid-afternoon and then return to the main rides, as the parks quieten down a little in late afternoon.

Finally, a word about shopping in Orlando – it's world class. Your battle plan should include at least half a day to visit one of the spectacular malls, as well as the discount outlets and speciality centres like Old Town in Kissimmee, the excellent Orlando Premium

BRIT TIP: In the first edition of the *Brit's Guide* for 1995, a typical burger-and-chips park meal cost around $5.65. Now it is more likely to be $8–10.

Outlets, and the likes of Pointe*Orlando and Festival Bay that grace I-Drive.

Clothing and comfort

The most important part of your holiday wardrobe is your footwear – you will spend a lot of time on your feet, even during the off-peak periods. The smallest of the parks covers 'only' 100 acres (40ha), but that is irrelevant to the amount of time you will spend queuing. This is not the time to break in new sandals or trainers! Comfortable, well-worn shoes or trainers are essential.

Otherwise, you need dress only as the climate dictates. T-shirts and shorts are quite appropriate in all of the parks (swimwear is not acceptable away from pool areas) and nearly all restaurants will happily accept informal dress.

BRIT TIP: The water IS safe to drink in the US but it may not taste great, as they tend to put a lot of fluoride in it.

If, after a long day, you feel the need for a change of clothes or a sweater for the evening, take advantage of the handy lockers (unlimited use all day, even if you change parks). All the parks are also well equipped with pushchairs (or strollers) for hire, and baby services are located at regular intervals.

It is absolutely vital to use high-factor sun creams at all times, even during the winter months when the sun may not feel that strong but can still burn. Nothing is guaranteed to ruin your holiday like severe sunburn. Orlando has a sub-tropical climate and requires higher factor sun creams than even the Mediterranean. Use sun blocks on sensitive areas like your nose and

2

BRIT TIP: If you fear the onset of blisters, head to the nearest supermarket or chemist (drug store) and seek out some moleskin footpads from the footcare counter. They work wonders on tender skin.

ears, and splash on the after-sun lotion liberally at the end of the day; you will need waterproof sun cream for swimming. Skincare products are widely available and usually inexpensive (especially at Wal-Mart or Kmart).

Wear a hat if you are out in the hottest part of the day, and try to avoid alcohol, coffee and fizzy drinks until the evening as they can dehydrate and make you susceptible to heatstroke. You will need to increase your fluid intake *significantly* during the summer months in Orlando, but stick to still soft drinks such as Gatorade, a squash-like energy drink, or water.

Want to see more?

If, like me, you want to make the most of every holiday opportunity, you could travel a little further afield in America with the help of their highly efficient low-cost airline system. Orlando now represents an excellent base from which to explore the delights of New York, Chicago,

BRIT TIP: One of the best ways to keep cool in the Florida sun is to visit a supermarket and buy a simple mist spray fan (about $7.99) which you carry with you and just refill with water.

Atlantic City and Puerto Rico in the Caribbean, all of which are only 2 hours' flight away, or go even further to glittering Las Vegas or Los Angeles. With the benefit of cheap hotel deals (check out www.hotels.com), you can seriously spread your wings (ahem) by using the likes of **Spirit Airlines** (from Orlando International and Tampa Airports) and **TransMeridian Airlines** (from Orlando Sanford Airport). Slip ahead to pages 301 and 302 for more details on how to extend your holiday. Repeat visitors may like to consider this, and it represents only a small additional investment after having gone all the way to Florida.

Medical aid

Should you require medical treatment, whether for sunburn or other first aid, consult your tour company's information about local hospitals and surgeries. In the event of a medical, or other, **emergency**, dial 911 as you would 999 in Britain.

It cannot be over-stressed that you should have comprehensive travel and health insurance (see page 35) for any trip to America as there is NO National Health Service and ANY form of medical treatment will need to be paid for – and is usually

Minnie meets mini-Minnie!

© Disney

Top 10 things to do for free

While Orlando has a magnificent array of paid-for attractions, there are still many things you can do which don't cost a cent.

1) Peabody Duck March: turn up at 11am or 5pm at the Peabody Hotel to see the resident mallards get the Red Carpet Treatment as they either arrive or leave their lobby fountain 'home'.

2) Lakeridge Winery and Vineyards: join a free wine-tasting tour and you'll know why Lakeridge (in nearby Clermont) has won more than 300 awards. Be sure to designate a driver as sample sizes are generous! 10am–5pm Mon–Sat, 11am–5 pm Sun (www.lakeridgewinery.com).

3) Disney's Boardwalk Resort: free nightly entertainment includes jugglers, comedy skits and live music. Time your visit to coincide with the 9pm IllumiNations fireworks extravaganza at nearby Epcot.

4) Orlando International Airport: bag some excellent photo opportunities at the many fine shops before you leave. Disney, Universal, SeaWorld, Kennedy Space Center and even the specialised Harley-Davidson store all feature some fun possibilities.

5) Pianoman Bob Jackson: *Disney's Port Orleans Riverside Resort* hosts some excellent free entertainment with Pianoman Bob on Wed–Sun evenings, doing the Chicken Dance and singing along with old favourites in a family-friendly atmosphere.

6) Lake Eola Park: take a walk on the mild side in the heart of downtown Orlando. The kids can play or feed the swans, and there is live musical entertainment in summer at the Disney Amphitheater (see Parks at www.cityoforlando.net).

7) Fort Christmas Historical Park: 20 miles (32km) east of Orlando in the town of Christmas is this replica of an 1837 US Army fort from the Seminole Indian Wars, with exhibits, video presentations and restored homes, and special events at some weekends; 10am–5pm Tue–Sat, 1pm–5pm Sun (www.nbbd.com/godo/FortChristmas).

8) Leu Gardens: just north of downtown Orlando, this sanctuary of peace and quiet, with wildlife, nature trails and the 1880s' Leu House Museum is free every Monday from 9am–noon (www.leugardens.org).

9) Sanford Museum: some quaint history is well presented through the personal collections of city founder Henry S Sanford (11am–4pm Tue–Fri). Combine a visit with a walking tour, including the new Riverwalk (www.ci.sanford.fl.us/cf03.html).

10) Old Town, Kissimmee: the biggest vintage car parade in the US every Saturday, with cars on display from 1pm and the parade at 8.30pm, a Friday Night Cruise (classic cars from 1978–85) at 8.30pm and Motorcycle Mania Thursdays at 6pm, plus live music (www.old-town.com). **SUSAN HAASS**

BRIT TIP: Don't be tempted to pack a lot of smart or formal clothing – you really won't need it in hot, informal Florida.

expensive. Keep all the receipts and reclaim on your return home.

Emergency out-patients departments can be found with **Centra Care** at Florida Hospital Medical Center in five locations and can provide hotel in-room services (407 238 2000) and free transport (407 239 6463). Open from 8am–5, 6, 7, 8 or 9pm, Centra Care can be found at 12139 South Apopka-Vineland Road, and 12500 Apopka-Vineland Road, next to Eckerd Drugs in The Shoppes at Lake Buena Vista, and next to Turner Drugs, near the Crossroads shopping centre, at Lake Buena Vista (the latter is open until midnight on weekdays – 407 239 7777 or 407 934 2273); 7848 West Irlo Bronson Memorial Highway (192), in Formosa Gardens Village just off West Highway 192 (407 397 7032); 6001 Vineland Road, near Universal Studios (407 351 6682); and 4320 West Vine Street, near Medieval Times (407 390 1888). Sand Lake Hospital on 9400 Turkey Lake Road also has an **emergency out-patients** department, 407 851 6478.

The **East Coast Medical Network** (407 648 5252) and **House Med Inc** (407 239 1195) both make hotel 'house calls' 24 hours a day. House Med also operates **MediClinic**, a walk-in facility on 2901 Parkway Boulevard, Kissimmee (open daily 9am–9pm) and Orlando Regional Healthcare System (operator of Sand Lake Hospital) has **Walk-In Medical Care** centres on I-Drive (407 351 3035 and 407 239 6679) open 8am–8pm.

A 24-hour tourist-orientated

dentist is located at J Antonellis on W Colonial Drive (407 292 8767).

The two largest **chemists** (drug stores in America) are Eckerd Drugs and Walgreens, and their branches at 908 Lee Road and 6201 I-Drive are both open 24 hours.

If you are taking regular prescription drugs, check with your doctor or pharmacist to see if they have a different name in the US. Many do (adrenaline is known as epinephrine) and it is worth finding out and carrying the drug with both names in case of an emergency. (Many thanks to Valerie Mulcare-Tivey for this advice.) Another reader points out the American term for paracetamol is acetaminophen.

Travel insurance

Having said you should not travel without good insurance, you should also not pay over the odds for it. Tour operators are notoriously expensive or may imply you need to buy their insurance policy when you don't. In all cases make sure your policy covers you in the USA for: **medical cover** of at least £2 million; **personal liability** up to £2 million (though this won't cover driving abroad; you would still need Supplementary Liability Insurance with your car-hire firm); **cancellation** or **curtailment** cover up to £3,000; **personal property** cover up to £1,500 (but check on expensive items, as most policies

BRIT TIP: The summer is mosquito time. Buy a spray-on insect repellent. Alternatively, try any of Avon's Skin So Soft skincare products, which can work wonders at keeping bugs at bay.

Park attendances 2003

(As estimated by Amusement Business magazine)

1 *Magic Kingdom*, 14 million (no change on 2002)
2 *Epcot*, 8.6 million (up 3.6%)
3 *Disney-MGM Studios*, 7.9 million (down 1.25%)
4 *Disney's Animal Kingdom*, 7.3 million (no change)
5 Universal Studios, 6.9 million (no change)
6 Islands of Adventure, 6.1 million (no change)
7 SeaWorld, 5.2 million (up 4%)
8 Busch Gardens, 4.3 million (down 4.4%)

limit single articles to £250); **cash and document** cover, including your passport and tickets; and finally that the policy gives you a 24-hour **emergency helpline**. If you want to go bungee jumping or even horse riding, check your policy includes **dangerous sports cover**.

Shop around at reputable dealers like **American Express** (0800 700 737), **AA** (0870 606 0483), **Bradford & Bingley** (0800 435642), **Club Direct** (0800 0744 558), **Columbus** (0845 330 8518), **Direct Travel** (01903 812345), **Norwich Union** (0800 121007), **Options** (0870 876 7878), **Premier Direct** (0990 133218), **Thomas Cook** (0845 600 5454), **Worldcover Direct** (0800 365121) and **Worldwide Travel Insurance** (01892 833 338).

Florida with children

I am often asked what I think is the right age to take children to Orlando, and there is no set answer, I'm afraid. Some toddlers take to it instantly, while some 6- or even 7-year-olds are left rather bemused. Quite often, the best attractions for young children are the hotel swimming pool or the tram ride to a park's front gates! Some love the Disney characters at first sight, while others find them frightening. There is simply no predicting how they will react, but I do know my oldest boy at 4½ loved just about every second of his first experience (apart from the fireworks – see page 37) and still talks about it. Yes, a 3-year-old may not remember much, but they WILL have fun and provide you with some great memories, photos and video.

Here are some top tips for travelling with youngsters – with thanks to the folks at www.wdwinfo.com for chipping in (additional tips are given in the theme parks chapters):

The flight: try to look calm (even if you don't feel it) and relaxed. Small children soon pick up on any anxieties and make them worse. Pack a bag with plenty of little bits for them (comics, sweets, colouring books, small surprise toys, etc) and keep vital 'extras' like Calpol (in sachets, if possible), change of clothes, small first-aid kit (plasters, antiseptic cream, baby wipes), sunglasses, hat and sunscreen in your hand luggage.

Once you're there: take things slowly and let your children dictate what pace you go at, to a large extent. In hot, humid summer, only the most placid children (and few under 5s, in my experience) will happily queue for an hour or more at a ride, so use Disney's FastPass system (see page 91) and Universal's equivalent (see page 141). The heat, in particular, can result in grizzly kids in no time, so take breaks for

BRIT TIP: Avoid making phone calls from your hotel room – it's very expensive. It's cheaper to buy a local phonecard and use a normal payphone (see page 43).

drinks and splash zones or head for attractions with air-conditioning. Remember to carry your small first-aid kit with you. Things like baby wipes always come in handy, and it is a good idea to take spare clothes, which you can leave in the lockers at all the main parks. Going back to the hotel for an afternoon snooze is a good idea – the late afternoon/early evening is usually the best time at the parks in terms of cooler temperatures, less crowds and pure fun.

In the sun: carry sun cream and sun block at all times and use it *frequently*, in queues, on buses, etc. A children's after-sun lotion is also advisable. And make sure they drink a lot of water or non-fizzy drinks. Tiredness and irritability are often a result of mild dehydration.

Dining out: look for the 'kids eat free' deals in many places, as they can apply to children up to 12, and take advantage of the many buffet options (see Chapter 10, Dining Out) to fill the family up or for picky eaters. 'Many restaurants do Meals To Go if you want a quiet meal in your own accommodation without the worry of the kids playing up!' says Lisag on www.wdwinfo.com. Try to let your children get used to the characters and the size of them before you go to one of the many fab Disney character meals.

Having fun: allow your children do some of the decision-making and be prepared to go with the flow if they find something unexpected they like (the many squirt fountains and splash zones in the main parks are an example – bring along swimsuits and/or a change of clothes!). The Orlando rule of 'You Can't Do It All' applies especially with children. And beware the evening fireworks at many of the parks, as they are loud and young children can get quite distressed (my eldest – then 4 – had to be taken out of *Epcot* in a hurry!). The resort hotels around the *Magic Kingdom* Park offer safer ways to view the fireworks – at a distance!

All the parks have **Baby Centers** for nursing mothers and can provide baby food and nappies on request (check the park map for the locations). The centres can even provide spare children's underpants for those little 'accidents'! All of Disney's resort hotel gift shops stock baby food and nappies. Expectant mothers are strongly advised not to ride some of the more dynamic attractions and coasters, and there will be clear warnings on park maps and at the rides themselves. Basically, the rides to avoid are: *Magic Kingdom* Park: Space Mountain, Splash Mountain; *Epcot:* Test Track, Body Wars, Maelstrom, Mission: SPACE; *Disney-MGM Studios:* Tower of Terror, Rock 'n Roller Coaster starring Aerosmith, Star Tours; *Disney's Animal Kingdom Park:* Dinosaur!, Primeval Whirl, Kali River Rapids, Kilimanjaro Safaris; *Universal Studios Florida:* Back To The Future – The Ride, Men In Black – Alien Attack, Revenge of the Mummy, Earthquake, Jimmy Neutron ride; *Islands of Adventure:* Incredible Hulk Coaster, Dr Doom's Fearfall, Popeye and Bluto's Bilge-Rat Barges, Dudley Do-Right's Ripsaw Falls,

Great shopping at Lake Buena Vista

American-speak

Many words and phrases have a different meaning across the Atlantic. For instance, when Americans say the first floor, they mean the ground floor, the second floor is really the first, and so on. (NB: NEVER ask for a packet of fags. Fag is a crude, slang term for homosexual.) Here are a few everyday words to help you:

American	English		American	English
Check or tab	Bill		Diaper	Nappy
Restroom	Public toilet		Stroller	Pushchair
Bathroom	Private toilet		Faucet	Tap
Eggs 'over easy'	Eggs fried both sides but soft		Collect call	Reverse charge phone call
			Gas	Petrol
Eggs 'sunny side up'	Eggs fried on just one side (soft)		Trunk	Car boot
			Hood	Car bonnet
Biscuit	Savoury scone		Fender	Car bumper
Seltzer	Soda water		Freeway	Motorway
Soda	Fizzy drink		Divided highway	Dual carriageway
Broiled	Grilled		Denver boot	Wheel clamp
Shrimp	King prawn		Turn-out	Lay-by
Eggplant	Aubergine		No standing	No parking OR stopping
Zucchini	Courgette		Ramp	Slip road
Chips	Crisps		Intersection	Junction
Entree	Main course		Yield	Give way
Graham cracker	Digestive biscuit		Purse	Handbag
Crib	Cot		Quarter	25 cents
Cot or rollaway	Fold-up bed		Dime	10 cents
			Nickel	5 cents

Jurassic Park River Adventure, Dueling Dragons; *SeaWorld:* Wild Arctic (avoid simulator ride), Journey to Atlantis, Kraken. *Busch Gardens:* Gwazi, Kumba, Montu, The Python, The Scorpion, Congo River Rapids, Stanley Falls Log Flume, Tanganyika Tidal Wave, The Phoenix, Sandstorm, Crazy Camel, Akbar's Adventure Tours.

BRIT TIP: Pushchairs are essential, even if your children are a year or two out of them. The walking involved wears kids out quickly and a pushchair can save a lot of discomfort (for dads especially!). You can take your own, hire them at the parks or, better still, buy one at a local supermarket for around £12.

Travellers with disabilities

The parks pay close attention to the needs of holiday-makers with disabilities. There are few rides that cannot cater for them, while wheelchair availability and access is almost always good. For hearing-impaired guests, there are assistive listening devices and reflective captioning at attractions where a commentary is part of the show, and guidebooks in Braille are available, plus rest areas for guide dogs. All Disney hotels have disabled-accessible rooms – call 407 939 7807 or visit www.disneyworld.com – and Disney publishes a *Guidebook for Disabled Guests* (as does Universal), available in all three main parks (and online). Life-jackets are always on hand at the water parks, and there are special tape cassettes for blind guests. If you require help while queuing for rides or have children with special needs, call in at any Disney guest relations office to ask about what provisions are available.

Disabled drivers should take their orange car badge with them as this is honoured in the US and there are designated parking areas at all theme parks. For local assistance, **Walker Medical & Mobility Products** (407 518 6000) specialises in 3-wheeled electric scooters and wheelchair rentals, with free delivery and pick-up even from holiday villas. **Rainbow Wheels** (407 977 3799, www.rainbowwheels.com) hires out full-size or mini vans equipped for wheelchair users. The discussion forums on www.wdwinfo.com also include a board geared to visitors with disabilities.

Reader Les Willans confirms: 'Orlando is superb when it comes to accessibility for wheelchair users like myself, but Americans often use quite offensive language, such as the term "handicapped", when referring to the disabled.'

Orlando for grown-ups

It may sound daft to include information specifically for adults, but it is an often overlooked aspect that you don't need to have kids in tow to enjoy Orlando. In fact, I've often felt the place is actually too good for kids! There is so much clever detail and imagination, it is usually the grown-ups who get the

BRIT TIP: If you have a fridge in your hotel, put drink cartons in the freezer overnight and they will be cool for much of the next day in your back-pack. Better still, buy a cheap cool bag, freeze it with some water bottles in, and leave it in the car – great after a day in the parks.

most out of the experience. In fact, as many couples and singles visit the parks as families.

Certainly, when you look at some of the entertainment on offer at places like *Pleasure Island* and CityWalk, the downtown district and Pointe*Orlando, the great range of bars and the proliferation of fine restaurants in recent years, with a good number of romantic offerings, it is easy to see the attraction for those 21 and over. As well as Florida being a key honeymoon destination, its friendly, social atmosphere provides an ideal place for singles, while couples without children can also take advantage of the late opening hours at the parks and clubs like Jellyrolls at *Disney's Boardwalk Resort.*

Orlando for seniors

The more mature traveller can also benefit from a healthy dose of the Sunshine State. And, if my parents (both in their 60s) are any guide, they will have just as much fun, within slightly different parameters. For the older person, staying in a Disney hotel is highly recommended as it removes the stress of driving. The extra cost is offset, my parents felt, by the beauty and convenience of their surroundings.

In the parks, they found there was still plenty for them to do, even if they weren't keen on most of the thrill rides (although just watching can be entertainment enough!). *Epcot* and Disney's *Animal Kingdom Theme Park* both have much to engage the older visitor, while the shows of *Disney-MGM Studios* make that a popular choice, too, and the *Magic Kingdom* Park, while 'probably the noisiest of all the parks', still represents an essential experience.

The *Downtown Disney* area can feel a bit frenetic for the senior crowd, but *Disney's Boardwalk Resort* is popular and the whole of the *Epcot*

Top 10 Romantic Restaurants

1. Tchoup Chop, Universal's Royal Pacific Resort
2. California Grill, *Disney's Contemporary Resort*
3. Todd English's bluezoo, *Walt Disney World Dolphin Resort*
4. Arthur's 27, Wyndham Palace Resort
5. Jiko, *Disney's Animal Kingdom Lodge*
6. The Boheme, Grand Bohemian Hotel
7. Manuel's on the 28th, Bank of America building, downtown Orlando
8. Old Hickory Steakhouse, Gaylord Palms Resort
9. Atlantis, Renaissance Orlando Resort
10. Bice Ristorante, Universal's Portofino Bay Hotel

resort area offers much in the way of fine dining and relaxation. In fact, this is often a prime area for seniors, notably the quieter *Disney's Yacht and Beach Club Resorts*, and the superb Swan-Dolphin complex.

For my parents in particular, the attractions they highlight for their age group are: Jim Henson's Muppet Vision 3-D and Fantasmic! at *Disney-MGM Studios;* Kilimanjaro Safaris, the Maharajah Jungle Trek and Festival of the Lion King at *Disney's Animal Kingdom Theme Park;* Spaceship Earth, Universe of Energy, Test Track and IllumiNations at *Epcot* (plus the

wonderful gardens and architecture); The Haunted Mansion, Jungle Cruise, Pirates Of The Caribbean and the monorail ride to the *Magic Kingdom* Park; watching the children at the many parades and character greetings; dinner at the California Grill in *Disney's Contemporary Resort;* shopping at Orlando Premium Outlets; most of Universal Studios, but less of Islands of Adventure (although they were wowed – as most are – by the Amazing Adventures of Spider-Man).

Weatherwise, March was just about ideal for them, but they wouldn't be keen to visit in the summer. Seniors can also take advantage of many discounts and special deals for their age group at the attractions as well as at many restaurants and hotels. The Official Visitor Center on I-Drive (see page 47) publishes a brochure of all the deals (www.orlandoinfo.com).

Repeat visitors

Repeat visitors create a large part of the Orlando market and are always on the lookout for something new after they have done all the main parks. To that end, our Off the Beaten Track chapter (see pages 214–42) is largely designed with them in mind. Listed here are ten things worth doing once you have Been There and Done That:

1) Behind the scenes tours at the Disney parks
2) Pony rides at *Disney's Fort Wilderness Resort* and carriage rides at both Fort Wilderness and *Disney's Port Orleans Resort*
3) A weekend visit to *Disney's Wilderness Preserve* in Poinciana, Kissimmee
4) The scenic boat ride at Winter Park
5) Historic Bok Sanctuary in Lake Wales
6) Lunch or dinner (and a visit to the soup cannery!) at the eclectic

The Gaylord Palms Wedding Pavilion

Chalet Suzanne – also Lake Wales

7) Breakfast at East Lake Fish Camp, plus an airboat ride
8) Sunset celebration at the Key West area inside Gaylord Palms Resort
9) Jazz evenings in Bosendorfer Lounge at The Grand Bohemian Hotel downtown
10) Friday night rodeo at Kissimmee Sports Arena.

Measurements

American clothes sizes are smaller than ours, hence a US size 12 dress is a UK size 14, or an American jacket sized 42 is really a 44. Shoes are the opposite: a US 10 should fit a British size 9 foot. Their measuring system is also still imperial and NOT metric.

Wedding bells

Florida is a place increasingly sought after by couples looking to tie the knot (some 20,000 couples a year at the last count). Orlando offers a terrific range of wedding services, from ceremony co-ordinators, photography and flowers to a wonderfully scenic range of venues such as Cypress Grove Park, Winter Park and Leu Gardens. More unusual ones include getting married in a hot-air balloon, helicopter, on the beach or a luxury yacht or in the pit-lane of the Richard Petty Driving Experience at *Walt Disney World Resort in Florida* or even at 145mph (233kph) around the speedway itself!

Walt Disney World's Wedding Pavilion offers true fairytale romance, with the backdrop of Cinderella Castle and Seven Seas Lagoon. You can opt for traditional elegance in this Victorian setting with up to 260 guests or the full Disney experience, arriving in Cinderella's glass coach with Mickey and Minnie among the guests. Disney's wedding organisers can tailor-make the occasion for individual requirements (407 828 3400). Universal provides a wedding service based at their beautiful **Portofino Bay Hotel**. Call 407 503 1120 for their wedding specialist.

All the main tour operators feature wedding options and co-ordinated services, and offer a variety of ceremonies. Prices vary from around £595 per couple (Cypress Grove Park in Orlando – Thomson) to £1,980 (Disney's Premium Intimate Wedding package – Virgin).

You can also **do it yourself** by calling at the new Osceola County Courthouse, Courthouse Square, Suite 2000, Kissimmee (just off Bryan Street in downtown Kissimmee) 8.30am–5pm Mon–Fri (407 343 3500). In Orange County, apply to the Orange County Courthouse on 425 North Orange Avenue 8am–5pm, Mon–Fri (407 836 2067). Both parties must be present to apply for the marriage licence, which costs $88.50 (in cash) and is valid for 60 days, while the ceremony (equivalent to a British

Cinderella-style wedding

© Disney

register office) can be performed at the same time by the clerk for an extra $20 (8–11am or 2–4pm Mon–Fri). Passports and birth certificates are required and, after acquiring a marriage licence, a couple can get married anywhere in Florida. Neither witnesses nor blood tests are necessary.

The County's Marriage Department can also supply names of public notaries to conduct the ceremony if you want to marry elsewhere, at one of the more picturesque resort hotels for example. Call the Orlando/Orange County Convention & Visitors Bureau for an info pack (407 363 5872), visit www.orlandoweddinglocations.com or call 407 876 6433. Another site worth visiting is www.getmarriedinflorida.com, or call 407 384 0848.

If you would prefer to get married in a church or other place of worship, contact the **Center of Light Church & Spiritual Center** on East Robinson Street (407 228 0101), the **First Baptist Church** on John Young Parkway (407 425 2555), **St Nicholas Catholic Church** on Sand Lake Road (407 351 0133) or **Trinity Lutheran Church** on East Livingston Street downtown (407 422 5704, www.trinitydowntown.org).

Disney special occasions

Birthday badges: free badges can be found at City Hall in the *Magic Kingdom* Park and Guest Services at *Epcot, Disney-MGM Studios* and *Disney's Animal Kingdom Theme Park.* Cast Members like to make a fuss over children (and adults!) wearing a birthday badge.

Birthday cakes: contact room service at your resort, or Guest Services at one of the parks. All Disney restaurants can offer cakes

> BRIT TIP: If you shop at any Wal-Mart store in America, you can return faulty or wrong-size goods to your local Asda for a refund, provided you keep your receipts.

(starting at $7.99). Be sure to tell the Cast Member at check-in (or when you make your hotel reservation) as well as hostesses and/or servers in restaurants, if someone in your party has a birthday. While it is not guaranteed, Disney staff often go out of their way to make the day special. If characters know it's a birthday when they sign a child's autograph book, they may add a special birthday wish.

Birthday cruise: the IllumiNations cruises (to *Epcot*) and the motorboat *Breathless* (from *Disney's Yacht and Beach Club Resorts*) both host birthday events, with cake and refreshments, and the boat can be decorated (by Disney). Small boat holds eight guests for $150 (plus tax), a large pontoon boat holds 12 at $220 (plus tax).

Birthday parties: *Disney's Yacht and Beach Club Resorts* arrange birthday parties for ages 4 and up. A 3-hour party for up to 12 guests is $300. Decorations, birthday cake, use of the games at the Sandcastle Club, arcade games (free), video games, Disney movies on TV and access to Stormalong Bay are included. Parties can be booked at either 11am or 12 noon. Menu is pizza, hot dogs, hamburgers, chips, and soda. Call 407 934 3750.

The *Winter-Summerland Miniature Golf* hosts 2-hour birthday parties for 10 or more, including pizza, sodas, cake, party favours and a round of mini golf. Cost is $16.95 a head, plus tax. Call 407 WDW-PLAY, and you need to book at least one week ahead.

DisneyQuest has Birthday Tickets at $33 for adults, $27 per child (3–9), which includes admission, one meal coupon, one $5 Prize Play card and 20 per cent off merchandise at the Emporium (good only for the day of the event).

Ice Cream Social: for a birthday or anniversary event, or for no occasion at all, at just $6.75, the Garden Grill at The Land pavilion in *Epcot* serves up a huge ice cream creation with Mickey, Pluto and Chip 'n Dale. Offered twice daily at 3 and 3.30pm, the Social can easily replace a meal and provides good character interaction at a price far below a typical character meal. Booking is advisable, though, on 407 WDW-DINE.

Safety first

While crime is not a serious issue in central Florida, this is still big-city America and, as with all big cities, you need to keep your wits about you. You don't leave your common sense at home.

The area has its own Tourist Oriented Policing Service (or TOPS), centred on I-Drive, with more than 70 officers patrolling purely the main tourist areas, arranging crime prevention seminars with local hotels and generally ensuring Orlando takes good care of its visitors. You will often see the local police in these areas out on mountain bikes, and they are a polite, helpful bunch should you need their assistance or to ask them directions. Tourism is such a vital part of the local economy the authorities cannot afford to be seen not taking an active role against crime, hence the area has a highly safety-conscious attitude.

However, it would be foolish not to stick to the usual safety guidelines when travelling abroad.

BRIT TIP: For your journey to the US, use a business address rather than your home address on all your luggage. It is less conspicuous and safer should any item be stolen or misplaced.

Emergencies

General: for police, fire department or ambulance, dial 911 (9-911 from your hotel room). It is a good idea to make sure your children are aware of this number, while for smaller-scale crises (mislaid tickets or passports, rescheduled flights, etc) your holiday company should have an emergency contact number in the hotel reception. If you are travelling independently and run into passport or other problems that require the assistance of the British Consulate in Orlando, their office is located in Sun Bank Towers, 200 South Orange Avenue, with walk-in visitors' hours 9.30am–noon and 2–4pm, or phone 9.30am–4pm on 407 426 7855.

Phonecards which you need to make a call from a local payphone – and are much cheaper than using your hotel room – are available from most 7-Eleven stores or from your tour rep.

Hotel security

While in your hotel, motel or guesthouse, you should always use door peepholes and security chains whenever someone knocks at the door. DON'T open the door to strangers without asking for identification, and check with the hotel desk if you are still not sure.

It is stating the obvious, but keep doors and windows locked at all times and always use deadlocks and

Phones and 2-way radio rentals

Mobile phones and 2-way radios are among the most useful gadgets at the best of times, but they take on a popular new role in Orlando, in terms of both safety and convenience. Many families now hire a mobile phone or radio to keep in touch around the parks and it is common to see them in use. And, when it comes to either one, a *Brit's Guide* partner provides an excellent service in this field. **Action Radio & Cell** at 7611 South Orange Blossom Trail rents both mobile phones (cellphones, as they are known in the US) and radios at $10/day, $30/week or $75/month, with minute usage at $1/minute, and calls back to the UK at an additional $1.75/minute (much cheaper than any hotel rate). For the more advanced Nextel phone/radio, it is $15/day or $50/week with the same per minute call charges. Action Radio & Cell can be found just north of the Florida Mall, and they will deliver to your hotel. For more details, call 407 354 4890 outside the US or freephone 1-800 717 3717 in Florida, www.radiogirlz.com.

security chains. It is still surprising how many people forget basic precautions on holiday (the local police never cease to be amazed at people leaving their common sense at home!). Always take your cash, credit cards, valuables and car keys when you go out (or put them in the safe), and don't leave the door open at any time, even if you are just popping down the corridor to the ice machine.

Make a point of asking hotels about their safety precautions when you make a reservation: do their rooms have electronic card-locks (which can't be duplicated) and do they have security staff? Most hotels can offer the use of safes and deposit boxes, and many rooms now have mini-safes installed to safeguard non-essential valuables.

Don't be afraid to ask reception staff for safety advice for the surrounding areas or if you are travelling somewhere you are not sure about. Safety is a major issue for the Central Florida Hotel/Motel Association and hotel staff are usually well briefed to be helpful. Using a bumbag (the Americans call them fanny packs!) is a better bet than a shoulder bag or handbag.

Nothing is guaranteed to get the local police shaking their heads in disbelief than the tourist who goes round looking like an obvious tourist. The map over the steering wheel is a giveaway, but other no-nos are wearing large amounts of jewellery, carrying lots of camera equipment or flashing wads of cash around. The biggest giveaway is leaving a camera or camcorder on view in the car (which is also

Lost River Voyage at Silver Springs

BRIT TIP: If your room has already been cleaned before you go out for the day, hang the 'Do Not Disturb' sign on the door. Always keep your valuables out of sight, whether in the hotel room or the car.

inadvisable as the heat build-up in a car in summer can ruin some photographic equipment).

Finally, and this is VERY strong police advice, in the unlikely event of being confronted by an assailant, DO NOT resist or 'have a go', as it can often result in making the situation more serious.

Money matters

It is useful to know that dollar travellers' cheques can be used as cash and can be readily replaced if lost or stolen, so it is not necessary (as well as not being advisable) to carry large amounts of cash around. However, sterling travellers' cheques can only be cashed in major banks – most outlets will not accept them.

Having a credit card is almost essential as they are accepted everywhere and provide an extra degree of buying security. In some cases, notably car hire, you can't operate without your flexible friend. Visa, Mastercard and American Express are all widely accepted.

It is worth separating the larger notes from the smaller ones in your wallet to avoid flashing all your money in view. Losing £200 of travellers' cheques shouldn't ruin your holiday – but losing $300 in cash might. The Sun Bank in *Disney's Magic Kingdom* Park and *Epcot* is open 7 days a week should you need financial help.

Take note, all Orlando prices, both in this book and on every price tag you see, do not include the 6–7 per cent **Florida Sales Tax**. There is also a 4–5 per cent **Resort Tax** on hotel rooms.

Car safety

Car crime is one of the biggest forms of criminal activity in America and has led to some of the most lurid headlines, especially in the Miami

BRIT TIP: All American banknotes are the SAME green colour and size. It is only the picture of the president and denomination in each corner that change.

area in the mid-1990s. Once again, it pays to make basic safety checks before you set off. The first thing is to familiarise yourself with the car's controls BEFORE driving off for the first time – which button for the air-conditioning, which control operates the indicators and where are the windscreen wipers, etc.

Also, try to memorise your route in advance, even if it is only a case of knowing the road numbers. Most hire firms now give good directions to all the hotels, so check them before you set off – trying to drive with the map over the steering wheel is just asking for trouble.

Check the petrol tank is well filled and never let it get near empty. Running out of 'gas' in an unfamiliar area holds obvious hazards. If you stray off your pre-determined route, stick to well-lit areas and ask directions only from official businesses like hotels and petrol stations or better still, a police patrol. Always try to park close to your destination where there are plenty of lights and DO NOT get out if there are any suspicious characters lurking around. Always keep your windows closed (you have

Feeding giraffes at Busch Gardens

Let us plan your holiday …

… with our Personalised Itinerary Planner

In conjunction with the new *Brit's Guide* website – www.askdaisy.net/orlando – our *Personalised Itinerary Planner* will help you get the very most out of your time in central Florida. For just £10, we will design an itinerary tailored to your individual plans for the parks and attractions of Orlando. In your planner, we will indicate the best days to visit the parks to avoid the crowds, all the show and parade times for the days you are there, a touring plan for each park, any rides that may be closed for refurbishment, a shopping guide, a weather forecast, updates on new rides, etc, and up-to-the-minute advice right from the source of the fun, plus a host of additional Brit Tips and Brit Picks (our special favourites) which we can't fit into the book.

All you have to do is visit the *Brit's Guide* website and click on the *Personalised Itinerary Planner* link. Fill out the online form with your travel dates, hotel details and what you would like to fit in to your visit. Submit the form, along with your payment, and you will receive an immediate acknowledgement of your requirements. A week before you go, you will receive by e-mail your Personalised Itinerary Planner, which will consist of:

1) An official *Brit's Guide* welcome from Simon Veness and Susan Haass.
2) A full day-by-day plan for the length of your holiday.
3) A touring strategy for ALL eight main parks, the water parks and shopping centres, avoiding the crowds and taking advantage of the latest developments.
4) An alternative plan in case of bad weather.
5) All the park show and parade times for the days you are there.
6) A list of any rides/shows that are closed during your visit.
7) A special selection of Brit Tips and local advice specifically for you.
8) Your individual holiday weather forecast.
9) Our Brit Picks – a guide to a range of personal favourites from restaurants to shops – which we feel may appeal to you most.
10) The ultimate insider knowledge, as both Simon and Susan are based in the heart of the Orlando magic and are fully up-to-date on all developments.

All in all, it adds up to the most comprehensive package of specialised holiday info anywhere, and it represents the secret to the most fun, in the most hassle-free way in the most exciting place on earth. What more could you ask for? Just check us out on www.askdaisy.net/orlando and we'll do the rest for you.

air-conditioning, remember?), and don't hesitate to lock the doors from the inside if you feel threatened (larger cars have doors that lock automatically as you drive off). And don't forget to lock up when you leave the car. Not many rental cars have central locking, so it's wise to double check.

Miami crooks have developed the habit of trying to get cars to stop by trying to look official or deliberately bumping into hire cars from behind.

The easily identified hire car number plates have now been phased out, but still NEVER stop for a non-official request. Go instead to the nearest petrol station or police station, and always insist on ID before getting out of your car for an official.

It is comforting to know that a unique aspect of driving in Orlando is that none of the main tourist areas have any no-go areas. The nearest is the portion of the Orange Blossom Trail south of downtown Orlando.

2

BRIT TIP: If you want to be extra safety conscious, you can hire mobile phones, pagers and 2-way radios from as little as $50 a week from Action Radio & Cell (see page 44).

This houses a selection of strip clubs and 'adult bars' that can be downright seedy at night.

For more information on safety, contact the Community Affairs office of Orange County Police on 407 836 3720 or the TOPS office on 407 351 9368.

Know before you go

You can contact these organisations for advance tourist information. Florida Tourism (www.flausa.com) have an info line on 0900 1600 555 (60p/minute) that lists all Florida destinations and gives other consumer lines in the UK, while they have a free information pack if you call 01737 644882 (plus some more great ideas on www.culturallyflausa.com). The Orlando Tourism Bureau in London has a 24-hour information line on 0800 018 6760, on which you can request their free *Destination Imagination* info pack or visit www.orlandoinfo.com/uk. You can also visit the Kissimmee Convention & Visitors Bureau at www.floridakiss.com.

When you arrive in the area, it is also worth checking out Orlando's ONLY official **Visitor Center** at 8723 International Drive (407 363 5872) for discounted attraction tickets, free brochures and accommodation advice and free information pamphlets and maps. The Kissimmee Convention of

Visitors Bureau is at the eastern end of the Highway 192 tourist drag (407 847 5000 or 1-800 327 9159 in the States) and they have a toll-free accommodation line in the US on 1-800 333 KISS.

You'll find information on all things Orlando and Disney on the fun and info-packed www.wdwinfo.com, to which I also contribute. The creation and maintenance of this independent site is a mind-boggling feat. It provides up-to-the-minute advice and assistance, including the complete range of theme park info (right down to park hours and ride height requirements), restaurant info, news, weather, facts, figures and tips, plus discounts throughout Orlando, discussion boards and a chat forum.

BRIT TIP: Don't forget our new website, www.asakdaisy.net/orlando, for all the latest updates.

The official sites are pretty good, too, with Disney's being the pick of the bunch: www.disneyworld.co.uk (check opening hours, parades and book online). Then there are www.universalorlando.com, www.seaworld.com and www.buschgardens.com. The local newspaper has a Calendar 'what's on' section (www.orlandosentinel.com) and the free *Orlando Weekly* (www.orlandoweekly.com) is full of helpful info.

Among the many unofficial websites (not approved by Disney) are www.wdwmagic.com (great for Disney trivia and rumours), the well-designed www.wdisneyw.co.uk (with more pages for UK visitors) and www.orlandorocks.com (for all theme park addicts).

3

Driving and Car Hire
(or, The Secret of Getting Around on Interstate 4)

For the vast majority, introduction to Orlando proper comes immediately after clearing the airport via the potentially bewildering road system in a newly acquired, left-hand drive hire car. Yet driving here is a lot more simple and, on the whole, enjoyable than driving in the UK. In fact, anyone familiar with the M25 should find Orlando's roads far less stressful.

Before you get to your hire car, however, a quick note about what you need to be aware of on arrival at Orlando International and Orlando Sanford Airports (see also Chapter 12).

Orlando International – which completed a major refurbishment in 2004 – is one of the most modern and enjoyable airports in the world, but it does have a bewildering double baggage collection system for international arrivals. You disembark at a satellite terminal and collect your luggage straight after going through Immigration, then put it on another baggage carousel that takes it to the main terminal while you ride the shuttle.

Once in the main terminal you will be on Level 3 and need to descend to Level 2 (split into the A

The Orlando airport shuttle

and B sides) for baggage reclaim. Porters can help you to Level 1 for car pick-up (remember the $1/bag tip), while trolleys need $1 in change – or a credit card – to operate. Taxis and limos are also on Level 1. Several tour operators have help desks here, too. The public bus system, Lynx (see next page), operates from the A side of Level 1, in spaces A32–34. If you are arriving late, consider staying at the **Hyatt Regency** hotel (see page 80) inside the airport rather than driving off tired. You'll feel far more refreshed to drive the next day.

The main hire companies with check-in desks at the airport are Dollar, National, L & M, Budget, Avis, and of course *Brit's Guide* partners Alamo, and all offer a comprehensive service (Alamo used to work out of a depot but is now on site in the airport, boosting the firm's all-round efficiency). However, a phone desk at Level 1 connects to another 12 companies at off-airport depots, including Hertz, Value, Payless and Enterprise.

The off-airport rental firms will have a free shuttle outside on Level 1 to take you to their depots, which will give you a preview of the roads before you take to them. Hertz and Avis are the biggest companies in the US, but Dollar and Alamo are tops for tourist business. Dollar is included in typical packages by Thomson, Airtours, Virgin, Style Holidays, Travel City and First Choice, while Alamo is the main client for Unijet, Funway, Jetlife, Jetsave, Kuoni, British Airways Holidays and Thomas Cook.

BRIT TIP: If you are hiring a car from one of the on-airport companies, save time by going to their desk to complete the paperwork BEFORE collecting your luggage on Level 2.

ORLANDO WITHOUT A CAR

Although being mobile is advisable, it is possible to survive without a car. However, few of the attractions are within walking distance of hotels and taxis can be expensive. You also need to plan your campaign with greater precision to allow for extra travelling time (and, with children, taking buses can be tiring). If you decide not to drive, your best base is either *Walt Disney World Resort in Florida* (free transport throughout, but harder to get to the rest of Orlando) or International Drive (I-Drive) for its location, good pavements and the great I-Ride Trolley. Many hotels have free shuttles to some of the parks or a cheap regular mini-bus service.

There are basically three different transport routes: public transport, shuttle services and taxis.

Public transport

The reliable, cheap, but slightly plodding **Lynx bus system** (407 841 8240, www.golynx.com) covers much of metro Orlando. Ask for a copy of their excellent System Map, which shows all their routes (or 'Links') and the main attractions. Worth noting are **Link 42** from Orlando International Airport to I-Drive; **Links 56** and **304**, respectively from Kissimmee and the I-Drive area to *Walt Disney World Resort in Florida*; **Link 18** from Kissimmee to downtown Orlando; **Link 55**, which covers a large part of Highway 192

in Kissimmee from Osceola Square Mall all the way west to Secret Lake Drive; **Link 38**, I-Drive to downtown Orlando; and **Links 50** and **300**, which both operate from Disney to downtown Orlando.

BRIT TIP: Don't want to drive? Consider a multi-centre stay within Orlando itself, staying first at, say, International Drive or Universal Orlando and then a Disney resort, to get the best out of the free or cheap transport options.

Lynx fares are $1.25 a ride (transfers are free) or $10 for a weekly pass (children 6 and under go free with a full-fare passenger). The service is every 30 minutes in the main areas, every 15 minutes from 6–9am and 3.30–6.30pm, but remember to have the right change. Lynx bus stops are marked by pink paw-print signs and all buses are wheelchair accessible. There can be long queues for the Lynx buses out of Disney at closing time, and it may be more worthwhile getting Disney transport to *Downtown Disney*, spending some time there, then getting a cab back to your hotel (about $25 to I-Drive).

The I-Drive area also has the great-value **I-Ride trolley**, which operates two routes along a 14-mile

The I-Ride trolley

(23-km) stretch of this tourist corridor. The *Main Line* runs from the Universal Orlando resort area of Windhover Drive and Major Boulevard in the north, via Belz shopping centre at the top of I-Drive, to SeaWorld via Westwood Boulevard and Sea Harbor Drive, and on to Orlando Premium Outlets in the south. The *Green Line* basically covers Universal Boulevard, from the Orange County Convention Center up to the junction of I-Drive and Kirkman Road (407 354 5656, www.iridetrolley.com). Running every day, 7am–10.30pm at roughly 15-minute intervals (30 minutes on the Green Line), it costs 75c per trip (25c for seniors) – please have the right change – or you can buy Unlimited Ride passes for 1, 3, 5, 7 or 14 days at $2, $3, $5, $7 or $14. You can buy a 14-day pass at the official Visitor Center on I-Drive (see page 47) by Austrian Court and save $2. If you need to transfer between routes, ask for a transfer coupon when you board (transfers are free with Unlimited Ride passes). Kids 12 and under go free with an adult, and all trolleys have hydraulic lifts for wheelchairs. Passes are sold at 75 locations in the I-Drive area, including most hotel service desks.

One other regular service worth noting is from SeaWorld to Busch Gardens in Tampa, with six departure points daily from 8.15–9.30am. Called the **Busch Shuttle Express**, it costs $5 a person but is free if you have bought Busch tickets in advance (included in the 5-Park Orlando FlexTicket). For more details, see page 178.

Shuttle services

An alternative to public transport is the raft of well-organised firms that offer set-fee shuttles to the attractions and places like Kennedy Space Center and Busch Gardens and pick up at hotels. The main firms are Mears and Coach USA.

Mears (407 423 5566, www.mearstransportation.com) offers the most comprehensive service, from limousines to coaches, and typical round-trip shuttle fares would be: Airport–*Walt Disney World*, $29/person ($21/child, ages 4–11; or $17 and $13 one-way); Airport–I-Drive, $25/$18; $15 and $11 one way); Airport–Highway 192 in Kissimmee $32–41/$19–23; *Walt Disney World*–Universal Orlando, $14 round trip; I-Drive–*Walt Disney World*, $14; I-Drive or *Walt Disney World*–Kennedy Space Center, $21. Mears also offers a SuperPass service of 3, 4, 5, 6 or 7 days of unlimited service to and from the main area attractions (including airport transfers) from I-Drive or *Walt Disney World* for $63, $72, $85, $96, $107 ($56, $67, $78, $89, $100 per child 3–11). Additional days $15 each. You can book a Mears shuttle on arrival at one of their desks in the luggage halls, but it can be a long journey to your hotel if they have a full van.

Coach USA (407 826 9999, www.coachusa.com) offers a full-day's excursion to Kennedy Space Center (including entry) for $66 ($54 children 3–9; $30 transport only), or $30 for a day trip to Cocoa Beach. Coach USA also has shuttle services from Orlando Sanford Airport at $40 round trip (much further north, remember) to most of the tourist areas ($21 one way).

Quick Transportation (1-888 784 2522 in the US or 407 354 2456 outside the US www.quicktransportation.com) comes well recommended for its excellent luxury van (people carrier), town car and limousine service, plus tailor-made transport packages. They offer a highly personal and efficient alternative to taxis and shuttles for airport transfers and can be more economical for larger groups. Town cars (luxury saloons) will cope with a family of four, while the spacious vans cater for larger parties (plus the limos). Their friendly drivers meet you in the baggage hall (look for the green sign-board) and take you directly to the hotel (with a 30-minute grocery stop, if required, for an extra $17.50). Visit their excellent website for an insight into arriving at Orlando International. Luxury van rates (for up to seven) one way from the airport range from $41.50 to the I-Drive area up to $66.50 for the farthest parts of *Walt Disney World*. Up to 11 can use a van for a small additional fee per person. Larger parties may need a luggage trailer for $17.50 extra each way. Town car rates are $68.50 one way from the airport to anywhere in Greater Orlando and $136 round trip, while stretch limos are $106 and $208.75. They offer a personalised service to all the theme parks and attractions, plus round-trip transportation from Orlando to Port Canaveral for cruise connections. Every Tuesday they organise a shuttle to Kennedy Space Center for $25 round trip.

You can also try **Florida Tours** (1-800 790 6290, www.fltours.com), who operate town cars, luxury vans – for up to ten people – and limousines, or **Tiffany Town Car** (www.tiffany towncar.com), but Quick Transportation gets the official *Brit's Guide* seal of approval.

Excursion services are offered by Coach USA, Gray Line (303 433 9800, www.grayline.com), **International Divers** (407 352 5151, www.swimdolphins.com), Keith Prowse and Access USA.

Several shopping malls have their own shuttle or pick-up service. **Lake Buena Vista Factory Stores** collects guests free on a daily basis from more than 40 hotels in the Orlando and Kissimmee areas (check your hotel for details, or call 407 363 1093). **Orlando Premium Outlets**

(407 390 0000) provides a hotel shuttle with Maingate Transportation at $6 round trip from the Lake Buena Vista area and $9 from Kissimmee hotels. The **Florida Mall** has a free shuttle twice daily from hotels in I-Drive and Lake Buena Vista (check with your hotel concierge, call 407 851 6255 or visit www.florida-mall-fl.com).

Taxis

For groups of four or five, **taxis** can be a more cost-effective option than the shuttles. Orlando International to I-Drive would cost around $35 plus tip – making it about $8 each for five – $12 from I-Drive to Universal Orlando and $25 from I-Drive to *Downtown Disney*. You will find plenty of taxis waiting in ranks at the parks, hotels and shopping centres, but they don't cruise around looking for fares, so it is usually best to book one in advance. You also need to ensure you choose a reliable, fully insured company (Orlando has what are known as 'gypsy' cab drivers, who appear to be with reputable firms but often do not have full passenger insurance). Check that the name and phone number of the cab company is clearly displayed on the side, that the driver's ID and insurance are visible and their rates are shown on the window or inside the car. 'Gypsy' drivers look for fares in the airport baggage hall, which is strictly illegal – all legitimate taxis should be in the rank on Level 1.

The **Mears** group (407 699 9999) has three firms who work (via computer system) through them – Checker Cabs, Yellow Cabs and City Cabs – all of which are reliable. Most taxis are metered but it is also acceptable to ask what the fare is in advance. Other reputable firms include **Central Florida Taxis** (407 851 7523 or freephone 1-800 441

I-Drive by night

3276 in Florida), **Star Taxis** (407 857 9999), **Diamond Cab Co** (407 523 3333) and **Town & Country** (407 828 3035; they tend not to run meters but will happily do so if you ask, or just ask the fare in advance). Several hotels have town cars at their ranks, and these will not have meters, so you can either ask the fare or call one of the companies listed above yourself.

THE CAR

Ultimately, having a car is the key to being in charge of your holiday and, on a weekly basis, it tends to work out quite reasonable too.

Weekly rental rates can be as low as $100 for the smallest car, an **Economy** (or sub-compact), usually a Corsa-sized hatchback; next up is the **Compact**, a small family saloon like a Vauxhall Astra; the **Midsize** (or Intermediate) is a more spacious 4-door, 5-seater like a Vectra; and the **Fullsize** would be a large-style executive car like an Omega, and you can go up the scale still, with

BRIT TIP: The boot size of American cars tends to be smaller than the British equivalent. And you will not get seven adults PLUS all their luggage in a 7-seat people carrier (van)!

Premium, **Luxury** and **Convertible**, plus the **Minivan**, a Renault Espace or VW Sharan type.

But beware these low starting rates. There are a number of essential insurances, taxes and surcharges, and these can take the final weekly rate up to $300 or more. However, all the big rental companies now offer all-inclusive rates, which can work out significantly cheaper if booked in advance in the UK. Rates can be as low as £150 a week, and you also benefit from easier processing at the Orlando end, making the whole business quicker.

To book, call **Alamo** (see inside the front cover for our special readers' offer) or **Dollar** on 0800 252897. Or you could try **Avis** (0990 900 500); **Budget** (0880 181181); **Thrifty** (0990 168 238); **Hertz** (0990 906090); **National** (0345 222525); or **Suncars** (0990 005566).

The scale of the car-hire operation is huge, with as many as 400 visitors arriving at a time. Most British holiday companies offer 'free car hire', but that does not mean it won't cost you anything. It is only the *rental* cost that is free and you must still pay the insurance, taxes and other extras BEFORE you drive away (which makes the all-inclusive packages even more attractive).

Having a credit card is essential, and there are two main kinds of insurance, the most important being the Loss or Collision Damage Waiver (LDW or CDW). This costs around $20 a day and covers you for any damage to your hire car. You can manage without it, but the hire company will insist on a huge deposit in the order of $1,500 on your credit card (and you are also liable for ANY damage).

You will also be offered Supplemental Liability Insurance (SLI) or Extended Protection at around $13 a day. This covers you against being sued by any court-happy American you may happen to bump into (not essential, but good for your peace of mind).

Relatively new and again optional is the Underinsured Motorists Protection (in case somebody with only minimal cover runs into you) at around $6 a day. Drivers under 25 have to pay an extra $15–20 a day, while all drivers must be at least 21.

> **BRIT TIP:** Double-check that you have your driving licence BEFORE you leave home (both parts of it with the new photo-card type). Without it you will simply NOT be given a hire car.

Other rental costs include local and Florida state taxes, which add $7 a day to your final bill, and Airport Handling Tax and Access Fee at $6–7 a day. Then there's petrol, although this is still much cheaper than in the UK. Ask to return the tank full yourself, as this will save a few dollars on their fill-up option.

For those on a tight budget, you can cut costs by arranging travel insurance through specialists like Extrasure (020 7480 6871), whose Americasure policy offers both LDW and SLI at around £5 a day. You may still need to leave a credit card imprint with the hire firm, but they should accept these policies (but do still check in advance).

You may feel jet-lagged for a day or two, but this can be reduced by avoiding alcohol and coffee on the plane and drinking plenty of water.

> **BRIT TIP:** Be firm with the car hire company check-in clerk; some can push you into having extras, like car upgrades, that you don't need.

Most people soon find driving in America is a pleasure rather than a pain, mainly because nearly all hire cars are automatics and rarely more than a year old. And, because speed limits are lower (and rigidly enforced), you won't often be rushed into taking the wrong turn. Keep your foot on the brake when you are stationary as automatics tend to creep forward, and always put the automatic gear lever in 'P' (for Park) after switching off.

Controls

All cars have air-conditioning, which is essential for most of the year. Turn on the fan with the A/C button or it will not work! Don't worry if a small pool of liquid forms under the car – it's condensation off the A/C unit.

Power steering is common on many hire cars and larger cars have cruise control, which lets you set the desired speed and take your foot off the accelerator. There will be two buttons on the steering wheel, one to switch the cruise control on, the other to set the desired speed. To take the car off cruise control either press the first button again or simply touch the brake.

The handbrake may also be different. Some cars have an extra foot pedal to the left of the brake, and you need to push this to engage the handbrake. To release it, you pull the tab just above it, if there is one, or give a second push on the pedal. The car probably won't start unless the gear lever is in 'P'. To put the car in 'D' for Drive, you also have to depress the main brake pedal. D1

Highway 192 in Kissimmee

> BRIT TIP: With an automatic, you probably won't be able to take the keys out of the ignition unless you put the car in 'Park' first.

and D2 are extra gears for steep hills (none in Florida!). Few cars have central locking, so make sure you lock ALL the doors.

Getting around

Your car-hire company should provide you with a basic map of Orlando, plus directions to your hotel. Insist they give you these, as all the hire companies make a big point of this in their literature. Try to familiarise yourself with the main roads in advance and learn to navigate by the road numbers (as those are mainly given on the signposts) and the exit numbers of the main roads.

When you drive out of **Orlando International Airport** (or the hire company's off-airport depot) don't look for signs to 'Orlando' – the airport's new signage should be a big help here. The main tourist areas are all south and west of the city proper, so follow the appropriate signs for your hotel. For the International Drive area (or I-Drive), you want the Beeline Expressway (Route 528) all the way west until it crosses I-Drive just north of SeaWorld. The main hotel area of I-Drive is to the

> BRIT TIP: The Beeline Expressway (528) and Greeneway (417) are both toll roads, so keep some change in the car. Toll booths are reluctant to change notes above $20.

north, so keep right at the exit.

For western Kissimmee and Disney resorts go south out of the airport and take the Central Florida Greeneway (Highway 417) west until it intersects with State Route (SR) 536 at Exit 6 (for *Animal Kingdom* resorts, use Exit 3 and take Osceola Parkway). Then you take SR536 straight across into *Walt Disney World Resort in Florida* or Interstate 4 (I-4) west for one junction until it hits the main Kissimmee road, Highway 192 (aka the Irlo Bronson Memorial Highway).

For eastern Kissimmee, come off Highway 417 at Exit 11 with the Orange Blossom Trail (Highway 441), where going south brings you on to Highway 192 at the other end of the main tourist drag.

Leaving **Orlando Sanford Airport** is also a straightforward affair, boosted by the airport's simple design. Dollar and Alamo have made a big impression here with their British-dedicated operations, and Avis and Hertz are also on-site now, while Budget and Enterprise both have off-airport depots. The vast majority book with Alamo or Dollar, and you simply exit the baggage hall and walk straight across the road (to Dollar) or turn right and walk to the end of the concourse (for Alamo).

It may be further to the north and involve more driving (and taxis and shuttles are more expensive – a town car service would be $70 one-way to I-Drive and a taxi almost $60), but you usually save time overall by your quicker exit. Leave the airport on East Lake Mary Boulevard and quickly hit the junction with the Central Florida Greeneway (Highway 417) on which you head south. The slip road on to this toll motorway is just under the fly-over on your LEFT, and you will need about $4.50 to reach Kissimmee or *Walt Disney World Resort in Florida* or $3.75 to reach I-Drive (via the Beeline Expressway, Route 528).

You can avoid the tolls by staying on Lake Mary Boulevard for 6 miles (10km) until you hit I-4, but you may encounter the 4–6pm snarl-up through the city centre. The Greeneway is an excellent, easy-driving introduction to Orlando roads, even if it does cost an extra few dollars.

For radio traffic news and reports, tune in to 1680AM (if you have a mobile phone, dial 511 for traffic info on I-4).

Signs and road names

The system of signposting and road-naming can be confusing. For instance, you cannot fail to find the

> BRIT TIP: On the Greeneway (417) heading south, just after Exit 34, it appears to split into two where it meets Highway 408. Stay in the RIGHT lane to stay southbound.

main attractions, but retracing your steps back to the hotel can be tricky because they often take you out of the parks a different way. (Disney is notoriously poor at sign-posting to help find your way out. A good tip is to get a copy of their Transportation Guide/Map from Guest Services at any park to help navigation.)

It is vital to learn the main road numbers (and directions, either east–west or north–south) around the attractions so you know where you are heading, and whether you want I-4 east or west or 192 as you exit *Epcot* or *Disney-MGM Studios*.

Exits off I-4 and other main roads can be on EITHER side of the carriageway, not just on the right. This potential worry is offset by the fact you can overtake in ANY lane on multi-lane highways, not just the outside ones. Therefore, you can sit

in the middle lane until you see your exit. However, you don't get much advance notice of turn-offs.

Orlando has yet to come up with a comprehensive tourist map of its streets and the maps supplied by the car-rental companies tend to be simplified. It helps that none of the main attractions are off the beaten track, but the support of a front-seat navigator can be useful.

Around town, road names are displayed at every junction, hung underneath the traffic lights suspended ABOVE the road. This road name is NOT the road you are on, but the one you are CROSSING. Once again there is no advance notice of each junction and the road names can be difficult to read as you approach them, especially at night, so keep your speed down if you think you are close to your turn-off, to get in the correct lane. If you do miss a turning, most roads are based on a simple grid system so it is usually easy to work your way back.

Occasionally, you will meet a crossroads where no right of way is obvious. This is a **4-way stop**, and the priority goes in order of arrival, so when it's your turn you just indicate and pull out slowly (America doesn't have many roundabouts, so this is the closest you will get to one).

> BRIT TIP: The Osceola Parkway toll road which runs parallel to Highway 192 is a much easier route into *Walt Disney World Resort in Florida* from much of Kissimmee and costs only $1.50. Use Sherberth Road for Disney access from west 192.

© Disney

Getting around on two wheels

Tolls and traffic lights

For the toll roads, have some change handy in amounts from 25c to $1. They all give change (in the GREEN lanes), but you will get through much quicker if you have the correct money (in the BLUE lanes). On minor exits of Osceola Parkway and the Greeneway, there are auto-toll machines *only*, so keep some loose change in the car.

As well as the obvious difference of driving on the 'wrong' side of the road, there are also several differences in procedure. The most frequent British errors occur at traffic lights (which are hung above the road, not on posts). At a red light it is still possible to turn RIGHT, providing there is no traffic coming from the left and no pedestrians crossing, unless otherwise specified (signs will occasionally indicate 'No turn on red'). Turning left at the lights, you have the right of way with a green ARROW, but you have to give way to traffic from the other direction on a SOLID green.

The majority of accidents involving overseas visitors take place on left turns, so take extra care here. There is also no amber light from red to green, but there IS an amber

BRIT TIP: Be organised – get your directions in advance off the internet at excellent map sites like www.mapquest.com.

light from green to red. A flashing amber light at a junction means proceed but watch for traffic joining the carriageway, while a flashing red light indicates it is okay to turn if the carriageway is clear.

Restrictions

Speed limits are always well marked with black numbering on white signs and the police are pretty hot on speeding, with steep on-the-spot fines. Limits vary from 55–70mph (88–113kph) on the Interstates and can change frequently – where there is also a 40mph (64kph) *minimum* speed – to just 15 or 20mph (24 or 32kph) in some built-up areas.

Flashing orange lights over the road indicate a school zone and school buses must not be overtaken in either direction when they are unloading and have their hazard lights on. U-turns are forbidden in built-up areas and where there is a solid line running down the middle of the road.

It is illegal to park within 10ft (3 metres) of a fire hydrant or a lowered kerb, and never park in front of a yellow-painted kerb – they are stopping points for emergency vehicles and you will be towed away. Never park ON a kerb, either.

Seat belts are compulsory for all front-seat passengers, while child seats must be used for under 4s and can be hired from the car companies at around $5 a day (better still, bring your own). Children aged 4 or 5 must either use a seat belt, whether sitting in the front or back, or have a child seat fitted for them.

You must put your lights on in the rain, and park bonnet first. Reverse parking is frowned upon because number plates are often found only on the rear of cars and police then can't see them. If you park parallel to the kerb you must face the direction of the traffic. You must pull to the side of the road to allow emergency vehicles to pass when they have lights and/or sirens going.

Disabled drivers should note that their UK orange disabled badge IS recognised in Florida for parking in the well-provided disabled spaces.

Finally, don't drink and drive. Florida has strict laws, with penalties of up to 6 months in prison for first-time offenders. The legal blood-alcohol limit is lower than in Britain, so it is safer not to drink at all if you are driving. It is also illegal to carry open containers of alcohol in the car.

Bonus for AA members: your membership is recognised by the equivalent AAA in the US and you also benefit from a number of special offers. Take your AA card with you and, where you see the AAA 'Show & Save' signs in hotels, shops and restaurants, just produce it to enjoy the same money-saving benefits as the locals (notably a coupon book at the Orlando Premium Outlets). Visit www.aaasouth.com then click on the Savings link for the full low-down.

Accidents

In the unlikely event of having an accident, no matter how minor, you must contact the police before the cars can be moved (except on the busy I-4). Car-hire firms will insist on a full police report for the insurance. If you break down, there should be an emergency number for the hire company in their literature or, if you are on a major highway, raise the bonnet and wait for one of the frequent police patrol cars to stop (or dial *FHP on your mobile). Always carry your driving licence and hire agreement forms in case you are stopped by the police.

Key routes

The main route through Orlando is **Interstate 4** (or I-4), a 4-, 6- or 8-lane motorway linking the two coasts. Interstates are always indicated on blue shield-shaped signs. For most of its length, I-4 travels east–west but, around Orlando, it swings north–south, although directions are still given east (for north) or west (for south). All main motorways are prefixed I, the even numbers generally going east–west and the odd numbers north–south. Federal Highways are the next grade down and are all numbered with black numerals on white shields, while state roads are known as Routeways and prefixed SR (black numbers on white circular or oblong signs). All the attractions of *Walt Disney World Resort in Florida*, plus those of SeaWorld and Universal Orlando are well sign-posted from I-4. Historic Bok Sanctuary is a 45-minute drive from central Orlando (south) west on I-4 and Highway 27, while Busch Gardens is 75–90 minutes down I-4 to Tampa.

International Drive (or I-Drive) is the second key local roadway, linking a 16-mile (26-km) ribbon of hotels, shops, restaurants and attractions like Wet 'n Wild, The Mercado centre and Belz Factory Outlet. (I-Drive south, from Highway 192 north to Route 535, is NOT the main stretch, although they will eventually link up.) From

International Drive

I-4, take Exits 71, 72, 74A or 75A going (north) east, or 75B, 74A or 72 going (south) west. To the north, I-Drive runs into Oakridge Road and then the South Orange Blossom Trail, which leads to downtown Orlando (Junctions 82C–84 off I-4). I-Drive is also bisected by Sand Lake Road and runs into Epcot Drive, via Route 536, to the south, also convenient for Disney's attractions.

I-Drive is a major tourist centre and makes an excellent base, especially to the south of Sand Lake Road, near The Mercado, where you have the benefit of proper pavement. It's a 20-minute drive to Disney and 10 minutes from Universal. However, it can be congested at peak times, especially around Sand Lake Road in the evening, so try to use Universal Boulevard instead.

BRIT TIP: All Interstate exits have been renumbered recently, so repeat visitors must be aware that I-4 exit numbers may be different from the last time they were here.

The other main tourist area is the town of **Kissimmee**, south of Orlando and south-east of Disney and it's an attraction in its own right. Its features are grouped along a 19-mile (31-km) stretch of the Irlo Bronson Memorial Highway (192), which intersects I-4 at Junction 64B, and is only 10 minutes from *Walt Disney World Resort in Florida*, 20 from SeaWorld and 25 from Universal. The downtown area of Kissimmee is off Main Street, Broadway and Emmett Street and is ideal for walking.

A handy visual along **Highway 192** are the markers from Formosa Gardens (Number 4) to just past Medieval Times (Number 15). These highly visible signs are good locators for hotels, restaurants and attractions.

Fuel

At American petrol, or 'gas', stations you may have a choice of attendant or self-service. You do not tip the attendant but you do pay slightly more. Most gas stations will also require you to pay in advance at night, and will require the exact amount in cash or your credit card. Some pumps also allow you to pay by credit card without having to go into the cashier's office. The American gallon is smaller (by about a fifth) than the British version. Always use unleaded fuel and, to activate the petrol pump, first lift the lever underneath the pump nozzle. **RaceTrac** petrol stations are often the cheapest (even for soft drinks and cigarettes), although some don't take credit cards.

Local maps

The best and most up-to-date free maps are the bright orange Welcome Guide-Map (also full of discount coupons), available in the main tourist areas, and the pull-out map inside the Kissimmee-St Cloud Visitors' Guide (from the official Visitor Center on East Highway 192, call 407 847 5000). AA members are well catered for (see page 57), but the best paid-for maps are the Trakker series, with four products covering Orlando: the Pocket Map ($4.95) is almost as detailed as the AAA ones, while the City Slicker (a laminated fold-out of the main areas, $5.95) is useful in the car. Trakker also does a full Orlando Street Atlas ($19.95) (407 447 6485 in Orlando, www.trakkermaps.com).

Now, let's go on to your holiday accommodation...

Accommodation

(or, Making Sense of American Hotels, Motels and Condos)

To list all the accommodation in this area would fill a book. Metro Orlando has the second highest concentration of hotels in the world and more are being built all the time – with more than 112,000 rooms and still counting. Therefore what follows is a general guide to the bigger, better and budget types.

HOTELS

American hotels, particularly in the tourist areas, tend towards the motel type. The facilities and service are great, but you won't necessarily be located in one main building. Your room may be in one of several blocks arranged around the pool, restaurant or other facilities, making it more important to be security-conscious (see page 43). Room size rarely alters, even between 2- and 4-star accommodation; extra amenities and services give a hotel extra star rating. A standard room usually has two double beds and will comfortably accommodate a family of four (couples should ask for a king room, with an extra-size bed). Most hotels offer non-smoking rooms.

The other surprising feature of motel-type accommodation is the lack of a restaurant in some cases. This is because American hotels operate almost exclusively on a room-only basis – meals are usually extra – so you may have to drive to the nearest restaurant (of which there are many – see Chapter 10) just for breakfast. So check the dining facilities before you book.

Most Orlando hotels are big, clean, efficient and great value. You'll find plenty of soft-drink and ice machines, with ice buckets in all the rooms (although drinks from the machine may be more expensive).

All accommodation will be air-conditioned and, when it is really hot, you have to live with the drone of the A/C unit at night. *Don't* turn it off when you go out, even if it is cool in the morning, or the room will be like an oven by your return.

Note that the most expensive place from which to make a phone call is your hotel room! Nearly every

> BRIT TIP: Not all hotels provide hair-dryers, though they can often be ordered from the desk. For your own, you will need a US plug adaptor (with two flat pins). Their voltage is 110–120 AC (ours is 220) so appliances will be sluggish.

hotel adds a 45–70 per cent surcharge (Disney resorts add a $15 'connection fee') to every call (you can also be charged for a call even if no one answers, if it rings five or more times). Buy a phonecard instead (see page 43).

Remember, too, that hotel prices (in this book and in Orlando) are always *per room*. They will be cheaper out of the main holiday periods, but they can still vary from month to month, with special deals offered at times. Always ask for rates if you book independently and check if any special rates apply during your visit (don't be afraid to ask for their 'best rate' at off-peak times, which can be lower than published rates). There may be an additional charge ($5–15 per person) for more than two adults sharing the same room, plus there is a per-night state tax.

If you've just arrived and are still looking for accommodation, head for one of the two official Visitor Centers: International Drive just south of The Mercado (on the corner of Austrian Court, open daily 8am–7pm); or on the eastern stretch of Highway 192 in Kissimmee (open 8am–5pm), where they keep brochures and all the latest hotel deals. If you are happy with auction websites like www.priceline.com, you may pick up a bargain.

Know Before You Go (407 425 5387 or 1800 230 5938, www.knowbeforeugo.com) also deals in discounted accommodation as well as attraction tickets. Other booking agents are **Hotel Anywhere** (01444 410555, www.hotelanywhere.co.uk) and, in the US, **Hotels.com** (1-800 246 8357, www.hotels.com).

We place accommodation in four price bands to give you a rough reckoner, although bear in mind no price is set in stone:

$	=	up to $50 per night
$$	=	$51–99
$$$	=	$100–160
$$$$	=	$161-plus

Disney's Caribbean Beach Resort

© Disney

As there is no widely accepted star rating system for US hotels, we have given our own C grades, based on the number of facilities and extra comforts. Hence, a CCCCC grading will include the highest level of facilities and service, while a CC or C will be a more basic motel-type.

Resort hotels

Our review of Orlando's hotels starts with *Walt Disney World Resort in Florida*. Conveniently sited on the doorstep of the main attractions – and linked by an excellent free transport system of monorail, buses and boats – Disney's hotels, holiday homes and campsites are all magnificently appointed and maintained. They range from the five-star *Disney's Grand Floridian Resort & Spa* to the more basic but still fun style of the new *Pop Century Resort* – and their imagination and attention to detail are as good as the theme parks. There are some 28,000 rooms, while *Disney's Fort Wilderness Resort & Campground* has 1,190 sites.

Grand accommodation comes at a price, though. A standard room at the Grand Floridian can cost $500 a night in high season (suites can top $2,000!) and even the mid-range *Disney's Caribbean Beach Resort* can be over $150 a night. Dining at resort hotels is not cheap either, and you'll find few fast-food outlets on site.

Disney hotels come in four groups: **Deluxe** (*Grand Floridian, Polynesian Resort, Contemporary Resort, Yacht and Beach Club Resorts, Wilderness Lodge, Boardwalk Inn and Animal Kingdom*

© Disney

Disney's Pop Century Resort

Lodge); **Moderate** *(Caribbean Beach Resort, Coronado Springs and Port Orleans);* **Value** *(All Star Resorts and Pop Century);* and **Home Away From Home** *(Wilderness Lodge Villas, Old Key West, Boardwalk Villas,* the new *Saratoga Springs Resort & Spa* and *Fort Wilderness* cabins.

> BRIT TIP: It is usual in American hotels to tip the chamber maid by leaving $1 per adult each day before your room is made up.

Staying with the Mouse is one of the great thrills, for the style, service and extras. The 21 resorts offer a superb array of facilities, and children especially love being a part of Disney full-time. The benefits are: **Resort ID card:** every guest receives a card with which to charge almost all your food, gifts and services while on site to your room account. **Package delivery:** in conjunction with your ID card, you can have purchases sent back to your hotel gift shop. **Free parking:** with your ID card, there is no charge for your car at any of the parks. **Free transport:** forget the car and use the monorail-bus-boat network. **Refillable mugs:** all Disney resorts sell collectible drinking mugs, which

are well worth buying (about $11.99 each) as you can then help yourself to refills at their self-service cafés. **Dining priority:** guests can make Priority Seating bookings up to 90 days in advance (2 years for dinner shows). Call 407 939 3463 or dial *55 on any resort phone. Note: a Priority Seating (or PS) is not a reservation but a guarantee of the first available table when you turn up. **Priority golf:** the best tee times are reserved for resort guests and can be booked 90 days in advance on 407 939 4653. **Children's services:** all resorts have in-room or group baby-sitting (subject to availability, so book in advance on 407 827 5444) and the eight Deluxe resorts have supervised activity centres and dinner clubs (around $10/child per hour), usually open until midnight. **Mickey on call:** what better way to wake up than with an alarm call from the Mouse himself? **Extra Magic Hour:** this is the BIG bonus, the chance to get into one of the parks an hour early each day (see page 30) and do some rides before the crowds arrive. This was also being tested for evenings in 2004.

Magic Kingdom resorts

Around the *Magic Kingdom* Park are four of the grandest properties, plus the campground-style *Fort Wilderness.* The 15-storey **Disney's Contemporary Resort** has 1,030 rooms, a cavernous foyer, shops, restaurants, lounges, a real sandy

> BRIT TIP: Disney resort restaurants CAN (and should) be visited even if you are not staying there. You can book in advance at any of the parks, from any Disney phone (dial *55) or on 407-WDW-DINE.

4

beach, a marina, two pools (one with water-slide), six tennis courts, a video games centre and health club – and fabulous views, especially from the superb, hotel-top **California Grill** (one of the most romantic settings in Orlando; try to arrange a Priority Seating to coincide with the park's fireworks). Don't miss **Chef Mickey's** for a breakfast or dinner buffet with your favourite characters. There is the **Mouseketeer Club** for 4–12s, while the monorail runs *through* the hotel – fascinating for kids. Rooms are large, scrupulously clean and well furnished. Within walking distance of the *Magic Kingdom* Park, transport to the other parks is by bus. $$$$+, CCCCC.

> BRIT TIP: Watch the fireworks over the *Magic Kingdom* Park from the beach area of *Disney's Polynesian Resort*.

Disney's Polynesian Resort is a South Seas tropical fantasy with modern sophistication and comfort. Beautiful beaches, lush vegetation and architecture are home to 853 rooms built in wooden long-house style, all with balconies and superb views. Also on the monorail line, it boasts a stunning 3-storey atrium, with 75 varieties of tropical plants, parrots and a waterfall.

The resort offers excellent eating: **'Ohana** is an entertaining dinner venue, which also offers lively character breakfasts – plus there are canoe rentals, a beautiful pool area with water-slide, a games room, shops and children's playground. **The Neverland Club** caters for 4–12s (4pm–midnight). Catch the monorail or a boat to the *Magic Kingdom* Park, and buses to the others. The Poly is also home to the nightly *Spirit of Aloha* dinner show (see page 252), which is open to

non-resort guests and makes a great evening among the torch-lit paths and gardens. $$$$+, CCCCC.

> BRIT TIP: Dine in superb South Seas style at 'Ohana's but don't ask for the salt – unless you want to spark an amazing reaction…

Disney's Wilderness Lodge is one of the most picturesque resorts, one of my favourites and a great romantic destination. It is a detailed re-creation of a National Park lodge, down to the stream running through the massive wooden balcony-lined atrium into the gardens, past the swimming pool (with hot and cold spas) to a geyser that erupts each hour. Offering authentic backwoods charm with true luxury, the resort is connected to the *Magic Kingdom* Park by boat and bus only (and buses to the other parks). It also has two restaurants: the brilliant **Artist's Point** (lunch and dinner) and the **Whispering Canyon Café** (lively breakfast and huge all-you-can-eat buffets) – plus a snack bar and pool bar. The **Cubs Den** is for 4–12s (4.30pm–midnight). $$$$, CCCCC.

The Villas at Wilderness Lodge is a recent development of 136 studios and 1- and 2-bedroom villas. Facilities include living areas, fully equipped kitchens, private balconies and whirlpool baths. There is a quiet pool area, spa and health club.

Disney's Grand Floridian Resort & Spa is a hugely elaborate mock Victorian mansion with 867 rooms, an impressive domed and towered foyer and staff in Edwardian dress. The rooms are luxurious, hence mega prices, so it is worth a look even if you are not staying! It has six restaurants, including *Walt Disney World Resort in Florida's* top-of-the-range **Victoria and Albert's** (where the set, 6-course dinner with wine will cost $110+ each) and the chic seafood-based **Narcoossee's** (one of my favourites), with its excellent view over Seven Seas Lagoon and the nightly Electrical Water Pageant, plus four bars and impressive sporting and relaxation facilities. There's a wonderful new second pool area, complete with zero-depth entry and water-slide. The **Mouseketeer Club** caters for 4–12s (4.30pm–midnight) and the **1900 Park Fare** restaurant is one of the most popular for character breakfasts and dinners.

> BRIT TIP: Watch out for the free nightly **Electrical Water Pageant** on Bay Lake and Seven Seas Lagoon (see page 253), which you can see from all the *Magic Kingdom* resorts.

New in 2004 in the Garden View Lounge was **My Disney Girl's Perfectly Princess Tea Party** (10.30am–noon; daily except Tue and Wed), featuring Princess Aurora from *Sleeping Beauty* and with storytelling, sing-alongs and a princess parade, plus a princess doll and gifts for each child (3–11). The cost for one adult and child is a whopping $200 (reservations still advisable on 407 WDW DINE).

Transport to the *Magic Kingdom* is by boat and monorail; by bus to the others. $$$$+, CCCCC.

Camping Disney-style

Disney's Fort Wilderness Resort and Campground, on Bay Lake, opposite the *Magic Kingdom* Park, offers impressive camping facilities and chalet-style homes that can house up to six in a 750-acre (304-ha) spread of Florida countryside. Two 'trading posts' supply fresh groceries and there are two bars and cafés plus a range of on-site activities, including the thrice-nightly *Hoop-Dee-Doo Musical Revue*, campfire programme, films, sports, games and a prime position from which to view the nightly Electrical Water Pageant. You can rent bikes or take horse rides around the country trails, or go boating on Bay Lake, while the Tri-Circle D ranch offers a small petting zoo. Buses and boats link the resort with other areas (and a short boat ride to the *Magic Kingdom* is a great start to a day). $–$$$$, CCC.

Epcot resorts

The *Epcot* area features six hotels, including the best value ones. The unmistakable **Walt Disney World Swan** and **Dolphin** hotels are within walking distance of *Epcot* and *Disney-MGM Studios*, *Disney's Boardwalk Resort* and the Fantasia Gardens Miniature Golf Courses. The 'entertainment architecture' style is extensive and fun, they have the full range of resort benefits, facilities and style, yet are privately run so are a little cheaper than Disney's other Deluxe hotels. The Swan features a 45-ft (14-metre) statue on top and has 758 large rooms (including 55 suites), while the Dolphin (1,509 rooms, with 136 suites) is crowned by two even bigger statues. The duo make up one mega resort, and both were extensively refurbished in 2003–4 with a luxury look by the original architect, Michael Graves. They now feature the ever-popular Westin Heavenly Bed and unlimited access to high-speed in-room internet.

This extensive resort boasts 17 restaurants, four tennis courts, five pools (one an amazing grotto pool with hidden alcoves and water-slide), a kids' pool and white-sand beach, two health clubs, bike and paddle boat rentals, a great range of shops, video arcade and the **Camp Dolphin** centre for 4–12s (5.30–

4

midnight, $10/hour). Even for non-guests, the Italian **Palio** (Swan), **Shula's Steak House** and, new to the resort, celebrity chef Todd English's **bluezoo** (both Dolphin) are worth seeking out (with seafood-themed bluezoo one of the top restaurants recommended, see page 282). **Fresh**, the Dolphin's new Mediterranean-style market, serves breakfast and lunch, features all made-to-order menu items and both à la carte and tableside dining. At the Swan, the **Garden Grove Café** is set indoors in a tropical gazebo, with à la carte or buffet breakfasts – including character breakfasts on

Monorail at Disney's Polynesian Resort

this is very nearly the perfect resort. Visit www.swandolphin.com or call 407 934 3000. Transport is by boat (to *Epcot* and *Disney-MGM Studios*) and bus. $$$$, CCCCC.

The 45-acre (18-ha) **Disney's BoardWalk Inn and Villas Resort** is the most extravagant on-site property, featuring a 372-room hotel, 520 villas, four themed restaurants, a TV sports club and two nightclubs, plus an impressive array of unique shops, sports facilities and a huge, free-form swimming pool with a 200-ft (60-metre) water-slide, all on a semi-circular boardwalk around Crescent Lake. The effect is stunning, and the in-room attention to detail excellent. Highlights are the summer-cottage-style villas, Mediterranean restaurant **Spoodles** (tapas in the evening) and the **Big River Grille Brewing Company** for a great range of beers. Top of the range is the expensive but excellent seafood restaurant, the **Flying Fish**. It is a delightful resort to visit for a meal, the nightlife (especially **Jellyrolls** piano bar and the **ESPN Club**) or just to wander along the boardwalk. The **Harbor Club** caters for 4–12s (4pm–midnight). $$$$+, CCCCC.

Disney's Caribbean Beach Resort has more moderate prices for its 2,112 rooms spread over five Caribbean 'islands' (with inter-island bus service). Rooms are plainer (but

---

SPECIAL OFFER: Book a stay at the Walt Disney World Swan and Dolphin hotels June–Sept 2005 through any UK wholesale travel company and enjoy a FREE upgrade to a room with a magnificent lake view. Based on availability at the time of registration.

Saturday and Sunday. The restaurant is transformed in the evening into **Gulliver's Grill**, featuring à la carte menus, themed buffets and Disney characters every weeknight. **Tubbi's** in the Dolphin is open 24 hours.

At night, the complex looks truly magnificent. With its ideal location within walking distance of the two parks and the Boardwalk district,

Wilderness cabin

still comfortably sleep four), but the food court, main restaurant, **Shutters**, and outdoor activities (with a lakeside recreation area with themed waterfalls, slides and games arcade) are a big hit with children.

The six counter-service outlets in the food court at **Old Port Royale Town Center** (hub of this pretty resort and extensively refurbished in 2003) can get busy in the morning, and the Trinidad South and Barbados 'islands' are a fair walk from the centre. But it is an action-packed resort with some imaginative touches, like Parrot Cay Island Playground with its tropical birds and play area. Transport to the parks is purely by bus. $$$, CCCC.

Upmarket again, the refined, almost intimate, **Disney's Yacht Club Resort** has 630 nautical-themed rooms round an ornamental lake. For dinner, the **Yachtsman Steakhouse** offers friendly, polished and elegant dining. Sister hotel **Disney's Beach Club Resort** has 583 spacious rooms set along a man-made white-sand beach like a tropical island paradise. **Cape May Café** offers lovely character breakfasts and a nightly New England-style clambake buffet. You can go boating or catch a water-shuttle to *Epcot;* other transport is by bus. *Yacht and Beach Club* resorts share water fun at Stormalong Bay, a superb 2½-acre (1-ha) recreation area with water-slides and a sandy lagoon. The **Sand Castle Club** caters for 4–12s (4.30pm– midnight). Both $$$$+, CCCCC.

Disney's Animal Kingdom resorts

Disney's All-Star Resorts were Disney's first serious venture into the budget hotel market in 1997. Here, for just $77–109 a night year-round, you can stay in one of the five sports-themed blocks (Surfing,

Basketball, Tennis, Baseball and American Football) centred around a massive food court, two swimming pools, a games arcade and shops; the music-themed version (Jazz, Rock, Broadway, Calypso and Country); or the movies complex (Mighty Ducks, 101 Dalmatians, Fantasia, Love Bug and Toy Story). The latter is possibly the most imaginative, with its Fantasia pool and kids' play areas, and the most popular blocks are Toy Story and 101 Dalmatians (both non-smoking). All three centres, which total 5,760 rooms, have pool bars, shops, laundry facilities, video games rooms and a pizza delivery service. Bright and compact (if a little tight for families of four with older children), they are well designed for budget-conscious families who still want to enjoy all the Disney conveniences. Transport to the parks is provided by an efficient bus schedule. $$–$$$, CCC.

Disney's Coronado Springs Resort is possibly the best value of the moderate resorts (*Caribbean Beach* and *Port Orleans*) as it's the newest and has slightly more facilities for its 1,921 rooms spread over 125 acres (50ha): four pools, including the massive Lost City of Cibola, two games arcades, a boating marina, bike rentals, restaurant, food court and convenience store, lounge bar, gift shop, beauty salon and health club, business centre and two guest launderettes. Constructed in a scenic Mexican/Spanish theme in three 'villages' (Casitas, Ranchos and Cabanas), Coronado is an often-

Disney's BoardWalk Inn and Villas Resort

© Disney

4

overlooked treasure. Check out the **Maya Grill** and its New Latino cuisine. Coronado is 5 minutes from *Disney's Animal Kingdom Theme Park* and is well served by Disney's bus network. $$$, CCCC.

Disney's Animal Kingdom Lodge opened in 2001, a stunning private game lodge on the edge of a 33-acre (13-ha) animal-filled savannah, which many rooms overlook. The pervasive African theme is almost overwhelming, and the effect of opening your curtains to a vista of giraffes and zebras is immense. This wonderful creativity comes before you consider the amenities of this 1,293-room deluxe resort: two restaurants, café, bar, elaborately themed 'watering-hole' main pool (with water-slide) and kids' pool, massage and fitness centre, large gift shop, children's play area and an awesome 4-storey atrium. The main restaurant, **Jiko**, is spectacular, but there is also the

BRIT TIP: Jiko at *Disney's Animal Kingdom Lodge* offers an imaginative, African-tinged menu, attentive service and authentic ambience.

buffet-style **Boma**, a 'marketplace' restaurant featuring African dishes from a wood-burning grill and rotisserie for breakfast and dinner. The lavishness and detail are unmatched anywhere I have seen. Guides can tell guests about the 200 animals and their habitats, while children can listen to African folklore stories around the outdoor firepit or become junior safari researchers while Mum and Dad do some wine-tasting (the hotel boasts the largest US collection of South African wines). Rooms range from standard doubles (with the same slightly dated layout of the moderate resorts) to 1- and 2-bedroom suites, some which have bunk beds.

Simba's Cubhouse is for children aged 4–12 (4.30pm–midnight), and Disney transport is by bus. $$$$, CCCCC.

Disney's Pop Century Resort is in a similar style to *Disney's All-Star Resorts*, themed round the decades of the 20th century. There are 10 blocks with giant icons – such as yo-yos, Rubik's cubes and juke-boxes – and a riot of period sayings and visual gags. The first half of the resort (the Classic Years, 1950s–90s) opened in December 2003 and features a huge ten-pin bowling lane incorporating one of the three pools (the others are shaped like a computer and a flower), a huge table football set-up and open-air Twister mats. Blocks are grouped around a main building housing a spacious check-in area (with large-screen TV

BRIT TIP: To make a reservation at any *Walt Disney World* resort, call 407 934 7639. For information, visit www.disneyworld.co.uk.

showing Disney films of course), a large food court, a lounge (with quick-breakfast bar), a Disney store and games arcade. The 177-acre (72-ha) complex also features a central lake, while the Legendary Years, the 1900s–40s, will have identical facilities when it opens late in 2004. It adds significantly to Disney's budget-orientated offerings and has a well-organised bus service to the parks. The drawbacks? Long queues to check in build up for much of the afternoon and it has a rather hectic feel even late into the evening. You also need to request a hair-dryer from reception and rooms can feel comparatively small. $$–$$$, CCC.

Downtown Disney resorts

This is the other main resort accommodation centre. Here you will find: **Disney's Port Orleans Resort**, a 2-part complex (formerly Port Orleans and Dixie Landings) split into the 2,048-room Riverside – with a steamboat reception area, a great cotton mill-style food court, a full-service Cajun-themed restaurant and an old-fashioned general store (gift shop) – and the 1,008-room French Quarter, which has the **Sassagoula Floatworks and Food Factory** court, two bars, a games room and shopping arcade (the French Quarter was closed for refurbishment for much of 2004).

The Riverside includes **Ol' Man Island**, a magnificent 3½-acre (1.5-ha) playground with swimming pool, kids' area and a fishing hole, while the French Quarter has Doubloon Lagoon. Kids will especially enjoy the Mardi Gras dragon slide, alligator fountains and play area. The eye-catching landscaping and architecture vary from rustic Bayou backwoods to turn-of-the-century New Orleans. Transport for both sections is by bus or boat to *Downtown Disney*. $$$–$$$$, CCCC.

Disney's Old Key West Resort is a 5-star holiday ownership scheme (one of seven Disney Vacation Club properties), but the 1-, 2- or 3-bed studios in a Key West setting can also be rented nightly when not in use by members. Facilities include four pools, tennis courts, games room, shops and fitness centre plus **Olivia's** restaurant (for superb Key Lime Pie!). $$$$+, CCCC.

Disney's Saratoga Springs Resort & Spa is the newest member of the line-up, a 65-acre (26-ha) apartment complex opposite *Downtown Disney* with some wonderful views over the lake. When the third phase is completed in 2007, it will boast 828 units, from standard 2-bed hotel-style rooms to huge 2-storey, 3-bedroom apartments sleeping up to 12. The first phase of 184 rooms opened in May 2004, with another 368 due in 2005. The theme is the 1880s' New York resort of the same name, with a peaceful, gracious look and a great array of facilities, from the free-form, zero-depth entry main pool (with water-slide and squirt-fountain play area), the health-conscious dining room (the Artist's Palette, offering breakfast, lunch and dinner, as well as groceries), a large video arcade and a wonderful full-service spa and gym. This is Disney's answer to the vacation homes business, providing spacious, elegant accommodation for large groups. The standard 1-bedroom apartment can sleep four; the 2-bedroom version sleeps eight and the there's a 3-bedroom, 3-bath villa. All but the hotel-style studios have a fully-fitted kitchen (with dishwasher and microwave), washer, dryer, whirlpool bath and DVD player with TVs in the living room and each bedroom. It includes a guest services desk, room service, baby-sitting and child-minding services, and a water launch to the shops and entertainment of *Downtown Disney*. Rates for the 3-bedroom villas top $1,000 a night, but the 1-bedroom units are more modestly priced and, although it is a Disney Vacation Club property, some rooms will still be available to the general public. $$$$+, CCCCC.

Disney Hotel Plaza

In addition to the official hotels, there are another seven 'guest' hotels inside *Walt Disney World Resort in Florida* at the **Disney Hotel Plaza** on the doorstep of *Downtown Disney*. There's a free bus to the attractions and guaranteed admission to the parks, and you can make reservations for shows and restaurants before the public, but they are almost all more expensive than similar hotels outside Disney property (but being able to walk to *Downtown Disney* and Crossroads shopping plaza is worth a lot).

Top of the list (for service, mod cons and price) is the 10-storey, 814-room **Hilton** (407 827 4000; $$$$+, CCCC). With two excellent pools, seven restaurants and lounges and a health club, it fully deserves its 4-star, 4-diamond rating. It is also the only 'outside' hotel to enjoy

> BRIT TIP: No standard Disney Value or Moderate room will accommodate more than four. For larger groups, consider Old Key West, Saratoga Springs, the Boardwalk Villas, Wilderness Lodge Villas, Fort Wilderness cabins or one of the Deluxe resorts.

Disney's Extra Magic Hour feature. The outstanding **Benihana** restaurant offers sushi, sashimi, chicken and great steaks.

Also fairly expensive is the **Grosvenor Resort** (407 828 4444; $$$–$$$$, CCCC), with 626 fine rooms, exceptional service and colonial decor, plus a windmill-shaped pool area and a health spa, a daily Disney character breakfast at

Horse-drawn carriage at Fort Wilderness

Old Man Island in Disney's Port Orleans Resort French Quarter

Baskerville's, a sports bar and a 24-hour café, **Crumpets**. The standout property here is the **Wyndham Palace Resort & Spa** (407 827 2727; $$$$, CCCC), an elegant, 27-storey cluster offering 1,014 rooms, many with a view of *Epcot's* Spaceship Earth, a European-style spa, three heated pools, tennis courts, a marina with boat rentals and the superb **Arthur's 27** restaurant, with stunning views and a magnificent menu (opt for the set 4-course version at $66) for one of the most memorable dining experiences. Also try the **Top of the Palace Lounge** for a drink with a view! The chic **Watercress Café** is a great venue for breakfast and lunch, or a Sunday brunch with Disney characters (adults $22.95, children $12.95, no reservations needed). The **Laughing Kookaburra Lounge** is a smart nightclub open to non-residents, and the themed **Outback Steakhouse** is a one-off of this great chain restaurant.

The contemporary **Doubletree Guest Suites** offers 229 spacious family suites with every in-room convenience – from in-room safe to cookies! – and great kids' facilities, with their own check-in area, games room, pool, cinema and video arcade (407 934 1000; $$$$, CCCC).

The more modestly priced and tropically themed **Best Western Lake Buena Vista** has 325 rooms with views over the Marketplace, in-room coffee-makers and hair-dryers. The huge top-floor suites are magnificent. Garden-themed **Traders** is pleasant for breakfast or dinner, plus there is a quick-service deli, **Parakeets**, a lounge bar, and **Toppers** nightclub on the 18th floor (go during Disney firework shows!), plus a large pool, video arcade and small gym. The convenience marks this out as a real bargain. Like all the hotels in the Boulevard, it is perfectly positioned for a stroll to *Downtown Disney*, has free buses, guaranteed access to the parks, and preferred tee times at Disney golf courses (407 828 2424, www.orlandoresorthotel.com; $$$, CCC).

The well-priced **Holiday Inn in the Walt Disney World Resort** (formerly the Courtyard by Marriott) has 323 extra-large rooms in a 14-storey tower and 6-storey annex with glass-walled lifts, three heated swimming pools – including one for kids – small gym, games room, **Courtyard Café & Grill**, snack bar and lounge/bar, plus lovely gardens (407 828 8888; $$$, CCC).

Finally, the lovely **Hotel Royal Plaza** has a pleasant aspect, boasting 372 spacious and well-equipped rooms and 22 suites, with a full-service diner–restaurant, lounge bar, landscaped pool area, four tennis courts, a health club and Disney gift shop (407 828 2828; $$$, CCCC).

For more on hotels in the area, go to www.downtowndisneyhotels.com.

> BRIT TIP: To save time from the Hotel Plaza properties, walk to *Downtown Disney* Marketplace to catch the free bus to the theme parks.

Lake Buena Vista

As you move further away from *Walt Disney World Resort in Florida*, prices tend to moderate. You can still spend a small fortune, however, at the **Hyatt Regency Grand Cypress**. This 1,500-acre (608-ha) resort offers three 9-hole and one 18-hole golf course (designed by Jack Nicklaus), a swimming pool with waterfalls and slide, 21-acre (9-ha) boating lake, tennis complex, health club and equestrian centre. Rates START around $250, but the 750 rooms and suites are magnificently appointed and the resort is lovely. It also has five restaurants, three lounges and a poolside bar (407 239 1234; $$$$+, CCCCC).

Nearby, **Orlando World Center Marriott** is another personal favourite and an impressive landmark on Disney's outskirts, set in 200 landscaped acres (810ha) and surrounded by another golf course. An elaborate lobby, Chinese antiques and its sheer size (2,003 rooms, including 110 suites, seven restaurants, four pools, tennis courts and a health club) make it expensive, but it is conveniently situated and has one of the most picturesque pool areas, plus the whizziest glass-fronted lifts. It gets busy, especially with convention business. 'Try their Christmas Day Buffet,' says reader Roy Carlisle. 'Pricey but brilliant.' (407 239 4200; $$$$, CCCCC).

Disney's Contemporary Resort

© Disney

4

The Holiday Inn Sunspree Resort at Lake Buena Vista (507 rooms) is excellent for children's facilities, featuring a highly rated supervised childcare programme and a good range of other facilities. All rooms have kitchenettes. It also features the trademark 'Kidsuites' – a private playhouse/bedroom built into the hotel room, with its own TV, cassette player, video game player, clock, fun phone, table and chairs. They offer a fun alternative to normal hotel accommodation, down to the separate kids' check-in. Sunspree, perfectly situated for Disney and with free transport, also has a 2,100sq ft (195sq metre) Cyber Arcade, with access to the internet and other high-tech elements, while it has 50 two-room suites for more family comfort. Kids 12 and under eat free. (www.kidsuites.com, 407 239 4500; $$$, CCCC).

A novel choice is the African-themed **Sheraton Safari Hotel**, which sports the Python water-slide, a heated pool and kids' pool, with free transport to Disney parks and 'kids eat free' with parents at **Casablanca's** restaurant (breakfast buffet is highly recommended). Rooms are well equipped, with hair-dryers, coffee-makers and ironing boards, and all within walking distance of the Crossroads shopping centre, a good selection of shops and restaurants, and close to *Downtown Disney*. It has 489 safari-themed rooms, including 96 huge suites. With its great location and expansive style, it is an ideal mid-range family choice (www.sheratonsafari.com, 407 239 0444; $$$, CCC).

Some of the big hotel chains also have some of their smartest properties in this area, notably the **Radisson Inn Lake Buena Vista**, which has 200 rooms (407 239 8400; $$$, CCC) and the recently refurbished and fun-styled **Doubletree Club Hotel**, with 246 rooms, including kids' club suites.

The Doubletree's location at the entrance to *Downtown Disney*, pleasant bar and café, large pool deck and spacious, airy rooms mark this out as a real bargain (www.doubletreeclublbv.com, 407 239 4646; $$$, CCC½).

Kissimmee

Moving out along Highway 192 into Kissimmee, you will find the biggest choice of budget accommodation. Facilities vary little and what you see is what you get. All the big hotel chains can be found along this tourist sprawl, and rates can be as low as $29 per room off-peak, or $35 for a room with a kitchenette (what they call an 'efficiency'). Be prepared to shop around for a good rate (look for off-peak discounts), especially along Highway 192, where many hotels advertise rates on neon signs. As a rule, prices drop the further you go from Disney. Feel free to ask to see a room before you book (some of the motels can be pretty ordinary).

Chains

Among the leading chain hotels are **Best Western** (all with pools, family-orientated but large, in the $$–$$$ range); **Days Inn** (rather characterless and some without restaurants, but the newer properties are good value, mainly $$, and convenient, some rooms with kitchenettes); **EconoLodge** (akin to Best Western); **Howard Johnson** (a bit dearer, but with more spacious rooms and some with free continental breakfast); **Quality Inn** (sound, popular $–$$ chain); **Ramada** (rates vary between hotels in the $$–$$$ range, some offer free continental breakfast); and **TraveLodge** (another identikit, budget group, $–$$). The **Fairfield Inns** are the budget version of the impressive Marriott chain ($$).

The Marriott chain has three other family-friendly brands: the **Residence Inn by Marriott**, **SpringHill Suites** and **Courtyard by Marriott** (all $$$). The smart complex just off I-4 at Exit 68 features a Fairfield Inn, Courtyard and SpringHill Suites (www.marriottvillage.com), with 24-hour gated security, free *Walt Disney World* transport and great facilities.

The **Renaissance World Gate Hotel** (577 rooms; 407 496 1400; $$$, CCCC) scores high on value for money with its oversized rooms, excellent facilities and good service. In budget territory, the motel-type **Inns of America, Knights Inn, Motel 6, Comfort Inn** and **Super 8 Motel** brands all deliver a basic $ service, but the **Hampton Inn** and **Red Roof** groups manage a more quality-conscious approach in the same price band.

The **La Quinta Inn and Suites** series ($$–$$$) has six well-equipped new properties in the area, with two on I-Drive.

The **La Quinta Inn Lakeside** (formerly the Four Points by Sheraton Lakeside) on West Highway 192, is excellent value with three pools, tennis courts, kids' playgrounds, mini-golf, paddleboats and two restaurants and free Disney transport (651 rooms; 407 396 2222; $$–$$$, CCC½).

A firm personal choice is the **Holiday Inn Hotel and Suites Maingate East**, which also boasts Kidsuites rooms and Camp Holiday children's programmes, making it an outstanding family resort. Attention to detail (hair-dryers, coffee-makers, microwaves and fridges even in standard rooms), free Disney transport and its proximity to Old Town make for great flexibility and value (614 rooms and 110 suites; 407 396 4488; $$–$$$, CCC½). There's a children's check-in area, and under-13s eat free, as they do at **Holiday Inn Maingate West**, with

its tropical courtyard, free-form heated pool and kids' pool (287 rooms; 407 390 9063; $$, CCC).

The **Holiday Inn Nikki Bird Resort**, just west of Disney's Highway 192 entrance, is another good family-orientated property with its 23-acre (9-ha) tropical setting, three pools, basketball and volleyball courts and children's entertainment (529 rooms; 407 396 7300; $$, CCC). **Angel's Diner**, the hotel's outstanding restaurant, offers great breakfast and dinner buffets.

Equally, the **Radisson Resort Parkway** has above-average facilities and service after recent renovations. Just 1½ miles (2.4km) from Disney, with free transport, the resort boasts an elaborate free-form pool with waterfall, lovely rooms, and kids stay and eat free with their parents (718 rooms; 407 396 7000; $$$, CCCC).

Independent organisations

There are dozens of smaller, independent outfits that offer special rates from time to time. Look out in particular for 'kids eat free' offers. The budget-priced **Magic Castle Inn and Suites Maingate** take some beating with their range of amenities: free continental breakfast, free Disney transport to the parks, room fridges, kids' playground, guest laundry and picnic area (107 rooms and 15 suites; 407 396 2212 or 1-800 446 5669; $–$$, CC½).

Slightly off the beaten track, although well situated for all the parks and with extra charm, is the **Celebration Hotel** in the Disney-inspired town of Celebration. Just off Highway 192, the Central Florida Greeneway and I-4, this unique hotel offers a refreshing small-town America style. It has an elegant lounge and two reception desks, and you are a long way from the usual tourist hurly-burly. With 115 rooms in its 1920s' wood-frame design, the Celebration has a classy ambience and a wealth of high-quality touches, notably in the ultra-comfy rooms. These come in a choice of an attic-like Retreat, Traditional (with either one king or two queen-size beds), Studio or a 2-room Suite and are all beautifully furnished. Lovely artwork, courteous staff and a good array of facilities – pool, jacuzzi and fitness centre, plus the superb **Plantation Room Restaurant** (excellent buffet breakfasts and a range of 'new Florida' dishes) – mark this out as a real gem. It is also within a short stroll of the town's shops, restaurants and some good walks, and there's an inexpensive shuttle service to the parks. This member of The Kessler Collection Hotels Group (the Sheraton Safari, Doubletree Castle, Sheraton Studio City, Red Horse Inn and The Westin Grand Bohemian) is ideal for a quieter or romantic stay (407 566 6000, www.celebrationhotel.com; $$$$, CCC).

> BRIT TIP: Hotels designated Maingate East or Maingate West should be close to Disney's main entrance on Highway 192, although it is wise to check.

One of the newest – and possibly most dramatic – properties is the 1,406-room **Gaylord Palms Resort** on the junction of I-Drive South and Osceola Parkway (very convenient for Disney). A cross between a convention centre and a vast turn-of-the-century Florida mansion, it features 4½ acres (2ha) of indoor gardens, fountains and landscaped waters under a glass dome. Three intricately themed areas bear witness to a Disney-like creativity, and the resort offers every creature comfort, with an array of restaurants and bars, an adults-only pool, family activity

© Disney

Victoria & Alberts at Disney's Grand Floridian Resort & Spa

pool and beach (with octopus water-slide), full-service spa, children's daycare centre and a range of shops.

Standard rooms are some of the smartest and most spacious in the area, while the suites are enormous, and there is even a hotel-within-a-hotel, as the central Emerald Tower offers an even more upmarket room choice and concierge facilities.

One area is landscaped like the Everglades, with native plants, trees and animals (a new exhibit in 2004 added turtles and gators); another copies the old-world charm of St Augustine – with replica Spanish Fort – while the third reproduces the style and eclecticism of Key West, with a mock-up marina and sailboat (and a fun-themed daily **Sunset Celebration** with live entertainment) and the rooms are themed after each area. To walk into the resort's marbled lobby and cavernous interior at night is like entering a future world. A special Christmas celebration, **ICE!**, is another highlight, with 2 million pounds of ice sculpted into elaborate set-pieces, including a snowy forest and castle with ice slide. This is a separate ticketed event (early Nov to Jan 2) at $16.95 for adults, $13.95 for over 55s and $7.95 for 4–12s but is worthwhile for novelty value.

The elaborate settings add to the resort's signature fine dining, with the choice of **Old Hickory Steakhouse** (naturally aged Black Angus beef a speciality, with an

WALT DISNEY WORLD AND LAKE BUENA VISTA ACCOMMODATION

1 Disney's Contemporary Resort
2 Disney's Polynesian Resort
3 Disney's Wilderness Lodge
4 Disney's Grand Floridian Resort & Spa
5 Walt Disney World Swan
6 Walt Disney World Dolphin
7 Disney's Caribbean Beach Resort
8 Disney's Yacht Club Resort
9 Disney's Beach Club Resort
10 Disney's Boardwalk Resort
11 Disney's All-Star Resorts
12 Disney's Port Orleans Resort (French Quarter)
13 Disney's Port Orleans Resort (Riverside)
14 Disney's Coronado Springs Resort
15 Disney's Saratoga Springs Resort and Spa
16 Disney's Old Key West Resort
17 Disney's Fort Wilderness Resort and Campground
18 Disney's Animal Kingdom Lodge
19 Disney's Pop Century Resort
20 Hilton at Walt Disney World
21 Grosvenor Resort
22 Wyndham Palace Resort & Spa
23 Doubletree Guest Suites Resort
24 Best Western at Walt Disney World
25 Hotel Royal Plaza
26 Holiday Inn in the Walt Disney World Resort
27 Hyatt Regency Grand Cypress
28 Orlando World Center Marriott
29 Embassy Suites Resort Lake Buena Vista
30 Sierra Suites Hotel
31 Radisson Inn Lake Buena Vista
32 Summerfield Suites at Lake Buena Vista
33 Vistana Resort
34 Sheraton Safari Resort
35 Holiday Inn Sunspree Resort
36 Marriott Village
37 Doubletree Club Hoel

4

artisanal cheese course), **Sunset Sam's** (for fine seafood) and the wonderful Spanish buffet-style **Villa de Flora** (with six show kitchens). The Canyon Ranch Spa Club is one of the largest in central Florida with a state-of-the-art spa, a wide range of fitness facilities and a full-service beauty salon.

There are 13 retail outlets in the resort plus the **Planet Java** coffee shop, **Auggie's Jammin' Piano Bar**, the **Gaylord Yacht Bar** and the **St Augustine Piazza** (407 586 0000, www.gaylordpalms.com; $$$$, CCCCC).

International Drive

I-Drive is further from *Walt Disney World Resort in Florida*, but handy for Universal Orlando, SeaWorld and closer to downtown Orlando. It is hard to beat for location and value. It is thoughtfully laid out, some attractions are in walking distance, and is a good base for non-drivers.

Top of the range for quality is the **Peabody Orlando**, a luxurious, 891-room tower block, with an Olympic-size pool, health club, four tennis courts and some of the best Orlando restaurants, notably the gourmet **Dux** (jacket advisable) and the classy Italian **Capriccio**, plus the amazing **B-Line Diner** (see page 276) – all get high marks from the locals. Service is superb and the style is a cut above normal tourist fare – check out the Royal Duck Palace! Larger-than-average rooms and some huge suites add to the quality, but rates are impressive and convention business can make it hectic (407 352 4000, www.peabodyorlando.com; $$$$+, CCCCC).

The **Wyndham Orlando Resort** (1,052 rooms) is also extravagant but with less of the price tag. It boasts a formidable line-up of facilities – three swimming pools, a full-service restaurant and bar, a deli and an ice cream shop, two pool bars, a pool restaurant, tennis courts, a kids' club and game arcade, and a health club – in its beautifully landscaped grounds and is well situated at the junction of I-Drive and Sand Lake Road (with a 'back door' on to Universal Boulevard when I-Drive is busy). The resort covers 42 acres (17ha), which takes some getting around, but it is one of the best all-round hotels for the money (407 351 2420, www.wyndham.com; $$$, CCCC).

Going upscale again, the superb **Renaissance Orlando Resort** (788 rooms on Sea Harbor Drive) is a personal favourite. It boasts the world's largest atrium – ten storeys – and some equally enormous rooms and suites, an Olympic-size pool, tennis courts, fitness centre with

> BRIT TIP: For a novel attraction, don't miss Peabody's twice-daily, red-carpet Duck March, when their trademark ducks take up residence 11am–5pm in the lobby fountain.

sauna and steam room, and kids' play areas and activities. It is also home to one of the most romantic restaurants in town, the seafood-themed **Atlantis** (see page 281), plus a regular breakfast, lunch and dinner offering, **Tradewinds**, plus a coffee shop, pool bar/grill and a stupendous Sunday buffet. There is a choice of bars and shops, and all the rooms have recently been renovated to a high standard. There is even a 24-hour health club. The Renaissance offers some great packages in conjunction with SeaWorld, which is a 2-minute walk across the car park (407 351 5555, www.renaissance hotels.com; $$$, CCCCC).

Nearby, the recently remodelled **Sheraton World Resort** offers things on a slightly more modest budget, just off the main I-Drive. Set in 28 acres (11ha) and with 1,102 rooms and extra-large suites, the resort offers three pools, two kiddie pools, a playground and mini-golf and extremely well-furnished rooms. Dining options are fairly standard, but the tropically styled grounds give it a more upmarket feel (407 352 1100, www.sheratonworld.com; $$$, CCCC).

The remodelled 21-storey **Sheraton Studio City Hotel** is an I-Drive landmark close to Universal Orlando and features a startling 1950s' art deco film theme, from the shower curtains to the landscaping; even the staff give the impression of being 'on set'. Facilities include a heated outdoor pool and paddling pool, games room, mini-golf, fitness room, **Starlight Grille** restaurant and free shuttle to Universal, Wet 'n Wild (within walking distance) and SeaWorld. All rooms have hair-dryers, coffee-makers and Nintendo games (302 rooms; 407 351 2100, www.sheratonstudiocity.com; $$$, CCCC).

Next door, the **Red Horse Inn** (formerly the Universal Inn) is a fun budget choice, with a striking Southwestern design theme and 159 large, comfy rooms, all refurbished. There is a Cantina lobby bar (with free continental breakfast featuring Starbucks coffee) and a neat oasis-themed pool area that represents a nice haven on busy I-Drive. There is no restaurant but the neighbouring Sheraton Studio City is only a short walk and a 24-hour Denny's diner is next door (407 351 4100, www.redhorseorlando.com; $$, CC).

In the heart of I-Drive are two budget choices which both attract large numbers of Brits and make an excellent base in this area: the **Quality Inn International** (728 rooms, kids under 12 eat free, 407 996 1600; $$, CCC) and **Quality Inn Plaza**, a massive 1,020 rooms in multiple blocks with multiple pools

and another 'kids eat free' restaurant (407 345 8585; $–$$, CCC).

Another I-Drive landmark (next door to The Mercado) is the **Doubletree Castle Hotel**, a 9-storey fantasy modelled on Cinderella's castle at the *Magic Kingdom* Park. It features tower and turret rooms, a grand outdoor heated pool, hot tub, pool bar and grill, fitness centre, gift shop and a kids' play area. Rooms are immaculately furnished and there is a free shuttle to *Walt Disney World*, SeaWorld and Universal (216 rooms; 407 345 1511; $$$–$$$$, CCCC).

The other eye-catching property on I-Drive is the **Rosen Center Hotel**, the third largest hotel in Orlando, next to the Beeline Expressway. It caters primarily for the convention trade (it is next door to the massive Convention Center), but also offers excellent facilities with 1,334 rooms and 80 suites. It has a huge swimming grotto, tennis courts, exercise centre, two top-quality restaurants (including the seafood-based **Everglades**) and two bars (407 354 9840; $$$, CCCC).

The **Crowne Plaza Hotel** also offers a touch of elegance, with 304 rooms and 94 suites in two distinct, stylish blocks and a spectacular circular atrium. Two restaurants, a cocktail lounge, fitness centre, guest laundry and baby-sitting facilities, plus a huge heated pool, add up to excellent quality and value on Universal Boulevard's junction with Sand Lake Road (407 781 2107, www.crowneplazauniversal.com; $$$$, CCCC).

Universal Orlando

With the expansion of Universal as a resort destination has come the development of the surrounding locale on Kirkman Road and Major Boulevard, featuring Universal's own resort hotels, which are some of the best in the area. They also come with a rare theme-park privilege – **Universal Express**, front-of-line access to all the main attractions.

The **Portofino Bay Hotel** is the jewel in the crown, a splendid re-creation of the famous Italian port and a stunning resort with every facility – and more! The elaborate porticos, the genuine *trompe l'oeil* painting, lovely harbourside piazza and faithful ornamentation of the waterfront make it one of the most memorable settings in Florida, and the 750 rooms are impeccably appointed, with lashings of Italian style. Standard rooms are truly deluxe, with huge beds, spacious bathrooms, mini-bar and coffee facilities, ironing board and hair-dryer, while the exclusive Villa rooms feature butler service and a private pool area. There are 18 fun Kidsuites with separate themed rooms that include TV, CD player, Sony Playstation and play area.

The resort facilities are equally breathtaking – a Roman aqueduct-style pool with water-slide, a completely enclosed kids' play area and wading pool, a separate quiet pool, jacuzzis, a full (if expensive) health spa, business centre, gift shops (try Galleria Portofino for some magnificent art and jewellery) and video games room. There is also the **Campo Portofino** activity centre for kids 4–14, daily 5pm–11.30pm ($10/hour for the first child, $8/hour for each additional child).

For wining and dining, the Portofino boasts eight restaurants and lounges, including the 5-star (and very romantic) **Bice Ristorante**, the boisterous **Trattoria del Porto, Mama Della's**, an authentic Italian family dining experience (watch out for Mama herself!), an aromatic deli, a pizzeria and gelateria. It is only a short boat ride from Universal, but it feels light years away in terms of its tranquil ambience ($$$$+, CCCCC).

The **Hard Rock Hotel** is possibly the coolest hotel in Orlando. This home of rock chic is themed as a former rock star's home. It has 650 rooms and suites in California mission style. High ceilings, wooden beams, marble floors and eclectic artwork give an eye-catching and elegant style, with a rock-star theme to most public areas, with rock 'n' roll memorabilia, black-suited foyer staff and fairly constant music.

The 14-acre (6-ha) site includes three bars (the ultra-cool **Velvet Bar**, **Lobby Lounge** and **Beach Club** poolside bar and grill), two restaurants (the full-service **The Kitchen** and the 5-star, dinner-only **Palm Restaurant**), plus a take-away café and **Starbucks** counter, a fitness centre, gift shop (with live TV links to other HR Cafés around the world), **Camp Lil' Rock** (for the 4–14s, like Campo Portofino) and games room. The lido area that is the hotel's focus is terrific, with a large, free-form pool and 240-ft (73-metre) water-slide, two jacuzzis, a beach and volleyball court, shuffleboard, and life-size chess and draughts. The pool even has an underwater sound system! The rooms (including 14 Kidsuites) are big, modish, beautifully furnished in the hotel's chic style and wonderfully comfortable ($$$$, CCCC).

The 53-acre (21-ha), 1,000-room **Royal Pacific Resort** has an exotic South Seas feel, transporting you back to a 1930s' luxury hotel in the tropics, and you really feel as if you have stepped into another world as you cross the bamboo bridge, over

Portofino Bay Hotel

HIGHWAY 192 ACCOMMODATION

1 Country Inn & Suites at Calypso Cay
2 Buena Vista Suites
3 Caribe Royale Resort Suites
4 Radisson Resort Parkway
5 Renaissance World Gate Hotel
6 Summer Bay Resort
7 Omni Orlando Resort at Champions Gate
8 Magic Castle Inn & Suites Maingate
9 Holiday Inn Hotel & Suites Maingate East
10 Holiday Inn Maingate West
11 Holiday Inn Nikki Bird Resort
12 La Quinta Inn Lakeside
13 Celebration Hotel
14 Gaylord Palms Resort
15 Comfort Suites Maingate
16 Tropical Palms Funsuites
17 Nickelodeon Family Suites by Holiday Inn
18 Orange Lake Resort
19 Villages at Mango Key
20 Liki Tiki Village
21 Wonderland Inn
22 Comfort Suites Resort Maingate East
23 Hampton Inn Maingate West
24 Reunion Resort
25 Hampton Inn at Maingate East
26 La Quinta Inn & Suites Orlando Maingate
27 Quality Suites Maingate East

4

the rice terraces, into the elegant lobby, faced by the splendidly colourful Orchid Garden courtyard. The extensive use of rich, dark woods, cool stone floors and masses of greenery (58,000 plants and 2,500 trees) give the place an opulent, colonial feel, while the rooms and facilities are equally impressive. The spacious standard rooms all feature hand-carved Balinese furniture, among many refined touches, and there is also a Club level of accommodation, with separate lounge and extended facilities, and some superlative suites.

Islands Dining Room offers breakfast, lunch and dinner in a setting of oriental simplicity (children have their own buffet area with TV screen), while fine dining is taken to a new dimension by a magnificent restaurant run by top American chef Emeril Lagasse called **Tchoup Chop** (possibly the best in Orlando, see page 283). There is a pool snack bar, lobby lounge and Luau garden party area (with barbecue buffet on Saturdays, **Wantilan Luau**, featuring a Polynesian feast and dinner show; 6–9pm, $49.50 for adults, $29 for under 12s, and open to non-residents; book on 407 503 3463).

The huge free-form pool is ideal for kids, with zero-depth entry at one end and a boat-shaped interactive play area of squirting fountains, water jets, paddling pool, sandcastle pit and a 'lifeboat' that regularly fills with water and tips up. Add a health club (with Jacuzzi, sauna and gym), kids' club (with computer games, TVs and organised activities), video games room and two shops. ($$$$, CCCC.)

All Universal resort guests have a number of exclusive privileges: **resort ID** card (for buying food, merchandise and other items throughout Universal Orlando); **free water taxi** transport; **priority seating** at most restaurants (show your room key card); **package delivery** to your room; the chance to buy a special **Length of Stay pass** (for unlimited parks access while you are at the resort); and, most importantly, **Universal Express** no-wait access to all the rides all day just by showing your room key card.

For all Universal hotels, call 407 224 7117 or go to www.universalorlando.com.

Mid-range hotels

The choice around Universal is also growing. There are recent examples of the budget **Days Inn, Hampton Inn, TraveLodge** and **Country Inn** chains, plus the **Extended Stay America** group (good, clean studios with kitchenette, but few other amenities). However, there are two excellent mid-range hotels.

The **Doubletree Hotel Universal Orlando** (formerly the Radisson) is a twin-tower, 742-room complex which has a smart resort feel, with spacious, tropical-themed rooms, a large pool, kids' playground and jacuzzi, pool bar, video games room, hair salon, gym and sauna, plus a sports bar, full-service restaurant and food court. It also offers a free shuttle to Universal (across the road), SeaWorld and Wet 'n Wild (407 351 1000; $$, CCC).

The **Holiday Inn Hotel & Suites** is similar, with 256 rooms and 134 1- and 2-bedroom suites, a large heated outdoor pool and on-site TGI Friday's restaurant (407 351 3333; $$–$$$, CCC).

Best of the rest

A recent trend to provide more deluxe accommodation has also added a touch of class to the downtown scene with **The Westin Grand Bohemian**. Part of The Kesslar Collection Hotels Group, it features an early 20th-century Austrian theme, with the accent on fine art, fine dining and good service. Its 14 storeys make it a major landmark, and it boasts the sensational restaurant, **The Boheme**, one of the most stylish bars I have been to – the **Bösendorfer Lounge** – with great live entertainment nightly, and a 14th-floor concierge suite, plus an in-hotel Starbucks, a heated pool, spa and fitness centre, and the Grand Bohemian Art Gallery. The rooms are superbly appointed, with high-speed internet access, mini-bars, radio/CD players and huge interactive TVs, plus there are 36 sumptuous suites. All rooms feature the ultra-comfy Westin Heavenly Bed. The art collection, classic and modern, displayed throughout the public rooms, makes it more like a museum than a hotel (407 313 9000, www.grandbohemianhotel.com; $$$$, CCCC).

The luxury element is also fully displayed in the 500-acre (200-ha) **Grande Lakes Orlando**, a combination of a 584-room, 5-star Ritz-Carlton Hotel, a 1,000-room JW Marriott Hotel, a 40,000-sq ft (3,700-sq metre) health spa, an 18-hole Greg Norman-designed golf course, tennis centre and a range of shops and 11 restaurants, including the outstanding **Norman's**, featuring the 'new world' cuisine of celebrity chef Norman Van Aken. Located on the edge of a forestry preserve, it feels secluded and remote – quite a feat in this area. It is slightly off the beaten tourist track – at the junction of John Young Parkway and Central Florida Parkway – yet is only 2 miles (3km) from SeaWorld, 7 miles (11km) from Universal Orlando and 10 miles (16km) from Disney and Orlando International Airport.

The **Ritz-Carlton** is the first of the company's properties in central Florida, and the scale and detail are wonderful: lush gardens, abundant lakes and streams, Venetian-inspired architecture and a wealth of genuine antiques. It has a large, sloped-entry pool, kids' pool, three floodlit tennis courts, a signature shop and five restaurants, plus a separate children's check-in and the excellent **Ritz Kids Club** (for 5–12s; $10/hour, $55 full day, including lunch), while all the restaurants offer child menus. The rooms are gorgeous – beautifully furnished, with high-quality products in the marbled bathrooms – and feature large plasma-screen TVs, radio/CD, mini-bar, hair-dryer, slippers and robe, and all have balconies. There are 66 spacious suites and 92 Club rooms on the top

BRIT TIP: Head for the Ritz-Carlton's lobby lounge for afternoon tea or drinks in style with a magnificent view, especially at sunset.

two floors, with concierge and butler service, food and drink presentations in the Club Lounge, and Bulgari amenities. Two Kidsuites feature a separate bedroom and bathroom, with toys, games, TV and video games for great child appeal (and safety – the balcony is closed off).

Other Ritz-Carlton features are their **horse-drawn carriage rides** around the vast Grande Lakes property on Friday and Saturday ($40 for a family of six, including hot chocolate, souvenir photo and children's gift; $60 for a couple's starlight ride, with champagne, rose and photo; and $600 for the grand romantic experience, with a private dinner under the gazebo) and outdoor **concerts**, with a kids' playground and a firework finale.

The **JW Marriott** is the new flagship hotel for the Marriott group, with Spanish–Moorish design, a formal Italian restaurant, French brasserie, Starbucks coffee lounge and a pool bar and grill. It also has a unique 'lazy river' mini water park (providing the largest pool deck in Florida), plus a children's zero-depth-entry pool, a splash fountain and a separate kids' check-in. And, while the Marriott is more convention orientated, it is still well geared for families with all the facilities, a variety of shops and the option to use the Ritz Kids programme and dining options next door. Rooms are plush and ultra-comfortable, 70 per cent have balconies and there are 64 suites.

The golf course is immaculate, and every foursome is assigned a free caddie (virtually unknown for a public course in Florida). The beautiful citrus-tinged health spa is the best in the region, with a huge fitness centre and aerobics studio, lap pool (all free to guests at both hotels), lovely spa-cuisine restaurant and a huge array of massages and therapies, with a *sanitas per aqua* philosophy. The pricing is upscale, but it is a rare holiday treat (407 206 2400/2300, www.grandelakes.com; $$$$–$$$$$, CCCCC).

Another high-quality offering is the **Omni Orlando Resort at Champions Gate**, which was scheduled to open in October 2004. With 730 rooms and suites, and overlooking another superb golf set-up with two Greg Norman-designed courses, this is an imposing hotel with an impressive array of facilities, including a David Leadbetter golf academy, main swimming pool and activity pool (including a 'lazy river' feature and water-slides), four

Golf at sunset

restaurants (Asian, Mediterranean, sports bar and deli), three lounge bars, health club and spa.

Just 5 minutes south of Disney and right off I-4, this is well situated yet slightly off the beaten track for those looking for something different (especially golfers). Set in 1,200 landscaped acres (486ha), it suits the both business traveller and leisure-seeker alike (321 677 6664, www.omnihotels.com and www.championsgategolf.com; $$$$, CCCCC).

One final hotel worthy of note is the **Hyatt Regency** at Orlando International Airport, especially if you arrive late and could benefit from a first-night rest. It has two excellent restaurants – including the elegant **Hemisphere**, with monthly wine-tasting evenings and a great runway view – and a smart pool deck, plus a fitness room, lounge and business centre. The 446 rooms are superbly spacious, especially the corner rooms, and many feature internal balconies overlooking the 6-storey airport atrium. Surprisingly, there is no noticeable aircraft noise and none of the bustle you would expect of an airport hotel. There is valet and self-parking and staying there gives the added advantage of collecting your hire car in the morning rather than after a long flight (407 825 1234, http://orlandoairport.hyatt.com; $$$, CCC½).

Hard Rock Hotel

INTERNATIONAL DRIVE ACCOMMODATION

1 Peabody Orlando
2 Wyndham Orlando Resort
3 Renaissance Orlando Resort
4 Sheraton Studio City
5 Red Horse Inn
6 Days Inn Lakeside
7 Holiday Inn Express
8 Quality Inn International
9 Quality Inn Plaza
10 Embassy Suites Jamaica Court
11 Howard Johnson Plaza
12 Howard Johnson Inn
13 Rosen Plaza Hotel
14 Crowne Plaza Hotel
15 Enclave Suites
16 Quality Suites at Parc Corniche
17 Villager Premier
18 Staybridge Suites by Holiday Inn

19 Comfort Suites
20 The Doubletree Castle
21 Rosen Center Hotel
22 Hawthorn Suites
23 Holiday Inn & Suites at Universal
24 Best Western Plaza
25 Embassy Suites I-Drive/Conv. Center
26 Doubletree Hotel at Universal Orlando
27 Portofino Bay Hotel
28 Hard Rock Hotel
29 Amerisuites Convention Center
30 Sheraton World Resort
31 Sierra Suites
32 Homewood Suites
33 Country Inn & Suites
34 Royal Pacific Resort
35 Grande Lakes Orlando
36 Holiday Inn Convention Center

4

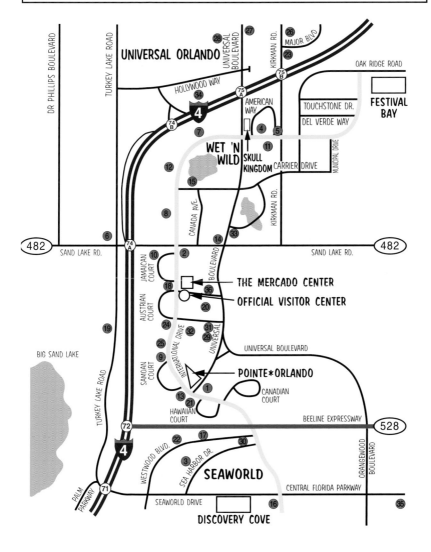

SUITES, RESORTS AND HOLIDAY HOMES

A fast-growing accommodation area in Orlando, suites hotels, purpose-built resorts and holiday homes provide a valuable way for large families and groups of friends to stay together and cut costs by self-catering. The homes, whether individual houses, collections of houses, resorts or condominiums (apartment blocks), usually have access to excellent facilities, such as pools and recreation, and are equipped with microwaves, TVs and washer-dryers. For these, a hire car is essential, but the savings are certainly quite significant.

Suite things

Suites hotels are virtually unknown in the UK but provide a combination of hotel and apartment, with extra value for large families or groups. Typically, a suites room gives you a living room and kitchenette, including microwave, coffee-maker, fridge, cutlery and crockery, while many offer a complimentary continental breakfast (or better). All have pools and grocery stores or snack bars. They vary only in the number of bedrooms and can usually sleep six to ten people.

They include the **Comfort Suites** on West Highway 192 (407 397 7848) and on Turkey Lake Road (407 351 5050), adjacent to I-4 and I-Drive, plus a smart recent 198-room development behind Old Town in Kissimmee, which even offers a fitness centre (407 397 7848; $$–$$$, CCC); the **Tropical Palms Funsuites**, on Holiday Trail, next to Old Town (407 396 4595; $$–$$$, CCC½) with well-equipped studio and 2-bedroom suites; the 2-bedroom, 2-bath studios of **Enclave Suites** (on Carrier Drive, off Kirkman Road, $$–$$$, CCC½)

where kids eat free with their parents; or the **AmeriSuites** group (on I-Drive, in Lake Buena Vista and by the airport, 1-800 833 1516; $$–$$$, CCC), each with a pool, fitness centre and free breakfast.

The **Country Inn & Suites** offers four new properties in the I-Drive area, Lake Buena Vista, Kissimmee and by Orlando International Airport. Good value, with large, clean rooms, free continental breakfast, local phone calls, Disney transport, pool and fitness centre. The property on **Universal Boulevard** is possibly the best, with 170 standard rooms with in-room safe, coffee-maker, hair-dryer and iron/ironing board; while the 48 king suites include microwave and fridge. It is 1 mile (1.6km) from Universal Orlando and half that from Wet 'n Wild, yet much quieter than many I-Drive hotels (407 313 4200, www.jaytelhotels.com; $$–$$$, CCC).

A property in transition is the **Holiday Inn Family Suites** at Lake Buena Vista (almost opposite Orlando World Center Marriott, on I-Drive South) which, in May 2005 becomes the **Nickelodeon Family Suites**. This is being transformed from what was already a wonderful holiday choice into something even more striking and kid-friendly. It's receiving a $20-million infusion of water attractions, newly themed suites, banquet space and a show room. Characters from the Nickelodeon TV station adorn strategic points and there is plenty of live character interaction (notably at breakfast). Suites are coming complete with bunk or twin beds, a TV and video-console system. The existing water features have been enhanced to form two sprawling pools with water-slides, flumes, poolside game areas and a games room, plus alarm calls from Nickelodeon stars such as Spongebob Squarepants and Jimmy Neutron.

The resort's current suites feature two bedrooms, a living room and bathroom, microwave and fridge. New suites are also being introduced featuring three bedrooms, two baths and a fully functional kitchen.

Designers promise a 'cruise-ship-on-land' atmosphere with a nationally branded food court, scheduled activities for all ages, a recreation team and live nightly Nickelodeon entertainment (407 387 5437, www.hifamilysuites.com, then www.nickhotel.com; $$$–$$$$, CCCC).

Other one-off suites properties worthy of note include the well-appointed **Buena Vista Suites** (407 239 8588; $$$, CCC) and the eye-catching **Caribe Royale Resort Suites** (407 238 8000, www.cariberoyale.com; $$$$, CCCC½), both at the lower end of I-Drive, with a choice of 1-bedroom suites and 2-bedroom villas, super pool area with water-slide and one of the best free breakfast buffets in town. Their new Venetian Room has quickly become a treat for lovers of fine continental cuisine, and there are four other cafés and lounges. The **Hawthorn Suites** (three places in Orlando), **Homewood Suites** (two in Lake Buena Vista and one on I-Drive) and the **Sierra Suites** (Lake Buena Vista and I-Drive) offer a more upmarket feel with mid-range pricing ($$–$$$, facilities vary).

Highly recommended

The two **Staybridge Suites by Holiday Inn** (on I-Drive, 407 352 2400, and Lake Buena Vista, 407 238 0777, www.staybridge.com) are another fine example, with suites sleeping up to eight, appetising free breakfast, convenience store and fresh, inviting ambience ($$$, CCC). The LBV site features a deli, while the I-Drive property also offers a lobby bar. The 1-bedroom suite is very spacious for a family of four, the standard 2-bedroom adds a second bathroom, and the 2-bedroom trio suite is ideal for eight. Both have relaxing pool decks, with kids' pool and whirlpool, are perfectly situated for the attractions and offer a relaxing retreat after a busy day.

The Embassy Suites group boasts eight properties around Orlando, but arguably the best is the **Embassy Suites International Drive/Convention Center** (407 352 1400, www.embassysuitesorlando.com; $$$, CCCC). This is the most prominent and consistently gets good reader feedback. 'I would strongly recommend the Embassy Suites,' says Gary Baldwin. 'It includes an all-you- can-eat buffet breakfast, which is great when planning a day at a theme park. Also, there are free drinks and snacks from 5.30–7.30 every evening.' It is exceedingly smart, with excellent service, and spacious rooms (either standard 2-room suites sleeping four or double-doubles, sleeping six) providing two TVs, coffee-maker, fridge and microwave. There's a neat outdoor pool deck, kids' splash pool and indoor pool, plus a sauna, steam room and gym. The Southwestern-style **Sedona Café** and **Hurricane's Lounge** give a real edge in dining options, irrespective of their great I-Drive location. They also offer a free Disney shuttle service and transport to the other parks from $4–8/person.

Holiday resorts

Another accommodation type, which combines the best of hotels, suites and private villas, is the handful of resort-style, purpose-built complexes, some of which double as timeshare resorts (or 'vacation ownership'). A cross between condominiums and motels, they have the advantage of great in-resort facilities. These include the extensive **Orange Lake Resort** (4½ miles/7km west of Maingate on

Highway 192, 407 239 0000;
$$$–$$$$, CCCC), with a mixture
of 2-bedroom, 2-bath villas and
suites, golf, water sports and cinema,
and the **Villages at Mango Key** (on
Lindfields Boulevard, 4 miles
(6.4km) west of Maingate, 407 397
2211; $$$, CCC), smart, new 2- and
3-bedroom townhouses, with pool,
Jacuzzi, tennis and volleyball.

Liki Tiki Village on the western
fringe of Highway 192 is a timeshare
set-up that often has good-value
apartments to rent on a weekly basis.
Their newest blocks offer huge 2-
bedroom flats, with well-equipped
kitchens (with coffee- and ice-
makers), while the 64-acre (26-ha)
complex boasts two pools, a mini
water park, tennis courts, paddle
boats, bikes, poolside bar and grill
and free continental breakfast
Mon–Fri when timeshare
presentations are held – but you
don't have to attend the timeshare
hard-sell (407 239 5000,
www.islandone.com; $$$, CCCC).

Another extensive operation is the
Sheraton Vistana Resort, just off
the lower end of I-Drive in Lake
Buena Vista, where facilities include
fitness centres with steam and sauna
rooms, seven pools and 13 tennis
courts, basketball, volleyball and
shuffleboard, games rooms, bike
rental and mini-golf to back up their
luxurious 1- and 2-bedroom villas
sleeping four to eight (407 238 5000,
www.starwoodvo.com; $$$–$$$$,
CCCCC). The relatively new
Windsor Palms Resort (formerly
the Wyndham Palms, just off West
Highway 192 in Kissimmee) is also
popular, offering private owner-
operated 3-, 4-, 5- and 6-bedroom
pool homes and 2- and 3-bedroom
condos with a clubhouse with gym,
tennis courts, an Olympic-sized
heated pool, a separate kiddie pool
and spa, basketball, billiard room,
playground and a 50-seat cinema
showing recent films (www.windsor-
palms-florida.net; $$$–$$$$; CCCC).

Three of the best

The following properties all strike
me as outstanding: the **Bahama Bay
Resort**, on Lake Davenport in
Kissimmee (at the west end of
Highway 192, by Highway 27),
opened in 2003 and is spread over 70
acres (28ha), with 498 condos (of
one, two and three bedrooms, all
with balconies) in 38 buildings, two
and three storeys high. The resort-
style community is woven with
tropical landscaping that includes
water features, a recreation centre
and clubhouse, restaurant and snack
bar, internet café, fitness centre,
sauna and spa (the fabulous
Eleuthera Spa & Salon), tennis,
basketball and volleyball, four heated
pools and kiddie pools. You can fish
in the lake, which has a sandy beach,
plus there is a video arcade and small
cinema. There's a regular shuttle to
the theme parks for a small charge.

The four types of condo offer 2-
bedroom, 2-bath (sleeping six, with a
sofa-bed in the lounge) and 3-
bedroom, 2-bath (sleeping eight,
again with sofa-bed), with fitted
kitchen, laundry room/washer-dryer,
living room and dining area. The
Grand Bahama 3-bedroom condo
boasts 1,739sq ft (162sq metres) of
space and is one of the most elegant
(call 0779 911 6540 in the UK, or
visit www.orlandorentalhome.co.uk;
$$–$$$, CCCC).

The **Summer Bay Resort** (also
on West Highway 192) is a mixture
of budget motel (The Inn at
Summer Bay), a moderate hotel (an
award-winning Holiday Inn
Express), some 3-bedroom vacation
homes and new 1-, 2- and 3-bed
villas and condos. The 700 rooms,
spread over 64 acres (26ha) are smart
enough, plus the facilities include
outdoor, heated pools and kiddie
pools, an elaborate children's water-
play area, mini-golf, clubhouse with
volleyball, tennis, basketball,
shuffleboard and fitness room, video

arcade, gift shop and snack bar. The lake provides jet-skis, paddle boats, water-skiing and more, plus daily kids' activities and organised sports. Even those in The Inn and Holiday Inn (which has its own pool deck and breakfast area) benefit from the clubhouse facilities, while there is a Denny's diner and Publix grocery next door. It represents amazing value at the budget end, and wonderful accommodation in the condos, and is still only 15 minutes from Disney (1800 654 6102, www.summerbayresort.com; $$–$$$$, CCCC½).

The final option is arguably the grandest, the **Reunion Resort and Club**, of keen interest to golfers and all who appreciate the 5-star touch. On Highway 532 in Kissimmee, just off Exit 58 of I-4 south of Disney (the exit for Champions Gate), this fledgling 'community' will boast 8,000 units when complete, with hotels, condos and luxury homes set around three superb golf courses (designed by Arnold Palmer, Tom Watson and Jack Nicklaus). There will be an area of restaurants and shops, a water park, riding stables, swimming pools and other recreation, while every unit will have room service, personal concierge (for dining, tee times, stocking the fridge, etc) and airport escort. The homes range from a modest 3-bedrooms to grand 8-bedrooms (costing over $750,000), but all are available for rent (and some for sale).

The condos vary from 1- to 3-bedroom, 2-bath apartments, all immaculately furnished and with some stunning views over the golf courses. Much is still to be finished in the next 2 years, but two golf courses are working, plus an array of condos and homes. Only those who stay here can play on the courses, but the scale and imagination of the resort make it awesome (1877 738 6466, www.reunionresort.com; $$$$+, CCCCC).

Holiday homes

Vacation homes to rent are big business in central Florida and now account for a huge slice of the British market as they are ideal for repeat visitors, large groups and those who like their own privacy and facilities. They tend to be grouped in newly built estates and several are 'gated' communities for added security. Nearly all offer a private pool and the largest can sleep up to 16. Some are classed as executive homes, and this usually means more facilities (DVD, games consoles, barbecues, etc) rather than any increase in size. If you are booking independently, there are several key questions to ask before you book.

Do you need to go to an office some way away to pick up the keys or do they have a combination-lock box at the house? Is there a local contact if anything goes wrong (some private owners do not live in Florida) or is the property maintained by an on-the-spot company? Do they offer a security bonding for your cash booking, and are they members of a reputable organisation like the Better Business Bureau of Central Florida? If it's winter, is the pool heated, and how much do they charge for heating? Finally, are they as close to Disney as they say – some homes can be down in Polk County, 20–45 minutes' drive away. One final warning – once you have sampled pool-at-home life, you may never go back to a hotel!

The bottom line is you need to do your homework and shop around as you would for any significant

Nickelodeon Family Suites

purchase, and check with organisations like the Central Florida Property Managers' Association (www.cfpma.com). The following all pass the *Brit's Guide* credibility test.

Welcome Homes USA have condos, villas and private homes to rent in the Kissimmee area, with some smart properties at a broad range of prices. Their houses (three to five bedrooms) come with communal or private pools. Homes are only 10–15 minutes' drive from *Walt Disney World* in residential areas and feature everything from dishwashers to spoons but not hair-dryers (407 390 9000, www.welcomehomesusa.com; $$–$$$$, CC).

For similar great value and excellent properties, **Alexander Holiday Homes**, also in Kissimmee, manages 260 properties, from standard condo villas to ultra-luxury executive homes sleeping up to ten, all with pools and immaculately furnished, within 15 minutes of *Walt Disney World Resort*. This company was the first of its kind in Orlando, and still offers a friendly, efficient service. They were only the third management company in Florida to earn a prestigious AAA rating (the American Automobile Association) and have new offices on Highway 192 near the I-4 junction. They also show prices in UK and US currency (407 932 3683 or, in the UK, 0871 711 5371, www.floridasunshine.com; $$–$$$, CC).

Premier Vacation Homes offers a great range of spacious properties with two to six bedrooms, sleeping up to 14, in secure residential communities within a 15-minute drive of *Walt Disney World Resort*. The homes are privately owned and have been purchased and furnished as vacation homes, with screened pools, two TVs, fully equipped kitchens (including dishwasher, washer-dryer, microwave and coffee-maker), at least one king or queen

bed, and free local phone calls. Maid service can be provided for an additional fee. The **Luxury** homes (2- to 4-bedroom) are their standard accommodation, while **Executive** homes (3- to 6-bedroom) are bigger, with an extra TV, VCR and a gas barbecue (407 396 2401, or 0500 892634 in the UK, www.premier-vacation-homes.com; $$$, CC).

A company I have got to know well and can highly recommend is British-owned **Florida Leisure** that pays great attention to detail. With some 90 homes (2- to 7-bedroom) in the Kissimmee area (most barely 2 years old) available for rent, they pride themselves on a personal touch and offer some of the biggest and newest properties. Many are in the Executive range, which means the fullest range of amenities in addition to their large, private, screened pools, and often in a secure, gated community. You can see them all on their website (in photo and video) plus lots of local info, especially for restaurants and golf. Their office is in the Lake Buena Vista Factory Stores, and you can call Nigel or Marion on 407 870 1600 (www.floridaleisure.com; $$–$$$$, CCC).

An alternative, UK-based company is **Sun Villas Florida Direct**, launched in September 2001 by a former managing director of Lunn Poly to provide a bespoke holiday offering villa accommodation, flights, attraction tickets and car hire. They have a variety of properties from Orlando down to Sarasota and Naples, and maintain consistently high standards. (Sun Villas Florida Direct on 01926 33661; www.SVFDirect.com.)

ResortQuest is a new name here, but not a new company. The former Advantage Vacation Homes is now part of a nationwide umbrella providing a growing list of properties throughout Florida. None of their 2- to 6-bedroom homes (the majority on West Highway 192 and Highway 27 in Clermont and Davenport) are more than 5 years old, while many are 1–2 years at most. They also manage an increasing portfolio of condos (in the Bahama Bay and SunLake Resorts), with plans for a big new development next to their offices on West Highway 192. They offer 24-hour management, with a courteous and efficient staff at their HQ (plus an attraction ticket service), open 9am–10pm daily. Their holiday homes are rated Bronze, Silver, Gold or Platinum, with the difference in quality measured in the extras rather than size or facilities (larger-screen or plasma TVs, tiled floors rather than carpeting and perhaps a jacuzzi). All include private, screened pools, fully equipped kitchens, hair-dryer, iron/ironing board, washer-dryers and the usual supply of linens and kitchen equipment. A typical, spacious 3-bedroom home would comfortably cater for six to eight, while the largest house sleeps 12 in style.

> **BRIT TIP:** You'll find Marmite, Ribena and McVitie's biscuits at the Publix supermarkets on Highway 192, or the 24-hour Goodings stores at Crossroads and on I-Drive.

Their newest properties on Highway 27 usually have communal playgrounds and tennis courts. Extra options include gift baskets, daily or mid-stay cleaning, welcome food pack and airport meet-and-greet (407 396 2262 or 1-800 527 2262, www.resortquest.com; $$$–$$$$+, CCC).

An accreditation agency aiming to take away some of the mystery and concern over booking private, rented accommodation are the UK-based **Accredited Florida**, who look to ensure every home on their list meets a required standard and is inspected and re-accredited every year. They have official recognition with both the Kissimmee and Polk County visitor centres and are members of the CFPMA. They are not a booking agency but their website lists all their officially accredited homes, with photos and links to the owners (01278 459058, www.accreditedflorida.org).

Finally, **Florida Choice Vacation Homes** provides townhouses (three to four bedrooms with communal pools and recreation facilities), standard and executive homes (3- to 7-bedroom private properties), some with heated pools and with free local phone calls. Optional maid service and cot and highchair rentals (407 847 0284, www.floridachoice.com; $$$–$$$$, CCC).

Bed and breakfast

Bed and breakfast in Orlando is offered in a more upscale, almost boutique style. Principle among them is the **Wonderland Inn** in Kissimmee, an 11-room, restored Historic Registry property off the beaten track but only 10 minutes from the Highway 192 area. Each room has a delightful, individual touch, and several are designed for singles as well as doubles, plus one honeymoon suite. The staff are wonderfully attentive and even the lovely gardens have an old-fashioned charm light years from the hectic tourist whirl. They also offer a 4-course Romantic Candlelight Dinner served in the gazebo (weather permitting) and a Romantic Getaway Package that includes a 3-hour limo service, dinner, breakfast in bed, a massage or two, champagne and chocolates (1-877 847 2477, www.wonderlandinn.com; $$$, CC).

The pretty Lake Eola district downtown has two fine B & Bs. **The**

Veranda has 12 intimate, cottage-style rooms, ranging from Queen Studio and King Suites to a lovely honeymoon suite in landscaped gardens with a private courtyard, pool and spa area. Breakfast offers fresh pastries, seasonal fruits, juices, tea and coffee, and it's a quiet spot, although it's an easy walk to some good restaurants and shops (407 849 0321; $$$–$$$$, CCC).

The nearby **Eõ Inn** is a genuine boutique hotel and spa (with a huge range of treatments), featuring 17 deluxe rooms. The lush grounds, rooftop terrace and lake vistas provide a refreshing alternative to the hotel experience (407 481 8485, www.eoinn.com; $$$–$$$$, CC).

Babysitting

For those who want an evening off from parenthood to take advantage of Orlando's nightlife, babysitting is a ready option. The two most relied on, trained and licensed companies are **KinderCare** (contracted to *Walt Disney World Resort* and Airtours, 407 827 5444) and **Fairy Godmothers** (407 939 3463). Both will visit hotels, motels, condos or homes.

BUYING A HOLIDAY HOME

The quality of life, a favourable exchange rate and the fabulous weather are all compelling reasons to consider acquiring your own vacation home, for holidays, investment, a winter retreat or a retirement home. But, apart from

A typical holiday pool-home

the fact that it is easy to be starry-eyed after a wonderful holiday, there are companies willing to exploit the naivety of tourists. Therefore, you need to do your homework, especially to understand the terminology of US property buying.

If you have looked in the window of a realtor (a US estate agent), you will have seen the tempting price differential compared with the UK. In the third quarter of 2002, the average price of a single family home in Florida rose by 8 per cent (to $141,300) on the same period in 2001, making the idea even more alluring. Another key element is new homes can often be cheaper than a comparable older property owing to modern construction techniques and the number being built, but this also means the quality can vary, so you need to find a trustworthy builder.

Greater Homes of Orlando (407 869 0300, www.greaterhomes.com) has an unimpeachable reputation and gets *Brit's Guide* approval. It is a family-run company that has been building here since 1965 and has sold more than 2,000 homes to British owners. It is a reliable and quality-conscious firm and their website carries essential info for anyone considering buying here (including mortgage terminologies). Their latest development, **Eagle Creek**, is a golf-community collaboration with British builder Jones Homes about 10 minutes from Orlando International Airport with prices from $250,000. The highest recommendation I can offer is that I bought a Greater Home in 2004 and could not be more satisfied with my purchase, the ease with which it was conducted and the after-sales care.

You will also find useful info on the **Alexander Holiday Homes** site (www.floridasunshine.com) and the Real Estate links on **Florida Leisure** (www.floridaleisure.com), a registered realtor that publishes a free *Home Buying Guide*, available

BRIT TIP: Florida Leisure has a cruise booking agency, Cruise Planners, so if you fancy a week in Orlando and a week at sea (highly recommended), visit www.gocruiseplanner.com.

from their website. Other builders worth considering are **Beazer Homes** and **KB Homes**, both rated well above average for build quality.

Owning a piece of the Magic is tempting, but you must get all the facts first, then look for a company that specialises in selling to British buyers. A dozen or so firms primarily offer vacation-style properties, and several deal mainly with British buyers. Consider investigating one of the firms that allows you to fund your mortgage in sterling, through a UK bank, rather than the dollar equivalent. If you live in the UK and are paid in sterling, a US dollar mortgage can be costly and inconvenient. For instance, US mortgage companies often 'sell' newly arranged mortgages to another lender shortly after closing a loan, making it hard to track. Repayment of a dollar mortgage with sterling is also subject to changing exchange rates. Two publications to note are *International Homes* and *Homes Overseas*, which both have Florida sections.

One company I have got to know well through my contacts with the British–American Chamber of Commerce, and am happy to recommend, is **British Homes Florida Group**. This is a well-established, specialist Orlando-based firm and (just as important) a certified realtor, dealing almost exclusively in finding investment property, whether a short-term rental own-to-let holiday home in the Disney area or an exclusive private coastal retreat. Through

subsidiaries British Homes Florida-Sales Inc. and British Home Florida-Loans Inc., they have a one-stop package. The Home Loans division works with various low-cost sterling mortgages, including UK flexible trackers, fixed-rate and interest-only options. With **British Mortgages Abroad**, a GE Consumer Finance company, you can ensure your mortgage is arranged via a UK currency loan at UK rates.

British Homes Florida is also *independent* of any UK or US builder or seller. It has both UK and US real estate and mortgage professionals, who I can confirm are expert in all British and American procedures. It is a member of both the Florida Association of Mortgage Brokers and British–American Chamber of Commerce. Call them (in Florida) on 407 396 9914, or (in the UK) on 0800 096 5989 (24 hours), e-mail bhlflorida@earthlink.net or visit www.britishhomeloansflorida.com, or their offices in Orlando at 2960 Vineland Road, Kissimmee (above the Edwin Watts golf shop at the T-junction of Routes 535/192).

Whoever you go with, ensure they can refer you to experts in UK and US taxation, immigration, hazard insurance, structural warranties and other areas *essential* to hassle-free home-ownership in Florida. Property in Orlando has increased in value by 10–12 per cent over the last ten years, but there is never any guarantee, and rates can fluctuate.

Bob Mandell (Chairman of Greater Homes) offers these buying tips: get references from UK owners, check management company references; look up the Better Business Bureau for Central Florida; ensure the product has a warranty; walk through the community and talk to people there; ensure the documentation allows you to let it on a short-term basis; make sure you have all the proper US fees, registrations and taxes.

5 The Theme Parks – Disney's Fab Four

(or, Spending the Day with Mickey Mouse and Co.)

By now you should be prepared to deal with the main business of any visit to Orlando: *Walt Disney World Resort in Florida* and the other main theme parks of Universal Orlando, SeaWorld and Busch Gardens.

If you have only a week, this is where you should concentrate your attention but even then you may decide Busch Gardens is a bridge too far. If you have less than a week, you should focus on seeing as much of *Walt Disney World Resort* as possible. There is SO much packed into every park and the main tourist areas, even 2 weeks is scarcely enough to give first-timers more than an outline of central Florida.

BRIT TIP: Offers of 'Free' Disney tickets usually means timeshare firms, who also have several 'official' visitor centres. I-Drive has the *only* genuinely Official Visitor Center.

Buying your tickets in advance is highly advisable, but work out your requirements first – you wouldn't get full use out of, say, a 7-Day Park Hopper Plus AND a 5-Park Orlando FlexTicket in just a 2-week holiday. There are so many ticket outlets these days, you need to check what measure of security they offer (ABTA bonding, etc) and what they do in the case of lost or stolen tickets during shipping. Try to use your credit card for all purchases – there is built-in additional security here (for our list of recommended ticket outlets, see page 13). You will also find **discount coupons** in tourist publications distributed in Orlando for many of the smaller attractions (or from the Guest Services desk at your hotel – it's worth asking), while the **tour operators'** welcome meetings usually have special offers and tickets for the latest excursions.

The **Official Visitor Center** at 8723 International Drive (in the Gala Center on the corner of Austrian Row; 407 363 5871, www.orlandoinfo.com; see map on page 81) is also worth checking out for discounts. Equally, the **Universal Attractions** booths at several shopping malls (notably Orlando Premium Outlets) have great deals (3 days for the price of 2, 2-for-1 drinks, etc) on many attractions. It IS possible to pick up free tickets for attending timeshare presentations, but they can easily take up half a day of your precious holiday. Other sites worth visiting for discounts, etc, are the *Orlando Sentinel*'s info-based www.go2orlando.com, www.orlandosavings.com and www.orlando.floridacouponsavings.com for free coupons.

Ratings

All the rides and shows are judged on a unique rating system that splits them into the **thrill rides** and

BRIT TIP: If you DO want to check out timeshare options, look first at Disney Vacation Club for the guaranteed way to secure memorable holidays. Call 407 566 3300 or visit http://dvc.disney.go.com/dvc

scenic rides. Thrill rides earn T ratings out of five (hence a TTTTT is as exciting as they get) and scenic rides get A ratings out of five (an AA ride is likely to be over-cute and missable). Obviously, it is a matter of opinion to a certain extent, but you can be sure a T or A ride is not worth your time, a TT or AA is worth seeing only if there is no queue, a TTT or AAA should be seen if you have time, but you won't miss much if you don't, a TTTT or AAAA ride is a big-time attraction that should be high on your list of things to do, and finally a TTTTT or AAAAA attraction should not be missed! The latter will have the longest queues and so you should plan your visit around them. Some rides are restricted to children over a certain height and are not advisable for people with back, neck or heart problems, or for expectant mothers. Where this is the case I have just noted 'Restrictions: 3ft 6in/106cm', and so on. Height restrictions (strictly enforced) are based on the average 5-year-old being 3ft 6in/ 106cm tall, 6s being 3ft 9in/114cm and 9s being 4ft 4in/132cm.

Disney's FASTPASS Service

Another essential aid to queuing here is **Disney's FASTPASS Service**. A number of the main attractions at the parks now have this wonderful service that allows you to roam while you wait for your allotted time to ride. How it works: insert your main park entrance ticket into the FASTPASS (FP) turnstile (to the side of the attraction's entrance) and you get another ticket giving you a period of time in which to return for your ride with only a minimal wait (NB: you need one FP ticket for every person who wants to ride, not just one per party). You can hold only one FP ticket per 2-hour period, although once you've used it you can get another. If you start by going to one of the FP rides, collecting your ticket and returning later, you can by-pass a lot of standing in line. You can also get another FP as soon as your 'window' opens: if your time slot for Space Mountain in *Magic Kingdom* Park is 10–11am, you could get another FP for, say, Buzz Lightyear's Space Ranger Spin at 10.05am and then go and ride Space Mountain! Many people still miss this, but it is FREE (FASTPASS rides are indicated by FP in attraction descriptions).

BRIT TIP: If you have pre-paid vouchers for park entrance rather than the actual tickets, you have to exchange them at a ticket booth. Go to the Guest Relations window and you will avoid the queues.

Pal Mickey

If you want the ultimate theme park friend, to help you queue, offer tips, play games and help find the characters, just ask Mickey – Pal Mickey, that is. This is a high-tech 10½-in (27-cm) tall cuddly toy that talks to you (using wireless communication at strategic points around the parks) as a kind of tour guide, with helpful hints (eg in

5

Disney-MGM Studios: 'Fantasmic! will be starting in about an hour'), insider info (on Main Street USA: 'See the names written on those second-storey windows? Those folks helped Walt build his Magic Kingdom!') and interactive games while you wait in a queue (and which still work when you get back home). Pal Mickey can be rented (at $8, plus tax, a day, with a $60 refundable deposit) or you can buy one for $56.33 plus tax.

Cast Members

Disney Cast Members (or CMs) are renowned for their helpful and cheerful style and are always willing to assist, offer advice or just stop and chat. Interaction with CMs often provides some of the best memories of a visit. So, if you've had exceptional service or a CM has gone out of their way to help you, let Disney know as they value such feedback (and CMs get credit for it, too). Call in at Guest Relations on your way out (or City Hall at the *Magic Kingdom* Park) and record your vote of thanks. Better still, write to: Walt Disney World Guest Communications, PO Box 10000, Lake Buena Vista, Florida, 32830-1000, USA, or e-mail via www.disneyworld.com (go to the Contact Us link). You can even download a form to say thanks at www.whatwouldwaltdo.com.

Wishes fireworks display

Baby swap

Where families have small children, but Mum and Dad both want to try a ride, you DON'T have to queue twice. When you get to the front of the queue, tell the operator you want to do a 'baby swap'. This means Mum can ride while Dad looks after junior and, on her return, Dad can have his go.

Many children get a big thrill from collecting autographs from the various Disney characters, and most shops sell **autograph books**.

50th Anniversary Celebration

May 2005 sees the 50th anniversary of *Disneyland Resort in California* in Anaheim, Los Angeles, Walt's original theme park, and to celebrate there will be special events in every Disney park around the world. Billed as *The Happiest Celebration on Earth*, each of the Florida parks will unveil a major new attraction in the course of the **18-month festival** and there will be some elaborate theming, commemorative events and additional gala elements throughout the *Walt Disney World Resort in Florida*. The *Magic Kingdom* Park will debut **Cinderellabration**, a lively stage show from *Disneyland Tokyo*; *Epcot* will open the amazing **Soarin'** ride from *Disney's California Adventure* (in Los Angeles); *Disney-MGM Studios* gets **Lights! Motors! Action!™ Extreme Stunt Show**, the sensational stunt show from *Walt Disney Studios* (Paris); and *Disney's Animal Kingdom* will boast **Everest**™ as arguably THE great new ride. There are sure to be other festive events added nearer the time, so visit www.askdaisy.net/orlando, www.wdwinfo.com and www.disneyworld.co.uk for updates.

Character dining

Having a meal with Mickey and Co. (or Winnie the Pooh, or Cinderella or Mary Poppins) is one of the great Disney experiences – even if you don't have children! It is also often the best way to meet your favourite characters without long, hot waits. All bookings – Priority Seating (PS) times – can be arranged up to 90 days in advance by phoning 407 WDW DINE (939 3463), calling at any Guest Services desk, or by touching *55 on a Disney resort phone. A credit card is also required for a PS on any American public holiday.

Some meals are difficult to get. Cinderella's Royal Table at the *Magic Kingdom* sells out 90 days in advance, within the first few *minutes*. Chef Mickey's and the Princess Storybook Breakfast also go quickly. If you cannot get a PS in advance, try calling the day you'd like to dine or, as a last resort, show up at the restaurant to see if there have been any cancellations.

You must check in at the podium 5 minutes prior to your PS time and you will be given the next available table. Some characters don't enter the restaurant so, if they are in the lobby, you'll want to meet them before you are seated. Dining is all-you-can-eat, served buffet, pre-plated or family-style.

Inside the restaurant, characters circulate among the tables giving attention to each party (particularly when children are holding the camera!). Character interaction is top-notch, especially if you dine off-hours when the restaurant is a bit slower. Be sure to bring your autograph book, a fat pen or marker (easier for the characters to hold) and plenty of film or an extra digital card for your camera. Some characters are huge and small children may be put off by them. If you aren't sure how they'll react, see how they are with the characters in the park before booking a character meal.

Price range: breakfast $16.99–19.99 for adults, $8.99–9.99 for children; lunch $17.99–19.99 and $9.29–9.99; dinner $21.99–25.00 and $9.99–10.99.

The meals

Magic Kingdom: **Crystal Palace** (breakfast, lunch or dinner with Winnie the Pooh, Tigger, Eeyore and Piglet – especially good for smaller children); **Cinderella's Royal Table** (now called Once Upon a Time Breakfast, with Cinderella, Fairy Godmother, Belle, Jasmine and Snow White. Credit card needed for PS, $10/$5 charged for no-shows); **Liberty Tree Tavern** (dinner with Chip 'n Dale, Meeko, Minnie and Pluto).

Epcot: **Garden Grill** (lunch or dinner with Farmer Mickey, Pluto, Chip 'n Dale); **Ice Cream Social** (also at the Garden Grill; ice cream creations with Farmer Mickey, Chip 'n Dale and Pluto at 3, 3.10 and 3.20pm for $6.99 per person – a good option for shy children who want to meet Mickey in a quieter atmosphere); **Princess Storybook Breakfast** (an alternative to Once Upon A Breakfast, with Belle, Jasmine, Snow White, Sleeping Beauty and Mary Poppins but NOT Cinderella. Credit card needed for PS, $10/$5 charged for no-shows).

Disney's Animal Kingdom: **Donald's Restaurantosaurus** (breakfast with Donald, Goofy, Pluto and sometimes Mickey).

Disney Resorts: **Chef Mickey's** (Contemporary Resort; breakfast or dinner with Mickey, Goofy, Chip 'n Dale – peak times book up quickly); **1900 Park Fare** (Grand Floridian Resort and Spa; breakfast with Alice and her Wonderland Friends, dinner with Cinderella, Perla, Suzy, Fairy Godmother and, sometimes, Prince Charming – again, book early); **Wonderland Tea Party** (Grand Floridian Resort and Spa; 1.30–2.30pm Mon–Fri, 3–10s only, $28.17, lunch, activities and storytelling with Alice and friends); **'Ohana** (Polynesian Resort; breakfast with Mickey, Minnie and Chip 'n Dale); **Cape May Café** (Beach Club Resort; breakfast with Goofy, Chip 'n Dale and Pluto); **Mickey's Backyard Barbecue** (Fort Wilderness; $39 and $25, games, storytelling, live entertainment, music and dancing with Mickey and Co; unlimited beer, wine, iced tea and lemonade – seasonal); **Walt Disney World Swan** (Garden Grove Café; Sat breakfast with Goofy and Pluto. Gulliver's Grill; 6pm dinner with Timon and Rafiki Mon–Fri, Goofy and Pluto Sat and Sun).   **SUSAN HAASS**

Magic Kingdom Park

The starting point for any visit has to be the *Magic Kingdom*, the park that best embodies the spirit of delight that Disney bestows on its visitors. It's the original development that sparked the tourist boom in Orlando back in 1971. In comparative terms, the *Magic Kingdom* Park is similar to the *Disneyland Parks* at *Disneyland® Resort Paris* and *Disneyland Resort in*

California in Los Angeles. Outside those, it has no equal as an enchanting and exciting day out for all the family. However, although superficially some rides are the same as those in Paris or LA, there are key differences, notably on Pirates of the Caribbean, Big Thunder Mountain Railroad and the Haunted Mansion. And Space Mountain here is a completely different ride.

The Magic Kingdom Park at a glance

Location	Off World Drive, Walt Disney World
Size	107 acres (43ha) in 7 'lands'
Hours	9am–7pm off peak; 9am–10pm Washington's birthday (see page 19), spring school holidays; 9am–11pm high season (Easter, summer holidays, Thanksgiving and Christmas)
Admission	Under 3 free; 3–9 $43.75 (1-day ticket), $176 (4-Day Park Hopper), $226 (5-Day Park Hopper Plus); adult (10+) $54.75, $219, $289. Prices do not include tax.
Parking	$8
Lockers	Yes; under Main Street Railroad Station; $7 ($2 refund)
Pushchairs	$8 and $15 (Stroller Shop to right of main entrance, $1 deposit refunded)
Wheelchairs	$8 ($1 deposit refunded) or $40 ($10 deposit refunded) (Main Ticket Centre or Stroller Shop)
Top Attractions	Splash Mountain, Space Mountain, Mickey's PhilharMagic, Stitch's Great Escape, most rides in Fantasyland
Don't Miss	Share A Dream Come True Parade, SpectroMagic Parade (certain nights) and Wishes fireworks (certain nights)
Hidden Costs	**Meals** Burger, chips and coke $7.68 3-course dinner $35 (Cinderella's Table) Kids' meal $3.49
	T-shirts $19–28
	Souvenirs $1–325
	Sundries Spray fan (handy when it's hot) $15.96

BRIT TIP: For the smoothest entry by road from West Highway 192, take Seralago Boulevard opposite the Holiday Inn Hotel & Suites next to Old Town, turn left on to a non-toll stretch of Osceola Parkway and follow the signs to your chosen park. On East 192, turn off on Sherberth Road, go north to the first traffic lights and turn right, then pick up the Disney signs.

I will now attempt to steer you through a typical day at the parks, with a guide to the main rides, shows and places to eat, how to park, how to avoid the worst of the crowds and how much you should expect to pay.

This essential park takes up just 107 acres (43ha) of Disney's near 31,000 acres (12,555ha) but attracts almost as many visitors as the rest put together. It has seven separate 'lands', like slices of a large cake, centred on Florida's most famous landmark, Cinderella Castle. More than 40 attractions are packed into the park, not to mention numerous shops and restaurants (although the eating opportunities are less impressive than in *Epcot* and *Disney-MGM Studios*).

It's easy to get overwhelmed by it all, especially as it does get so busy (even the fast-food restaurants have serious queues in high season), so study the notes and plan your visit around what most takes your fancy.

Location

The *Magic Kingdom* Park is situated at the innermost end of the vacation kingdom, with its entrance booths in Toll Plaza three-quarters of the way along World Drive, the main entrance road off Highway 192. World Drive runs north–south through *Walt Disney World Resort in Florida*, while the Interstate 4 (I-4) entrance, Epcot Drive, runs east–west. Unless you are staying at a Disney resort, you will have to pay your $8 parking fee at the Toll Plaza and that brings you to the car park (or 'parking lot' in American-speak) that has room to accommodate more than 10,000 cars.

BRIT TIP: Staying at a Disney resort? You can sometimes ride up front on the monorail (and be given a 'driver' certificate!) if you ask a Cast Member on the platform.

The majority arrive between 9.30 and 11.30am, so the car parks can be pretty busy then, which is another good reason to get here EARLY. If you can't make it by 9am during peak periods, you might want to wait until after 1pm, or even later when the park is open as late as 11pm (in high summer and Christmas). Remember to note on your parking

BRIT TIP: Reader Roy Williams says: 'We bought a bright, 3-in plastic ball that we fixed to our car aerial in the car park, enabling us to find it easily on our return.' You could also leave a familiar, non-valuable item in the window for extra help. Visit www.aerialbuddies.co.uk for a selection of fun aerial accessories!

5

ADVENTURELAND
1 Swiss Family Treehouse
2 Jungle Cruise
3 Pirates Of The Caribbean
4 The Enchanted Tiki Room (under new management)
5 Magic Carpets of Aladdin

FRONTIERLAND
6 Splash Mountain
7 Big Thunder Mountain Railroad
8 Country Bear Jamboree
9 Raft To Tom Sawyer Island

LIBERTY SQUARE
10 Goofy's Country Dancin' Jamboree
11 Liberty Square Riverboat
12 The Haunted Mansion
13 The Hall of Presidents

FANTASYLAND
14 'It's a Small World'
15 Dumbo The Flying Elephant
16 Mad Tea Party
17 The Many Adventures Of Winnie The Pooh
18 Snow White's Scary Adventures
19 Cinderella's Golden Carrousel
20 Mickey's PhilharMagic
21 Peter Pan's Flight
22 Castle Forecourt Stage – Cinderellabration
23 Cinderella's Royal Table
24 Ariel's Grotto
25 Fairytale Garden

MICKEY'S TOONTOWN FAIR
26 Mickey's Country House
27 Minnie's Country House
28 Toontown Hall of Fame
29 The Barnstormer at Goofy's Wiseacre Farm
30 Donald's Boat

TOMORROWLAND
31 Space Mountain
32 Tomorrowland Indy Speedway
33 Astro Orbiter
34 Walt Disney's Carousel of Progress
35 Tomorrowland Transit Authority
36 Stitch's Great Escape
37 Buzz Lightyear's Space Ranger Spin
   (Disney/Pixar)
38 The Timekeeper
39 Galaxy Palace Theater

TRANSPORT
40 Walt Disney World Railroad
41 Boat Dock
42 Monorail Station
43 Bus Station

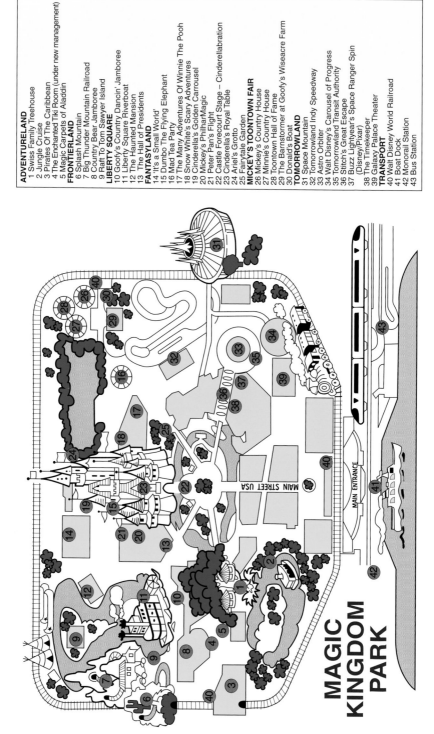

MAGIC KINGDOM PARK

MAIN STREET USA

MAIN ENTRANCE

© Disney

Cinderella Castle

ticket exactly what area you parked in and the row number, e.g. Mickey, Row 30. You will struggle to remember otherwise, and all hire cars look exactly the same!

A system of motorised trams carries you from the car park to the Transportation and Ticket Center at the heart of the operation. Unless you already have your ticket (which will save you valuable time), you will have to queue up at the ticket booths to go any further. From here, the monorail or a ferryboat will bring you to the doorstep of the *Magic Kingdom* Park itself. The monorail (dead ahead of you) is quicker, if there isn't a long queue, otherwise bear left and take a slower ferryboat. If you are staying at a Disney hotel, one of the complimentary resort buses will deliver you to the park's front door (or the monorail or boat will if you are staying at one of the *Magic Kingdom* resorts).

The *Magic Kingdom* is a 'dry' park, i.e. there is no alcohol on sale. This is the only Disney park with this restriction. One final note, in all the parks you may find one or two attractions closed for refurbishment to mark the constant process of keeping things fresh, but you will never be short of things to do!

Main Street USA

Right, we've finally reached the park itself… but not quite. Hopefully you've arrived early and are among the leading hordes aiming to swarm through the main entrance. The published opening times may say 9am, but the gates to the *Magic Kingdom* Park are likely to open up to 45 minutes before then.

You will find yourself in **Main Street USA**, the first of the seven lands. At opening time, there is an informal Welcome Parade, with costumed singers and dancers, and the Character Train then arrives at Main Street Station to bring a variety of characters for a friendly meet-and-greet in Town Square (get those autograph books ready!). A family is then chosen at random to sprinkle some 'pixie dust' on the *Magic Kingdom* to officially open the park for the day. Immediately on your right is **Exposition Hall**, a photographic centre featuring archive film material, a mini cinema showing Disney classics and a series of interactive games, plus some cartoon photo opportunities. On your left is **City Hall**, where you can pick up a park map and daily schedule (if you haven't been given one at the entrance booths) and make reservations for the main restaurants (highly advisable at peak periods). You can also find out where the characters will be appearing and when. Ahead of you is **Town Square**, where you can take a one-way ride down Main Street USA on

5

Main Street USA

© Disney

> BRIT TIP: Save paying up to three times more for your drinks by bringing your own bottled water in a back-pack to all the parks and use the many drinking fountains for refills.

a horse-drawn bus or fire engine and visit the **Car Barn** mini museum. The Street itself houses some of the best shopping in the *Magic Kingdom* Park (check out the massive Emporium), plus the **Walt Disney World Railroad** (AAA), a Western-themed steam train that circles the park and is one of the better attractions when the queues are long elsewhere (although – be warned – Town Square station is the busiest).

For dining, you have lunch and dinner at **Tony's Town Square Restaurant**, specialising in Italian meals, **The Plaza Restaurant** (lunch and dinner, sandwiches, salads and sundaes) and **The Crystal Palace** (breakfast, lunch and dinner, buffet-style food with Winnie the Pooh, Tigger and Co.). Quick bites can be bought from **Casey's Corner** (hot dogs, chips and soft drinks), **Main Street Bakery** (coffee and pastries), **Main Street Cinema** and **Main Street Confectionary** (chocolate and sweets) and the **Plaza Ice Cream Parlor**. Disney characters also appear periodically outside Exposition Hall.

Look out for the **Guest Information Board** at the top of Main Street USA (on the left) that gives waiting times for all the attractions through the day. The **Baby Center** (for nursing mothers) can also be found at the top of Main Street, to the left next to the Crystal Palace, along with the park's **First Aid** station.

Unless you are a late arrival, give Main Street no more than a passing glance and head for the end of the street to the real entrance to the park. This is where you must await the official opening hour for the famous 'Rope drop', and you should adopt one of three tactics here, each aimed at doing one or two of the most popular rides before the queues become substantial (waiting times of an hour or more for Splash Mountain are not unknown).

One: if you fancy the 5-star, log-flume ride Splash Mountain, keep left in front of the Crystal Palace with the majority of the crowd, who will be heading for the same place.

Two: if you have young children who can't wait to have a ride on Cinderella's Golden Carrousel (and yes, it really IS spelt that way) or the other Fantasyland rides, stay in the middle and make your way through the castle.

Three: if the thrills of the indoor roller-coaster Space Mountain appeal first, move to the right by The Plaza Restaurant and you'll get straight into Tomorrowland.

Now you will be in pole position for the opening rush (and it will be a rush, believe me; take care if you're here with small children).

Find the characters

Can't find Mickey and Co? Check in at **City Hall** first and they will be able to tell you where they can be found (which is often one of the main laments of those who come in unprepared). In fact, City Hall is your best friend for a variety of queries, from the location of baby facilities to meal bookings (there are NO baby facilities at City Hall, though). Character meet-and-greets are also shown on all park maps with a Mickey's glove icon.

Adventureland

If you head to the left (effectively going clockwise around the park – always a good idea), you will enter Adventureland. If you're going to Splash Mountain first, you pass the Swiss Family Treehouse on your left and bear right through an archway (with restrooms on your right) into Frontierland, where you turn left and you will see Splash Mountain straight in front of you. Stopping in Adventureland, however, these are the attractions:

Swiss Family Treehouse: this imitation Banyan tree is a clever replica of the treehouse from Disney's 1960 film *Swiss Family Robinson*. It's a walk-through attraction where the queues (rarely long) move steadily if not quickly, providing a fascinating glimpse of the ultimate treehouse, complete with kitchen, rope bridges and running water! AAA.

Jungle Cruise: it's not so much the scenic, geographically suspect boat ride (where the Nile suddenly becomes the Amazon) that is so amusing here as the patter of your boat's captain, who spins a non-stop yarn about your adventure that features wild animals, tropical plants, hidden temples and sudden waterfalls. Great detail but long queues, so visit either early morning (opens at 10am) or late afternoon (evening queues are shortest, but you'll miss some of the detail in the dark). AAAA (FP).

> BRIT TIP: When you are faced by more than one queue for an attraction, head for the left-hand one. Almost invariably, for some reason, this moves slightly quicker than the one on the right.

Pirates of the Caribbean: one of Disney's most impressive attractions that involves their pioneering work in audio-animatronics, life-size figures that move, talk and, in this instance, lay siege to a Caribbean island! Your underground boat ride takes you through a typical pirate adventure and the wizardry of the special effects is truly amazing. It's worth having several rides here, although it may be a bit spooky for very young children. Queues are rarely long and almost non-existent late in the day. AAAAA.

The Enchanted Tiki Room – Under New Management: a bird-laden, audio-animatronics venture features Iago (from *Aladdin*) and Zazu (from *The Lion King*). They head a colourful, lively 16-minute revue that will appeal especially to younger children. Queues are rare here. AAA.

Magic Carpets of Aladdin: here, in an Agrabah-themed area styled after the animated film, the latest ride spins you up, down and around as you try to dodge the spitting camel! Your 'flying carpet' tilts as well as levitates, but it is basically simple stuff geared towards younger children (and virtually identical to the Magic Carpets of Agrabah in the *Walt Disney Studios* in *Disneyland® Resort Paris*). TT (TTTT under 5s).

Shrunken Ned's Junior Jungle Boats: this costs an extra 50c for kids to try their hand at steering rather tame toy boats. T.

Disney characters also turn up outside the Pirates of the Caribbean and Magic Carpets rides, while the best of the shopping is in the Pirates Bazaar here.

For food, you have **Aloha Isle** (yoghurt and ice cream) and **Sunshine Tree Terrace** (fruit, snacks, yoghurt, tea and coffee), plus the more substantial Mexican bites of tacos, nachos and taco salads of **El Pirata y el Perico Restaurante**.

5

Frontierland

Passing through Adventureland brings you to the target for many of the early birds. This Western-themed area is one of the busiest and is best avoided from late morning to late afternoon.

Splash Mountain: based on the 1946 classic Disney cartoon *Song of the South*, this is a watery journey into the world of Brer Rabbit, Brer Fox and Brer Bear. The first part is all jolly cartoon scenery and fun with the main characters and a couple of minor swoops in your 8-passenger log boat. The conclusion, a 5-storey plummet at 45 degrees into a mist-shrouded pool, will seem like you are falling off the edge of the world! A huge adrenalin rush, but busy almost all day (try it first thing or during one of the parades to avoid the longest queues). You will also get VERY wet! Restrictions: 3ft 4in/ 101cm. TTTTT (FP).

Big Thunder Mountain Railroad: when Disney does a roller-coaster you can be sure it will be one of the classiest, and here it is, a runaway mine train that swoops, tilts and plunges through a mock abandoned mine filled with clever scenery. You should ride at least

Cinderella's Golden Carrousel

The Jungle Cruise

twice to appreciate all the detail, but again queues are heavy, so go first thing (after Splash Mountain) or late in the day. Restrictions: 3ft 4in/ 101cm. TTTT (FP).

Country Bear Jamboree: now here's a novelty, a 16-minute musical revue presented by audio-animatronic bears! It's great family fun with plenty of novel touches (watch for the talking moose-head). Again, you'll need to beat the crowds by going early morning (open at 10am) or early evening. AAAA.

Frontierland Shootin' Arcade: this is the only other attraction in the park to cost extra (50c), as you shoot the animated targets. TT.

Tom Sawyer Island: take a raft over to an overgrown playground of mysterious caves, grottos and mazes, rope bridges and Fort Sam Clemens, where you can fire air guns at passing boats (open at 10am). A good get-away in the early afternoon when the crowds are at their biggest, while **Aunt Polly's Dockside Inn** is a refuge within a refuge for snacks and soft drinks. TT.

Frontierland shops sell cowboy hats, guns and badges as well as Native American and Mexican handicrafts. For food, try **Pecos Bill Café** (salads, sandwiches and burgers), **Frontierland Fries** (McDonald's fries and drinks) or the **Turkey Leg Cart** (massive, smoke-grilled turkey legs). For shopping here, try the nicely themed **Briar Patch** and the **Prairie Outpost** for some interesting gifts.

© Disney

The Mad Tea Party

Liberty Square

Continuing the clockwise tour brings you next to a homage to post-Independence America. A lot of the historical content will go over the heads of British visitors, but it still has some great attractions.

Goofy's Country Dancin' Jamboree: at the old Diamond Horseshoe Saloon, this is a new character sing-along as Goofy and his pals (Chip 'n Dale, plus *Toy Story* trio Woody, Jessie and Bullseye) lead an 18-minute show designed purely for the young 'uns. The 'country music dance party' promises young guests the chance to learn classic dances like *Boot Scootin' Boogie* and *Electric Slide* while Mum and Dad take pictures from the second-floor gallery. AAA (under 8s only).

Liberty Square Riverboat: cruise America's 'rivers' on an authentic paddle steamer, be menaced by Indians and thrill to the stories of How the West Was Won (open at 10am). This is also a good ride to take at the busiest times of the day, especially early afternoon. AAA.

The Haunted Mansion: a clever delve into the world of ghost train rides that is neither too scary for kids nor too twee for adults. Not so much a thrill ride as a scenic adventure. Watch out for the neat touch at the end when your car picks up an extra 'passenger'. Longish queues during much of the day,

however (so a good one for a FASTPASS). AAAA or TTTT for under 6s (FP).

The Hall of Presidents: this is the attraction that is likely to mean least to us, a 2-part show that is first a film about the history of the Constitution and then an audio-animatronic parade of all 43 American presidents (open at 10am). Technically it's impressive, but dull for young children, although it is another air-conditioned haven. AAA.

Shopping here includes **Ye Olde Christmas Shoppe** and **The Yankee Trader**, while eating opportunities consist of the full-service **Liberty Tree Tavern** (serving hearty soups, steaks and traditional dishes like meatloaf and pot roast, plus dinner with Mickey and Co), **Columbia Harbour House** (for counter-service fried chicken or shrimp, fish and salads) and **Sleepy Hollow** (a picnic area serving an assortment of snacks, fresh fruit and drinks).

Fantasyland

Leaving Liberty Square, you walk past Cinderella Castle and come into the park's spiritual heart, the area with which young children are most enchanted. The attractions are designed with kids in mind, but some of the shops are quite sophisticated.

5

Magic Carpets of Aladdin

© Disney

'It's a Small World' (NB: being refurbished until May 2005): this could almost be Disney's theme ride, a family boat trip through the different continents, each represented by hundreds of dancing, singing audio-animatronic dolls in delightful set-piece pageants. It sounds twee but it actually creates a surprisingly striking effect, accompanied by an annoyingly catchy theme song which young children adore. Crowds peak in early afternoon. AAAA.

Dumbo the Flying Elephant: parents hate it but kids love it and all want to do this 2-minute ride on the back of a flying elephant that swoops in best Dumbo style (even if the ears do not flap). Ride early here or expect a long queue. TT (TTTT under 5s).

Mad Tea Party: again the kids will insist you take them in these spinning, oversized tea cups that have their own 'steering wheel' to add to the whirling effect. Actually, they're just a heavily disguised fairground ride. Again, go early or expect serious crowds. Characters from *Alice In Wonderland* also visit from time to time. TT (TTTT under 5s).

The Many Adventures of Winnie the Pooh: building on the timeless popularity of Pooh, Piglet and Co., this family ride offers a musical jaunt through Hundred Acre Wood with some clever special effects (get ready to 'bounce' with Tigger!) and another original soundtrack. AAA (AAAAA under 5s) (FP).

Snow White's Scary Adventures: this lively, fast-paced ride tells the cartoon story of Snow White with a few ghost train effects that may scare small children. Good fun, though, for parents and kids. Again, you will need to go early or late (or during the main afternoon parade) to beat the queues. TTT (TTTTT under 5s).

Cinderella's Golden Carrousel: the centrepiece of Fantasyland shouldn't need any more explanation other than it is a vintage carousel ride which kids adore. Long queues during the main part of the day. T (TTT under 5s).

Mickey's PhilharMagic: this dramatic and utterly fun 3-D 10-minute film show (replacing *Legend of the Lion King*) has a host of in-theatre special effects as Donald tries to conduct the Enchanted Orchestra à la Sorcerer Mickey – to suitably comic effect. Set in the PhilharMagic Concert Hall, it features a 150-ft (46-metre) wide screen to immerse guests in the richly animated 3-D world of *Beauty & The Beast, The Little Mermaid, The Lion King, Peter Pan* and *Aladdin*, with the hapless Donald surviving a string of adventures with each before Mickey brings him back to earth. The lavishness of the theatre, the artistry of the all-new animation, the interweaving of the special effects (you can even 'smell' the food on-screen!) and the all-round family entertainment on offer add up to one of the most enjoyable Disney attractions. There is no scare factor at work here (although the sudden plunge into darkness at one point and the sheer noise of the 'orchestra' can sometimes spook young children), while you'll be enchanted when Tinkerbell seems to fly right out of the screen to hover in front of you. AAAAA (FP).

Peter Pan's Flight: don't be fooled by the long queues, this is a rather tame ride, although it is still a big hit with kids. Its novel effect of flying up with Peter Pan quickly wears off, but there is still a lot of clever detail as your 'sailing ship' journeys over London to Neverland. AA (AAAAA under 6s) (FP).

In addition to the rides, there are different musical shows daily on the **Castle Forecourt Stage**, while the *Sword In The Stone* show is re-enacted several times a day near

Cinderella's Golden Carrousel.

Cinderellabration: as part of the *50th Anniversary Celebration*, this elaborately staged spectacular debuts in May 2005, picking up where the classic animated film ends. Mickey and Minnie join in to help Cinderella in becoming a princess, with the Fairy Godmother sprinkling her 'magic' around the Castle Forecourt with some beautiful lighting and other special effects. A variety of entertainers begin the grand dance, and Cinderella and Prince Charming ride their horse carriage around the Plaza. AAAA.

Ariel's Grotto, behind Dumbo, offers the chance to meet The Little Mermaid (which draws a queue at peak periods), while periodically in the **Fairytale Garden**, on the corner of the Castle facing Tomorrowland, you can listen to *Storytime with Belle*.

Eating opportunities are at **The Pinocchio Village Haus** (salads, burgers and hot dogs), the **Enchanted Grove** (ice drinks and juices), **Scuttle's Landing** and **Mrs Potts' Cupboard** (for ice creams and sundaes). **Cinderella's Royal Table** is a fine setting for a meal, be it lunch, dinner or the much sought-after character breakfast. The majestic hall, waitresses in costume and well-presented food – salads, seafood, roast beef, prime rib and chicken – provide a memorable experience. It's a touch pricey for dinner, though.

Shop at **Tinkerbell's Treasures**, the excellent **Sir Mickey's, Fantasy Faire** and **Pooh's Thotful Shop**.

Mickey's Toontown Fair

In the top corner of Fantasyland (just past the Mad Tea Party) is the shrub-lined entrance to **Mickey's Toontown Fair** (area open at 10am). It is easy to miss, but it does have a station on the railroad. Its primary appeal is to young children, as they can meet their favourite Disney characters. Exceptionally kid-friendly and well landscaped, it features a huge merchandising area, the **County Bounty** – wallets beware!

Mickey's Country House: here is a walk-through opportunity to see Mickey at home and have your picture taken with him in the Judge's Tent. AAAA (plus TTTTT for the photo opportunity.

Minnie's Country House: this is a chance to view Minnie's home and 'unique memorabilia', all designed in a Country and Western style. AAA.

Mickey's Toontown Fair Hall of Fame: three opportunities to meet a host of other Disney favourites in the Villains Room, Mickey's Pals and Famous Faces. TTTTT (for kids!).

The Barnstormer at Goofy's Wiseacre Farm: a mini roller-coaster just for the young 'uns (although possibly a bit too much for the under 5s) and is another masterpiece of design as it swoops through the barn, even if it is a pretty short ride after all the queuing. TTT (TTTTT for 5–9s). Restrictions: 3ft/91cm.

Donald's Boat: parents beware, youngsters get seriously wet here! If you've seen the dancing fountains at *Epcot* between Future World and World Showcase (see page 113), prepare for more watery delights as this boat-themed fountain spouts off in all sorts of wonderful ways. Ideally, bring a change of clothes or swimsuit for your offspring. It's a great place to revitalise tired or irritable children. AAAA (under 10s). Check out the **Toontown Farmers Market** for fruit, snacks, and beverages.

Tomorrowland

The last of the seven 'lands,' this has a cartoon-like space-age appearance, guaranteed to appeal to youngsters, and some of the more original shops.

Space Mountain: this is one of the three most popular attractions, and its reputation is deserved. It is a

5

fast, tight-turning roller-coaster completely in the dark save for occasional flashes as you whiz through 'the galaxy'. Don't do this after eating! The only way to beat the crowds is to go either first thing, late in the day or during one of the parades (or, of course, get a FASTPASS). Restrictions: 3ft 8in/ 111cm. TTTTT (FP). Children will also gravitate to the **Tomorrowland Arcade** as you exit the ride.

Tomorrowland Indy Speedway: despite the long queues, this is a rather tame ride on supposed race tracks that just putt-putts along on rails with little real steering required. Restrictions: children must be 4ft 4in/132cm to drive alone. T (TTTT under 6s).

Astro Orbiter: a jazzed-up version of Dumbo in Fantasyland, this ride is just a bit faster, higher and on 'rockets'. Large, slow-moving queues are another reason to give this a miss unless you have children. TT (TTTT under 10s).

Walt Disney's Carousel of Progress: this will surprise, entertain and amuse. It is a 100-year journey through modern technology with audio-animatronics and a revolving theatre that reveals different stages in that development. Its 22-minute duration is rarely threatened by crowds. AAA (only at peak periods)

Tomorrowland Transit Authority: a neat 'future transport system', the TTA gives an elevated view of the area, with a glimpse inside Space Mountain, in electro-magnetically powered cars. Queues

Barnstormer at Goofy's Wiseacre Farm

Disney's Agrabah Bazaar

are usually short, so give it a go. AAA (TTT for under 8s).

Stitch's Great Escape!: opening in October 2004, this 15-minute experience replaces the Alien Encounter and is sure to be a hit with all the family (although not perhaps for children frightened by the dark or loud noises). In many ways a prequel to the animated hit *Lilo & Stitch*, it is a unique audio-animatronic 'show' into the cartoon world of the Galactic Federation (including Captain Gantu, the Grand Councilwoman and the hapless Pleakley). Visitors become recruits for the Federation prison service but things go hilariously wrong as a new prisoner arrives (Stitch, or Experiment 626 as he is still known) and proceeds to cause havoc. There are two pre-show areas and then the 'recruits' are ushered into a sit-down (with shoulder restraints) chamber where Stitch is let loose to bounce, dribble and, yes, even belch over the unsuspecting audience. Kids will love it and even grown-ups may laugh out loud at some of the jokes and special effects. Restrictions: 3ft 4in/101cm. AAAAA (expected; FP).

Buzz Lightyear's Space Ranger Spin (Disney/Pixar): kids will not want to miss this chance to join the great *Toy Story* character in his battle against the evil Emperor Zurg. Ride into action against the robot army – and shoot them with laser cannons!

Buzz Lightyear's Space Ranger Spin

A sure-fire family winner, especially as you get to keep score. Watch out for a gift shop and ride photo opportunity as you exit. TTT (TTTTT for under 8s; FP).

The Timekeeper: a combination of high-tech audio-animatronics and 360-degree film wizardry gives you an amusing plunge into time travel in the company of the zany robot Timekeeper (voiced by Robin Williams) and his camera-equipped assistant Nine-eye. AAAA (only at peak periods).

The Galaxy Palace Theater hosts live musical productions, featuring Disney characters and talent shows, at various times of the day. For food, **Cosmic Ray's Starlight Café** has burgers, chicken and salads, **The Plaza Pavilion** does pizza, subs and salads, **Auntie Gravity's** (ouch!) **Galactic Goodies** serves ice cream and juices, the **Lunching Pad** (double ouch!) offers smoked turkey legs, snacks and drinks, and the **Cool Ship** provides various drinks. Shopping highlights include **Mickey's Star Traders** and **Merchant of Venus**.

Having come full circle you are now back at Main Street USA and it's best to return here in early afternoon to avoid the crowds and have a closer look at the impressive array of shops.

The afternoon highlight, however, is the **Share A Dream Come True** parade. This six-part extravaganza,

> **BRIT TIP:** To watch a parade, sit on the left side of Main Street USA (facing the Castle) to stay in the shade if it's hot. People start staking out the best spots here up to an HOUR in advance.

along Main Street and through Frontierland, is designed as a flurry of classic Disney moments frozen inside giant snow globes full of special effects. All the favourite characters feature, along with a new musical score, plus some lighting tricks. Watch out for the chance to join in as the parade stops to allow characters to select people to dance and play act with. The globes themselves feature some outstanding effects, with Aladdin taking to the air on his flying carpet, the Wicked Queen turning into the evil old hag, and snow in the leading globes. It is a dazzler for all ages, but is especially popular with children. AAAAA.

There's more

If you think the park looks good during the day, prepare to be amazed at how wonderful it appears at night – some of the lighting effects are astounding. When the park is open in the evenings (during the main holiday periods and weekends), you can see the **SpectroMagic parade** (when there are two a night, the second is less crowded), which is a mind-boggling light and sound festival full

SpectroMagic Parade

of glitter and razzamatazz, with the Disney characters at the centre of a multitude of sparkling lights and fibre-optic effects. It is difficult to do it justice in words, so just make sure that you see it.

Firework finale

Most nights at the *Magic Kingdom* Park conclude with the stunning **Wishes** firework show, behind the Castle and with a broad vista to the rear of the park.

With a clever soundtrack narrated by Jiminy Cricket and featuring memorable moments from an array of Disney classics, it is magnificently choreographed and culminates in a sequence of pyrotechnic explosions (many of them designed especially for this show), which truly dazzle the eyes and mind. Starting with an appearance by Tinkerbell (from the Castle's top turret), it continues for 12 minutes of typical Disney emotional heart-tugging and is the perfect pixie-dust farewell to a day at this park.

At Easter and Christmas, the daily parade takes on extra seasonal charm with appearances by the Easter Bunny and Father Christmas.

If the crowds get too heavy, you CAN escape by leaving the park in the early afternoon (get a hand-stamp for re-admission and keep your car park ticket, which is valid all day) and returning to your hotel for a few hours' rest or a dip in the pool.

BRIT TIP: After the fireworks crowd exits, you are often allowed to take the Resort Only monorail back to the Transportation & Ticket Center, rather than stand in the queues for the main monorail.

BRIT TIP: Main Street USA closes half an hour after the rest of the park, so you can avoid the mad rush for the car parks by lingering here and enjoying an ice cream or coffee.

Halloween and Christmas

Two additional annual events in the *Magic Kingdom* Park are **Mickey's Not So Scary Halloween Party** (on selected dates in October) and **Mickey's Very Merry Christmas Party** (late November and December) which provide a separate, party-style ticketed event from 7pm to midnight, with most of the rides open and extra themed fun and games. The Halloween event sees many visitors dress up for the typical American trick-or-treat fun, and there are plenty of treats and sweets for youngsters on the way. With special music, story-telling, parades and fireworks (and some wonderful lighting effects), plus a free family photo, tickets go on sale about six months in advance and sell out quickly. The Christmas party sees regular 'snow' on Main Street and an array of magnificent festive decorations and theming. There are free hot chocolate and cookies, plus a family photo, as well as a parade and more fireworks. The whole atmosphere is truly enchanting, although the evening is occasionally liable to some unfriendly Florida weather. Halloween party tickets cost $34.95 for adults and $28.95 per child on the day (or $31.95 and $25.95 in advance), while the Christmas party is $42.95 and $32.95 (or $35.95 and $25.95 in advance). Book in advance on 407 934 7639.

Finally, one of the park's little-known 'secrets' is the **Keys to the**

Kingdom, a 4–5-hour guided tour of many backstage areas, including the service tunnel under the park, and entertainment production buildings. It costs an extra $58 (including lunch; not available for under 16s). Call 407 939 8687 for more information. **Disney's Family Magic Tour** is a 2-hour guided adventure that takes you on a search for clues throughout the park at $25/person or you can experience **Disney's The Magic Behind Our Steam Trains** tour ($40/person; no under 10s) as you join the crew who prepare the park's trains each day.

MAGIC KINGDOM PARK with children

Here is a rough guide to the rides which appeal to different age groups. Obviously, children vary enormously in their likes and dislikes but, as a general rule, you can be fairly sure the following will have most appeal to the ages concerned (height restrictions have been taken into account):

Under 5s
Walt Disney World Railroad, Main Street Vehicles, Jungle Cruise, The Enchanted Tiki Room – Under New Management, Country Bear Jamboree, Liberty Square Riverboat, 'It's a Small World', Peter Pan's Flight, Mickey's PhilharMagic, Cinderella's Golden Carrousel, Dumbo The Flying Elephant, Many Adventures of Winnie The Pooh, Mickey's Country House, Donald's Boat, Tomorrowland Indy Speedway (with a parent), Buzz Lightyear's Space Ranger Spin (Disney/Pixar), Tomorrowland Transit Authority.

5–8s
Walt Disney World Railroad, Pirates of the Caribbean, Jungle Cruise, Swiss Family Treehouse, The Timekeeper, Magic Carpets of Aladdin, The Enchanted Tiki Room – Under New Management, Country Bear Jamboree, Goofy's Country Dancin' Jamboree, Liberty Square Riverboat, Tom Sawyer Island, Big Thunder Mountain Railroad, Splash Mountain, Haunted Mansion, Mickey's PhilharMagic, Snow White's Scary Adventures, Mad Tea Party, Many Adventures of Winnie The Pooh, Mickey's Country House, Donald's Boat, The Barnstormer at Goofy's Wiseacre Farm, Tomorrowland Indy Speedway (with parent), Tomorrowland Transit Authority, Buzz Lightyear's Space Ranger Spin (Disney/Pixar), Walt Disney's Carousel of Progress, Astro Orbiter, Stitch's Great Escape! and Space Mountain (with parental discretion).

9–12s
Pirates of the Caribbean, Big Thunder Mountain Railroad, Splash Mountain, Country Bear Jamboree, Goofy's Country Dancin' Jamboree, The Haunted Mansion, Mad Tea Party, Mickey's PhilharMagic, The Barnstormer at Goofy's Wiseacre Farm, Tomorrowland Indy Speedway (without parent), Buzz Lightyear's Space Ranger Spin (Disney/Pixar), Stitch's Great Escape!, The Timekeeper, Astro Orbiter, Space Mountain.

Over 12s
Pirates of the Caribbean, Big Thunder Mountain Railroad, Splash Mountain, Mickey's PhilharMagic, Haunted Mansion, Buzz Lightyear's Space Ranger Spin (Disney/Pixar), The Timekeeper, Stitch's Great Escape!, Mad Tea Party, Astro Orbiter, Space Mountain.

5

Epcot

Amaze and annoy your friends by revealing *Epcot* stands for 'Experimental Prototype Community Of Tomorrow' (or the visitor's version: Every Person Comes Out Tired!), once you have marvelled at the magnificent entertainment value of this 300-acre (122-ha) playground. Actually, it is not so much a vision of the future as a look at the world of today, with a strong educational and environmental message which children are quick to pick up on. At more than twice the size of the *Magic Kingdom* Park, it is more likely to require a 2-day visit (although under 5s might find it less entertaining) and your feet in particular will notice the difference!

Location

Epcot is located off Epcot Drive and the parking fee is again $8 as you drive into its main entrance (there is a separate entrance for guests at the *Epcot* resort hotels, called International Gateway). It opened in October 1982 and its giant car park is big enough for 9,000 vehicles, so a tram takes you from your car to the main entrance (although if you are staying at a Disney hotel you can catch the monorail, boat or bus service to its gates). And don't forget to note where you are parked (e.g. Create, row 78). Once you have your ticket, you wait by the turnstiles for the opening moment (often accompanied by a Disney character or two) and are then admitted to the central plaza, between the two Innoventions centres.

Epcot is divided into two distinct parts arranged in a figure of eight and there are two tactics to help you avoid the worst of the early morning crowds. The first or lower half of the '8' consists of **Future World**, with seven different pavilions arranged around Spaceship Earth, which dominates the *Epcot* skyline) and Innoventions. The second part, or the top of the '8', is **World Showcase**, a potted journey around the world via 11 internationally presented pavilions that feature a taste of each country's culture, history, shopping, entertainment and cuisine.

Once you are through the gates, start by heading for the Future World pavilions to your left (Universe of Energy, Wonders of Life, Test Track and Mission: SPACE) and then continue up into World Showcase. This way you will visit some of the best rides in *Epcot* ahead of the main crowds. Alternatively, if the rides don't appeal quite so much as a visit to such diverse cultures as Japan and Morocco, spend your first couple of hours in the Innoventions centres (busy from mid-morning), then head into World Showcase as soon as it opens at 11am and you will be ahead of the crowds for several hours. If you time your journey around the Showcase (which is a 1½-mile/2km walk) to arrive back in Future World by late afternoon, you will find the worst of the milling throng will have passed through (except for Test Track and Mission: SPACE).

The other thing you should do early on is book lunch or dinner at one of the many fine restaurants around World Showcase (Mexico, Morocco, Canada and Japan are all highly recommended). The best reservations go fast, but check in at Guest Relations (on the left of the Innoventions plaza) and they can give advice and make a Priority Seating (see page 61).

Mission Space at Epcot

© Disney

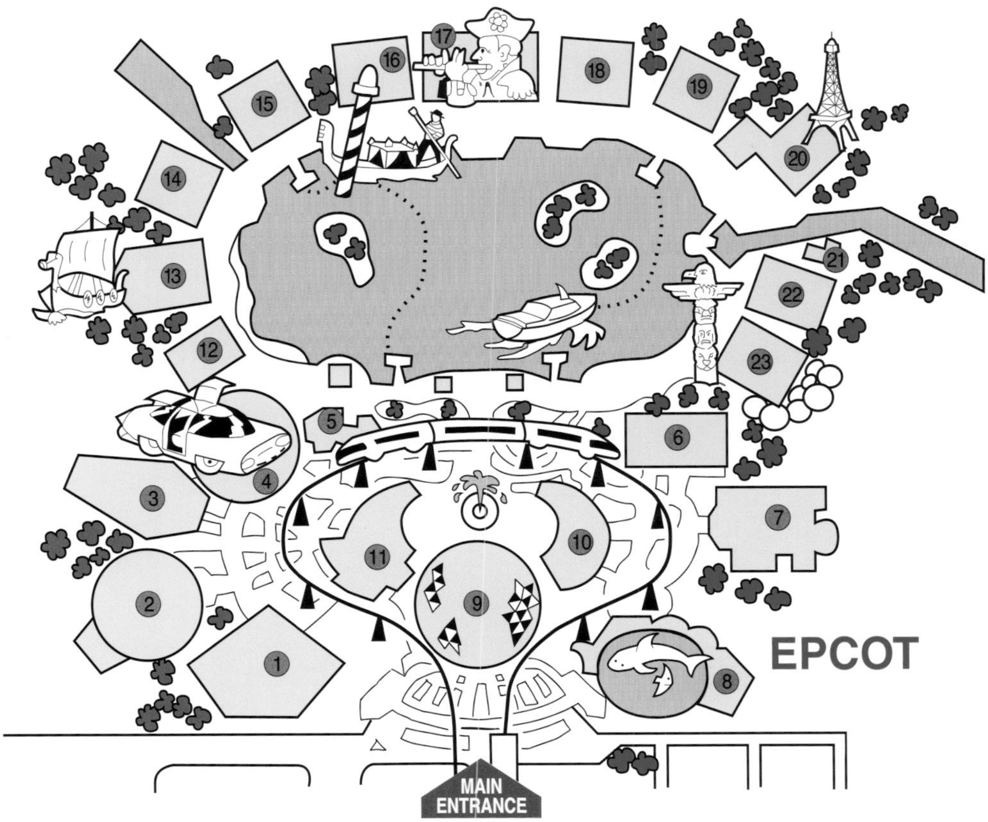

FUTURE WORLD

1 Universe Of Energy
2 Wonders Of Life
3 Mission: SPACE
4 Test Track
5 Odyssey Center
6 Imagination! (Including Honey, I Shrunk The Audience)
7 The Land
8 The Living Seas
9 Spaceship Earth
10 Innoventions West
11 Innoventions East

WORLD SHOWCASE

12 Mexico
13 Norway
14 China
15 Germany
16 Italy
17 The American Adventure
18 Japan
19 Morocco
20 France
21 International Gateway (To Epcot Resort Hotels)
22 United Kingdom
23 Canada

5

EPCOT

MAIN ENTRANCE

Epcot at a glance

Location	Off Epcot Drive, *Walt Disney World*
Size	300 acres (122ha) in Future World and World Showcase
Hours	9am–6pm Future World (except Test Track, Innoventions, Spaceship Earth, Honey I Shrunk the Audience, 9am–9pm), 11am–9pm (World Showcase)
Admission	Under 3 free; 3–9, $43.75 (1-Day ticket), $176 (4-Day Park Hopper), $226 (5-Day Park Hopper Plus); adult (10+) $54.75, $219, $282. Prices do not include tax
Parking	$8
Lockers	Yes; to left underneath Spaceship Earth and International Gateway; $7 ($2 refund)
Pushchairs	$8 and $15 ($1 deposit refunded); to the right underneath Spaceship Earth and International Gateway
Wheelchairs	$7 ($1 deposit refunded) or $40 ($10 deposit refunded), same location as pushchairs
Top Attractions	Mission: SPACE, Test Track, Spaceship Earth, Soarin'™, 'Honey, I Shrunk the Audience', Maelstrom, Universe of Energy, American Adventure
Don't Miss	IllumiNations: Reflections of Earth, Disney character bus (around World Showcase), live entertainment (including Off Kilter in Canada, JAMMitors in Innoventions plaza and Miyuki in Japan), and dinner at any of the World Showcase pavilions
Hidden Costs	**Meals** — Burger, chips and coke $7.68 / 3-course dinner $33 (Le Cellier, Canada) / Kids' meal $3.49
	T-shirts — $19–32
	Souvenirs — $1–975
	Sundries — Epcot 'Passport' $9.95

Future World

Here is what you will find in the first part of your *Epcot* adventure:

Universe of Energy: there is just the one attraction here but it is a stunner. **Ellen's Energy Adventure** is a 45-minute show-and-ride with comedienne Ellen DeGeneres and Bill Nye the Science Guy exploring the creation of fuels from the age of dinosaurs to their modern-day usages. The film elements convince you that you are in a conventional theatre, but then your seats rearrange themselves into 96-person solar-powered cars and you are off on a journey through the sights, sounds and even smells of the prehistoric era, with some realistic dinosaurs! Queues are steady but not overwhelming from mid-morning. AAAAA.

Wonders of Life: this used to be one of Future World's most popular pavilions, but is now often quiet in the afternoon as the crowds flock to other attractions nearby. It is also often closed at off-peak times. **Body Wars** is a hectic simulator ride through the human body, as in the film *Fantastic Voyage*. It is quite a violent adventure, too, hence it is not recommended for people who suffer from motion sickness, anyone with neck or back injuries, or pregnant women. Restrictions: 3ft 4in/101cm. TTTT. **Cranium Command** is a hilarious theatre show set in the brain of a 12-year-old boy, showing how he negotiates a typical day. It is both audio-animatronic and film-based. See how many famous TV and film stars you can name in the 'cast'. AAAA. **The Making of Me** is a sensitive film on the creation of human life and will therefore require parental discretion for children as it has its explicit moments, although not without humour. AAA.

> BRIT TIP: The Wonders of Life pavilion is a good place in which to spend time if you need to cool down, or if it's raining.

The Fitness Fairground, with hands-on exhibits like exercise bikes, gives you the chance to see just how far all the holiday fun has taken its toll on your body!

Mission: SPACE: this is the new cutting edge of Disney's attraction technology, a journey 30 years into the future to join the International Space Training Center. The space-age building alone prepares you for a major adventure and you enter through Planetary Plaza, with its giant replica planets (check out the model showing the Moon landings).

At the main entrance you have a choice of four queues – FASTPASS Collection, Stand-by (the main queue), Single riders and FASTPASS return, and the clever organisation keeps lines to a minimum (it is the first ride built with FASTPASS in mind, and queues are seldom a problem). As you enter the 'training facility', there are some superb models and graphics (like the giant revolving Gravity Wheel) to look at while you queue, passing the Training Operations Room (the cleverly disguised ride controllers) and the story of 75 Years of Space Flight (this is now 2036, remember) to reach Team Despatch. Here the four 'ready rooms' form you into teams of four for the ride itself, and you will be either the Navigator, Engineer, Pilot or Commander, each having different functions to perform, so pay attention!

Once briefed (by actor Gary Sinise), you enter the Preparation Room to learn your mission – a flight to Mars. And then it is quickly into the ride vehicle – capsules that close down tightly with outer doors, shoulder restraints and screens that move forward to just 18in (46cm) from your face (this is NOT the ride for you if you suffer from claustrophobia). The sense of realism, with the control consoles, individual speakers and the countdown is magnificent, and the blast off feels VERY real as you experience some of the genuine forces of a rocket launch (it is part ride and part simulator).

Each member of the team has to perform their duties on cue (Sinise will 'prompt' you if you forget) and you experience a cleverly simulated sling-shot flight around the Moon and on to Mars, where the landing is an adventure in itself. It is a truly original, ultra-dynamic ride, but you should heed the advice to keep your head still and look straight into the screen or you'll feel sick.

It is way too intense for younger children, and there is no backing out once you blast off (parents could try it first to see if their children would

5

BRIT TIP: If Mission: SPACE and Test Track appeal to you most, head here FIRST when you arrive, grab a FASTPASS for Test Track, then ride the other. When you have done your FP ride, consider grabbing another FP to re-ride your favourite!

enjoy it), while it is definitely not a ride for expectant mothers. Restrictions, 3ft 8in/112cm. TTTTT+ (FP).

As you exit the attraction, there is an elaborate four-part post-show with even more activities. **Space Base** is an excellent play area for children who can't ride (and those who just like to explore, climb, slide and crawl – enter through the gift shop if you just want to play here); **Space Race** is a game for two teams of 60 players, working in pairs, to propel their rocket to Mars with a series of on-screen challenges; **Expedition Mars** is a computer game to rescue stranded astronauts; and **Postcards from Space** gives you the chance to send someone a video e-mail of yourself in one of eight space 'scenes.' There is then the inevitable (and well-stocked) gift shop to negotiate on the way out. All in all, it is a mind-boggling experience, and a real taste of space 'exploration' without leaving the building!

Test Track: this is another big production, a 5½-minute whirl along

Disney's longest and fastest track to date. It starts with a pre-show into the world of General Motors' quality and safety techniques to prepare riders for a taste of vehicle testing. The way the cars whiz around the outside of the building (at up to 60mph/97kph) provides a glimpse of what's in store. The reality is pretty good, too, as you are taken on a tour of a GM proving ground, including a hill climb test, suspension test (hold on to those fillings!), brake test, environment chamber, barrier test (beware the crash test dummies!) and the steeply banked, high-speed finale.

For those who manage to regain their breath, there is a post-show area with a multimedia film, an animated presentation featuring future GM products and technological innovations, with a hint of virtual-reality driving, and the chance to view the latest GM models. Along with a smart gift store and photo opportunity, it all adds up to an extremely involved exhibit (although a bit technical for youngsters).

The downside is the HUGE queues it attracts, topping 2 hours at times, while the available FP service often runs out. Head straight here after opening or return in the evening to keep your queuing to bearable levels. If you are on your own, you can save time by using the Singles Queue. Restrictions: 3ft 4in/101cm. TTTT (TTT for teens) (FP).

The Odyssey Center next door offers baby-care and first-aid facilities, telephones and restrooms.

Imagination!: The 2-part attraction here starts with **Journey Into Imagination with Figment**, a recently revamped ride into experiments with imagination, in the company of Eric Idle (as Dr Nigel Channing of the Imagination Institute) and the cartoon dragon, Figment. The sight laboratory sees Figment having fun with a vision chart, the sound lab is a symphony

Koutoubia Minaret at World Showcase

© Disney

of imaginative melodies and Figment's house is a truly topsy-turvy world (and watch out for the skunk in the smell lab!). It is gentle fun and rarely draws a crowd. AAA. (For fans of the original Dreamfinder ride here, Figment is highly prominent once again, while the ride's theme song, 'One Little Spark', makes a welcome return).

You exit into **Image Works – The Kodak 'What If' Labs**, an interactive playground of unusual sights and sounds, which will probably amuse children more than adults (although you may be tempted to part with more money on various cartoon images and select-your-own CDs).

Come out of the building and turn right for the fabulous 3-D experience of **'Honey, I Shrunk The Audience'**, as Rick Moranis reprises his hapless inventor character Wayne Szalinski. A neat 8-minute pre-show is the perfect prelude to the fun and games in store. If you have seen Jim Henson's Muppet*Vision 3-D at *Disney-MGM Studios* you'll have an idea of what to expect. Special effects and moving seats add to the feeling you have shrunk in size. And beware the sneezing dog! AAAAA (FP).

Outside, kids are always fascinated by the **Jellyfish** and **Serpentine Fountains** that send water squirting from pond to pond, and there is always one who tries to stand in the way and 'catch' one of the streams of water. Have your cameras and camcorders ready!

The Land: this pavilion features three elements that combine to make a highly entertaining but educational experience on food production and nutrition – plus the new Soarin'™ ride which is a pure thrill.

Living with the Land is an informative 14-minute boat ride that is worth the usually long queue. A journey through various types of food production may sound a dull idea, and it may not appeal to younger children, but adults and school-age kids will sit up and take notice of the three ecological communities, especially the greenhouse finale. AAAA (FP).

Having ridden the ride, you can also walk the walk on the **Behind The Seeds** guided tour through the greenhouse complex and learn even more about Disney's horticultural projects. It takes an hour ($6 for adults, $4 for 3–9s), but you have to book in person at the desk near the Green Thumb Emporium.

The Circle of Life is a 15-minute live-action/ animated story, featuring characters from the film *The Lion King*, that explains environmental concerns and is easily digestible for kids. Queues not a problem here, either. AAA.

Soarin'™ (due to open in May 2005) is a clone of the Soarin' Over California simulator ride in *Disney's California Adventure* in Los Angeles and is a bold addition here. It offers a novel 'flight' over the notable landmarks of California, complete with aroma-vision (smell those orange groves!) and sea spray. An elaborate queuing area is arranged like an airport departure lounge, with the 'passengers' embarking on rows of seats that are then hoisted up into the air over a giant screen. The feeling is somewhat akin to setting off on a hang-glider ride as the special film and the sounds (and smells) become all-encompassing. Feet dangling, you genuinely soar over the Golden Gate Bridge, sweep through a redwood forest and glide above Napa Valley with the wind in your hair. The finale includes a close

5

Soarin'™

encounter with a certain Disney theme park in LA! The ride's realism, magnificent music and superb technology ensure a 5-star experience, and it is likely to draw some serious queues, so head here early or make it a FASTPASS choice. Restrictions, 3ft 4in/102cm. AAAAA (FP).

The **Sunshine Season Food Fair** offers the chance to eat some of Disney's home-grown produce, and there are healthy alternatives to the usual fast-food fare, while the **Garden Grill** restaurant is a slowly revolving platform that offers more traditional food, including pasta, seafood and delicious rotisserie chicken.

The Living Seas: this pavilion does for the sea what The Land Pavilion does for terra firma. A 7-minute pre-show film leads on to a short journey to Sea Base Alpha by 'Hydrolator' (imagine an undersea lift simulator) and an elaborate marine research facility centred around a 5.7 million-gallon (25.9 million-litre) aquarium, with sharks, stingrays and other impressively large denizens of the deep. This 2-level development takes you through six modules that present stories of undersea exploration and marine life, including a research centre that provides a close-up encounter with the endangered manatee. Plenty of interactive elements and educational touch-screens are on offer, plus additional fish tanks displaying Caribbean reef fish, jellyfish and the curious cuttlefish, while there is also an excellent real-life demonstration of a diving chamber. Crowds build up steadily through the day, but queues rarely get too long. AAA.

The pavilion also includes the highly recommended **Coral Reef Restaurant** that serves magnificent seafood, as well as providing diners with a grandstand view of the massive aquarium. Dinner for two will cost around $70, which isn't cheap, but the food is first class.

Spaceship Earth: spiralling up 18 storeys, this attraction tells the story of communication from early cave drawings to modern satellite technology. It is one of the most popular rides in the park, largely because of its visibility and location, hence you need to do it either first thing or late afternoon when the crowds have moved on from Future World into World Showcase. The highlight is the depiction of Michelangelo's painting of the Sistine Chapel, which will be lost on small kids, but it's an entertaining 15-minute journey all along. AAAA.

As you leave, you enter the **Global Activity Center**, with a host of interactive educational communications exhibits.

Innoventions West and East: these two centres of hands-on exhibits and computer games – subtitled **The Road to Tomorrow** – were revamped for the Millennium celebrations and include a glimpse of Disney's latest investigations into virtual reality entertainment and other demonstrations of current and future technologies, especially the internet and computers, by the likes of IBM, Xerox, Compaq, Motorola and General Motors. Both sides are routed like a journey into the future and will reward enquiring minds in areas like People At Play and Mouse House Jr.

In Innoventions West, the kids will gravitate to the free **Video Games of Tomorrow selection** presented by Disney Interactive and they may take a bit of moving along! Also worth waiting for are the 20-minute **Ultimate Home Theater Experience**, presented by Lutron, and the **Thinkplace** presented by IBM, featuring a demonstration of IBM's voice recognition technology.

In Innoventions East, you can send a video e-mail to friends in the **Internet Zone**, check out **The Underwriters Lab**, which offers an interactive area with various testing stations and Video D-Mail, and take the 15-minute walk through the **House of Innoventions**, full of smart gadgets and new technologies. You must also take a look at the latest form of transport here – the wonderful two-wheeled Segway Human Transporter (which you can also pay to ride – see page 119).

Musical entertainment is provided periodically in the Innoventions plaza, along with other innovative live acts (look out for the unique **JAMMitors** percussion group and the unusual **Kristos** dance troupe, while the majestic fountains are choreographed to an hourly music performance. Food outlets include the self-service **Electric Umbrella Restaurant** for lunch and dinner (sandwiches, pizza, burgers and salads) and the **Fountain View Espresso and Bakery** for tea, coffee and pastries. At **Ice Station Cool**, presented by Coca-Cola™, you'll be given some free product samples and the chance to encounter real snow! You'll also find the huge gift shop **Mouse Gear** in Innoventions East, featuring stacks of quality *Epcot* and Disney souvenirs (and some wacky ceiling architecture!).

World Showcase

If you found Future World a huge experience, prepare to be amazed also by the more down-to-earth but equally imaginative pavilions around the World Showcase Lagoon. Each features a glimpse of a different country in dramatic settings. Several have either amusing rides or films that show off the tourist features of their country, while in nearly every case the restaurants offering national fare are some of the best in Orlando.

Mexico: starting at the bottom left of the circular tour of the lagoon and moving clockwise, your first encounter is the spectacular pyramid that houses Mexico. Here you will find the amusing boat ride along **El Rio del Tiempo**, the River of Time, which gives you a potted 9-minute journey through the people and history of the country. Queues here tend to be surprisingly long from mid-morning to late afternoon. AAA. The rest of the pavilion is given over to a range of shops in the **Plaza de los Amigos**, which vary from pretty tacky to sophisticated, and the **San Angel Inn**, a dimly lit and romantic full-service diner offering traditional and tempting Mexican fare. Outside, on the lagoon, is the **Cantina de San Angel**, a fast-food counter for tacos, chilli and burgers. As in all the World Showcase pavilions, there is live entertainment and music.

> BRIT TIP: The Cantina in 'Mexico' is a great spot from which to watch the nightly IllumiNations fireworks and laser show, but you need to arrive at least an hour early.

Norway: next up is Norway, which probably has the best ride in World Showcase, the Viking-themed **Maelstrom**. This 10-minute longboat journey through the history and scenery of the Scandinavian country features a short waterfall drop and a North Sea storm. It attracts longish queues during the day, so the best tactic is to go soon after World Showcase's 11am opening. TTT (FP). There are periodical Norwegian-themed exhibits in the reconstructed **Stave Church** and twice-daily guided tours (sign up at the Tourism desk), while kids can play on the Viking boat. The pavilion also contains a clever reproduction of Oslo's Akershus Fortress. The popular **Restaurant Akershus** offers lunch and dinner buffets and the **Kringla Bakeri Og Kafé** serves open

5

sandwiches, pastries and drinks.

China: the spectacular architecture of China is well served by the pavilion's main attraction, the stunning **Reflections of China**, a brand new (in May 2003) 20-minute, 360-degree film in the circular Temple of Heaven. Here you are surrounded by the sights and sounds of one of the world's most mysterious countries in a special cinematic production, the technology of which alone will leave you breathless. Queues build up to half an hour during the main part of the day (but the waiting area is fully air-conditioned). AAAA.

Land of Many Faces is an exhibit introducing China's ethnic peoples. Two restaurants, the **Nine Dragons** (table service, decent if unremarkable food) and the **Lotus Blossom Café** (self-service, fairly predictable spring rolls and stir-fries), offer tastes of the Orient, while the **Yong Feng Shangdian Department Store** is a virtual warehouse of Chinese gifts and artefacts. Don't miss the periodic shows of Oriental music and acrobatics (including the stunning Dragon Legend Acrobats) on the plaza in front of the temple.

The **Outpost** between China and Germany features hut-style shops and snacks, with entertainment from Africa and the Caribbean.

Germany: this provides more in the way of shopping and eating than entertainment, although you still find strolling players and a magnificent re-creation of a Bavarian **Biergarten**, with lively Oktoberfest shows featuring the resident brass band at regular intervals. It also offers hearty portions of German

BRIT TIP: The lunch and dinner menus at the Nine Dragons restaurant are similar, so choose the lunch version – it's cheaper!

sausage, sauerkraut and rotisserie chicken. The **Sommerfest** is fast food German-style (bratwurst and strudel). This pavilion has more shops than any of the others in *Epcot* and includes chocolates, wines, porcelain, crystal, toys and cuckoo clocks. An elaborate outdoor model railway is popular with children.

Italy: similarly, Italy has pretty, authentic architecture (including a superb reproduction of St Mark's Square in Venice), lively music and amusing Italian folk stories, three tempting gift shops (including wine, Perugina chocolates, Armani collectables, fine crystal, porcelain and Venetian masks), and a 5-star restaurant, **L'Originale Alfredo di Roma Ristorante**. It's a touch expensive, but the atmosphere and decor add extra zest to the meals, which include fettucine, chicken, veal and seafood. Expect a 3-course meal to cost about $38.

America: at the top of the lagoon and dominating World Showcase is **The American Adventure**, not so much a pavilion as a celebration of the country's history and Constitution. A colonial fife and drum band and wonderful *a cappella* group (Voices Of Liberty) add authentic sounds to the 18th-century setting, overlooked by a faithful reproduction of Philadelphia's Liberty Hall. Inside you have the spectacular American Adventure show, a magnificent film and audio-animatronic production lasting half an hour, which details the country's struggles and triumphs, its presidents, statesmen and heroes. It's a glossy, patriotic performance, featuring some pretty outstanding

China pavilion

© Disney

audio-animatronic effects and, while some of it will leave foreign visitors fairly cold, it is difficult not to be impressed. Avoid at midday because of the queues. AAAA. If you have time pre-show, check out the new **American Heritage Gallery** and its first full-time exhibition, Echoes of Africa, which explores the influence of African art on contemporary African–American artists.

Outside, handcarts provide touches of American nostalgia and antiques, along with the **Heritage Manor Gifts** store, while the **Liberty Inn** offers fast-food fare for lunch and dinner. **The America Gardens Theater**, facing the lagoon, presents Disney fun and musical performances from worldwide artists.

Japan: next up on the clockwise tour, you will be introduced to typical Japanese gardens and architecture, including the breathtaking Chi Nien Tien, a round half-scale reproduction of a temple, some magnificent art exhibits (notably the Bijutsu-kan Gallery), musical shows and dazzling live entertainment (especially child-friendly **Miyuki**, a lovely lady who spins amazing candy creations out of toffee sugar). For one of the most entertaining meals in *Epcot*, the **Teppanyaki Dining Rooms** and **Tempura Kiku** both offer a full, table-service introduction to Japanese cuisine while **Yakitori House** is the fast-food equivalent and the **Matsu No Ma Lounge** features sushi and cocktails. The restaurants are run by Mitsukoshi, as is the superb department store here. Periodic live music features the **Matsuriza** traditional drummers.

Morocco: as you would expect, this is a real shopping experience, with bazaars, alleyways and stalls selling a well-priced array of carpets, leather goods, clothing, brass ornaments, pottery and antiques (seek out that Magic Lamp!). All of

BRIT TIP: Kids, to get the best autographs from your Disney favourites, use a thick pen or pencil, as some characters have trouble writing otherwise!

the building materials were faithfully imported for the pavilion, which was hand-built to give Morocco a great degree of authenticity, even by World Showcase's high standards. You'll be unable to keep your eyes off the clever detail around the winding alleyways and gardens, which can be enjoyed on daily (free) 45-minute walking tours.

The **Gallery of Arts and History** offers more historical and cultural insight into the country, while the **Fez House** depicts the style of a typical Moroccan home.

Restaurant Marrakesh provides a full Moroccan dining experience, complete with traditional musicians and a belly dancer. It's slightly pricey ($59 for the Moroccan feast for two) but the atmosphere is lively and entertaining. **Tangierine Café** offers Mediterranean-style foods (hummus, tabouleh, couscous, roast lamb, lentil salad and Moroccan breads) at more down-to-earth prices, and with several vegetarian options ($6.95–10.95). Watch out, too, for characters from Disney's film *Aladdin* and a new live musical show, **MoRockin'** with a variety of Arabic rhythms served up in fun style.

BRIT TIP: The Tangierine Café in Morocco is a peaceful little haven in which to enjoy a quiet and healthy lunch, especially if you are a vegetarian, while there is also a tempting coffee and pastry counter.

France: France is predictably overlooked by a replica Eiffel Tower, but the smart streets, buildings and the sheer cleanliness of France is a long way from modern-day Paris! This is pre-World War One France, with official buskers and comedy street theatre acts adding to the rather dreamy atmosphere. Don't miss **Impressions de France**, another stunning big-film production that serves up all the grandest sights of the country to the accompaniment of the music of Offenbach, Debussy, Saint-Saëns and Satie. Crowds get quite heavy from late morning (although kids might feel left out). AAAA.

This is also the pavilion for a gastronomic experience with three restaurants, of which **Chefs de France** and **Bistro de Paris** are major discoveries. The former is an award-winning, full-service, and therefore expensive, establishment featuring top quality cuisine created by French chefs on a daily basis, while the latter, upstairs, offers more intimate bistro dining, still with an individual touch (and, if anything, slightly more expensive) and plenty of style (starters from $9–17, main courses $29–35). The Bistro books only 30 days in advance. Alternatively, the **Boulangerie Patisserie** is a sidewalk café offering more modest fare (and some wonderful pastries, as you'd expect) at a more modest price. Shopping is also suitably chic, with a Guerlain perfumery, wine shop and patisserie.

United Kingdom: the least inspiring of all the pavilions, and certainly with little to entertain those who have been inside a traditional pub before or shopped for Royal Doulton or Burberry goods. It is partly offset by some good street entertainers and the excellent Beatles tribute band, the **British Invasion**, but that really is the sum total here. **The Rose and Crown Pub** is antiseptically authentic, but you can get better elsewhere for these prices (ploughman's $10.79, cottage pie $12.99, fish and chips $14.79, and a pint of Bass, Harp Lager or Guinness for a whopping $6.75). There is also a take-away **Harry Ramsden's** fish and chippie. Other shops are the Tea Caddy, the Magic of Wales, the Queen's Table, Crown And Crest (perfumes, heraldry) and the Toy Soldier (traditional games and Disney toys).

Canada: completing the World Showcase circle, the main features here are **Victoria Gardens**, based on the world-famous Butchart Gardens on Vancouver Island, some spectacular Rocky Mountain scenery, a replica French gothic mansion, the Hôtel de Canada, and another stunning 360-degree film, **O Canada!** As with China and France, this showcases the country's sights and scenery in a terrific, 17-minute advert for the Canadian Tourist Board. It gets busiest from late morning to late afternoon. AAA. Resident band **Off Kilter** are also one of the most entertaining acts I've seen anywhere. Want to hear rock 'n' roll bagpipes? This is the group for you! **Le Cellier Steakhouse** is a modestly priced dining room offering steaks, prime rib, seafood, chicken and several vegetarian dishes for lunch and dinner.

Around World Showcase are 11 **Kidcot Fun Stop** activity centres, at which children can play games and collect a special Epcot Passport to get stamped at each pavilion. Kids will also want to pick up **Goofy's Epcot Guide** booklet at the main entrance which asks them to answer various questions around World Showcase and solve Goofy's dilemma.

Disney characters put on a show several times a day at **Showcase Plaza**, just across the bridge from Future World to World Showcase, and you can take their sight-seeing bus on tour to several locations in

World Showcase, so have those autograph books handy!

For those who enjoy new technology, World Showcase offers a morning **Around The World At Epcot** tour on the innovative two-wheeled Segway Human Transporter. It costs a hefty $80/person extra but the 2-hour tour includes full instruction and plenty of travel time on these amazing contraptions, which can go up to 12.5mph (20kph). It is open to only 10 guests a day (minimum age 16) and it's advisable to book in advance on 407 WDW TOUR.

Planning your visit

If you plan a 2-day visit, it makes sense to spend the first day in World Showcase, arriving early and going straight there while everyone else goes to Future World, booking your evening meal around 5.30pm, and then lingering around the lagoon for the evening entertainment.

For your second visit, try arriving in mid-afternoon and then doing Future World in a more leisurely fashion than it would be earlier. Queues at most of the pavilions are almost non-existent for rides like Universe of Energy, Body Wars and The Land, although Test Track stays busy all day as does Mission: SPACE.

You CAN do *Epcot* in a day – if you arrive early, put in some speedy legwork and give some of the detail a miss. But, of all the parks, it is a shame to hurry this one. In the shops (almost 70 in all), try to save your browsing for when most people are on the rides.

IllumiNations: Reflections of Earth

The day's big finale is an absolute show-stopper. **IllumiNations: Reflections of Earth** is a firework and special-effect extravaganza, awesome even by Disney standards.

> BRIT TIP: The Rose and Crown dining room in the UK pavilion is a great place from which to see the nightly IllumiNations fireworks spectacular.

British composer Gavin Greenaway provides original music for a 15-minute performance of vivid brilliance. Some 2,800 firework shells are launched as a celestial backdrop to a series of fire-and-water effects on the World Showcase lagoon. The central icon is a 28-ft (9-metre) video globe of Earth that opens in a spectacular climax of choreographed pyrotechnics. Truly magnificent. However, people start staking out the best lagoon-side spots up to 2 HOURS in advance.

The ultimate way to view IllumiNations: Reflections of Earth is by private boat on one of three **speciality cruises** from *Disney's Boardwalk* or *Yacht/Beach Club Resorts* (for non-residents, too). They vary from $120–350 per boat (holding 4–12 guests) and can be used for special celebrations. The basic cruise costs $120 and the pontoon boat holds up to 12. The level-1 cruise adds soda, sandwiches, water and snacks and costs $200 for up to four guests and $20 for each additional person. The level-2 cruise adds fruit, cheese and dessert, costing $275 for 4 and $35 for each additional guest. A level-3 cruise adds alcohol and boat decoration, costing $350 for up to four people, plus $50 per additional person. Call 407 939 7529 up to 90 days in advance to book. Be aware that cruises launch regardless of whether fireworks are taking place.

Behind the scenes

Epcot also has some special behind-the-scenes tours (but not for under-16s). **Dolphins In Depth** ($150,

5

including souvenir photo, T-shirt and refreshments) is a 3½-hour delve into the backstage and research areas of the Living Seas pavilion, including a chance to meet the resident dolphins (ages 13–17 must be accompanied by an adult). **Gardens of the World** ($59) is a 3-hour botanical tour of the gardens in *Epcot*, and includes tips for your own garden. **Hidden Treasures** is a 3-hour tour ($59) of the 11 countries of World Showcase. **Undiscovered Future World** is a 4½-hour journey into the creation of *Epcot*, Walt's vision for the resort and backstage areas like IllumiNations ($49). **Dive Quest** ($140/person, ages 10 and up) is a 2½-hour experience, with a 30-minute dive into the Living Seas aquarium, plus a behind-the-scenes look at the facility and training involved at either 4.30 or 5.30pm every day, and you need to have scuba certification (T-shirt and certificate for all participants; theme park admission not required). The new **Aqua Seas Tour** ($100/person, ages 8 and up; under 18s must be accompanied by an adult; inclusive of T-shirt and group photo; again, theme park admission is not required for this tour) is similar to Dive Quest but without the scuba diving element (daily at 12.30pm).

The most comprehensive tour, **Backstage Magic** ($199; ages 16 and up), goes behind the scenes of *Epcot*, *Magic Kingdom* Park and *Disney-MGM Studios* on a 7-hour foray into little-seen aspects, such as watching the animators at work in *Disney-MGM Studios* and the tunnels below the *Magic Kingdom* Park. These tours must be booked on 407 WDW TOUR (407 939 8687).

Annual festivals

There are two other annual *Epcot* events to watch out for. The **International Flower and Garden Festival** literally puts the whole park in full bloom with an amazing series of set-pieces, seminars and mini-exhibitions from mid-April to June (expanded to 7 weeks in 2004). All the exhibits and lectures are free and it adds a beautiful aspect to an already scenic park. The **Food and Wine Festival** was also extended in 2004, to 45 days from October 1 to November 14. It showcases national and regional cuisines, wines and beers, with the chance to attend grand Winemakers Dinners and Tasting Events, or just sample the inexpensive offerings of more than 20 food booths around World Showcase.

EPCOT with children

Here is our rough guide to the attractions which appeal to different age groups in this park:

Under 5s
Spaceship Earth, Universe of Energy, Journey Into Imagination with Figment, The Living Seas, Living with the Land, Circle of Life, El Rio del Tiempo.

5–8s
All the above, plus Body Wars, Cranium Command, Test Track, Innoventions, 'Honey, I Shrunk The Audience' (with parental discretion), Image Works, Maelstrom (Norway), The American Adventure.

9–12s
All the above, plus Soarin'™, Behind the Seeds tour, Mission: SPACE, Treasures of Morocco tour, Impressions de France, Wonders of China, O Canada!

Over 12s
All the above, plus Land of Many Faces (China), Bijutsu-kan Gallery, Norway guided tours, Off Kilter (Canada), British Invasion (UK).

Disney-MGM Studios

Welcome to Hollywood – well, the *Walt Disney World Resort in Florida* version of it. When it opened in May 1989, Michael Eisner, chairman of the Walt Disney Company, insisted it was 'the Hollywood that never was and always will be'. Sounds double Dutch? Don't worry, all will be revealed in your day-long tour of this real-life combination of theme park and working TV and film studio. The most common question about *Disney-MGM Studios* is 'Are they really working studios?', and yes, there are film and TV productions going on even while you're riding around the park peering into the backstage areas.

Rather bigger than the *Magic Kingdom* Park at 154 acres (62ha) but substantially smaller than *Epcot*, *Disney-MGM Studios* is a different experience yet again with its combination of attractions, spectacular shows (including the unmissable Fantasmic!), street entertainment, film sets and smart gift shops. Like the *Magic Kingdom* Park, the food on offer may not win awards, but some of the restaurants (notably the **Sci-Fi Dine-in Theater** and '**50s Prime Time Café**) have imaginative settings. The park also has rather more to occupy smaller children than *Epcot*, but you can still easily see all of it in a day unless the crowds are heavy.

Location

The entrance arrangements will be fairly familiar if you have already visited any of the other parks. *Disney-MGM Studios* is located on Buena Vista Drive (which runs between World Drive and Epcot Drive) and the parking fee is $8. Remember to make a note of where you park before you catch your tram to the main gates, where you must wait for the official opening hour. If the queues build up quickly, the gates will open early, so be ready for a running start.

Once through the gates, you are into Hollywood Boulevard, a street of mainly gift shops, and you have to decide which of the main attractions to head for first, as these are the ones where the queues will be heaviest nearly all day. Try to ignore the lure of the shops as it is better to browse in the early afternoon when the attractions are at their busiest.

Incidentally, if you thought Disney had elevated queuing to an art form in their other parks, wait until you see how cleverly arranged they are here. Just when you think you have got to the ride itself, there is another twist to the queue you hadn't seen or an extra element to the ride which holds you up. The latter are 'holding pens' which are an ingenious way of making it seem like you are being entertained instead of queuing. Look out for them in particular at the Great Movie Ride, Twilight Zone™ Tower of Terror and Jim Henson's Muppet*Vision 3-D.

An up-to-the-minute check on queue times at all the attractions is kept on a **Guest Information Board** on Hollywood Boulevard, just past its junction with Sunset Boulevard, where you can also book for the restaurants. The **Baby Center** here is located just inside the main gates on the left, next to Guest Relations, along with **First Aid**.

Disney-MGM Studios is laid out in a rather more confusing fashion than

5

Lights! Motors! Action!™ Extreme Stunt Show

© Disney

Disney-MGM Studios at a glance

Location	Off Buena Vista Drive or World Drive, Walt Disney World
Size	154 acres (62ha)
Hours	9am–7pm off peak; 9am–10pm high season (Easter, summer holidays, Thanksgiving and Christmas)
Admission	Under 3 free; 3–9 $43.75 (1-Day Ticket), $176 (4-Day Park Hopper), $226 (5-Day Park Hopper Plus); adult (10+) $54.75, $219, $282. Prices do not include tax
Parking	$8
Lockers	Yes; next to Oscar's Super Service, to right of main entrance; $7 ($2 refundable)
Pushchairs	$8 and $15 ($1 deposit refunded) from Oscar's Super Service
Wheelchairs	$8 ($1 deposit refunded) or $40 ($10 deposit refunded); same location as pushchairs
Top Attractions	Twilight Zone™ Tower of Terror, Rock 'n Roller Coaster Starring Aerosmith, Star Tours, The Great Movie Ride, Who Wants To Be A Millionaire – Play It!, Voyage of the Little Mermaid, Jim Henson's Muppet*Vision 3-D, Lights! Motors! Action!™ Extreme Stunt Show (May 2005)
Don't Miss	Disney Stars and Motor Cars Parade, Indiana Jones™ Epic Stunt Spectacular!, Fantasmic!

Hidden Costs	**Meals**	Burger, chips and coke $7.98 3-course lunch $23 (Prime Time Café) Kids' meal $3.49 and $4.99
	T-shirts	$19–30
	Souvenirs	$1.25–900
	Sundries	Roller Coaster Starring Aerosmith ride photo $16.95; poster-size $22

its counterparts, which have neatly packaged 'lands', so you need to consult your map often to ensure you're going in the right direction.

The main attractions

The opening-gate crowds will all surge in one of four directions, which will give you a pretty good idea of where you want to go. By far the 'biggest' attraction here is the **Twilight Zone™ Tower of Terror**, a magnificent haunted hotel ride that culminates in a 13-storey drop in a lift, where queues can build up to 2 hours at peak periods. So, if the Tower appeals to you, do it first! Head up Hollywood Boulevard then turn right into Sunset Boulevard where you'll see it at the end, looming ominously over the park. It's a FASTPASS (FP) ride (see page 91) like the **Rock 'n Roller Coaster**

Starring Aerosmith, at the end of Sunset Boulevard on the left, which is another huge draw, so you can get a pass for one and ride the other.

Star Tours, the great Star Wars™ simulator ride, and **Voyage of the Little Mermaid** are also serious queue-builders and FP attractions. If you are not up for the really big thrills, grab a FP for Mermaid (straight up Hollywood Boulevard, past Sunset, turn right into Animation Courtyard), then head for Star Tours (back across the main square past the Indiana Jones™ show). Finally, the new **Who Wants To Be A Millionaire – Play It!** attraction is a major success, but has only ten shows (accommodating 1,600 people a time) a day, hence FPs can run out quickly. So, if this appeals to you, head here first (past the Little Mermaid and along Mickey Avenue).

Opening in May 2005 is the blockbuster new **Lights! Motors! Action!™ Extreme Stunt Show**, which will play 3–5 times a day. This is sure to draw a serious crowd, so keep an eye out for fluctuations.

Here's a full rundown of the attractions, in a clockwise direction:

The Great Movie Ride: this faces you (behind the hat icon) as you walk in along Hollywood Boulevard and is a good place to start if the crowds are not too serious. An all-star audio-animatronics cast re-creates a number of box office smashes, including Jimmy Cagney's *Public Enemy*, Julie Andrews in *Mary Poppins*, Gene Kelly in *Singing in the Rain* and many more masterful set-pieces as you undertake your conducted tour. Small children may find the menace of *The Alien* too strong, but otherwise the ride has universal appeal and features some clever live twists I won't reveal (there are two slight variations on this ride, a cowboy and a gangster version – ask a Cast Member if you especially

want to do either one). AAAA.

ABC Sound Studio 'Sounds Dangerous' Starring Drew Carey: a sound FX special which features American comedian Drew Carey in an instalment of a spoof undercover police show *Sounds Dangerous*. Most of the 12-minute show is in the dark – which upsets some children – and is centred on your special headphones as Carey's stakeout goes wildly wrong. Clever and amusing – if a bit tame for older children – you exit into the Sound Works Studio to try out some well-known sound effects. AAA.

Indiana Jones™ Epic Stunt Spectacular!: consult your park map for the various times for when this rip-roaring stunt cavalcade hits the stage. A specially made movie set creates three different backdrops for Indiana Jones'™ stunt people to put on a dazzling array of clever stunts, scenes and special effects from the Harrison Ford film epics. Audience participation is an element and there are some amusing sub-plots. Queues for the 30-minute show begin to form up to half an hour beforehand, but the auditorium holds more than 2,000 so everyone usually gets in. TTTT (FP).

Star Tours: anyone remotely amused by the *Star Wars*™ films will enjoy just queuing for one of my own favourites, a breathtaking 7-minute spin in a Star Speeder. The elaborate walk-in area is full of *Star Wars*™ gadgets and gizmos that will make the long wait (sometimes up to an hour) pass quickly. From arguing robots C-3PO and R-2D2 to your robotic 'pilot', everything has a brilliant sense of space travel, and the ride won't disappoint! Restrictions: 3ft 4in/101cm, no children under 3. TTTT (plus AAAAA) (FP).

Jim Henson's Muppet*Vision 3-D: the 3-D is crossed out here and 4-D substituted in its place, so be warned that strange things will be

5

DISNEY-MGM STUDIOS

1 Parade Route ... Disney Stars And Motor Cars Parade
2 Sorcerer Mickey
3 The Great Movie Ride
4 ABC Sound Studio 'Sounds Dangerous' Starring Drew Carey
5 Indiana Jones™ Epic Stunt Spectacular!
6 Star Tours
7 Jim Henson's Muppet*Vision 3-D
8 Honey, I Shrunk The Kids Movie Set Adventure
9 Catastrophe Canyon On Disney-MGM Studios Backlot Tour
10 Disney-MGM Studios Backlot Tour
11 Meet Mickey Mouse
12 Who Wants To Be A Millionaire – Play It!
13 Walt Disney: One Man's Dream
14 Voyage Of The Little Mermaid
15 The Magic Of Disney Animation
16 Playhouse Disney – Live On Stage!
17 Rock 'n Roller Coaster Starring Aerosmith
18 The Twilight Zone™ Tower Of Terror
19 Beauty and the Beast – Live On Stage
20 Fantasmic!
21 Guest Information Board
22 Toy Story Pizza Planet
23 Lights! Motors! Action!™ Extreme Stunt Show (May 2005)

DISNEY-MGM STUDIOS

The Twilight Zone™ Tower of Terror

happening! A wonderful 10-minute holding-pen pre-show takes you into the Muppet Theater for a 20-minute experience with all of the Muppets, 3-D special effects and more – when Fozzie Bear points his squirty flower at you, prepare to get wet! It's a gem, and the kids love it. Queues build up through the main parts of the day, but Disney's queuing expertise makes them seem shorter. AAAAA (FP).

Honey, I Shrunk the Kids Movie Set Adventure: this adventure playground gives youngsters the chance to tackle gigantic blades of grass that turn out to be slides, crawl through caves, investigate giant mushrooms and more. However, some may turn round and say 'Yeah. A giant ant. So what?' and head back for the rides. There can be long queues here, too, so arrive early if the kids demand it (and bring plenty of film). TT (TTTT under 9s).

Lights! Motors! Action!™ Extreme Stunt Show: a direct import from the *Walt Disney Studios* in Paris (and due to open in May 2005 as part of Disney's *50th Anniversary Celebration*) is this truly amazing live action stunt spectacular, featuring cars, motorbikes and jet-skis. It is one of the most remarkable shows you will see anywhere, full of genuine high-risk stunts that will leave you shaking your head in amazement. Seating starts 30 minutes prior to a show, and there is some amusing pre-show chat and freestyle show-boating by one of the bike riders before the serious stuff starts. Various audience members are recruited to help in one of the scenes and a roving cameraman picks out people from the crowd to highlight on the video screen in the 'town square'. The set is based on a typical Mediterranean village and is magnificently crafted.

5

BRIT TIP: In the Paris version of Lights! Motors!, Action!™ queuing starts a good half-hour before seating, and the midday shows are always full. It is better to aim for the first performance, or wait until later.

Once the preliminaries are completed, you are treated to a 40-minute extravaganza of daredevil stunts, with a Car Ballet sequence, a Motorbike Chase and a Grand Finale that features some surprise pyrotechnics to complete an awesome presentation (keep your eyes on the windows below the video screen at the end!). Each scene – featuring a secret agent 'goody' and various baddies – is explained by a movie 'director' and the results of each 'shoot' are played back on the

Rock 'n Roller Coaster Starring Aerosmith

video screen to show how each effect was created and spliced together. All the cars were specially created for the show by Vauxhall, and there are some extra tricks in between the main scenes. The whole thing was designed by Frenchman Rémy Julienne, the doyen of film car stunt sequences, who has worked on James Bond films *Goldeneye* and *Licence to Kill* and other action-packed epics such as *The Rock*, *Gone In 60 Seconds* and *Enemy Of The State*.

> BRIT TIP: If you have young children, be aware there is some (loud) mock gunfire in the Motors! Action! show, which can upset sensitive ears, while the motorbike scene includes a rider catching fire, which can be frightening for them too.

Finally, the exit can be quite a scrum as 5,000 people have to leave together, and it can take 10–15 minutes to clear the auditorium, hence if you can sit towards the front of the grandstand, you will be out rather quicker. The fact it involves so much genuine, live co-ordination makes for a truly thrilling experience and the kids are sure to want to see it more than once (mine certainly did), which is another reason to see it early on. TTTTT.

The Disney-MGM Studios Backlot Tour: before you board the special trams for a look at the off-limits part of the studios in this 35-minute walk-and ride tour, you are treated to some special effects (involving an amusing water tank with a mock Pearl Harbor attack!). The tram takes you round the production backlot and then to **Catastrophe Canyon** for a demonstration of special effects that

try both to drown you and blow you up! AAA (plus TTTT). You exit into the **American Film Institute Showcase** of costumes and props from recent films. Nearby, **Goofy's Prop Stop** is a neat photo stall with Disney images ($12.95 and $16.95).

Who Wants To Be A Millionaire – Play It!: Disney's live version of the hit TV show is based on the US programme, but is still effectively the same show. The great twist is EVERYONE gets to play – all 1,600 members of the audience. Whoever is fastest with the put-them-in-order question starts in the hot seat and, as you play along, you build up a score, with the top ten shown on screen at various stages. Then, when a contestant loses out, the person with the highest score is next up. The hosts do a terrific job of maintaining the TV 'illusion' and there are the usual rules and lifelines, which add to the sense of reality here (although you play for Disney points towards some great souvenirs). One difference is there can be no Phone A Friend. Instead, you have Phone A Complete Stranger, when a passer-by is grabbed off the street outside! It is addictive fun, and the only drawback is it is so popular the FASTPASS tickets run out quickly, so try to get here early. AAAAA (FP). As you come out, look for the **Meet Mickey Mouse** character greet nearby.

Walt Disney: One Man's Dream: this interactive show-and-tell exhibit chronicles Walt himself and his lifetime of accomplishments. From archive school records to a model of the Nautilus from *20,000 Leagues Under The Sea*, the story of the man behind the Mouse comes to vivid life. The homage concludes with a preview of Disney's future developments, plus a 10-minute film encapsulating everything Walt achieved and dreamed about. AAAA.

Voyage of the Little Mermaid: a 17-minute live performance which is primarily for children who have seen

BRIT TIP: Try to sit at least halfway back in the Mermaid Theatre, especially with young children, as the stage front is a bit high for little 'uns.

the Disney cartoon. It brings together a creative mix of live actors, animation and puppetry to re-create the highlights of the film. Parents will still enjoy the clever special effects, but queues tend to be long, so go early or late. Those in the first few rows may also get a little wet. AAA (AAAAA under 9s) (FP).

The Magic of Disney Animation: an amusing and entertaining 35-minute tour through the making of cartoons. It's up to you how you pace it, but don't miss Robin Williams in a special cartoon, *Back to Neverland*, and the fascinating view of some of Disney's animators at work. It concludes with a film of some of the highlights of Disney's many animated classics. Queues are rarely serious here, so it's a good one for the afternoon. AAAA.

Playhouse Disney – Live On Stage!: straight out of several popular kids' TV series comes this 20-minute live show with pre-school favourites *Bear in the Big Blue House, Rolie Polie Olie, The Book of Pooh* and *Stanley*. Much of this can be seen only on cable or satellite TV in the UK, but it is still colourful and entertaining. AAA (AAAAA under 5s).

Rock 'n Roller Coaster Starring Aerosmith: Disney's first big-thrill inverted coaster is a sure-fire draw for the high-energy ride addicts, with a magnificent indoor setting and nerve-jangling ride. It features a clever 3-D film show starring rock group Aerosmith in their recording studio. That preamble leads to the real fun, set to specially recorded tracks from the band itself and with outrageous

speaker systems, as riders climb aboard Cadillac 'cars' for this memorable whiz through a mock Los Angeles setting (watch out for a close encounter with the 'Hollywood' sign!). The high-speed launch and inversions ensure an up-to-the-minute coaster experience. Go first thing or expect serious queues. Restrictions: 4ft 1in/124cm TTTTT (FP).

The Twilight Zone™ Tower of Terror: the tallest landmark in *Walt Disney World Resort in Florida* (at 199ft/60 metres) invites you to experience another dimension in this mysterious Hollywood Tower Hotel that time forgot. The exterior is intriguing, the interior is fascinating, the ride is scintillating and the queues are serious! Typically, just when you think you are through to the ride itself, there is another queue, but the inner detail is so clever you can spend the time inspecting how realistic it all is. The ride was also revamped in 2003 to add a new, random element to the drop sequence, with other special effects, and lap bars have been replaced with seat-belts for a more hair-rising experience! Restrictions: 3ft 4in/101cm. TTTTT (FP).

Beauty and the Beast – Live on Stage: an enchanting live performance of the highlights of this Disney classic will entertain the whole family for 20 minutes in the nearby Theater of the Stars. Check the schedule for showtimes. AAA.

Fantasmic!: this special-effects spectacular is simply not to be missed. Staged every night in a 6,900-seat amphitheatre behind the Tower of Terror™, it features the 'dreams' of Mr M Mouse, portrayed as the Sorcerer's Apprentice, through films such as *Pocahontas, The Lion King* and *Snow White*, but hijacked by various Disney villains, leading to a tumultuous battle with Our Hero emerging triumphant. Dancing waters, shooting comets, animated fountains, swirling stars and balls of

5

fire combine in a breathtaking presentation – but beware of the giant, fire-breathing dragon! The 25-minute show begins seating up to 90 minutes in advance and it is advisable to head there at least 30 minutes before (watch out for the splash zones!). AAAAA.

Daily parade

In keeping with the park's movie-star style, the daily parade (another designed for the *100 Years of Magic* celebration) is **Disney Stars and Motor Cars**, and is one of the highlights. The theme is a Hollywood film premiere of the 1930s and '40s, with a series of genuine vintage cars and clever replicas being used to mount a riotous cavalcade of Disney showbiz favourites. It features 15 crazily customised cars – including a 1929 Cadillac – that provide the likes of *Aladdin, Mary Poppins, Mulan*, the Muppets and new films like *Atlantis* and *Monsters Inc.* with a chance to show off in larger-than-life fashion. Watch out for the *Star Wars*™ 'Land Speeder' with a radio-controlled R-2D2 in the largest parade ever staged in *Disney-MGM Studios*. The lead car also features any special guests at the Studios that day – or a visiting family instead. AAAA.

Disney characters are out and about along Mickey Avenue as are performing 'actors and actresses' in Hollywood Boulevard.

Places to eat

While the choice of food may not be wide, there is plenty of it and at reasonable prices. **The Hollywood Brown Derby** offers a full-service restaurant in fine Hollywood style (reservations necessary – special Early Evening Value meals 4–6pm), while **Mama Melrose's Ristorante Italiano** is a wonderful table-service Italian option (one of my favourites).

Beat the crowds by booking a Fantasmic! dinner package when you enter the park (or on 407 939 3463). Just make an early-evening Priority Seating for the Hollywood Brown Derby, Mama Melrose's or Hollywood and Vine and you get VIP seating later for the show. Make sure you ask for the dinner package when you book.

The **Sci-Fi Dine-In Theater Restaurant** is a big hit with kids as you dine in a mock drive-in cinema, with cars as 'tables', waitresses on roller skates and a big film screen showing corny old black-and-white science fiction clips. The **'50s Prime Time Café** is another hilarious experience as you sit in mock stage sets from American TV sitcoms and eat meals 'just like Mom used to make'. (The waiters all claim to be your brother and warn you to take your elbows off the table, etc. Good fun.) Priority Seatings are necessary. The fast-food eateries consist of the **ABC Commissary** (breakfast till 10.30am), **Backlot Express** (excellent burgers and hot dogs), **Rosie's All-American Café** (chicken, burgers, salads) and the **Toy Story Pizza Planet** (pizza, salads and drinks). A good buffet lunch (high season only) and dinner is also available at **Hollywood and Vine Cafeteria of the Stars**.

BRIT TIP: I always recommend the Sci-Fi Dine-In Theater Restaurant or '50s Prime Time Café for a main meal with a difference.

Shopping

There are 21 gift and speciality shops around the Studios – six of them along Hollywood Boulevard – worth checking out in early afternoon. Sid Caheunga's **One-of-a-Kind** (just to the left of the main gates as you enter) stocks rare movie and TV items, including many celebrity autographs. Try the **Legends of Hollywood** (on Sunset Boulevard) for some different souvenirs and **AFI Showcase Shop** (in the Backlot) with MGM logo products and movie-related gifts. **Keystone Clothiers** (at the top of Hollywood Boulevard) offers some of the best Disney apparel.

Studios at Christmas

At Christmas (in fact, from late November to January 1), one of the most amazing spectacles anywhere is the **Osborne Family Lights**, which are switched on every evening in the New York street area. The display of 5 million twinkling, themed fairy lights draws a huge crowd twice a night (try to go during a Fantasmic! performance to avoid the worst of the throngs) and is simply stunning.

Skywalker and Co.

Star Wars™ film fans will want to make a beeline for the Studios during weekends in the latter half of May when the park becomes a playground for characters, film stars, photo-opportunities, competitions and other memorabilia based on anything to do with Luke Skywalker and Co. There is no additional fee to rub shoulders with (and get autographs from) various *Star Wars*™ personalities, and the Studios take on an extra (Space) dimension each weekend.

5

DISNEY-MGM STUDIOS with children

Here is our general guide to the rides that appeal to the different age groups in this park (and it is, possibly, the best spread of all).

Under 5s
Playhouse Disney – Live On Stage!, Voyage of the Little Mermaid, Beauty and the Beast – Live on Stage, Disney Stars and Motor Cars parade, Fantasmic!.

5–8s
Voyage of the Little Mermaid, Beauty and the Beast – Live On Stage, Honey I Shrunk the Kids Movie Set Adventure, 'Sounds Dangerous' Starring Drew Carey, Jim Henson's Muppet*Vision 3-D, *Disney-MGM Studios* Backlot Tour, Disney Stars and Motor Cars parade, Lights! Motors! Action!™ Extreme Stunt Show (with parental discretion), Fantasmic!

9–12s
'Sounds Dangerous' Starring Drew Carey, Indiana Jones™ Epic Stunt Spectacular!, Lights! Motors! Action!™ Extreme Stunt Show, The Great Movie Ride, Star Tours, Jim Henson's Muppet*Vision 3-D, *Disney-MGM Studios* Backlot Tour, The Magic of Disney Animation, Beauty and the Beast – Live On Stage, Rock 'n Roller Coaster Starring Aerosmith, Twilight Zone™ Tower of Terror, Fantasmic!

Over 12s
Indiana Jones™ Epic Stunt Spectacular, Star Tours, The Great Movie Ride, Lights! Motors! Action!™ Extreme Stunt Show, Jim Henson's Muppet*Vision 3-D, *Disney-MGM Studios* Backlot Tour, Who Wants To Be A Millionaire – Play It!, The Magic of Disney Animation, Rock 'n Roller Coaster Starring Aerosmith, Twilight Zone™ Tower of Terror, Fantasmic!

Disney's Animal Kingdom Theme Park

The newest, smartest and most radical theme park at *Walt Disney World Resort in Florida* opened in 1998 and represents a completely different experience. With an emphasis on nature and conservation, it largely eschews the non-stop thrills and attractions which mark out the other parks, and instead offers a change of pace, a more relaxing motif, as well as Disney's usual seamless entertainment style – plus two excellent thrill attractions (three when the under-construction blockbuster Expedition: Everest™ opens in 2006).

The attractions are relatively few, just five out-and-out rides, plus two scenic journeys, two nature trails, five shows (including the hilarious 3-D film *It's Tough to Be a Bug!* and the full-blown theatre of *Festival of The Lion King*), an elaborate adventure playground, conservation station and petting zoo, and a Disney character greeting area. It's a far cry from the hustle-bustle of the *Magic Kingdom* Park, and it carries a strong environmental message that aims to create a greater understanding of the world's ecological problems.

School-age children should find it quite educational, though under 5s may be a little left out. It is outrageously scenic, notably with the 145-ft (44-metre) Tree of Life and the Kilimanjaro Safaris, but it won't overwhelm you with Disney's usual grand fantasy. Rather, it is a chance to experience a part of the world that is both threatened and threatening in a safe, secure manner. It is obviously not the Real Thing but it provides a glimpse of some of the world's most majestic areas in a manner that allows ecology and the commercial world to co-exist happily and meaningfully.

The most conclusive word on Disney's first full-blown animal adventure goes to Professor David Bellamy, who told me: 'This park has been designed and looked after by the best animal welfare people you can think of. Bad zoos are bad news and should be closed down, but good zoos are good news and the only hope for keeping about 500 species of animal alive in the future.'

The park does get crowded, however, and the walkways can be congested. There are also fewer places to cool down. It is definitely a good idea to be here on time and use FASTPASS (FP) to minimise queuing (see page 91).

Getting there

If you are staying in the Kissimmee area, *Disney's Animal Kingdom Theme Park* is the easiest to find. Just get on the (toll) Osceola Parkway and follow it all the way to the toll booths, where parking costs $8. Alternatively, coming down I-4, take the new Exit 65 which puts you on Osceola Parkway. If you are driving from West Highway 192, come in on Sherberth Road (turn right at the first traffic lights).

If you arrive early (which is advisable), you can walk up to the Entrance Plaza. Otherwise, the usual tram system will take you in, so make a note of the area in which you park (e.g. Unicorn, row 67). The Plaza is overlooked by the mountainous **Rainforest Café**, with its 65-ft (20-metre) waterfall, which is a must for an early lunch or dinner (rarely busy). With Orlando so hot through the summer months, you need to be here as early as possible to see the animals before they disappear into the shade.

For the early birds, here is your best plan of campaign. Once through the gates, animal lovers

Disney's Animal Kingdom Theme Park at a glance

Location	Directly off Osceola Parkway, also via World Drive and Buena Vista Drive		
Size	500 acres (203ha) divided into six 'lands'		
Hours	9am to 5 or 6pm		
Admission	Under 3 free; 3–9 $43.75 (1-Day Ticket), $176 (4-Day Park Hopper), $226 (5-Day Park Hopper Plus); adult (10+) $54.75, $219, $282. Prices do not include tax		
Parking	$8		
Lockers	Yes; either side of Entrance Plaza; $7 ($2 refundable)		
Pushchairs	$8 and $15 ($1 refundable) at Garden Gate Gifts, through entrance on right		
Wheelchairs	$8 ($1 refund) and $40 ($10 refund); with pushchairs		
Top Attractions	DINOSAUR!, Kilimanjaro Safaris, It's Tough To Be A Bug!, Kali River Rapids, Festival of The Lion King; Expedition: Everest™ (2006)		
Don't Miss	Pangani Forest Exploration Trail, Maharajah Jungle Trek, Rafiki's Planet Watch, Tarzan Rocks!, Mickey's Jamming Jungle Parade, Lucky the dinosaur, dining at Rainforest Café		
Hidden Costs	**Meals**	Burger, chips and coke $7.48 Kids' meal $3.49	
	T-shirts	$19–32	
	Souvenirs	$1.99–275	
	Sundries	Caricature drawings $16.95–33	

should head first for Kilimanjaro Safaris, through the Oasis, Discovery Island and into Africa. After the Safari, go straight to Pangani Forest Exploration Trail and you will have experienced two of the park's best animal encounters. Alternatively, thrill-seekers should turn right in Discovery Island for DinoLand USA, where the DINOSAUR! ride is the big attraction. With that one safely under your belt before the serious crowds arrive, head back through the Island to Asia and Kali River Rapids raft ride, followed by the scenic Maharajah Jungle Trek. The best combination for the first arrivals is to get a FASTPASS (FP) for DINOSAUR! then head straight for Kilimanjaro Safaris, and, once you have done that (and depending on your FP time), either do your DINOSAUR! ride (followed by a Kali River Rapids FP) or go straight to the Rapids. Check your show schedule for *Festival of The Lion King* and try to catch one of the first two performances as the later ones draw sizeable queues. The 'wait time' board at the entrance to Discovery Island is also helpful. The opening

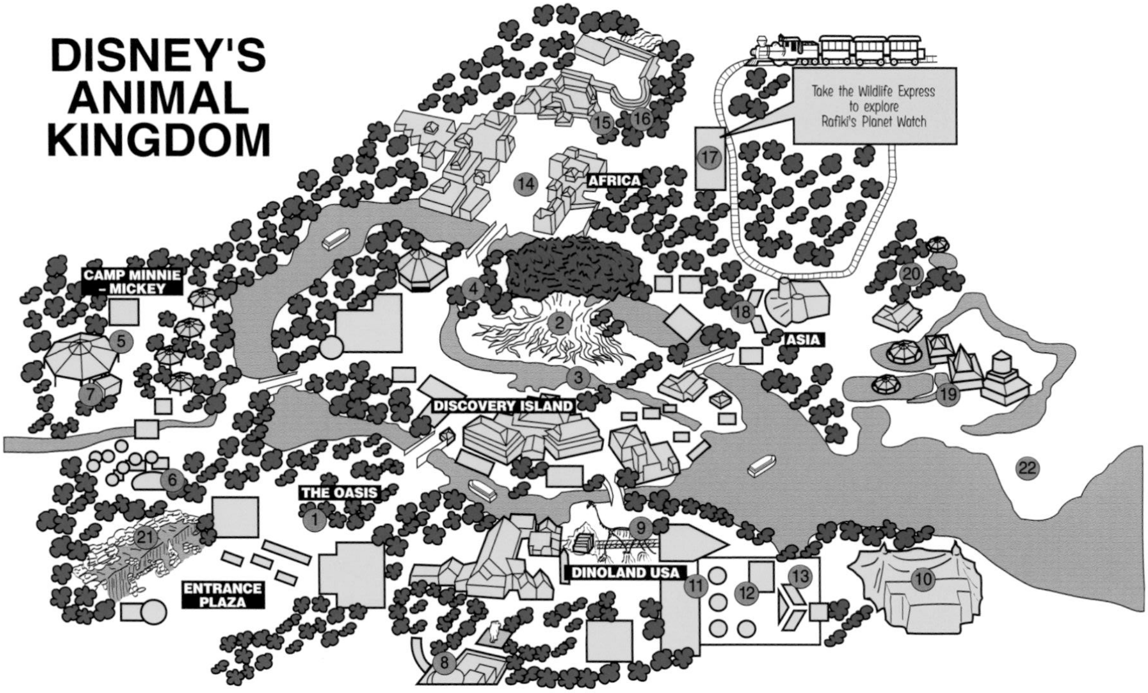

THE OASIS
1 The Oasis Tropical Garden

DISCOVERY ISLAND
2 The Tree Of Life
3 It's Tough To Be A Bug!
4 Discovery Island Trails

CAMP MINNIE-MICKEY
5 Character Greeting Trails
6 Pocahontas And Her Forest Friends
7 Festival Of The Lion King

DINOLAND USA
8 Dinosaur!
9 The Boneyard
10 Tarzan™ Rocks!
11 Chester & Hester's Dino-Rama!
12 TriceraTOP Spin
13 Primeval Whirl

AFRICA
14 Harambe
15 Kilimanjaro Safaris
16 Pangani Forest Exploration Trail
17 Rafiki's Planet Watch

ASIA
18 Flights Of Wonder
19 Kali River Rapids
20 Maharajah Jungle Trek

21 Rainforest Café
22 Expedition: Everest™ (2006)

DISNEY'S ANIMAL KINGDOM

Take the Wildlife Express to explore Rafiki's Planet Watch

THE OASIS

DISCOVERY ISLAND

CAMP MINNIE MICKEY

AFRICA

ASIA

DINOLAND USA

ENTRANCE PLAZA

Carvings on The Tree of Life

in early 2006 of Expedition: Everest™ will probably distort this picture and make this blockbuster new ride a must-do early on.

Right, those are your main tactics, here is the full rundown.

The Oasis

The Oasis Tropical Garden is a gentle, walk-through introduction to the park, a rocky, tree-covered area featuring several animal habitats, studded with streams, waterfalls and lush plant life. Here you will meet miniature deer, macaws, parrots, iguanas, sloths and tree kangaroos in a wonderfully understated environment that leads you across a stone bridge to the main open park area. AAA.

Discovery Island

This colourful 'village' is the park hub, themed as a tropical artists' colony, with animal-inspired artwork, four main shops and two eateries.

> BRIT TIP: The early start is especially advised for Kilimanjaro Safaris. You will see far more animals in the first few cooler hours of the day than during the hotter afternoon.

The Tree of Life: this 145-ft (44-metre) high arboreal edifice is the park centrepiece, an awesome creation that seems to give off a different perspective from wherever you view it. The 'trunk' and 'roots' are covered in 325 animal carvings representing the Circle of Life, from the dolphin to the lion. Trails lead round the tree, interspersed with animal habitats showcasing flamingos, otters, ring-tailed lemurs, macaws, axis deer, cranes, storks, ducks and tortoises. The tree canopy spreads 160ft (49 metres), the trunk is 50ft (15 metres) wide and the roots spread out 170ft (52 metres) in diameter. It has 103,000 leaves (all attached by hand) on more than 8,000 branches! AAAA.

> BRIT TIP: The dark, special effects and creepy-crawlies often scare young ones in It's Tough To Be A Bug beneath the big tree.

It's Tough To Be A Bug!: winding down among the Tree's roots brings you 'underground' to a 430-seat theatre and another example of Disney's artistry in 3-D films and special effects. This hysterically funny 10-minute show, in the company of Flick from the Disney/Pixar hit film *A Bug's Life*, is a homage to 80 per cent of the animal world, featuring grasshoppers, beetles, spiders, stink bugs and termites (beware the 'acid'

A rhino in the savannah

spray!) as well as a number of tricks I couldn't possibly reveal. Sit towards the back in the middle of a row (allow a good number of people in first as the rows are filled up from the far side) to get the best of the 3-D effects. Queues build up from midday, but they do move quite steadily. Don't miss the 'forthcoming attractions' posters in the foyer for some excruciating bug puns on well-known films. AAAAA (FP).

Shopping is at its best here, with a huge range of merchandise, souvenirs and gifts (notably in **Disney Outfitters** and **Island Mercantile**), while the two counter-service restaurants, **Pizzafari** and **Flame Tree Barbecue**, are both good choices. Indeed, provided it is not too hot, the Flame Tree is a relaxing and picturesque option, set among some pretty gardens, pools and fountains on the edge of Discovery River.

Camp Minnie-Mickey

A woodland retreat featuring gently winding paths and more of Disney's clever scenery – the benches, lighting and the gurgling stream, with Donald Duck and his nephews hiking down the side, that develops into a series of kid-friendly squirt fountains.

Character Greeting Trails: four trails lead to a series of jungle encounters with Disney characters such as Mickey and Minnie (naturally), Winnie the Pooh and Tigger, Chip 'n Dale, Baloo and King Louie, Timon and Rafiki. AAAAA (for kids).

Pocahontas and Her Forest Friends: based on characters from the Disney film *Pocahontas*, this 15-minute show sees various animals – racoons, rabbits, cranes, a skunk, armadillo and porcupine – interacting with the central actress and Mother Willow in the question of 'Who can save the forest?' However, it doesn't seem to do much for small children, there is not much shade in summer and it is standing room only once the 350 seats have been filled. AAA.

Festival of The Lion King: not to be missed, this high-powered 40-minute production brings the hit film to life in spectacular fashion with giant moving stages, huge animated figures, singers, dancers, acrobats and stilt-walkers. All the well-known songs are given an airing in a coruscation of colour and sound, and it serves to underline the quality Disney brings to live shows. People begin queuing 30 minutes in advance for the 1,000-seater theatre, so try to take in one of the earlier shows. AAAAA.

DinoLand USA

Rather at odds with the natural theming of the rest of the park, DinoLand USA is a full-scale palaeontology exercise, with this mock 'town' taken over by a university fossil dig. Energetically tongue-in-cheek (the 'students' who work in the area have the motto 'Been there, dug that', while you enter under a mock brachiosaurus skeleton, the 'Oldengate Bridge' – groan!), it still features some glimpses into dinosaur research and artefacts. Here you will also meet Disney's newest creation, Lucky the dinosaur from May 2005 as part of the 50th Anniversary Celebration. This truly amazing 9-ft (3-metre) high audio-animatronic figure walks on two legs and pulls a cart of flowers as he greets guests and even signs autographs with his four-leaf clover signature. This free-roaming creature is as 'real' as dinosaurs can get and is sure to captivate children of all ages.

DINOSAUR!: renamed after Disney's big animated film, its original fast, jerky ride has been toned down a little for a more family-friendly experience (although the dinosaur menace is too scary for many young children). It is a wonderfully realistic journey back to the end of the Cretaceous period and the giant meteor that put paid to dinosaur life. You enter the high-tech Dino Institute, 'A discovery centre and research lab dedicated to uncovering the mysteries of the past', for a multimedia show of dino history that leads to a briefing room for your 'mission' 65 million years in the past to view Cretaceous life.

However, one of the Institute's scientists 'hijacks' your journey for his own project, to capture a dinosaur before the fateful meteor's arrival, and you go careering back to a prehistoric jungle in your 12-passenger Time Rover. The threat of a carnivorous carnotaurus (quite frightening for some children; try to sit them on the inside of the car) and the impending doom of the meteor add up to a breathtaking whiz through a stunning environment. You will need to ride it at least twice to appreciate all the clever detail, but queues build up quickly, so go either first thing or late in the day. Restrictions: 3ft 4in/101cm. TTTT plus AAAA (FP).

The Boneyard: a hugely imaginative adventure playground, it offers kids the chance to slip, slide and climb through the 'fossilised' remains of triceratops and brontosaurs, explore caves, dig for bones and splash through a mini-waterfall. The amusing signage will go over the heads of most kids, but it is ideal for parents to let their young 'uns loose for up to an hour (although not just after the neighbouring Tarzan show has finished). TTTT (kids only).

Tarzan™ Rocks!: and he really does. This amazing show is basically a 30-minute rock concert showcasing the songs from the

BRIT TIP: At Tarzan™ Rocks! try to grab a seat by the rails that divide the auditorium, as the roller-skating monkeys will come and dance by you!

animated film, with special effects provided by dancers, acrobats and roller bladers, all in wonderful costumes and superbly choreographed. Tarzan and Jane make only a brief appearance, and then mainly as acrobats (ladies – no staring at that loincloth!). Its loud, high-energy style may not be everyone's cup of tea (especially for sensitive small children) but it is visually stunning as is the quality of the performers. AAAA.

Chester & Hester's Dino-Rama!: this mini-land of rides, fairground games and stalls adds a rather garish element to DinoLand USA. Its main icon is a towering Concretosaurus (!), and it is designed to have a quirky, tongue-in-cheek style reminiscent of 1950s' American roadside attractions. The top rides are:

TriceraTOP Spin: another version of the Dumbo/Aladdin rides in the *Magic Kingdom* Park, a flying, twirling, spinning top bounces you up and down with a surprise at the top. AA (or TTTT for under 5s).

Primeval Whirl: coaster fans will definitely get a laugh out of this wacky offering that sends its riders through a maze of curves, hills and (quite sharp) drops that make it seem much faster than it actually is. It is basically a fairground lampoon of the DINOSAUR! ride, a mock journey 'way back in time', with plenty of cartoon frippery. The extra fun is provided by the cars free-spinning, which means an extra, unpredictable element to each 3-minute ride (plunging through the jaws of a skeleton dino at one point!). The queuing area is a riot of visual gags, but the ride itself is not recommended for anyone with back or neck problems. Height restriction 4ft/122cm. TTTT (FP).

The **Fossil Fun Games** are six fairground-type stalls, each costing a rather hefty $2, to tempt you into trying to win a large cuddly dinosaur, all with the larger-than-life Dino-Rama trademark. Dining options include the (you've guessed!) **Restaurantosaurus**, counter-service burgers and hot dogs (presented by McDonald's, so you get McDonald's fries, Chicken McNuggets and Happy Meals but no Big Macs) and a snack bar. Any shopping is centred on the huge **Chester and Hester's Dino-Rama! – Dinosaur Treasures**, the 'Fossiliferous Gift Store' with groan-inducing slogans like Merchandise of Extinction, Prehistoric Prices and Last Stop for 65 Million Years!

TriceraTop Spin

Maharajah Jungle Trek

Africa

The largest land in the park, it re-creates magnificently the forests, grasslands and rocky homelands of equatorial Africa's most fascinating residents in a richly landscaped setting that is part rundown port town setting and part endless savannah. In this part of the park, the outside world seems thousands of miles away and there is hardly a glimpse of it anywhere.

Harambe: a reconstruction of a Kenyan port village, complete with white coral walls and thatched roofs, is the starting point of your adventure. The Arab-influenced Swahili culture is depicted in the native tribal costumes and architecture. Here you will find two more shops, including the **Mombasa Marketplace/Ziwani Traders**, where you can suit up safari-style, and the counter-service **Tusker House Restaurant** for rotisserie chicken, fresh fish, salads, vegetarian sandwiches and a special African dish (a healthier offering than most, but a touch expensive), plus four snack and drink bars, notably the **Kusafiri Coffee Shop**. The splendid **Karuka Acrobats** also perform here on select days.

Kilimanjaro Safaris: the queuing area alone earns high marks for authenticity, preparing you for the sights and sounds of the 110-acre (45-ha) savannah beyond. You board a 32-passenger truck, with your

The amazing Festival of The Lion KIng

5

driver/guide relaying information about the flora and fauna on view and a bush pilot overhead relaying facts and figures on the wildlife, including the dangers threatening them in the real world. Hundreds of animals are spread out in various habitats, with no fences in sight – the ditches and barriers are all well concealed – as you splash through fords and cross rickety bridges, and you should get some good close-ups of rhinos, elephants, giraffes, zebras, lions, baboons, antelope, ostriches and hippos.

Halfway round, your journey becomes a race to stop elephant poachers, though the outcome is fairly obvious. Once again, the authentic nature of all you see (okay, some of the tyre 'ruts' and termite mounds are concrete and the baobab trees are fake) is quite awesome with the spread of the vegetation and the landscaping, and the only drawback is the lack of photo stops along the way (and the ride can be bumpy). The animals also roam over a wide area and can disappear from view. Not recommended for expectant mothers or anyone with back or neck problems. AAAAA (FP).

Pangani Forest Exploration Trail: as you leave the Safari, you turn into an overgrown nature trail that showcases gorillas, hippos, meerkats and rare tropical birds. You wander the trail at your own pace

BRIT TIP: The best (i.e. the most jolting) ride with the Kilimanjaro Safaris is at the back of the truck, although there's nothing much to see from midday to late afternoon when many animals take a siesta.

Kali River Rapids

and visit several research stations to learn more about the animals on display, including the underwater view of the hippos (check out the size of a hippo skull and those teeth!) and the savannah overlook, where giraffe and antelope graze and the amusing meerkats frolic. The walk-through aviary gives you the chance to meet the carmine bee-eater, pygmy goose, African green pigeon, ibis and brimstone canary, among others, but the real centrepiece is the silverback gorilla habitat, in fact, two of them. The family group is often just inches away from the plate-glass window, while the bachelor group further along can prove more elusive. Again, the natural aspect of the trail is breathtaking and it provides a host of photo opportunities. It is best to visit early on to see the animals at their most active (and because it quickly becomes quite crowded). AAAAA.

Rafiki's Planet Watch: the little train journey here, with its peek into some of the backstage areas, is just the preamble to the park's interactive and educational exhibits. The 3-part journey starts with **Habitat Habit!**, where you can see cotton-top tamarins and learn how conservation begins in your own back garden. **Conservation Station** is next up with a series of exhibits, shows and hands-on information stations about the environment and its ecological dangers, which are aimed primarily at children.

Look out for *Sounds of the Rain Forest*, the story of endangered species at the **Mermaid Tales Theater** and the Eco-Heroes (who can be quizzed on screen) trying to redress the balance, then take a self-guided tour of the park's backstage areas such as the veterinary treatment centre, the hatchery and neo-natal care area. You can easily spend an hour absorbing the environmental message here, along with that of Disney's Wildlife

Conservation Fund. Plus, youngsters can meet Rafiki and some of his animal chums. The **Affection Section**, a petting zoo of lambs, goats, donkeys, sheep and guinea pigs, completes the Planet Watch line-up.

Asia

The final 'land' of the park is elaborately themed as the gateway to the imaginary south-east Asian city of Anandapur, with temples, ruined forts, landscape and wildlife.

Flights of Wonder: another wildlife show, this portrays the talents and traits of a host of birds, built into a production of mythical proportions, as a treasure-seeking student meets Phoenix, the birds' guardian, in a crumbling, fortified town. Vultures, eagles, toucans, macaws and many other feathered friends take a bow as Phoenix reveals the treasures of the avian world. The Caravan Stage is not air-conditioned, though, and is fiendishly hot in summer. AAA.

Kali River Rapids: part thrill-ride, part scenic journey, this bouncy, raft-ride journey will get you pretty wet (not great for early morning in winter). It starts out in tropical forest territory before launching into a scene of logging devastation, warning of the dangers of clear-cut burning. Your raft then plunges down a waterfall (and one unlucky soul – usually the rider with their back to the drop – gets seriously damp) before you finish the journey more sedately, albeit with a few more watery encounters. Queues can be long through the main part of the day, so make use of FASTPASS here. You will probably want to experience the ride twice to appreciate all the clever detail. Restrictions: 3ft 6in/106cm (a few rafts have adult-and-child seats allowing smaller children to ride). TTT (plus AAAA) (FP).

Maharajah Jungle Trek: Asia's version of the Pangani Forest Trail is another picturesque walk past decaying temple ruins and various animal encounters. Playful gibbons, tapirs, Komodo dragons and a bat enclosure (including the flying fox-bat, the world's largest variety) lead up to the main viewing area, the 5-acre (2-ha) Tiger Range, which includes a pool and fountains and is a popular playground early in the day for these magnificent big cats. An antelope enclosure and walk-through aviary complete this breathtaking trek (which rarely draws heavy crowds). AAAAA.

Expedition: Everest™: another major new attraction which is scheduled to open in early 2006, this roller-coaster takes you deep into the Himalayas for an encounter with the mythical Yeti. The queuing area alone will convince you of its authentic location (try to do the main queue at least once rather than FASTPASS to appreciate all the fine detail) as it delivers you to an old abandoned tea plantation train station (at least, that's the clever theme). Here you undertake the ride to the foothills of Mount Everest, but you must first brave the Canyons of the Yeti to get there. Will the mythical beast be in evidence – you bet! The ride becomes a typically fast-paced coaster whiz (although with no inversions), both forwards AND backwards, as you attempt to escape from the Yeti's domain. It promises to be another fabulous new ride experience, with plenty of twists and turns, but it is also sure to draw a crowd, so make it one of the first things you do. Restrictions: 4ft/ 122cm. TTTTT (expected; FP).

Finally, returning to the front entrance gives you the chance to sample or just visit (and shop at) the **Rainforest Café**, the second on Disney property. If you haven't seen the one at *Downtown Disney* Marketplace, you should definitely call in to witness the amazing jungle interior with its audio-animatronic animals, waterfalls, thunderstorms and aquariums. A 3-course meal will set you back about $28 (kids' meals at $6.99), but the setting alone is definitely worth it and the food is above average.

DISNEY'S ANIMAL KINGDOM PARK with children

Here is our general guide to the rides which appeal to the different children's ages in this park.

Under 5s
Character Greetings Trails, Festival of The Lion King, Discovery Island Trails, Kilimanjaro Safaris, Pangani Forest Exploration Trail, Affection Section, Maharajah Jungle Trek, TriceraTOP Spin, The Boneyard.

5–8s
All the above, plus Pocahontas and Her Forest Friends, Habitat Habit!, Conservation Station, Kali River Rapids, Flights of Wonder, It's Tough To Be A Bug! and DINOSAUR! (with parental discretion).

9–12s
All the above, plus Expedition: Everest™ (2006), Primeval Whirl and Tarzan™ Rocks!

Over 12s
Festival of The Lion King, It's Tough To Be A Bug!, Kilimanjaro Safaris, Pangani Forest Exploration Trail, Kali River Rapids, Maharajah Jungle Trek, Flights of Wonder, DINOSAUR!, Tarzan™ Rocks!, Primeval Whirl, Expedition: Everest™ (2006).

Jammin' Jungle Parade

The daily highlight is a tour de force called **Mickey's Jammin' Jungle Parade**. Here, the Imagineers have created a series of fanciful 'Expedition Rovers' that give various Disney characters the chance to celebrate all the animals who live here. The parade is enhanced by stilt-walkers, puppets, mobile sculptures and different 'party animals', plus live percussionists as it snakes down a narrow path from Harambe, around Discovery Island and back. Set to a memorable musical backing, it sounds truly delightful, while 25 park guests are chosen to take part each day, travelling on the back of amusingly designed rickshaws which follow each of the character jeeps.

Finally, for a behind-the-scenes look at the park, **Backstage Safari** is

© Disney

Mickey's Jammin' Jungle Parade

a wonderful 3-hour journey into the handling and care of all the animals ($65, not for under 16s), while **Wild By Design** offers a 3-hour tour of the park's art, history and architecture and how it was all created ($58, not for under 14s). Book on 407 939 8687.

WALT DISNEY WORLD RESORT IN FLORIDA at Christmas

If you can visit prior to the seriously busy days from just before Christmas Day to New Year's Day, you get the benefit of all the added decorations and atmosphere and none of the overwhelming crowds. Each of the parks takes on a festive character, with the addition of artistic artificial snow, Christmas lights and a huge, magnificently decorated fir tree.

Disney-MGM Studios also features the eye-popping Osborne Family Lights while, at the **Magic Kingdom** Park, Main Street USA is transformed into a Christmas extravaganza, dominated by a 60-ft (18-metre) tree. The unmissable **Mickey's Very Merry Xmas Parade** replaces the main 3pm parade in December and is a positive delight for its lively music and eye-catching costumes. Another seasonal extra is the colourful *'Twas the Night before Xmas* show at the Galaxy Palace Theater.

Epcot is the jewel in the Christmas crown, though, with two outstanding features. At 6pm, the daily Christmas tree lighting ceremony is quite breathtaking as the rest of the park lights go out and then the World Showcase bridge and the tree itself are illuminated in dramatic stages to some grand musical accompaniment. The nightly **Candlelight Processional** also draws a crowd, with a guest narrator telling the story of Christmas to the backdrop of a large choir and elaborate candle parade. It is tasteful, dramatic and eye-catching, but you should arrive early as people start queuing almost 3 HOURS in advance. However, you can get a reserved seat if you buy the *Candlelight Processional Dinner* Package (variously $28.99, 34.99, and 41.99, plus tax, depending on which World Showcase restaurant you select, and $10.95 for children 3–11), by calling well in advance on 407 939 3463 (credit card details required).

Five More of the Best
(or, Expanding Orlando's Universe)

It is time to leave the wonderful world of Disney and venture out into the rest of central Florida's great attractions. And, believe me, there is still a terrific amount in store.

For a start, they don't come much more ambitious than Universal Orlando. The area that used to consist of just the one theme park, Universal Studios Florida®, is fast developing into a fully fledged resort of similar scope to Disney's. Their second park, Universal's Islands of Adventure, opened in 1999, hot on the heels of the CityWalk entertainment district. The first resort hotel, the Portofino Bay, made its debut in 1999, followed by the Hard Rock Hotel in 2000, and the Royal Pacific Resort in 2002.

A waterway network connects the hotels to the CityWalk hub, while the multi-storey car parks, for more than 20,000 vehicles, have done away with the need for any other transport system, and it is quite convenient to move between parks.

The marketing tie-up with SeaWorld and Busch Gardens, plus their purchase of the Wet 'n Wild water park, has also proved a success, with the 14-day Orlando FlexTickets giving excellent value. The opening of Islands of Adventure has added 2- and 3-Day Tickets (which include a CityWalk Party Pass), allowing movement between both Universal parks. In summer 2004, both these tickets had special offers for extended visits – seven consecutive days in the case of the 2-Day Ticket, and an amazing 14 days in the case of the 3-Day, effectively 11 days free! See pages 10–13 for more ticket details.

They have also introduced their **Universal Express** system for most rides. Similar to Disney's FASTPASS, it allows guests to 'reserve' one ride at a time and then another once you have done that attraction, and so on. You just present your park entry ticket at the Distribution Center next to the Universal Express ride or show of your choice, then return at the allotted time for a 15-minute wait (instead of an hour or more at peak periods).

Universal hotel guests benefit from Express ride priority ALL DAY by producing their room key. A new feature is **Universal Express Plus**, a day pass that provides one-time access to the top rides with minimal queuing – for an extra $15.90 per person. A limited number go on sale an hour after park opening and they sell fast! NB: at peak periods, Universal hotel guests are limited to one Express ride at the five main attractions in each park until 3pm.

In addition, many rides have **Single Rider** queues which can save time if you want to go on one by yourself. Once again, any height restriction is noted and Universal Express attractions are shown by UE.

The entrance to Universal Studios

Universal Studios Florida®

Universal opened its Florida park in June 1990 (its original Los Angeles site has been open to the public since before World War Two) and quickly became a serious competitor to Disney. For the visitor, it means a consistently high standard and good value in everything on offer (although the choice is quite bewildering!). If you have been to the LA Universal Studios, this one is quite different.

The obvious question here is do you need to do *Disney-MGM Studios* as well as Universal? The answer is an emphatic YES! Universal is a very different kettle of fish to Disney, with a more in-your-face style that goes down well with older kids and younger adults. Younger children are also well catered for in Woody Woodpecker's KidZone.

Universal parks can also require more than a full day in high season. As at Disney, the strategies for a successful visit are the same. Arrive EARLY (up to 30 minutes before the official opening), do the big rides first, avoid main meal times, and step out for a few hours in the afternoon (try shopping or dining at CityWalk) if it gets too crowded.

> BRIT TIP: Reader Tom Burton advises: 'If you buy an Orlando FlexTicket giving you 14 consecutive days at Universal, etc, try going to their parks a couple of times in the evenings only. There are virtually no queues this late in the day and I went on the Hulk Coaster (in Islands of Adventure) five times in an hour!'

Location

Universal Studios Florida® is sub-divided into six main areas, set around a huge, man-made lagoon, but there are no great distinguishing features, so you need a map. The main entrance is just off the new exit on Interstate 4 (I-4) or by the Universal Boulevard link from International Drive (I-Drive) by Wet 'n Wild. Parking costs $8 in their massive multi-storey car park and there is quite a walk (with some moving walkways) to the front gates.

Once through, your best bet is to turn right on to Rodeo Drive, along Hollywood Boulevard and Sunset Boulevard and into World Expo for Back To The Future… The Ride and Men In Black – Alien Attack. From there, head across the bridge to Jaws, then go back along the Embarcadero for Earthquake and into New York for Revenge of the Mummy. This will get most of the main rides under your belt before the crowds build up, and you can then take it a bit easier by seeing one of the shows or taking advantage of Universal Express. Alternatively, try to be among the early birds flocking to the new Shrek 4-D film show in Production Central and the Revenge of the Mummy in New York to avoid the queues that build up here, then use Universal Express for the likes of Terminator 2, Back To The Future and Men In Black.

Here's a full blow-by-blow guide to the Studios. For the rundown on CityWalk, see Chapter 9.

Production Central

Coming straight through the gates brings you immediately into the administrative centre, with a couple of large gift stores (have a look at these in mid-afternoon) plus **Studio**

Universal Studios Florida® at a glance

Location	Off Exits 75A and 74B from I-4; Universal Boulevard and Kirkman Road
Size	110 acres (45ha) in seven themed areas
Hours	9am–7pm off peak; 9am–10pm high season (Washington's birthday, Easter, summer holidays, Thanksgiving, Christmas)
Admission	Under 3 free; 3–9 $44.95 (1-Day Ticket), $88.95 (2-Day Ticket), $101 (3-Day Ticket), $145.95 (4-Park FlexTicket), $179.95 (5-Park FlexTicket); adult (10+) $54.75 $99.95, $114, $179.95, $214.95; Universal Bonus Pass (5 consecutive days, online sales only) $94.95 adult and child.
Parking	$8
Lockers	Yes; immediately to left in Front Lot; $7
Pushchairs	$10 and $16, next to locker hire
Wheelchairs	$10 and $40 (with photo ID as deposit), same location as pushchairs
Top Attractions	Revenge of the Mummy, Men In Black, Jaws, Back to the Future, ET, Earthquake, Shrek 4-D, Terminator 2
Don't Miss	Curious George Playground (for kids), The Blues Brothers

Hidden Costs	**Meals**	Burger, chips and coke $8.28 3-course dinner $21.50 (Finnigan's) Kids' meal $5.50–7.50 (Finnigan's and Lombard's Seafood Grill only)
	T-shirts	$17.95–23.95
	Souvenirs	$0.99–199
	Sundries	Portrait studio photo $24.95 and $28.95

6

Sweets. Call at **Guest Services** here for guides for disabled visitors, TDD and assisted listening devices, and to make restaurant bookings. If you are here early, you can sign up to be in the audience for one of Universal's TV shows at the **Studio Audience Center. First aid** is available here (and on Canal Street between New York and San Francisco), while there are facilities for nursing mothers at **Family Services** by the bank through the gates on the right.

Coming to the top of the Plaza of the Stars brings you to the business end of the park.

Shrek 4-D: replacing the old Alfred Hitchcock Theater, this adds a whole new dimension to the genre of 3-D film shows as the original cast of the Oscar-winning *Shrek* movie (Mike Myers, Eddie Murphy, Cameron Diaz and John Lithgow) returns for a 13-minute fun-fest that picks up where the original left off. The evil but vertically challenged

PRODUCTION CENTRAL
1 Guest Services
2 Shrek 4-D
3 Nickelodeon Studios
4 Jimmy Neutron's Nicktoon Blast

NEW YORK
5 Twister
6 Revenge of the Mummy
7 The Blues Brothers
8 Finnegan's Bar and Grill

SAN FRANCISCO/AMITY
9 Earthquake — The Big One
10 Jaws
11 All-New Beetlejuice Revue
12 Central Lagoon
13 Lombard's Seafood Grill

WORLD EXPO
14 Back To The Future…. The Ride
15 Men In Black – Alien Attack

WOODY WOODPECKER'S KIDZONE
16 Animal Planet Live!
17 Fievel's Playland
18 A Day In The Park With Barney
19 ET Adventure
20 Woody Woodpecker's Nuthouse Coaster
21 Curious George Goes to Town

HOLLYWOOD
22 Universal's Horror Make-Up Show
23 Terminator 2: 3-D Battle Across Time
24 Lucy: A Tribute

UNIVERSAL STUDIOS FLORIDA

Shrek 4-D

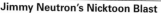

Lord Farquaad is back in ghost form to welcome visitors to his 'dungeons' and reveal his plan to ruin the honeymoon of swamp-dwelling Shrek and Princess Fiona. The amusing 7-minute pre-show film leads into the 500-seat main theatre, where you don your 'Ogre Vision' 3-D glasses and prepare to enter a new technological world.

The film is funny enough (and acts as a bridge between the original and Shrek 2) as Shrek and Donkey have to rescue the Princess, but the addition of a host of special effects (watch out for the 'spiders'!) and 'moving' seats mean this is almost a ride as much as a show, and the effect is both startling and hugely entertaining. State-of-the-art digital projection and audio systems, lighting effects, fog and smoke (plus a hilarious finale featuring an out-of-

control Tinkerbell) ensure high quality all round. It is a major draw, so try to go first thing in the day or expect waits well in excess of an hour. AAAAA+ .

Nickelodeon Studios: a lot of this American kids' TV series will be lost on us (although it's on satellite TV in Britain) as visitors go behind the scenes into the production set. Most kids will welcome the chance to get gunged in green slime by the Gakmeister and they'll love the restrooms which feature green slime 'soap' and sirens when you flush the loo. Long queues build up quickly. AAAA (for children only) (UE).

Jimmy Neutron's Nicktoon Blast: anyone not familiar with the cartoon antics of Jimmy Neutron (Boy Genius) and other members of the Nicktoon stable (Rugrats, the Fairly Odd Parents and SpongeBob Squarepants) might be bemused by the antics here in this rather noisy simulator ride experience. It revolves around Jimmy tangling once again with the evil (but hapless) emperor Ooblar and battling to save the world, with the help of his zany inventions and cartoon friends. It is a big hit with under 10s and the ride is quite dynamic. It quickly draws a queue as it is one of the first you encounter through the gates. There is no height restriction as long as a

6

Jimmy Neutron's Nicktoon Blast

child can sit unassisted, but it is not recommended for anyone with heart, neck or back problems. TTTT (UE).

The main eating outlet here is the magnificently themed **Monsters Café**, specialising in salads, pasta, pizza and chicken. The counter-service area is done up like Frankenstein's lab, with the dining areas sub-divided into Swamp, Space, Crypt and Mansion Dining, all to the accompaniment of old black and white horror film clips on the many video screens. Shopping includes **On Location** (film, sundries, apparel, 2-way radio rentals), **Nickstuff** (Toon merchandise with Jimmy Neutron, SpongeBob Squarepants and Dora the Explorer), **Surf Hut** (the latest in beach wear) and **It's A Wrap**.

New York

From Production Central you head on to New York and some great scene-setting in the architecture and detail of the buildings and streets. It's far too clean to be authentic, but the façades are first class.

Twister: this experience, based on the hit film, brings audiences 'up close and personal' with the awesome destructive forces of a tornado. The 5-storey terror will shatter everything in its path (okay, so it's pretty tame compared with the real thing), building to a shattering climax of destruction (watch out for the flying cow!). The noise is stunning, but it's a bit much for young children (parental discretion advised for under 13s). The pre-show area is almost a work of art but, unless you do it early, save this for late in the day. TTT (UE).

Revenge of the Mummy: this awesome new (May 2004) offering in Orlando's roller-coaster catalogue is a high-tech, high-thrill, high-fun journey into the highly successful world of *The Mummy* film series,

replacing the old King Kong attraction. It features an indoor spin into Ancient Egypt that fuses brand-new coaster technology with space-age robotics and special effects. It starts out as a 'dark ride' (a slow journey through the shadowy, curse-ridden interior of Hamunaptra, The City of the Dead, as created by *Mummy* writer–director Stephen Sommers) but soon evolves into something far more dynamic – with a breathtaking launch sequence.

BRIT TIP: For the best ride experience on Revenge of the Mummy, try to sit in the back row. You are not allowed to carry anything on the ride – loose items must be left in the lockers provided.

The basic premise of the film studio entrance morphing into a fully-fledged archaeological discovery is a good one, and the transition from dark ride to coaster is ingenious, with a host of special effects and eye-popping audio-animatronics as you brave the realm of The Mummy. The high-speed whiz into the dark (backwards to start with) does not involve any inversions but is still a real thrill with its tight turns and sudden dips, while there are several clever twists which I won't reveal (the front row may get slightly damp!). It is a superb, immersive experience and, with the elaborately themed queuing area, adds a real 5-star attraction to the park. However, it is probably a touch too dark and threatening for under 8s. Restrictions: 4ft/122cm. TTTT½ (UE).

The Blues Brothers: fans of the film will not want to miss this live show as Jake and Elwood Blues (well, pretty good doubles, anyway) put on a stormin' performance on

New York's Delancey Street four or five times a day. They cruise up in their Bluesmobile and go through a selection of the film's hits before heading off into the sunset, stopping only to sign a few autographs. Terrific entertainment. AAAA.

For dining, you have two main restaurants. **Finnegan's Bar and Grill** offers the likes of shepherd's pie, fish and chips, corned beef and cabbage along with more traditional New York fare like prime rib, burgers, fries and a good range of beers, plus Irish-tinged entertainment and Happy Hour from 4 to 7pm (half price domestic beer; 10 per cent off imported beer). **Louie's Italian Restaurant** (and **Starbucks**) has counter-service pizza and pasta, Italian ice cream and tiramisu. For shops, you have **Sahara Traders** for *Mummy* souvenirs, as well as jewellery and toys, **The Aftermath** for Twister souvenirs, and **Second Hand Rose** for Coca-Cola™ merchandise and sweets. New York also boasts a noisy amusement arcade.

San Francisco/Amity

Crossing Canal Street brings you all the way across America to San Francisco/Amity and two more serious queues.

Earthquake – The Big One: this three-part adventure gets busy from mid-morning until late. Go behind the scenes first to two stage sets where, with audience help, some of the special effects of the Charlton Heston film are explained. Then you enter the Bay Area Rapid Transit underground and arrive in the middle of a full-scale earthquake that shakes you to your boots. Tremble as the walls and ceilings collapse, trains collide, cars fall in on you and fire erupts all around, followed by a seeming tidal wave of water. It's not for the faint-hearted (or small children), while those who have bad

backs or necks, or are pregnant, are advised not to ride. Restrictions: 4ft/122cm (unless accompanied by an adult, with parental discretion). TTTT (UE).

Jaws: the technological wizardry alone will amaze you here, and queues of an hour are common at peak times. The man-made lagoon holds 5 million gallons (23 million litres) of water; nearly 2,000 miles (3,219km) of wire run throughout the 7-acre (3-ha) site, which required 10,000cu yd (7,646cu metres) of concrete and 7,500 tons of steel. Yes, this is no ordinary ride, and its 6-minute duration will seem a lot longer as your hapless boat guide steers you through an ever more spectacular series of stunts, explosions and menace from the Great White. I defy you not to be impressed – and just a little scared! TTTT (UE).

Beetlejuice's Graveyard Revue: Disney-MGM Studios has *Beauty and the Beast* and *The Little Mermaid*, Universal goes for *Dracula*, *Frankenstein*, *The Wolfman* and *Frankenstein's Bride* in this recently revamped, 20-minute shock 'n' roll extravaganza, compered by Beetlejuice himself. It eschews the twee prettiness of Disney's attractions yet still comes up with a fun family show with lots of laughs, as the 'Graveyard' characters perform specially adapted rock and pop anthems with a mock-horror theme in a great setting. AAAA (UE).

San Francisco also has the park's best dining choice, with **Lombard's Seafood Grill** the highlight (reservations accepted). Great seafood, pasta and sandwiches are accompanied by a good view over the main lagoon, and there's a separate pastry shop for desserts and coffee. **Richter's Burger Co** offers a few interesting burger variations. For a quick snack, **Chez Alcatraz** provides seafood and hot sandwiches, **Captain Quint's**

6

Seafood and Chowder House Restaurant offers fresh chowder and coastal seafood, and the **San Francisco Pastry Co** serves sweet snacks and speciality coffees.

For shopping, try **Quint's Surf Shack** (men's and women's clothing), **Shaiken's Souvenirs** for more upmarket mementoes and apparel, **Oakley** (sunglasses) and the **San Francisco Candy Factory**. An added attraction is a boardwalk of fairground games (which cost an extra few dollars to play), including a Guess Your Weight stall which usually attracts a good crowd for the fun patter of the person in charge.

Men in Black – Alien Attack

World Expo

Crossing the bridge from Amity brings you to a rather nondescript area, but home to the park's other 5-star thrill attraction.

Back To The Future... The Ride: simulators just do not come more realistic than this journey through space and time in Dr Emmit Brown's time-travelling De Lorean. The queues are immense, but a lot of time is taken up by some attention-grabbing pre-ride info on

the TV screens above you. Once you reach the front, there is more information to digest and clever surroundings to convince you of the scientific nature of it all. Then it's into your time-travelling car and off in hot pursuit of baddie Biff, who has stolen another time-car. The huge, wraparound screen and violent movements of your vehicle bring the realism of the ride to a peak, adding up to a huge experience.
Restrictions: 3ft 4in/101cm.
TTTTT (UE).

Men In Black – Alien Attack: this combination thrill/scenic ride takes up where the original hit film,

Revenge of the Mummy

The Terminator

you survive? Only your collective shooting skills can save the day, and there are numerous ride variations according to your accuracy as each rider's score is totted up. Will Smith and Rip Torn are your on-screen hosts, and Will returns at the end to reveal if your score makes you Galaxy Defenders, Cosmically Average or Bug Bait!

> BRIT TIP: For a big score in Men in Black, when you meet the Big Bug – push the big red button!

starring Will Smith, left off. Visitors are secretly introduced to the MIB Institute in a wonderfully inventive mock-futuristic setting and enrolled as trainees for a battle around the streets of New York with a horde of escaped aliens. Your six-person car is equipped with laser zappers for an interactive shoot-out that is like a real-life arcade game, and the aliens can also shoot back and send your car spinning. The finale features a close encounter with a 30-ft (9-metre) bug that is all mouth – will

Fast, frantic and a bit confusing, this will have you coming back for more until you can score more than 250,000 (Defender status). Restrictions: 3ft 6in/106cm. TTTT. (UE) Beat my best score – 265,550!

The International Food and Film Festival here is a food court-style indoor diner offering burgers, sandwiches, meatball subs and salads (in air-conditioned comfort). For gifts, there is **MIB Gear** (apparel, jewellery, toys, sunglasses, towels) and the **Back to the Future Store.**

6

Twister

Woody Woodpecker's KidZone

Animal Planet Live!: this highly amusing show comes from the Animal Planet satellite TV channel. Several children are invited to take part and present a series of unlikely feats and stunts featuring a whole range of fairly tame wildlife, from a racoon to a snake, and on to cats and dogs. Many have been rescued from animal shelters and gone on to feature in films before finding a home at Universal. The big theatre provides an escape from the afternoon crowds. AAAA (UE).

> **BRIT TIP:** Along the lagoon in the World Expo/KidZone area is Central Park, a quiet spot where you can escape the theme park whirl for a while.

Fievel's Playland: strictly for kids (and gives parents a break), this playground, based on the enlarged world of the cartoon mouse, offers youngsters the chance to bounce under a 1,000-gallon hat, crawl through a giant cowboy boot, climb a 30-ft (9-metre) spider's web and shoot the rapids (a 200-ft/61-metre water-slide) in Fievel's sardine can. TTTT (young 'uns only!).

A Day in the Park with Barney: again strictly for the younger set (ages 2–5), the purple dinosaur from the popular kids' TV show is brought to super-dee-duper life on stage in a large arena that features a pre-show before the 15-minute main event, plus an interactive post-show area. Parents will cringe, but the youngsters love it. NB: check out the amazing restrooms! AA (AAAAA under 5s) (UE).

ET Adventure: this is as glorious as scenic rides come, with a picturesque queuing area like the pine woods from the film and then a spectacular leap on the trademark flying bicycles to save ET's home planet. Steven Spielberg (Universal's creative consultant) has added some special effects and characters, and you have an individual ET greeting at the end. Queues top an hour at peak periods, so try to do this one either early or late (or, again, through UE). There is a height restriction of 4ft/122cm, but smaller children can ride with parents. AAAAA (UE).

Woody Woodpecker's Nuthouse Coaster: anchoring this excellent under-10s' adventure land is this child-sized but still quite racy roller-coaster. The brilliant red 800-ft (244-metre) track reaches only 28-ft high (8 metres) and 22mph (35kph), but it seems the real deal to young 'uns. There is still a height restriction of 3ft/91cm, however. TTTT (juniors only).

Curious George Goes to Town: this American children's book character means little to me, but kids of all ages just love this amazing adventure playground and huge range of activities – and plenty of opportunities to get wet (bring swimsuits or a change of clothing for them here). It combines toddler play, water-based play stations and a hands-on interactive ball area, and is a real bonus for harassed parents. The town theme includes buildings to climb, pumps and hoses to spray water, a ball factory in which to shoot, dump and blast thousands of foam balls and – the tour de force – two 500-gallon (2,275-litre) buckets of water which regularly dump their contents in spectacular fashion on the street below. TTTTT (under 12s).

Curious George himself roams the KidZone from time to time, while other characters make regular appearances. For snacks, **Animal Crackers** offers hot dogs, chicken fingers, smoked sausage hoagies and frozen yoghurt. Shop at the

Cartoon Store, Barney Store or ET's Toy Closet and Photo Spot.

Hollywood

Finally, your circular tour of Universal brings you back towards the main entrance via Hollywood (where else?). Here, you'll find **Universal's Horror Make-Up Show** (not recommended for under 12s), which demonstrates some of the often amusing ways in which films have attempted to terrorise us. It's a 20-minute show, queues are rarely long and the special effects secrets are well worth discovering. AAA (UE).

Terminator 2: 3-D Battle Across Time: another first-of-its-kind attraction, this is hard to describe. Part film, part show, part experience but all action, it cost $60 million to produce and is guaranteed to leave its audience in awe. The 'Wow!' factor works overtime as you go through a 10-minute pre-show that represents a trip into the workshops of the Cyberdyne Systems from the *Terminator* films and then into a 700-seater auditorium for a 'presentation' on their latest robot creations.

Needless to say, nothing runs to plan and the audience is subjected to a mind-boggling array of (loud) special effects, including indoor pyrotechnics, real actors interacting with the screen and the audience, and a climactic 3-D film finale that takes the *Terminator* story a step further. The original cast, including Arnold Schwarzenegger and director James Cameron, all collaborated on the 12-minute movie (which, at $24 million, is some of the most expensive frame-for-frame film ever made) and the overall effect of this technological marvel is dazzling. However, you need to arrive early or expect queues in excess of an hour all day (parental discretion for under

12s). TTTTT (UE).

The last attraction (or first, depending on which way you go round the park) is **Lucy: A Tribute**, which will mean little to all but devoted fans of the late Lucille Ball and her 1960s' TV comedy *The Lucy Show*. Classic shows, home movies, costumes and scripts are all paraded for close viewing, but youngsters will find it tedious. AA.

If you haven't eaten by now there is a choice of four contrasting but highly enjoyable eateries. **Mel's Drive-In**, a re-creation from the film *American Graffiti*, serves all manner of burgers, hot dogs and milkshakes, while **Café La Bamba**, offers rotisserie chicken, ribs, salad and burgers, plus Margaritas and beer (Happy Hour 3–5pm). **Schwab's Pharmacy** provides sandwiches, old-fashioned milkshakes, sundaes and ice cream and the **Beverly Hills Boulangerie** does baked breakfast treats, pastries, juices and coffee. Shop for hats in the **Brown Derby**, *Terminator* gifts and clothing in **Cyber Image** and for movie memorabilia in **Silver Screen Collectibles**.

Street entertainment

Watch out for various interactive street shows around the park. **The Swashbucklers** engage in some amusing swordplay and stunts (that eventually include some of the guests).

Extreme Ghostbusters: The Great Fright Way, stars Beetlejuice

BRIT TIP: Universal's trademark Halloween Horror Nights programme (see page 162) is now shared between the Studios and Islands of Adventure. Check www.universalorlando.com for updates.

6

Curious George Goes to Town

and the Ghostbusters in a clever song and dance act in the New York street backlot; then there is the **MIB Agents** show (enrolling YOU in a humorous screen test) plus the gravity-defying **Street Breakz** dancers on Park Avenue (opposite Revenge of the Mummy).

Universal characters appear at regular intervals for autographs and photo sessions, notably **Spongebob Squarepants** (inside the Nickstuff Store), **Shrek** (in Ye Olde Souvenir Shoppe at the exit to the show) and **Star Toons** (by Fievel's Playland).

Special programmes

Universal Studios features some brilliant extra seasonal entertainment for Mardi Gras (a major parade, plus music, street entertainment and authentic New Orleans food each night at 6pm from mid-February to April 1), as well as a major party for **New Year's Eve** and the **4th of July**, when the park swings into full fiesta mode.

In summer 2004, there was also a **Shooting Stars** fireworks finale each night over The Central Lagoon and a **Watercraft Stunt Show** four times daily, and the intention is to do something similar in 2005.

UNIVERSAL STUDIOS with children

Our guide to the rides which generally appeal to the different age groups.

Under 5s
Nickelodeon Studios, Animal Planet Live!, A Day In The Park With Barney, Curious George Goes To Town, Fievel's Playland, ET Adventure.

5–8s
Nickelodeon Studios, Animal Planet Live!, Curious George Goes To Town, Fievel's Playland, ET Adventure, Woody Woodpecker's Nuthouse Coaster, Jimmy Neutron's Nicktoon Blast, Shrek 4-D, Men In Black, as well as Earthquake – The Big One (with parental discretion).

9–12s
Jimmy Neutron's Nicktoon Blast, Shrek 4-D, Terminator 2: 3-D Battle Across Time, Twister, Earthquake – The Big One, Animal Planet Live!, Curious George Goes To Town, Woody Woodpecker's Nuthouse Coaster, ET Adventure, All-New Beetlejuice Revue, Jaws, Men In Black – Alien Attack, Back To The Future… The Ride, plus the new Revenge of the Mummy (with parental discretion).

Over 12s
Terminator 2: 3-D Battle Across Time, Universal's Horror Make-Up Show, Jimmy Neutron's Nicktoon Blast, Shrek 4-D, Twister, Revenge Of The Mummy, Earthquake – The Big One, The Blues Brothers, ET Adventure, All-New Beetlejuice Revue, Jaws, Men In Black – Alien Attack, Back To The Future… The Ride.

Islands of Adventure

In May 1999, Universal's creative consultant Steven Spielberg officially opened the £1 billion Islands of Adventure, or IoA as the park is known, with the words: 'These are not just theme park rides, these are entertainment achievements beyond anything I have ever seen anywhere else in the world.'

And that's only the beginning. Here is the most complete and thrilling theme park on offer. Complete, because the park offers a genuinely rounded and consistent concept that has been carried through to the full extent of its designers' aims. And thrilling because it contains more T-rides per square metre than almost all the others combined.

It has a full range of attractions from the real adrenalin overloads to pure family entertainment. The shopping and eating opportunities are above average and it even *sounds* good – with some 40 pieces of original music, you can buy the CD of the theme park!

Okay, so they are not really islands (the six themed 'lands' form a chain around the central lagoon), but that's the only illusion. And you get a lot for your money here, unless you have extremely timid children or under 5s, in which case the *Magic Kingdom* is still your best bet. However, Seuss Landing will keep them amused for several hours while Camp Jurassic is a clever adventure playground for the 5–12s, but the rest of the park, with its seven 5-star thrill rides and other standout attractions, is primarily geared to kids of 8-plus, their parents and especially teenagers. There are five elements that look truly alarming (two of which produce moments of supreme terror), but don't be put off – they all deliver immense fun. There is also a great deal of spectator value here!

If there is one ride that sums up IoA, it is the Amazing Adventures of Spider-Man, the world's first moving 3-D simulator ride. It is sure to leave you in awe of its technological wizardry and imagination, and it is the only ride I have been on where people applaud at the end!

6

Night lights at Islands of Adventure

Islands of Adventure at a glance

Location	Off Exits 75A and 74B from I-4; Universal Boulevard and Kirkman Road
Size	110 acres (45ha) in six 'islands'
Hours	9am–7pm off peak; 9am–10pm high season (Washington's birthday, Easter, summer holidays, Thanksgiving, Christmas)
Admission	Under 3 free; 3–9 $44.95 (1-Day Ticket), $88.95 (2-Day Ticket), $101 (3-Day Ticket), $145.95 (4-Park FlexTicket), $179.95 (5-Park FlexTicket); adult (10+) $54.75, $99.95, $114, $179.95, $214.95; Universal Bonus Pass (5 consecutive days, online sales only) $94.95 (per person)
Parking	$8
Lockers	Yes; immediately to left through main gates; $7
Pushchairs	$10 and $16; next to locker hire
Wheelchairs	$8 and $40 (with photo ID as deposit); same location as pushchairs
Top Attractions	Amazing Adventures of Spider-Man, Dueling Dragons, Incredible Hulk Coaster, Jurassic Park River Adventure, Dudley Do-Right's Ripsaw Falls
Don't Miss	Eighth Voyage of Sindbad, Jurassic Park Discovery Centre, If I Ran the Zoo playground, Firework Finale (high season only), dining at Mythos
Hidden Costs	**Meals** — Burger, chips and coke $8.28 $29.94 (Confisco Grille) Kids' meal $5.95–6.99
	T-shirts — $17.95–25.95
	Souvenirs — $0.99–400
	Sundries — Caricature drawings $15–36

Private nursing facilities, an open area for feeding and resting (with high-chairs) and nappy-changing stations, can be found at the **Family Service Facility** at Guest Services (to the right inside the main gates), while ALL restrooms throughout the park are equipped with **nappy-changing** facilities. **First aid** is provided in Sindbad's Village in the Lost Continent, just across from Oasis Coolers.

Port of Entry

You arrive for IoA as you do for Universal Studios Florida® in the big multi-storey car parks ($8) off Universal Boulevard and either walk or ride the moving walkways into CityWalk, where you continue through to the entrance plaza (head for the 130-ft (40-metre) high Pharos Lighthouse).

Once through the gates, the

lockers, pushchair and wheelchair hire are all immediately to your left as the **Port of Entry** opens up before you. This elaborate 'village' consists of shops and eateries, so push straight on until you hit the main lagoon. Later in the day, you can return to check out the fully themed retail experience at places like the **IoA Trading Company** and **Ocean Trader Market**. Enjoy a snack from **Cinnabon** (cinnamon rolls and pastries) or the **Croissant Moon Bakery**, or chill out with a soft drink or ice cream from **Arctic Express**. Alternatively, sit down for lunch or dinner (great steak, pasta, burgers and salads) at **Confisco Grille** and grab a beverage at the **Backwater Bar** (Happy Hour 3–5pm). There is also a **Character Breakfast** at Confisco Grille (9–10.30am Thur–Sun) with Spider-Man and the Cat in the Hat at $15.95 for adults and $9.95 for children (call 407 224 4012 to book).

Above all, take a closer look at the wonderful architecture, which borrows from Middle East, Far East and African themes and uses bric-a-brac from all over the world.

At the end, you are faced with three choices and this is where you need a plan of campaign. There are five attractions where the queues build up quickly and remain that way. If you are here for the big thrill rides, turn left into Marvel Super-Hero Island and head straight to Spider-Man, then do Dr Doom's Fearfall and the Incredible Hulk Coaster, taking advantage of the Universal Express (UE) system.

Alternatively, dinosaur fans should head straight around the lagoon to Jurassic Park, where you should be able to do the River Adventure before the majority arrive. Once you are nice and wet, you might as well go to Toon Lagoon and get Ripsaw Falls and the Bilge-Rat Barges under your belt. Or, if you have younger children, turn right into the amazing multi-coloured world of Seuss Landing and enjoy the Cat In The Hat and other family-type rides prior to the crowd build-up.

Marvel Super-Hero Island

Taking the journey clockwise, you arrive first in the elaborate comic-book pages of the super-heroes. As with all the islands, the experience is total immersion. The amazing façades of this world surround you with an utterly credible alternative reality that is one of the park's triumphs – and that's before you have tried the rides.

The Incredible Hulk Coaster: roller-coasters don't come any more dramatic than this giant green edifice that soars over the lagoon, blasting 0–40mph (64kph) in 2 seconds, and reaches a top speed of 65mph (105kph). It looks awesome, sounds stunning and rides like a demon as you enter the gamma-ray world of Dr David Banner, aka the Incredible Hulk and zoom into a weightless inversion 100ft (30 metres) up!

Just watching is quite mind-boggling, and the after-effects are distinctly brain-scrambling. You will need to deposit ANY loose articles (sunglasses, cameras, coins, etc) in the lockers at the front of the building as the ride is guaranteed to shake everything out of your pockets. Crowds build up rapidly, but the queues seem to move quite quickly. Restrictions: 4ft 6in/137cm. TTTTT+ (UE).

BRIT TIP: At the Incredible Hulk Coaster keep left where the queue splits up and you will be in the right queue for the front car for an even more extreme Hulk experience.

6

PORT OF ENTRY
1 Ocean Trader Market
2 Confisco Grille

MARVEL SUPER-HERO ISLAND
3 Incredible Hulk Coaster
4 Doctor Doom's Fearfall
5 Café 4
6 Captain America Diner
7 The Amazing Adventures Of Spider-Man
8 Storm Force Accelatron

TOON LAGOON
9 Me Ship, The Olive
10 Popeye & Bluto's Bilge-Rat Barges
11 Dudley Do-Right's Ripsaw Falls
12 Comic Strip Café
13 Amphitheater
14 Toon Lagoon Beach Bash

JURASSIC PARK
15 Jurassic Park River Adventure
16 Camp Jurassic
17 Pteranodon Flyers
18 Triceratops Encounter (closed 2004)
19 Discovery Center
20 Thunder Falls Terrace

THE LOST CONTINENT
21 Dueling Dragons
22 The Flying Unicorn
23 The Eighth Voyage of Sindbad
24 Poseidon's Fury
25 The Enchanted Oak Tavern (and Alchemy Bar)
26 Mythos Restaurant
27 The Mystic Fountain

SEUSS LANDING
28 Caro-Seuss-el
29 One Fish, Two Fish, Red Fish, Blue Fish
30 The Cat In The Hat
31 If I Ran The Zoo
32 Circus McGurkus Café Stoo-pendous
33 Green Eggs and Ham Café
34 Guest Services

ISLANDS OF
ADVENTURE

The Incredible Hulk Coaster

6

Dr Doom's Fearfall: stand by for one of those two moments of supreme terror I mentioned earlier. This is where, O hapless visitor, you wander into the lair of the evil Dr Doom – arch-enemy of the Fantastic Four – and his sinister cohorts. His latest creation is the Fearfall, a device for sucking every ounce of fear out of his victims, and YOU are about to test it. Four riders at a time are strapped into chairs at the bottom of a 200-ft (60-metre) tower, the dry ice rolls, and whoooosh! Up you go at breakneck speed, only to plummet back seemingly even faster, with an amazing split second in between when you feel suspended in mid air. Summon up the courage to do this and I promise a truly astonishing (if brief!) experience. Queues are substantial during the main part of the day. Restrictions: 4ft 4in/132cm, and I reckon this is way too scary for under 10s. TTTTT+ (UE).

You exit Fearfall into the inevitable high-energy video arcade,

or you may prefer to calm your nerves with a meal at the Italian buffeteria **Café 4** (pizza, spaghetti, sandwiches and salads) or a burger at the **Captain America Diner**.

Dr Doom's Fearfall

For shopping, each of the rides has its own character merchandise for sale, while the **Comic Book Shop** and **The Marvel Alternative Shop** sell other souvenirs.

The Amazing Adventures of Spider-Man: just queuing is a novel experience as your visit to the *Daily Bugle*, home of ace reporter Peter Parker (or Spider-Man to his enemies), unravels into a reporting secondment in one of the 'Scoop' vehicles. Prepare for an audio-visual extravaganza as the combination of 3-D and motion simulator takes you into a battle between Spidey and arch-villains like Dr Octopus with his anti-gravity gun, culminating in a 400-ft (122-metre) sensory drop off a skyscraper as the contest literally hots up. There are numerous jaw-dropping special effects and you will need to ride at least twice to appreciate it all. Ride early on or leave it till late in the day – queues often top an hour. Restrictions: 3ft 4in/101cm. TTTTT+ (UE).

Storm Force Accelatron: this ride, aimed primarily at youngsters, puts you in the middle of a whirling, twirling battle between X-Men super-heroine Storm and arch-nemesis Magneto, with a range of special effects. It is basically an updated version of a fairground spinning-cup ride, but with some great twists (there is a 3-way rotation when the cars look set to collide at any moment!). TTT (TTTTT under 12s) (UE).

You can also meet the **Marvel Super-Heroes** for autographs several times a day.

Toon Lagoon

The thrills continue here with a watery theme and more comic-book elements as the (American) newspaper cartoon characters take a bow. Children will love the chance to play with the fountains, squirt pools and overflowing fire hydrants, plus a purpose-built playland **Me Ship, The Olive**, a 3-storey boat full of interactive fun and games, including slides, bells and water cannons (with which to squirt riders on the Bilge-Rat Barges below) in best Popeye style. TTTT (youngsters only).

Popeye and Bluto's Bilge-Rat Barges: every park seems to have a variation on the white-water raft ride, but none is as outrageously themed and downright wet as this. It's fast, bouncy and unpredictable, with water coming at you from every direction, a couple of sizeable drops and a whirl through the Octoplus Grotto that adds to the fun. If you don't want to get wet, don't ride, because there is no escaping the deluge here. This is also one of the top five rides for queues, but it's worth the wait. Restrictions: 4ft/122cm. TTTTT (UE).

> **BRIT TIP:** A change of clothes is often advisable after riding the Barges, unless it's so hot you need to cool down in a hurry. Bring a waterproof bag for your valuables.

Dudley Do-Right's Ripsaw Falls: Universal's designers have again taken an existing ride concept and given it a new spin, as this becomes the first flume ride to send its passengers through the water surface and out the other side at high speed. You join guileless mountie Dudley Do-Right in a bid to save girlfriend Nell from the evil Snidely Whiplash. The action builds to an 'explosive' showdown at the top of a 60-ft (18-metre) precipice that drops you through the roof of a ramshackle dynamite shack and into the lagoon below. Just awesome – as are the queues from mid-morning to late afternoon. Wet? You bet! Restrictions: 3ft 8in/111cm. TTTTT (UE) You can also try the Water Blasters (for 25c) on the bridge overlooking the final drop to get Ripsaw riders even wetter!

After drying off, take a walk along **Comic Strip Lane** to meet up with characters like Beetle Bailey, Hagar the Horrible, Krazy Kat and Blondie (some of whom will mean little to a British audience). You go past the **Amphitheater** on your left (home to seasonal entertainment like the amazing bike riders of **Mat Hoffman's Crazy Freakin' Stunt Show** and the skateboarding prowess of the **Tony Hawks Spectacular**). There is the usual array of character shopping outlets, like **Gasoline Alley** and **Toon Extra**, while you can grab a truly humongous sandwich at **Blondie's: Home of the Dagwood**, a trademark hamburger or hot dog at **Wimpy's**, sample the **Comic Strip Café** food court (Mexican, Chinese, American and Italian) or tuck into something colder at **Cathy's Ice Cream**. Watch out for appearances at the **Toon Lagoon Character Zone** for a meet-and-greet with various cartoon characters.

Jurassic Park

Leaving the comic-book lands behind, you travel back in time to the Cretaceous age and the credible make-believe dinosaur film world. Again, the immersive experience is first class and the lavish scenery will have you looking over your shoulder for dinos.

Jurassic Park River Adventure: the mood change from scenic splendour to hidden menace is startling as your journey into this magnificent waterborne realm brings you up close and personal with the most realistic dinosaurs created to date. Inevitably, your passage is diverted from the safe to the hazardous, and the danger increases as the 16-person raft climbs into the heights of the main building – with raptors loose everywhere. You are aware of something large lurking in the shadows – will you fall prey to the T-Rex, or will your boat take the 85-ft plunge to safety (with a good soaking for all concerned)? Queues usually move quite briskly here. Restrictions: 3ft 6in/106cm. TTTTT (UE). The more adventurous can then try the **Rock Climbing Wall** (just outside River Adventure) for an extra $5.

Camp Jurassic: more excellent kids' fare here with the mountainous jungle giving way to an 'active' volcano for youngsters to explore, climb over and slide down. Squirt guns and 'Spitter' dinosaurs add to the fun. TTTT (children first, but parents may explore).

Pteranodon Flyers: the slow-moving queues are a major turn-off, especially for a fairly average ride, which glides gently over much of Jurassic Park. It is designed mainly for kids, though, and the height range of 3–4ft 8in (91–142cm) requires anyone OVER the upper limit (usually 11 or older) to be accompanied by a child of the right height! TT (TTTT under 9s).

Triceratops Discovery Trail: this face-to-face meeting with the park's resident 4-ton, 24-ft (7-metre) long 'living' dinosaurs was closed in summer 2004, with the probability that it would not re-open.

Discovery Center: the designers' imagination have gone into overdrive here with terrific results. Interactive opportunities include creating a dinosaur through DNA sequencing, mixing your own DNA with a dino via a computer touchscreen, seeing through the eyes of various large reptiles and even watching a baby raptor hatch, plus a host of other fun hands-on exhibits. Air-conditioned, this is a good place

6

to visit in the hotter part of the day (open 11am–5pm). AAAA.

Best of the shopping is in the Discovery Center itself, while you can chow down at the **Burger Digs** there, visit the **Pizza Predattoria** or the **Watering Hole**, or go for the rotisserie chicken at the rustic **Thunder Falls Terrace** (counter service), which boasts a great view of the River Adventure.

The Lost Continent

This is one of my favourite lands for its theming, gentle contrast after Jurassic Park; superb attractions, great eating options and a few amusing 'extras'.

Dueling Dragons: there is no disguising the intense nature of this magnificent double coaster, with its 100-ft (30-metre) drop, multiple loops, twists and three near-miss encounters. There is a lot more, too, as the queuing area is a real mind-boggler – 1,060yd (969 metres), most of it along a dark tortuous path through the ancient castle that is the domain of the dragons, Fire and Ice. You are given their story while you wait, and Merlin arrives in time to cast a spell to ensure you survive. You choose which dragon to ride (the tracks differ slightly), and you can join an additional queue for the front seats. Unlike the Hulk, this is a suspended coaster, so your legs dangle free, and the initial drop is like going into free-fall (Supreme Terror moment Number 2!). Coaster aficionados reckon the best

Dueling Dragons

ride is in the back of the Ice (Blue) dragon, but it's all pretty amazing. Restrictions: 4ft 6in/137cm, and you will need to leave all your loose belongings in the lockers provided to the left of the entrance. TTTTT+ (UE).

The Flying Unicorn: this junior-sized coaster is aimed primarily at youngsters and features a wizard's workshop, hidden in an enchanted wood, which is the gateway to a magical journey inspired by the Unicorn. There are no big drops, but it delivers a surprisingly fast-paced whirl. TTTTT (for 6–12s) (UE).

The Eighth Voyage of Sindbad: this stunt and special effects show is another marvel, as much for its elaborate staging as its performance. Mythical adventurer Sindbad and sidekick Kabob (a name that's the cue for a truly awful pun) tackle evil witch Miseria in a bid to rescue Princess Amoura, and the action springs up in surprising places. There are several loud bangs which could scare young children, but otherwise it is good, family fun. At peak times, arrive 20 minutes before showtime, but everyone usually gets in. There is also a great post-show feature where the cast reappear for photos and autographs. TTT/AAAA (UE).

Poseidon's Fury: a walk-through show that puts its audience at the heart of the action as you journey in the company of a hapless young archaeologist (who ignores all the various 'warnings') beneath the sea to the lost temple of Poseidon. The route passes through an amazing

The Flying Unicorn

water vortex and your 'expedition' takes a wrong turn, awakening an ancient demon. Again, there is an element of suspense, so I won't reveal what happens, but the showdown between Poseidon and the demon is amazing. Queuing is tedious, but at least you are inside in summer. TTT (UE).

For an extra dollar or two, try the **Pitch and Skill Games**, or shop at **The Coin Mint** (coins forged and struck before your eyes), or visit **Historic Families** (explore the history of your family name and coat of arms in a medieval armoury), **Pearl Factory** (pick an oyster), and **The Dragon's Keep** (dragon apparel, games, and toys).

The Fire-Eater's Grill (sausages, chips and drinks) and **Frozen Desert** (sundaes and sodas) provide the snacks, while you mustn't miss the magnificent **Enchanted Oak Tavern** (in the dark, cool interior of a vast, sculpted oak tree) and **Alchemy Bar** for counter-service meals (hickory-smoked chicken, ribs and salads). The elaborate **Mythos Restaurant** provides the best dining in IoA, though. Not only is the food first class (seafood, grills, pizza and pasta), but the setting, inside a dormant volcano with streams, fountains and clever lighting, is an attraction in its own right.

Finally, watch out for **The Mystic Fountain** in Sindbad's Village – it has the ability to get you very wet when you least expect it!

Seuss Landing

There is not a straight line to be seen in this vivid 3-D working of the books of Dr Seuss. The characters may not mean much to those unfamiliar with the children's stories, but everyone can relate to the fun here (although queues build up quickly). There is so much clever detail packed into the area, from squirt ponds to beach scenes, it can be easy to miss something, so take your time.

Caro-Seuss-el: this intricate carousel ride on some of the Seuss characters – like cowfish, elephant-birds and dog-a-lopes – has rider-activated features that are a big hit with the young ones. AAA (AAAA under 5s) (UE).

One Fish, Two Fish, Red Fish, Blue Fish: another fairground ride is given a twist as you pilot these Seussian fish up and down according to the rhyme that plays while you ride. Get it wrong and you get squirted! More guaranteed fun for the younger kids. TTT (TTTTT under 5s) (UE).

The Cat In The Hat: prepare for a ride with a difference as you board these crazy 6-passenger 'couches' to meet the world's most adventurous cat and his friends, Thing One and Thing Two. You literally go for a spin through this storybook world, and it may be a bit too much for very young children. The slow-moving queues are a bit of a drag, so try to get here early or leave it until much later in the day (or use the UE system). AAAA/TTT) (UE).

If I Ran The Zoo: interactive playgrounds don't get much more fun for the pre-school brigade than with the 19 different Seuss character scenarios, most of which can get them quite wet. Hugely imaginative and great fun just to watch. TTTTT (young 'uns only).

If you have been captivated by the land, you can buy the book at **Dr Seuss' All The Books You Can Read Store**, or visit the **Mulberry**

The Cat in the Hat

Street Store for all the characters. **Snookers and Snookers Sweet Candy Cookers** is a super sweet shop, while snacks and drinks can be had at **Hop on Pop Ice Cream Shop** and **Moose Juice Goose Juice**. The **Circus McGurkus Café Stoo-pendous** is a mind-boggling cafeteria for fried chicken, lasagne, pizza and spaghetti, complete with clowns and pipe organs, while **Green Eggs and Ham Café** is a must for all Seuss fans to try the meal of the same name. (And the eggs ARE green!)

Halloween Horror Nights

Now being spread between both IoA and the Studios park is Universal's massively popular Halloween celebration throughout October each year. The Horror Nights have become a real trademark and add a wonderfully bloodthirsty touch. The parks are transformed with some highly imaginative re-creations and set-pieces from various horror movies, with a parade and shows that include live (terrifyingly so, in some cases) character interaction. The rides are also all open (anyone for The Hulk and Dueling Dragons in the dark?), adding more novelty to the park experience, but this over-the-top (and occasionally downright grisly) extravaganza is definitely not for kids. It goes down a treat with adults with the right sense of humour, though, and begins every evening at 7.30pm. It is a separately ticketed even and coss $58.31 per person (or $91.06 for a day and evening ticket) and it is highly advisable to book in advance on www.universalorlando.com.

And that, folks, is the full low-down on arguably the world's best theme park. Miss it at your peril.

ISLANDS OF ADVENTURE with children

Our guide to the rides which generally appeal to the different age groups:

Under 5s
Caro-Seuss-el, If I Ran The Zoo, The Cat In The Hat, One Fish, Two Fish, Red Fish, Blue Fish, Eighth Voyage of Sindbad, Jurassic Park Discovery Center, Me Ship, The Olive.

5–8s
All the above, plus Flying Unicorn, Pteranodon Flyers, Camp Jurassic, Amazing Adventures of Spider-Man, Storm Force Accelatron, and Jurassic Park River Adventure (with parental discretion).

9–12s
The Cat In The Hat, Flying Unicorn, Dueling Dragons, Eighth Voyage of Sindbad, Camp Jurassic, Pteranodon Flyers, Jurassic Park River Adventure, Jurassic Park Discovery Center, Dudley Do-Right's Ripsaw Falls, Popeye and Bluto's Bilge-Rat Barges, Amazing Adventures of Spider-Man, Dr Doom's Fearfall, Storm Force Accelatron, Incredible Hulk Coaster.

Over 12s
Dueling Dragons, Eighth Voyage of Sindbad, Jurassic Park River Adventure, Jurassic Park Discovery Center, Dudley Do-Right's Ripsaw Falls, Popeye and Bluto's Bilge-Rat Barges, Amazing Adventures of Spider-Man, Dr Doom's Fearfall, Storm Force Accelatron, Incredible Hulk Coaster.

SeaWorld Adventure Park

SeaWorld is firmly established as one of the most popular parks with British visitors for its more peaceful and naturalistic aspect, the change of pace it offers and the general lack of substantial queues. It is a big hit with families in particular, but also possesses some dramatic rides and imaginative attractions.

An extensive development programme by owners Anheuser-Busch has given it the big-park treatment in recent years, with an impressive 12-acre (5-ha) entrance plaza and rebranding as an Adventure Park, and it now demands a full day's attention. The opening, in summer 2000, of sister park Discovery Cove, an exotic tropical island with dolphin, stingray and snorkelling adventures, has added still more.

Happily, the queues and crowds have yet to reach the monster

SeaWorld Adventure Park at a glance

Location	7007 SeaWorld Drive, off Central Florida Parkway (Junctions 71 and 72 off I-4)
Size	More than 200 acres (81ha), incorporating 25 attractions
Hours	9am–7pm off peak; 9am–10pm high season (Easter, summer holidays, Thanksgiving, Christmas)
Admission	Under 3 free; 3–9 $43.95 (1-Day Ticket), $145.95 (4-Park Orlando FlexTicket), $179.95 (5-Park FlexTicket), $80.95 (SeaWorld/Busch Gardens Combo ticket); adult (10+) $53.95, $175.95, $214.95, $89.95
Parking	$8, $10 preferred
Lockers	Yes, by main entrance; $1.50 (also by Shamu's Emporium)
Pushchairs	$10 and $17 ($2 refundable; from Information Center, to left of main entrance)
Wheelchairs	$8 and $32; same location as pushchairs
Top Attractions	Shamu Stadium, Shark Encounter, Journey to Atlantis, Kraken, Wild Arctic, Fusion
Don't Miss	Mistify at The Waterfront (high season), Manatees: The Last Generation?, Behind-the-Scenes Tours, Odyssea show, dining at Sharks Underwater Grill
Hidden Costs	**Meals** — Burger, chips and coke $10.58 / 3-course lunch (Sharks Grill) $22 / Kids' meal $5.69
	T-shirts — $8.99–26.95
	Souvenirs — 69 cents–$6,599.95(!)
	Sundries — Face painting $8–15

6

1 Information
2 Wild Arctic
3 Shamu Stadium
4 Dine with Shamu
5 Sea Lion and Otter Stadium
6 Key West Dolphin Fest
7 Atlantis Bayside Stadium
8 The Waterfront
9 Seaport Theater
10 Nautilus Theatre – Odyssea
11 Clydesdale Hamlet
12 Anheuser-Busch Hospitality Center
13 Manatees: The Last Generation?
14 Pacific Point Preserve
15 Shamu's Happy Harbor
16 Shark Encounter
17 Sharks Underwater Grill
18 Tropical Reef
19 Penguin Encounter
20 Key West At SeaWorld
21 Stingray Lagoon
22 Turtle Point
23 Dolphin Cove
24 Journey To Atlantis
25 Kraken
26 Dolphin Nursery

SEA WORLD

MAIN ENTRANCE

proportions of elsewhere, so this is a park where you can still proceed at a relatively leisurely pace, see what you want without too much jostling and yet feel you have been superbly entertained (even if mealtimes do get crowded in the restaurants).

SeaWorld is also a good starting point if this is your first visit to Orlando as it will give you the hang of negotiating the vast areas, navigating by the various maps and learning to plan around the showtimes. This park has a strong educational and environmental message, plus three 1-hour, behind-the-scenes tours (book up as soon as you enter), which provide a greater insight into SeaWorld's marine conservation, rescue and research programme, as well as their entertainment resources.

The Polar Expedition provides a close-up of the penguin and polar bear environments; **Saving A Species** showcases the park's animal rescue and rehabilitation programme, with a chance to hand-feed exotic birds in the free-flight aviary ($1 of the tour fee also goes to the SeaWorld and Busch Gardens Conservation Fund); and **Predators!** offers a backstage view of Shark Encounter. You pay an extra $15 ($12 for 3–9s) for these tours, but they are worth it and, if you take one early on, it will increase your appreciation of the park. You can also save 10 per cent on single-day tickets if you book online at www.seaworld.com, where you print your own tickets and save waiting in a queue. Periodically, SeaWorld also offers a Second Day Free if you sign up before you leave the park – check at the information kiosk just inside the main entrance.

Three additional programmes provide unique insights and experiences of the park's activities. The 6-hour **Adventure Express Tour** offers visitors their own guide to tour the park, with back-door

access to the rides, reserved seating at shows and animal feeding opportunities (an extra $89 for adults, $79 for 3–9s; book up first thing at the Guided Tours counter or call 1-800 406 2244);

SeaWorld's Marine Mammal Keeper Experience is a new option for two visitors daily (aged 13 or above) to find out about the intensive care necessary to rehabilitate injured manatees, plus bottle-feed some of them, meet the seals and walruses and prepare meals for the beluga whales. It starts at 6.30am and lasts around 8 hours for $389/person (including lunch at the Shark Encounter, T-shirt, special book, souvenir photo and 7-day SeaWorld pass); finally, **Sharks Deep Dive** is the most original and captivating experience of all, a chance to suit up and dive in a specially constructed cage into the huge shark aquarium, and spend half an hour up close and personal with these deadly but amazing creatures. The 2-hour programme includes a full and educational induction into the world of sharks, what they are and what makes them tick (with important pointers like never wear jewellery in the sea – sharks can be attracted by the glitter, mistaking it for the reflection off fish scales). Then you are equipped for the dive with wetsuit (the water IS chilly), gloves, dive belt and either mask and snorkel or air tank (if you can show a scuba certification) for the reinforced steel cage, that glides slowly from one end of the 125-ft (38-metre) long tank to the other

6

The main entrance at SeaWorld

and back. Getting a fish-eye view of these creatures is truly an astounding experience, and you never tire of the underwater panorama (which includes waving to folks walking through the shark tunnel!). It is an eye-opening and addictive programme, but the best part is you get to wear a really cool wetsuit with 'Scubapro' on the front! It costs $150 for the scuba experience or $125 to snorkel (including 2-day park admission, a great souvenir T-shirt and shark book; participants must be at least 10 years old).

Location

SeaWorld is located off Central Florida Parkway, between I-4 (Exit 71 going east or 72 heading west) and I-Drive, and the parking fee is $8. It is still best to arrive a bit before the officially scheduled opening time so you're in good position to book one of the backstage tours or dash to one of the few attractions that does draw a crowd, like Journey to Atlantis.

The park covers in excess of 200 acres (81ha), with nine shows (ten with the nightly **Makahiki Luau** dinner show at the Seafire Inn which costs $42.95 for adults, $27.95 for 3–9s; nightly, times vary, call 407 351 3600 or book online), nine large-scale continuous viewing attractions and nine smaller ones, plus the eye-catching new **Waterfront area**, relaxing gardens, a kids' play area and a smart range of shops (a noticeable feature of Anheuser-Busch parks).

Their hire pushchairs (strollers) are also the most amusing – shaped like baby dolphins. Be warned, though, the size of the park will take you by surprise and requires a lot of to-ing and fro-ing to catch the various shows. Keep a close grip on your map and entertainment schedule and try to establish your own programme that gives you

regular breaks to sit and enjoy some of the quieter spots.

For something different, you can sign up for the free 35-minute Anheuser-Busch **Beer School** at the Hospitality Center for a glimpse into beer-making (and tasting!). New in 2004 was **Shamu and Crew Character Breakfast**, a hearty character meal with a cuddly Shamu and friends such as Penny Penguin and OP Otter. $14.95 adults, $9.95 ages 3–9, from 8.45–10.15am at the Seafire Inn Wed–Sun in peak season; advanced booking on 1-800 327 2420 or www.seaworld.com.

The main attractions

Wild Arctic: this interactive ride-and-view experience provides a realistic environment that is both educational and thrilling. It consists of an exciting simulator jet helicopter journey into the Arctic wilderness arriving at a clever research base, Base Station Wild Arctic, where the 'passengers' are disgorged into a frozen wonderland to meet polar bears, beluga whales and walruses.

This one is not to be missed (but not just after a Shamu show when the hordes descend). Restrictions: 3ft 6in/ 106cm. TTTT plus AAAAA. Those who don't want to ride can just walk through to the Base Station.

Shamu Stadium: SeaWorld has long since outgrown its tag as just the place to see killer whales, but the Shamu show is still one of its most

> BRIT TIP: Reader David Snelling from Cheshire, warns, 'Gentlemen, do not volunteer to participate in the Shamu display – it will be chauvinistically humiliating.'

amazing sights. Watch the killer whales and their trainers pull off some spectacular stunts, as well as hearing everything you ever wanted to know about these huge, majestic creatures.

There are two distinct shows, the more humorous *Shamu Adventure* during the day (25 minutes) and the louder *Shamu Rocks America* at night (20 minutes). Both are worth seeing, and are easily the most popular events so do make an effort to arrive early (especially as there is an amusing pre-show). Also, the first 14 rows get VERY wet (watch out for your cameras) – when a killer whale leaps into the air in front of you, it displaces a LOT of water on landing! AAAAA.

Dine with Shamu: this recent offering gives guests a VIP experience 'backstage' with the killer whales and their trainers. An all-you-can-eat buffet on a covered terrace right alongside the main whale pool gives you the chance to ask questions of the trainers and watch some of the training sessions. It is $32 for adults and $18 for children, it's offered every day (twice daily in high season, at 4.45 and 7.30pm) and it is highly advisable to book in advance on 407 351 3600 or online at www.seaworld.com. All guests can take advantage of the **Underwater Viewing** area.

Sea Lion and Otter Stadium: the venue for a wonderful show, *Clyde and Seamore Take Pirate Island*, it features the resident sea lions who, with their pals the otter and walrus (plus a couple of humans as the fall guys), put on a hilarious 25-minute performance of watery stunts and gags. Arrive early for some first-class audience mickey-taking from the resident pirate mimic. In high season, there is a second evening show, *Clyde and Seamore Present Sea Lions Tonight*, which offers more fun as the resident duo serve up a parody of other SeaWorld shows. AAAA.

Next door is the **Xtreme Zone**, a Trampoline Jump and Rock Climbing Wall, for an extra fee (reservations required).

Key West Dolphin Fest: more breathtaking marine mammal stunts and tricks in a funky beach theme, with the accent again on informing and educating in a gentle manner on the current state of research into dolphins and false killer whales and the dangers they face. The show lasts almost 20 minutes and is rarely over-subscribed, but once again the first few rows face a soaking. AAAA.

Atlantis Bayside Stadium: **Fusion**: shown twice daily, this high-energy 'surf, sand and sky' show features jet-ski stunts, 5-tiered kites, high-diving, song, dance and water-skiing, plus the wonderful frisbee-catching dog! Especially geared to a youth audience but with guaranteed family appeal, it is an eye-catching 20 minutes of music, fun and watery tricks. There is also an imaginative pre-show aimed at children, with hula-hoops, a remote control surfer, giant beach balls and kites.

6

BRIT TIP: The weather may occasionally mean the outdoor entertainment is cancelled, but don't let it stop you enjoying yourself. Cheap, plastic ponchos will appear in the shops at the first sign of rain!

The Waterfront: not so much an attraction as a new 5-acre (2-ha) 'village' at the heart of SeaWorld, offering fine dining, smart shops, several shows and street entertainment. This area forms an arc around part of the central lake, is themed like an eclectic harbour and offers two excellent eateries (the **Seafire Inn**, for gourmet steak burgers, salads and coconut-fried shrimp, and the superb **Voyagers** for wood-fired pizzas, pasta and sandwiches, plus a low-carb option; not cheap but quite delicious), two snack bars (**Café de Mar** for pastries, coffees and soft drinks, and **Freezas** for frozen yoghurt and other drinks), four interlinked boutique-style shops (with some stylish souvenirs – check out **Allura's Treasure Trove** and **Under The Sun**) and some highly amusing street performers. Keep an eye out for the amazing percussive pots-and-pans rhythms of the **Groove Chefs**.

New additions in 2004 were the unique **The Oyster's Secret** shop (with resident pearl divers who can be viewed underwater as they collect the pearl-bearing oysters on request, to be incorporated into jewellery pieces by the shop's artisans) and **The Spice Mill**, a cafeteria-style restaurant offering some succulent (and spicy) variations on soups, sandwiches, grilled chicken and jambalaya.

> BRIT TIP: Grab an evening meal at The Spice Mill, head out on to their open-air terrace and you have one of the best seats in the house for the Mistify nightly finale.

Finally, in best fortress style, **The Tower** is the centrepiece of The Waterfront, with a 400-ft (122-metre) landmark offering slowly rotating rides (at an extra $3) up for a bird's eye view of the park. Here you will also find the **SandBar**, a lovely water's edge cocktail bar with live musicians throughout the day, and snacks like sushi, cheese plates, fresh fruit and shrimp cocktail. It's the perfect place to watch the sun go down (and the fireworks go up!). Kids can play in the two **squirt fountains** (remember those

Odyssea

swimming costumes) and the whole scene is characterised by lovely landscaping and even some ocean sound effects. AAAA.

Seaport Theater: just inside the Waterfront, this air-conditioned haven (during the hottest part of the day) hosts the *Pets Ahoy!* show, a genuinely cute 25-minute giggle featuring the unlikely talents of a menagerie of dogs, cats, birds, rats, pot-bellied pigs and others, the majority of which have been rescued from animal shelters. AAA.

Nautilus Theater – Odyssea: fans of the old Cirque de la Mer show here will be sad to know it has gone – but happy it has been replaced by something even smarter and equally as captivating. Odyssea is a 30-minute fantasy featuring some mind-boggling acrobatic feats, engaging live music, clever lighting and a host of in-theatre special effects. The show tells the spectacular, if stylised, story of a seaman who falls into the ocean and descends through various levels to the sea bed, encountering an assortment of creatures along the way. Think of a watery version of Cirque du Soleil® and you are not far wrong. When it's hot or wet, this is a great place to be! AAAAA.

The Nautilus Theater is also home to various weekend events through the year, notably **Jack Hanna's Animal Adventure**, the **Bud and BBQ** Country Music Festival as well as the **Viva La Musica** Latin weekends.

Clydesdale Hamlet: these massive stables are home to the Anheuser-Busch trademark Clydesdale dray horses. They make great photo opportunities when fully harnessed and there is a life-size statue outside, which also makes a good backdrop. The Hitching Barn shows how the horses are prepared for the twice-daily parade, including washing, grooming and braiding. AA.

Anheuser-Busch Hospitality Center: adjoining Clydesdale Hamlet, this offers the chance to sample the company's most famous product, beer (in fact, the world's Number 1 bottled beer, Budweiser, and its cousins). Sadly, it's only three small samples per visitor aged 21 or over, but you can enjoy it sitting outside on the terrace, which provides a pleasant break from all the hustle and bustle. AAA. You'll also find the **Beer School** here, while **The Deli** restaurant is an attractive proposition, serving fresh-carved turkey and beef, German sausage, sauerkraut, fresh-baked breads and delicious desserts.

Manatees: The Last Generation?: here is an exhibit that really tugs at your heartstrings as you learn of the tragic plight of this endangered species of Florida's waterways. Watch these lazy-looking creatures (half walrus, half hippo?) lounge around their man-made lagoon from above, then walk down the ramp to the special circular theatre where a 5-minute film with amazing 3-D effects will reveal the full dangers facing the harmless manatee. Then pass into the underwater viewing section, with hands-on TV screens offering more information. It's a magnificent exhibit and often provokes a few tears at the animals' uncertain future. It is also right behind Key West Dolphin Fest, so DON'T go just after one of their shows. AAAA.

Pacific Point Preserve: another SeaWorld first, this carefully re-created rocky coast habitat shows the park's seals and sea lions at their most natural. A hidden wave-making machine adds the perfect touch, while park attendants provide informative talks at regular intervals. You can also buy small packs of smelt to throw to the ever-hungry mammals. AAAA.

Shamu's Happy Harbor: 3 acres (1.2ha) of brilliantly designed adventure playground await youngsters of all ages here. Activities include a 4-storey net climb, two tented 'ball rooms' to wade through, and a giant 'trampoline' tent. It does get busy in mid-afternoon, but the kids love to love it at any time. Next door is the clever **Shamu Splash Attack** (water-balloon catapults), the inevitable video arcade and some funfair games for a few extra dollars. TTTT.

Shark Encounter: the world's largest collection of dangerous sea

The Waterfront at SeaWorld

creatures can be found here, brought dramatically to life by the walk-through tubes that surround you with more than 50 prowling sharks (including sand tigers, black tips, nurse sharks and sand bars), sawfish, tropical fish and gigantic groupers. It's an eerie experience (and perhaps too intense for young children), but brilliantly presented and, again, highly informative. You can also watch the intrepid souls in the Sharks Deep Dive cage as it traverses the aquarium (see page 165). Queues do tend to build up here at peak times, though. AAAA or TTTT.

Once you have ridden the moving walkway, head for the best restaurant in the park for another close-up at the **Sharks Underwater Grill**. Not only do you have an amazing backdrop for your meal in a clever, subterranean environment (check out the incredible bar which is a mini-aquarium!), but the upscale, full-service restaurant features a hugely appetising 'Floribbean'-style menu, blending both local and spicy Caribbean fare. The emphasis is on seafood – and wonderful creations with scallops, jumbo shrimp (king prawns), grouper and sea bass – plus pasta, oak-grilled filet mignon, chicken and pork, and a dessert menu to die for. Some refreshing (non-alcoholic) cocktails and menus for under 10s and teens complete the picture – it is a real treat on a hot day. Open from 11am to park

BRIT TIP: If the main adult portions look too big at the Sharks Underwater Grill – and they are pretty hefty – you can order from the Young Adults menu for smaller portions of four regular dishes. Check out the kids' dessert menu, too.

closing (VERY busy at lunch but quieter in late afternoon), it is advisable to book at the restaurant itself as soon as you arrive or on 407 351 3600 in advance. A 3-course meal will cost around $31.

Tropical Reef: after the dramas and amusements elsewhere, this may seem a little tame, but go and see it. Literally thousands of colourful fish inhabit the centrepiece 160,000-gallon (728,000-litre) tropical reef, while smaller tanks show off other intriguing species. AAA.

Penguin Encounter: always a hit with families (and one of the more crowded exhibits), the eternally comical penguins are brilliantly presented in this chilly showpiece. You have the choice of going close and using the moving walkway along the display or standing back and watching from a non-moving position. Both afford fascinating views of the 17 different species under water. Feeding time is the most popular time, so arrive early if you want a prime spot. There is also a question-and-answer session at 2pm every day – the winner gets to pet a penguin. AAAA.

Key West at SeaWorld: a whole collection of exhibits are grouped together here under the clever Key West theme. **Stingray Lagoon**, where you can feed and touch fully grown rays, includes a nursery for newborn rays, while the park's rescued and rehabilitated sea turtles can be seen at **Turtle Point**, which helps to explain the dangers to these saltwater reptiles. The centrepiece, the 2.1-acre (0.8-ha) **Dolphin Cove**, is a more spectacular, naturalistic development and offers the chance to get close enough to feed this community of frisky Atlantic bottlenose dolphins. There is an excellent underwater viewing area to the lagoon, which features waves, a sandy beach and a coral reef. Park photographers also patrol here, ready to snap you at play with the

BRIT TIP: Touching the rays and dolphins is an experience at SeaWorld you won't easily forget.

dolphins, and a 2-photo package (in a 5 × 7in/127 × 178mm stand-up frame) will set you back $22.99.

The whole area is designed in the tropical flavour of America's southern-most city, Key West, with beach huts, lifeguard chairs, dune buggies, themed shops and other eclectic lookalike elements, but it also underlines the environmental message of conservation through interactive graphics and video displays adjacent to the animal habitats, and children of all ages will find it a fun, educational experience. The selection of shops are above average, too. AAAA.

Journey to Atlantis: unique in Orlando, this terrific 'water-coaster' gave SeaWorld its first 5-star thrill attraction in 1998. The combination of extra elements here ultimately makes it a one-off, with some illusionary special effects giving way to a high-speed water ride that becomes a runaway roller-coaster. The 'discovery' of Atlantis in your 8-passenger 'fishing boat' starts gently through the lost city. But evil spirit Allura takes over and riders plunge into a dash through Atlantis, dodging gushing fountains and water cannons, with hundreds of dazzling holographic and laser-generated illusions, before the heart-stopping 60-ft (18-metre) drop, which is merely the entry to the roller-coaster finale back in the candle-filled catacombs. An amazing creation. Once again, be prepared to get soaked in the course of the ride, which is great in summer but not so clever first thing in the morning in winter. Restrictions: 3ft 6in/106cm. TTTTT. Riders exit into the **Sea Aquarium Gallery**, a combination

gift shop and huge aquarium full of sharks, stingrays and tropical fish (don't forget to look up).

Kraken: this member of the coaster family is the longest, fastest and highest in central Florida. Based on the mythical sea monster, Kraken is an innovative pedestal ride (you are effectively sitting in a chair without a floor – pretty exposed!) that plunges an initial 144ft (44 metres), hits 65mph (105kph), dives underground three times, adds seven inversions (including a vertical loop, a diving loop, a zero-gravity roll and a cobra roll) and a flat spin before riders escape the beast's lair. The ride from the front row, especially down that opening drop at an angle best described as ludicrous, is positively blood-curdling, and sitting in the rear seats is pretty amazing, too. Restrictions: 4ft 6in/137cm. TTTTT+.

SeaWorld specials

For extra fun, there is live entertainment daily around the Key West attractions, including the trademark **Sunset Celebration** street party. Throughout the summer high season, when the park is open as late as 10pm, there are often other live elements, leading up to the big **Mistify** finale on the Waterfront lagoon. This is a wonderful new piece of pyrotechnics and special effects, invoking giant sea creatures with dazzling laser images. The show mixes towering fountains (up to 100ft/30 metres high), mist sprays, flames and some unique fireworks (including some that burn under water), all with an epic soundtrack. By far the largest and most spectacular evening finale SeaWorld has yet produced, it doesn't quite rival Disney's Fantasmic! and IllumiNations, but it should not be missed.

As well as all the main set-pieces, several smaller ones can be equally

6

rewarding for their more personal touch. The **Dolphin Nursery** provides more close encounters with the park's (younger) dolphins, and there are the **Flamingo**, **Pelican** and **Spoonbill Exhibits**. The **Tide Pool** is another hands-on experience with starfish and sea anemones.

The flamingo pedal-boats, which rent for $6 per half-hour (for two people) in one corner of the lagoon, are also fun to do. Look out, too, for the best photo opportunity of the day as a big, cuddly Shamu will greet the kids just inside the main entrance.

Shamu the killer whale

You can choose to eat from a further ten different places, with the best of the bunch being the **Dockside Cafe** (barbecued, mesquite-grilled chicken and beef, chicken fingers and hot dogs), **The Deli** (in the Anheuser-Busch Hospitality Center, see page169), **Mama's Kitchen**, (sandwiches, salads, chilli, chicken fingers), **Smoky Creek Grill** (a Texas-style barbecue) and **Mango Joe's Café** (delicious grilled fajitas, speciality salads and sandwiches). As in the other main parks, try to eat before midday or after 2.30pm for a crowd-free lunch, and before 5.30pm if you want a leisurely dinner.

Your wallet will also be in severe peril in any of the 24 additional shops and photo kiosks. Make sure you visit at least **Shamu's Emporium** (for a full range of cuddly Shamu toys), **Manatee Cove** (more cuddlies), **Friends of the Wild** (dedicated to animal lovers everywhere) and **The Label Stable** for Anheuser-Busch gifts and merchandise (some of it extremely smart). Your purchases can be forwarded to Package Pick-up in Shamu's Emporium, to collect on your way out, provided you give them at least hour.

Finally, non-drivers will probably want to make a note of the special daily bus service from SeaWorld (and other points on I-Drive) direct to sister park Busch Gardens (see page 176), which you can book at Guest Relations.

SEAWORLD with children

The following gives a general idea of the appeal of SeaWorld's attractions to the different age groups.

Under 5s
Shamu Adventure Show, Key West Dolphin Fest, Clyde and Seamore Take Treasure Island, Pets Ahoy!, Wild Arctic (without the ride), Manatees: Last Generation?, Penguin Encounter, Tropical Reef, Pacific Point Preserve, Clydesdale Hamlet, Odyssea, Waterfront entertainment.

5–8s
All the above, plus Wild Arctic (with the ride), Odyssea, Mistify, Shark Encounter, Shamu's Happy Harbor.

9–12s
All the above, plus Kraken.

Over 12s
Kraken, Journey to Atlantis, Wild Arctic, Shark Encounter, Shamu Adventure Show, Clyde and Seamore Take Treasure Island, Odyssea, Mistify.

Discovery Cove

Fancy a day in your own tropical paradise, with the chance to swim with dolphins, encounter sharks, snorkel in a coral reef and dive through a waterfall into a tropical aviary? Well, Discovery Cove is all that and more. The only drawback is the price. This mini theme park comes at a premium because it is restricted to just 1,000 guests a day, creating an exclusive experience, and the admission fee reflects that. The flat rate entrance fee is $229 ($249 in the peak season) and the only reduction is $100 off for those not wishing to do the Dolphin Swim and for 3–5s; under 3s are free.

The **Trainer For A Day** programme adds an exciting opportunity to go behind the scenes into the training, feeding, health and welfare of the park's animals. You get to work with the experts as they interact with dolphins, birds, sharks, stingrays and tropical fish. The experience includes a behavioural training class, souvenir shirt, dolphin book and waterproof camera, and participants must be aged at least 6 and in good health. You need to book well ahead on 020 8668 4218 or online at www.discoverycove.com. The cost? A healthy $399 (increasing to $419 in 2005), including the main entrance fee, plus tax.

So, just what do you get for your money at Discovery Cove? Well, as you would expect, it is a supremely personal park. You check in as you would for a hotel rather than a theme park (the entrance lobby is wonderfully impressive), and you have a guide to take you in and get you set for the day.

All your basic requirements – towel, mask, snorkel, wet-jacket, lockers, beach umbrellas and lunch – are included in the price, and the level of service is excellent. A valuable 7-day pass for your choice of SeaWorld or Busch Gardens is also included. The lunch provided at the buffet-style **Laguna Grill** is pretty good, but you have to pay for any further snacks and drinks around the park, while the gift shop and photographic prices reflect the entrance fee – expensive.

Location

Situated on Central Florida Parkway, almost opposite the SeaWorld entrance (open year-round from 8.30am–5.30pm. Parking is free), the whole of the 30-acre (12-ha) park is magnificently landscaped, with lovely thatched buildings, palm trees, lush vegetation, brilliant white-sand beaches, gurgling streams and even hammocks. The overall effect is as if you have been transported to some Caribbean or South Sea oasis.

The usual tourist hurly-burly is left far behind. The 5-star resort feel is enhanced by a high staff-to-guest ratio (the lifeguards seem to outnumber guests at times). There should be no queues for anything (but the buffet-service restaurant may get busy at lunch) and the highlight dolphin encounter is world class. The ultimate effect is total relaxation, a veritable holiday from your holiday.

6

Snorkelling in Coral Reef

Visitors with disabilities are well catered for, with special wheelchairs that can move across the sand and into shallow water, and an area of the Dolphin Lagoon to allow those who can't enter the water still to be able to touch the dolphins.

The essence of a day here involves close encounters with all the animals – although not too close in the case of the sharks – plus a strong underlying conservation message.

The main attractions

Coral Reef: a huge rocky pool, filled with several thousand tropical fish, offers the most amazing man-made snorkelling experience you'll find. The water teems with silverjacks, angelfish and yellowtail snapper and, even if the 'coral' is hand-painted concrete, it is a clever environment. Some of the larger stingrays inhabiting the bottom of the reef are fascinating to watch. Swimmers also come within inches of sharks and barracuda – all safely behind a Plexiglass partition – which adds another novel element. If you stay reasonably still in the water, many of the tropical fish will crowd around to inspect their latest pool-mate! AAAA.

Ray Lagoon: another carefully sculpted pool provides the opportunity to paddle among several dozen southern and cownose rays, quite harmless, but with just a hint of menace to the fascination. AAAA.

Tropical River: this 800-yd (732-metre) circuit of gently flowing bath-warm water is a variation on the lazy river feature of many of the water parks, although with a far more naturalistic aspect and none of the inner tubes. It is primarily designed for snorkellers and features rocky lagoons, caves, a beach section, a tropical forest segment, sunken ruins and an underwater viewing window into the Coral Reef.

The lack of fish makes it seem a bit bland after the Tropical Reef and Ray Lagoon, but again, it is as much about relaxing as having fun. AAA.

Aviary: this recently enhanced 3-part adventure is both an area in its own right and a 40-yd (37-metre) section of the Tropical River. You can walk in off the beach or swim in through one of the two impressive waterfalls which guard each end, a beautifully scenic touch and fun for snorkellers. Some 200 tropical birds (plus tiny Muntjac deer) fill the main enclosure and, if you stand still for a while, they are likely to use you for a perch. An expansion in 2002 effectively doubled the size of the aviary by adding a small-bird sanctuary – full of finches, honeycreepers and hummingbirds – and a large-bird enclosure, featuring toucans and the red-legged seriema. Guides will introduce you to specific birds (which you can hand-feed) and tell you about their habits, habitats and conservation issues. AAAAA.

Dolphin Swim: the headline attraction at Discovery Cove is the encounter with the park's Atlantic bottlenose dolphin community. A 20-minute orientation programme in one of the four thatched beach cabanas, with a film and instruction from two of the animal trainers, sets you up for this deeply thrilling experience. Groups of six to eight go into the huge lagoon with careful supervision from the trainers and, starting off by standing in the waist-deep (slightly chilly) water as one of the dolphins comes to you, you gradually become more adventurous until you are swimming next to them. Timid swimmers are catered for and there are life-jackets for those who need them. The lagoon is up to 12ft (3.6 metres) deep so there is a real feeling of being in the dolphins' environment.

You will learn how trainers use hand signals and positive reinforcement to communicate with them, and get the chance to stroke, feed and even kiss (!) your dolphin. The encounter comes to a dramatic conclusion as you are towed back to shore by one of these awesome animals, which can weigh from 300–600lb (136–272kg), although the activities vary according to the dolphins' own attention span. You spend around 30 minutes in the water and it is totally unforgettable. Under 6s are not allowed into the dolphin lagoon. TTTTT+.

Truly, Discovery Park is an attraction with huge style and appeal – not to mention the stuff of which cherished memories are made – but it will take a big bite from your holiday budget. A family of four, with children of 6 or older who want to do the Dolphin Swim, could be paying up to $1,055 (including tax) for the day. Even with the 7-day SeaWorld pass included, it is a massive outlay. The charge for 3- to 5-year-olds is also pretty steep, in my opinion. Your sundries are likely to add up, too. An 8 x 10 or two 5 x 7 photos are $21.29. Then there are various photo packages at $29.99, $62.99 and $99.99, while the video of your experience (which includes 30 minutes of highlights of the whole park) costs $59.99. A CD with five images is $100, ten images are $150 and 20 images are $200.

The weather can get distinctly cool in the winter months, but the water is always heated (apart from the dolphin lagoon, which remains at 72°F/22°C) and full wetsuits are also available to keep out the chill. Their attention to detail is superb and guest satisfaction ratings remain extremely high (it is hugely popular with British visitors – up to 40 per cent of the daily attendance at times). However, if any element falls below expectations, it is worth bringing it to the attention of a manager as they are always keen to rectify any oversights.

Special occasions

For that extra special birthday, anniversary or for somewhere completely different to propose marriage, Discovery Cove has a range of options which involve extra dolphin interaction and private beach cabanas. The **Platinum Ring** (at an extra $474.95 per couple) includes sharing your special moment with a dolphin, who delivers a specialised message buoy, a private tent on the beach, Dom Perignon champagne, a dozen roses, chocolate-dipped strawberries, disposable waterproof camera, keepsake photo and frame, and a video of the occasion. The **Golden Ring Package** (at $224.95 per couple) and **Sweetheart Package** ($149.95), are scaled-down versions of the same. The **Birthday Package** ($74.95) includes dolphin activity, cake, photo and souvenir buoy, plus T-shirt and video, and a **Premium** version ($174.95) offers a T-shirt and video of the occasion. For more details, visit www.discoverycove.com. You can book online – preferably at least 3 months in advance at busy times – or call 407 370 1280 in the US.

NEW in 2004, when it was being tested for possible regular summer fare, was a **Twilight Discovery** programme – the chance to visit the park, be wined and dined in style, swim in the Coral Reef pool and enjoy a shallow-water dolphin encounter. The emphasis is on a refined tropical party experience, for just 100 guests a night from 7 to 11pm. The exclusive feel is enhanced by valet parking, a festive welcome reception, tropical drinks and live, Caribbean-style music, desserts on the beach and the special dolphin encounter. It includes a 7-day pass to either SeaWorld or Busch Gardens and a photo. The cost is still a whopping $249 but it's another unique opportunity.

6

Busch Gardens

When is a zoo not a zoo? When it is also a theme park like the 335-acre (136-ha) Busch Gardens in Tampa.

Busch Gardens, the second big Anheuser-Busch park in the area, started life as a mini-menagerie for the wildlife collection of the brewery-owning Busch family (Budweiser). In 1959, they opened a small, tropical-themed hospitality centre next to the brewery and now it is a major, multi-faceted family attraction, the biggest on Florida's west coast and a little more than an hour from Orlando.

It is rated among the top four zoos in America, with more than 2,700 animals representing more than 320 species of mammals, birds, reptiles, amphibians and spiders. But that's just the start. It boasts a safari-like section of Africa spread over 65 acres (26ha) of grassy veldt, with special tours to hand-feed some of the animals.

Interspersed among the animals are more than 20 bona fide theme park rides, including the mind-numbing roller-coasters **Kumba**, **Montu** and **Gwazi**, which guarantee fun for coaster addicts, plus the amusing and novel **Akbar's Adventure Tours**, yet another in the series of simulator rides; animal shows, comedians, musicians, strolling players and *KaTonga*, a new family show extravaganza in the impressive Moroccan Palace Theater, complete the picture. A new **Stanleyville Coaster** is being built for summer 2005, with a

substantial vertical drop (like Alton Towers Oblivion) and a water splash-down, but no other details were available as we went to press.

The overall theme is Africa, hence the park is subdivided into areas such as Nairobi and Congo, and the dining and shopping facilities are equal to most of the other theme parks. It doesn't quite have the pizzazz of an *Epcot* or Universal, and the staff are a bit more laid back. In a way, it is like the big brother of the Chessington World of Adventures in Surrey, although admittedly on a much grander scale (and in a better climate). But it has guaranteed, 5-star family appeal, especially with its selection of rides just for kids, and it is a big hit with the Brits.

Busch is the only park to offer 1-Day Tickets with a **Rain Guarantee**, which means if you get rained out on your visit, you can return FREE within 7 days.

Location

Busch Gardens is the hardest place to locate on the sketchy local maps and the signposting is not as sharp as it could be but, from Orlando, the directions are pretty simple. Head west on I-4 for almost an hour (it is 55 miles/88km from I-4's junction with Highway 192) until you hit the intersecting motorway I-75. Take I-75 north for 3½ miles (5.5km) until you see the exit for Fowler Avenue (Highway 582). Continue west on Fowler for another 3½ miles (5.5km), then just past the University of South Florida on your right, turn LEFT into McKinley Drive. A mile (1.6km) down McKinley Drive, Busch Gardens' car park will be on your left, where it costs $7 to park.

Those without a car can use the daily **Busch Gardens Shuttle Express** bus service, which makes

KaTonga

MOROCCO
1 Zagora Café
2 Marrakesh Theater
3 Moroccan Palace Theater
CROWN COLONY
4 Skyride Station
5 Clydesdale Hamlet
6 Crown Colony Restaurant and Hospitality Center
SERENGETI PLAIN
7 Edge of Africa
NAIROBI
8 Myombe Reserve
9 Rhino Rally
TIMBUKTU
10 Scorpion
11 The Phoenix
12 Sandstorm
13 Crazy Camel
14 Kiddie Rides
15 Carousel Caravan
16 Desert Grill
17 RL Stine's Haunted Lighthouse
CONGO
18 Kumba
19 Congo River Rapids
20 Ubanga-Banga Bumper Cars
21 Python
STANLEYVILLE
22 Stanley Falls Log Flume
23 Tanganyika Tidal Wave
24 Stanleyville Theater
25 Stanleyville Coaster (2005)
LAND OF THE DRAGONS
26 Dragon's Tale Theater
BIRD GARDENS
27 Bird Show Theater
28 Lory Landing
29 Aviary
30 Hospitality House/Beer School
31 Gwazi
EGYPT
32 Montu
33 Akbar's Adventure Tours
34 Tut's Tomb
35 Train Stations

BUSCH GARDENS

6

Busch Gardens at a glance

Location	Busch Blvd, Tampa; 75–90 minutes' drive from Orlando
Size	335 acres (136ha) in 11 themed areas
Hours	9 or 10am–6 or 7pm off peak; 9am–8pm Easter, Thanksgiving, Christmas; 9 or 9.30am–10.30pm summer
Admission	Under 3 free; 3–9 $44.95 (1-Day Ticket), $80.95 (Busch/SeaWorld Combo ticket), $179.95 (5-Park FlexTicket, including Universal Studios, SeaWorld and Wet 'n Wild); adults (10+) $53.95, 89.95, 214.95
Parking	$7
Lockers	Yes; in Morocco, Congo, Egypt and Stanleyville; $1
Pushchairs	$11 and $15 ($2 gift card refund; in Morocco)
Wheelchairs	$9 ($2 gift card refund) and $32, with pushchairs
Top Attractions	Rhino Rally, Gwazi, Kumba, Montu, Congo River Rapids, Tanganyika Tidal Wave, RL Stine's Haunted Lighthouse
Don't Miss	KaTonga, Myombe Reserve, Edge of Africa, Elephant Wash, Mystic Sheikhs band

Hidden Costs	**Meals**	Burger, chips and Pepsi $8.78 3-course meal $16–23; family-style diner $10.95 and $5.95 (Crown Colony House) Kids' meal $3.99 ($5.49 with souvenir bucket)
	T-shirts	$9.79–24.99
	Souvenirs	99 cents–$1,950
	Sundries	Ride photos $8.99

several round trips a day from Orlando at $5 a time (free if you have a 5-Park FlexTicket). You board the Shuttle at SeaWorld, The Mercado, Orlando Premium Outlets, Universal Studios or Old Town in Kissimmee and pick-up times range from 8–10.15am, returning at 6 or 7pm. Book at the **Guest Services** window at SeaWorld or call 1-800 221 1339.

You may think you have left the crowds behind in Orlando but, unfortunately, in high season you'd be wrong. It is still advisable to be here in time for opening, if only to be first in line to ride the amazing Rhino Rally or the dazzling roller-coasters, which all draw queues of up to an hour. The Congo River Rapids, Stanley Falls Log Flume ride and Tanganyika Tidal Wave (all opportunities to get wet!) are also prime rides. The relatively recent (summer 2003) **RL Stine's Haunted Lighthouse**, a 3-D film show, is also highly popular.

The queues do take longer to build up here, though, so for the first few hours at least you can enjoy a relatively crowd-free experience.

On your right as you approach the

main gates is the **Tours Centre** window, and you should go there straight away (or book in advance on 813 984 4043 or e-mail BGT.VIPTours@Buschgardens.com) if you'd like to do their wonderful Serengeti Safari or one of their other Adventure Tours (see page 185). Busch Gardens is divided into 11 main sections, with the major rides all being a bit of a hike from the main entrance.

Rhino Rally, which opened in summer 2001, is one of the prime attractions, so I would definitely head here first (especially as the animals are more visible early in the day). Bear right through Morocco, turn left into Nairobi, pass the train station and the Rally entrance is opposite the elephant habitat. **Gwazi**, the fabulous wooden double-coaster, is another to draw a crowd relatively quickly, so, if you are tempted by this first, bear left through Morocco past the Zagora Café and you will soon arrive in its own purpose-built area. Then go through Stanleyville to Congo for **Kumba**, and retrace your steps to do **Congo River Rapids**, the **Python** and the other two water rides. Alternatively, turn right through the main entrance and visit Egypt for **Montu** and **Akbar's**. Here is the full park layout going anti-clockwise.

Morocco

Coming through the main gates brings you first into **Morocco**, home of all the main guest services and a lot of the best shops. *Epcot's* Moroccan pavilion sets the scene rather better, but the architecture is still impressive and this version won't overtax your wallet quite as much as Disney does! For a quick meal try the **Zagora Café**, especially at breakfast when the marching, dancing, 8-piece brass band **Mystic Sheikhs** swings into action to entertain the early crowds.

Alternatively, the wonderfully enticing **Sultan's Sweets** serves coffee and pastries. Watch out, too, for the strolling Men of Note, a scintillating 4-piece *a cappella* group, and the costumed characters like TJ the Tiger and Hilda Hippo.

Turning the corner brings you to the first animal encounter, the alligator pen. Morocco is also home to two of the park's biggest shows. The **Marrakesh Theater** offers the 25-minute *Moroccan Roll* song and dance show, with live musicians, top-notch singers and energetic dancers all in an amusing pastiche of pop and rock with a desert theme (hence songs like *Midnight At The Oasis* and *Rock The Casbah*). AAA.

Moroccan Palace Theater: **KaTonga**: brand new in 2004 was this lavish Broadway-style spectacle, featuring an 18-strong cast of singers, dancers, acrobats and puppeteers. Sub-titled *Musical Tales from the Jungle*, this 35-minute theatrical extravaganza celebrates African animal folklore with an ingenious mix of live actor presentation, highlighted by the award-winning larger-than-life puppets of Michael Curry (who helped to create Disney's *The Lion King* show in London and New York). With 57 costumes, 45 puppets and troupe of stunning Chinese acrobats, it makes for a truly eye-catching performance, up to five times a day, that is way above usual theme park standards. It is also air-conditioned, a welcome relief in summer (you should also arrive a little early as the doors close right on time). AAAAA.

Crown Colony

This area sits in the park's bottom right corner and has five distinct components. Here, you can take the **Skyride** cable car (AAA) on a one-way trip to Congo (providing a great look at Rhino Rally). The

6

Clydesdale Hamlet is also here, but if you've seen the massive dray horses and their stables at SeaWorld, the set-up is pretty similar (AA).

The **Crown Colony Restaurant and Hospitality Center** is a large Victorian-styled building overlooking the Serengeti Plain. It offers counter-service salads, sandwiches and pizzas (downstairs) or a full-service restaurant upstairs with magnificent views of the animals roaming the plain. For a memorable meal (11.30am until an hour before park closing), head here for lunch (they don't take bookings) or, better still, come back for dinner in the early evening and see the animals come down to the waterhole.

Serengeti Plain

The Serengeti Plain itself is a 49-acre (20-ha) spread of African savannah that is home to buffalo, antelope, zebra, giraffe, wildebeest, ostriches, hippos, rhinos and many exotic birds, and can be viewed for much of the journey on the **Serengeti Express Railway**, a full-size, open-car steam train that chugs slowly from its main station in Nairobi to Egypt and all the way round to Congo, Stanleyville and back. It is a good ride to take during the main part of the day when queues build up at the thrill rides. AAA.

Edge of Africa: a 15-acre (6-ha) safari experience that guarantees a close-up encounter almost as good as the real thing. The walk-through attraction puts you in an authentic setting of natural wilds and native

> BRIT TIP: Edge of Africa offers some fantastic photo opportunities but, in the hot months, come here early in the day as many animals seek refuge from the heat later.

Edge of Africa

villages (right down to the imported plants and even the smells), from which you can view giraffes, lions, baboons, meerkats, crocodiles, hyenas, vultures and even get an underwater view of a specially designed hippopotamus habitat. Look out for the abandoned Jeep – you can sit in the front cab while lions lounge in the back! Wandering 'safari guides' and naturalists offer informal talks, and the attention to detail is wonderful. AAAAA.

Nairobi

Nairobi is home to the awesome **Myombe Reserve**, one of the largest and most realistic habitats for the threatened highland gorillas and chimpanzees of central Africa. This 3-acre (1.2-ha) walk-through has a superb tropical setting where the temperature is kept artificially high and convincing with the aid of lush forest landscaping and hidden water mist sprays. Take your time, especially as there are good, seated vantage points, and be patient to catch these magnificent creatures going about their daily routine. It is also highly informative, with attendants usually on hand to answer any questions. AAAAA.

Rhino Rally: this wonderfully dramatic and scenic ride starts out as an off-road Jeep safari and changes into an innovative raft adventure as your 17-passenger vehicle gets caught in a flash flood. The 8-minute whirl through the wilds of

Music show at Busch Gardens

Africa includes encounters with elephants, rhinos, crocodiles, antelope and more, as the off-road part of the ride is just about as 'real' as they can make it. Your driver adds to the fun with some amusing spiel about the rally and your purpose-built (by Land-Rover) vehicle, but it soon becomes clear your 'navigator' (the front seat passenger) has led you into a blind gully. An unused pontoon bridge is your only way out, but 'fate' has a unique twist in store, which opens the way to part two of the ride and the thrilling raging river section that is unlike any attraction I've experienced to date. Check this out (but you must get here early to beat the queues). Height restriction is just 3ft 3in/99cm. TTTT and AAAAA.

Back at **Myombe Gifts** you can buy your own cuddly baby gorilla (a toy, of course!) and you can get a snack or soft drink at the **Kenya Kanteen**. This is also the place to see the Asian elephants (check the advertised times for the **Elephant Wash**) and visit the **Nairobi Field Station**, an animal nursery and care centre which houses all manner of rehabilitating and hand-reared creatures.

Continuing round the nursery brings you to the **Reptile House** and **Tortoise Habitat**. The **Curiosity Caverns**, just to the left of the nursery, are easy to miss but don't if you want to catch a glimpse of some nocturnal and rarely seen creatures very much at home in a clever, cave-like setting.

Timbuktu

Passing through Nairobi brings you to the more ride-dominated area of the park, starting with Timbuktu. Here in a North African desert setting you will find many of the elements of a typical funfair, with a couple of brain-scrambling rides and two good shows.

Scorpion: a 50mph (80kph) roller-coaster, this features a 62-ft (19-metre) drop and a 360-degree loop that is guaranteed to dial D for Dizzy for a while! The ride lasts just 120 seconds, but seems longer. The queues build up here from late morning, and you must to be at least 3ft 6in/106cm to ride. TTTT.

Cheetah Chase: new in 2004, this family-orientated 'Crazy Mouse' style coaster is surprisingly energetic, rising as it does some 46ft (14 metres) and adding some tight turns and swift drops. Top speed is only 22mph (35kph), which won't excite Kumba fans, but it certainly *seems* faster and will thrill the younger lot. TTT (TTTTT for under 10s).

Other rides include **The Phoenix**, a positively evil invention, that involves sitting in a gigantic, boat-shaped swing which eventually performs a 360-degree rotation in dramatic, slow-motion style. Don't eat just before this one! Height restriction: 4ft/122cm; TTTT. **Sandstorm** is a fairly routine whirligig contraption that spins and

6

Scorpion in Timbuktu

levitates at fairly high speed (hold on to your stomach). Height restriction 3ft 6in/106cm; TTT.

A series of scaled-down **Kiddie Rides** are usually a hit with the under 10s (and give Mum and Dad a break as well). The **Carousel Caravan** offers the opportunity to ride a genuine Mary Poppins-type carousel, while there are the inevitable **Electronic Arcade** and a **Games Area** of side shows and stalls that require a few extra dollars.

Desert Grill is a new African-themed buffet diner here (offering large sandwiches, Italian sausage with grilled vegetables, salads and pasta, plus kids' meals in a souvenir bucket) set in a huge hall that provides some serious stage entertainment too. In summer 2004, it was the hot dance moves of **Burn The Floor**. AAA.

RL Stine's Haunted Lighthouse: the final element and a thoroughly fun 3-D film romp in the company of Christopher Lloyd that will appeal especially to children of all ages (although it may be a touch spooky for the youngest). The story centres on the two 'ghost children' of the Haunted Lighthouse and the real children who inadvertently come to visit. Cue a riot of 3-D visuals plus many clever (and hilarious) special effects (prepare to duck when Lloyd drinks a beer!). It also uses fog and wind effects, plus strobe lighting and a few 'surprises'. Based on a story by American kids' mock-horror writer RL Stine (of Goosebumps fame), it is an extremely well made 22-minute movie, with full surround-sound that draws a good crowd through the main part of the day, so go early or leave it until later on. AAAA.

Congo

You're into serious ride territory here, with the unmistakable giant turquoise structure of **Kumba**

looming over the area. First of all, it's one of the largest and fastest roller-coasters in the south-east United States and, at 60mph (97kph), it features three unique elements: a diving loop which plunges the riders a full 110ft (33 metres), a camelback, with a 360-degree spiral that induces a weightless feeling for 3 seconds, and a 108-ft (33-metre) vertical loop. For good measure, it dives underground at one point! It looks terrifying close up, but it is absolutely exhilarating, even for non-coaster fans. Restrictions: 4ft 6in/137cm. TTTTT.

Congo River Rapids: these look pretty tame after that, but don't be fooled. The giant rubber tyres will bounce you down some of the most convincing rapids outside of the Rockies, and you will end up with a fair soaking for good measure. Restrictions: 3ft 6in/106cm. TTTT.

Ubanga-Banga Bumper Cars: they are just that, typical fairground dodgems (height restriction: 3ft 6in/106cm; TT), and you won't miss anything by passing them by for the more daring **Python**, the fourth of Busch Gardens' roller-coasters, with this one featuring a double spiral corkscrew at 50mph (80kph) from 70ft (21 metres) up. Height restriction is 4ft/122cm, and the ride lasts just 70 seconds, but it's a blast. TTTT.

More **Kiddie Rides** are available for the smaller visitors. The **Vivi Restaurant** offers chicken fajitas, club sandwiches, salads and desserts, and there are two gift shops.

Stanleyville

You pass over Claw Island, home to the park's rare white **Bengal tigers**, to get to Stanleyville, which seems to merge into one area from the Congo. Here there are more watery rides, with the popular **Stanley Falls Log Flume** ride (almost identical to the ones at

Chessington, Legoland, Thorpe Park and Alton Towers), which guarantees a good soaking at the final drop (height restriction: 3ft 10in/116cm; TTT) and the distinctly cleverer **Tanganyika Tidal Wave**, which takes you on a scenic ride along 'uncharted' African waters before tipping you down a two-stage drop that really does land with tidal-wave force. Height restriction: 4ft/122cm. TTTT.

Stanleyville Theater: a good place to put your feet up as you watch the resident entertainers turn on the style. This varies seasonally; in 2003/04 it was the *Mapapa Acrobats*, a troupe of fun-loving African offbeat gymnasts and *Taganai*, an elaborate Cirque-style show. AAA½.

For a hearty, if messy, meal visit the **Stanleyville Smokehouse** – their wood-smoked ribs platter is a delight. As you leave Stanleyville behind, say hello to the Muntjac deer and orang-utans (who are rarely active during the day) in the large pens either side of the train station.

Land of the Dragons

Parents will want to know about this large, wonderfully clever area of activities, entertainment, rides and attractions purely for the young 'uns. It features a 3-storey treehouse complete with towers and maze-like stairways, a rope climb, ball crawl and outdoor **Dragon's Tale Theater**, which presents the 15-minute show *Dumphrey's Special Day* – a birthday special with the resident cuddly dragon. It is all good, knockabout, well-supervised stuff, and some of the kiddie rides are superbly inventive, as well as offering plenty of opportunity to get wet. TTTTT (youngsters only).

Bird Gardens

Your route around the park now brings you to the most peaceful area, and the original starting point of the park in 1959, the **Bird Gardens**. Here it is possible to unwind from the usual theme park hurly-burly.

BRIT TIP: Don't stand on the bridge into Orchid Canyon unless you want to catch the full weight of the Tidal Wave!

The exhibits and shows are all family-orientated, too, with the 30-minute *Wild Wings of Africa* presented in the **Bird Show Theater** (AAA) and the **Hospitality Patio**, where the resident band plays a mix of musical favourites, past and present. **Lory Landing** is a desert island-themed walk-through bird encounter featuring lorikeets, hornbills, parrots and more, with the chance to become a human perch and feed the friendly lorikeets (or have your ear nibbled!). A cup of nectar costs $1, but is a great investment for a memorable photo. Take a slow walk round to appreciate the lush, tropical foliage and special displays such as the walk-through **Aviary**, **Flamingo Island**, **Eagle Canyon**, plus the emus and the not-so-bird-like kangaroos. AAA.

A free taste of Anheuser-Busch products is on offer in **Hospitality House**, where you can enroll for the **Beer School**, a 40-minute lesson in the process of beer-making. It offers a fascinating glimpse into the brewery world, and is excellently explained, with the bonus of some tasting! You will also be presented with a Brewery Master certificate. AAA (21 and over only).

Gwazi: this is Busch's biggest roller-coaster, a massive 'duelling' wooden creation in the classic mould (i.e. no going upside down). The two sets of cars, the Gwazi Lion and Gwazi Tiger, each top 50mph (80kph) and generate a G-force of

6

up to 3.5 as they career around nearly 7,000ft (2,134 metres) of track with six fly-by encounters. You get to choose your ride in the intricately themed 8-acre (3-ha) village plaza and then you are off up the 90-ft (27-metre) lift for a breathtaking 2½ minutes. The shake, rattle 'n' roll effect of a classic coaster is cleverly re-created and the Lion and Tiger rides are slightly different, so you need to do both. Even if you don't like coasters, try this one. Height restriction: 4ft/122cm. TTTTT.

Next door is the **River Rumble** game for kids, a series of catapults that fire water-filled balloons. TTTT (for under 12s). This costs an extra $3 for a bucket of nine balloons (or $5 for two buckets). Children can also try the **bungee trampoline** and **rock-climbing wall** at $6 each or $9 for both.

Egypt

The final area of Busch Gardens is tucked away through the Crown Colony, so it is best visited either first thing or late in the day. **Egypt** is 8 acres (3ha) of carefully re-created pharaoh country, dominated by the roller-coaster Montu, named after an ancient Egyptian warrior god.

Montu: a truly breathtaking creation, this is one of the world's tallest and longest inverted coasters, covering nearly 4,000ft (1,219 metres) of track at speeds topping 60mph (97kph) and peaking with a G-force of 3.85! Like Kumba, it looks terrifying, but in reality is an absolute 5-star thrill as it leaves your

Cheetah Chase

legs dangling and twists and dives (underground at two points) for almost 3 minutes of brain-scrambling fun. Height restriction: 4ft 6in/137cm. TTTTT.

Akbar's Adventure Tours: this is actually located in Crown Colony because it replaced the Questor ride in 1998. Another in the array of simulator rides, it relies as much on fun as thrills. The TV pre-show leads its audience into the world of down-at-heel Akbar (brilliantly played by comedian Martin Short) and his home-made (and untried) excursion machine. It explores, in unconventional fashion, the secrets and treasures of ancient Egypt, but don't expect a smooth ride – a mysterious force suddenly takes control in the forbidden tomb and the trip takes a high-speed turn for the unexpected! It is not recommended for anyone with back or neck problems or for expectant mothers, while the height restriction is just 3ft 6in/106cm. TTTT.

You can travel back in time on a tour of **Tut's Tomb**, as it was when archaeologist Howard Carter discovered it, with clever lighting, audio and even aroma effects. AAA. Youngsters can also make their own excavations in a neat **Sand Pit** (with some little 'treasures' to be found!), while the shopping at **Golden Scarab** takes on a high-quality air with its hand-blown glass items and authentic cartouche paintings.

You should finally return to Morocco for a spot of shopping in the area's tempting bazaars. Middle Eastern brass, pottery and carpets will all tempt you into opening your wallet yet again at **Casablanca Outfitters**, **Genie's Bottle** and **Marrakesh Market**, while there is a full range of Anheuser-Busch products and gift ideas at the **Emporium** and **Label Stable**, if you haven't already fallen prey to the array of shops and cuddly-toy outlets around the park.

In addition...

The **Serengeti Safari** tour is a 30-minute excursion (five times a day, taking 20 people at a time) aboard flat-bed trucks that take you to meet the Serengeti Plain's giraffes, zebras, ostriches and rhinos close up and learn more about the park's environmental efforts. You book up at the Tour Office window just outside the main entrance, or at the kiosk in front of Casablanca Outfitters, for an extra $29.99, and places tend to fill up quickly (children must be at least 5 to take part, and 5–15s must be accompanied by an adult). New is the **Serengeti Dining Safari** which adds dinner at the Crown Colony House restaurant for $49.99 per adult and $39.99 per child.

The **Guided Adventure Tours** take 15 at a time on a VIP park trek (lasting 4–5 hours), with your own guide, reserved seating at *KaTonga*, front-of-line access for a number of rides (including Gwazi and Rhino Rally), counter-service lunch at Crown Colony and an up-close encounter with many of the animals and their staff, including the Serengeti Safari. They cost $69.99 ($64.99 for children) in advance or $74.99 ($69.99) on the day in addition to park entry. The new **Adventure Thrill Tours** are similar but substitute more rides – including the water rides – for the animal encounters ($59.99 and $54.99 in advance; $69.99 and $64.99 on the day). The 2-hour **Animal Adventures Tour** is a personal animal experience for seven to ten people a day. The next best thing to becoming a park zookeeper, it provides close encounters with the Clydesdales, black rhinos, hippos, giraffes and elephants, plus joining in animal behavioural sessions. It costs an extra $99.99/person.

Finally, the **Elite Adventure Tour** offers a personal, exclusive park tour, with front-of-line access to all rides, the Serengeti Safari, reserved seating at shows, free bottled water throughout, continental breakfast, lunch at the Crown Colony Restaurant, free parking and a free Fujifilm camera – all for an extra $149.99/person (ages 5 and up). Once again, all tours can be booked ahead on 813 984 4043. Busch Gardens is also now open till 10.30pm for their **Summer Nights** programme (July–Aug), which features live entertainment, music and DJs.

For a full family day out, you can combine Busch Gardens with the next-door water park **Adventure Island** (on McKinley Drive) which is particularly welcome when it hots up (provided you plaster on the sun cream). The 25 acres (10ha) of watery fun, in a Key West theme, offer a full range of slides and rides, such as the **Wahoo Run** adventure ride, the 76-ft (23-metre) free-fall plunge of the **Tampa Typhoon** and the spiralling **Calypso Coaster**, kids' playground, cafés, gift shops, arcades and volleyball, plus the wonderful **Splash Attack** adventure, a water activity maze culminating in a 1,000-gallon (4,550-litre) bucket dump on the unwary! Adventure Island is open from mid-February to late October (weekends only February to March and September to October) 10am–5pm (later in high season) and a combined Busch Gardens ticket costs $61.95 for adults and $52.95 for 3–9s.

Well, that's the low-down on all the main theme parks, but there is still more to discover...

Congo River Rapids

7 The Other Attractions

(or, One Giant Leap for Tourist Kind)

If you think you have seen everything Orlando has to offer by simply sticking to the theme parks, in the words of the song, 'You ain't seen nothin' yet'. It would be relatively easy to add the Kennedy Space Center to Chapter 6 because, although it's not strictly a theme park, it is adding new attractions all the time and is fast becoming a full day's excursion from Orlando to the east or 'space' coast.

Silver Springs, Historic Bok Sanctuary and a revamped Cypress Gardens will give you a taste of the more natural things Florida has to offer. The Kissimmee attraction Gatorland provides a completely contrasting experience, with its alligators, crocs and shows (great value, too), as do the one-off family centres like WonderWorks, the Orlando Science Center and Ripley's Believe It Or Not.

For more individual attractions, you have the unique aviation experience of Fantasy of Flight, the hair-raising haunted house walk-through of Skull Kingdom along with a magnificent array of water fun parks.

The choice is yours, but it is an immense selection. Let's start here with One Giant Leap for Mankind.

Kennedy Space Center

The recent change to a fully ticketed entrance fee is a reflection of the massive amount of new development that has taken place at the home of NASA's space programme. More than $120 million has been spent on revamping the Center's Visitor Complex in the last few years and, while it was always a great visit in the past, now it is simply unmissable, in my opinion, for its hugely imaginative depiction of the past, present and future of space exploration. The KSC also owns the nearby Astronaut Hall of Fame, and a Maximum Access pass provides entry to that as well.

There are five continually running shows or exhibitions, four static showcases, a kids' play area (and a new show designed specifically for them), an art gallery, the Astronaut Encounter, two splendid IMAX films and a full bus tour of the Space Center, which adds up to great value for the entrance fee. In addition, there are two separate guided tours, while the new **Astronaut Training Experience** provides a novel element to the Center.

You enter through the futuristic ticket plaza and can spend several hours wandering around the exhibits and presentations of the 70-acre (28-ha) Visitor Complex itself.

Robot Scouts is a walk-through display-and-show in the company of Starquester 2000, your robot host who will explain the history of NASA's unmanned space probes in a surprising and often amusing style.

Next door, the **Quest for Life** film – narrated by *Deep Space Nine* star Avery Brooks – provides another illuminating view in the Universe Theater. Head on out and see some of the hardware of space flight in the completely revamped **Rocket Garden**, which has a kids' water fountain and an Apollo space capsule gantry, to give you the feel of that last earthbound walk before the astronauts boarded the *Saturn V* rocket. Free guided tours are given twice a day. And don't forget to stop by the **Astronaut Memorial**, a stark, sombre but very moving tribute to the men and women who have died in advancing the space programme. **Shuttle Explorer** allows you to inspect a full-size replica space shuttle, while the **Launch Status Center** displays actual flight hardware, plus live mission briefings (once the programme is active again following the tragedy of the *Columbia*). Free walking tours are available several times a day.

Early Space Exploration is a clever and coherent walk-through trip into the recent past of the space programme, including the *Hall of Discovery*, the *Mercury Mission Control Room* – the original consoles from America's first manned space flights – and the *Hall of History*. The futuristic **Exploration in the New Millennium** exhibit provides more appeal for youngsters, with a fun educational element from the spaceship-like *Exploring Gallery*, the *Mars Rock* exhibit and a series of interactive panels.

New in 2001 was the kid-friendly **Mad Mission To Mars 2025** show, a mix of educational messages and pure fun theatricals, with lots of special effects, audience participation and even its own hip-hop song, *The Newton Rap*. Children aged 8 and up should have a laugh or two here.

Also here is **Nature and Technology** (which showcases the unique balance the Center maintains with the local environment), the **Center for Space Education** (an interactive learning and Teacher Resource Center), the **Space Walk of Honor**, and **NASA Art Gallery** (space exhibits and artwork).

Perhaps the most innovative feature, though, is the **Astronaut Encounter**, with personal briefings, Q&A sessions, video footage and anecdotes from various veterans of the Mercury, Gemini and Apollo programmes, plus several Space Shuttle astronauts. It is an amazingly insightful and engrossing feature, and takes place up to three times a day at the Center Plaza. You can even take things a step further with the **Lunch with an Astronaut** opportunity (12:30pm daily), whereby a small group gets to have lunch with the astronaut of the day. The featured astronaut will also give a special briefing adding extra insight into their space missions. Lunch and admission are $54.99 adults, $37.99 children (Maximum Access pass required), and tickets may be purchased online (see page 189) or by calling 321 449 4444. Young kids have their own playground, too, the **Children's Play Dome**, complete with a one-fifth scale space shuttle.

The air-conditioned **Coach Tour** (departures every 15 minutes), fully narrated throughout, makes two important stops in addition to driving around much of the working area of the Space Center, including the truly massive Vehicle Assembly Building. The first stop is the **LC39 Observation Gantry**, just 1 mile (1.6km) from shuttle launch pad 39A, a combination 4-storey observation deck and exhibition centre. The exhibits consist of a 10-minute film on the launch preparation of a shuttle, models and videos of a countdown and touch-screen information on the whole shuttle programme.

Next is the awesome **Apollo/ Saturn V Center**, one of the area's truly great exhibits, where you can easily spend 90 minutes. It highlights the Apollo programme

7

ORLANDO'S OTHER ATTRACTIONS

A Winter Park
B Aquatic Wonders Boat Tours
C Boggy Creek Airboat Rides
D Port Canaveral
E Leu Gardens
F Flying Tigers Warbird Museum
G Green Meadows Petting Farm
H Sanford-Rivership Romance
I WonderWorks
J Kissimmee Pioneer Museum
K Disney's Wilderness Preserve
L Orlando World Center Marriott
M Cypress Gardens Adventure Park
N Kissimmee Rodeo
O Richard Petty Driving Experience
P Black Hammock Fish Camp
Q Dave's Ski School
R Dolly Parton's Dixie Stampede

S Grand Cypress Equestrian Center
T Horse World Riding Stables
U Pirate's Dinner Adventure
V TD Waterhouse Center
W Citrus Bowl Stadium
X Osceola County Stadium
Y Central Florida Zoo
Z Sak Comedy Lab
A1 Sleuth's Mystery Dinner Shows
B1 Arabian Nights
C1 Florida Eco-Safaris
D1 Orlando Science Center
E1 Orange County History Center
F1 Lake Eola
G1 Medieval Times
H1 Hard Rock Vault/Titanic Exhibition
J1 Skull Kingdom
K1 Sanford Museum

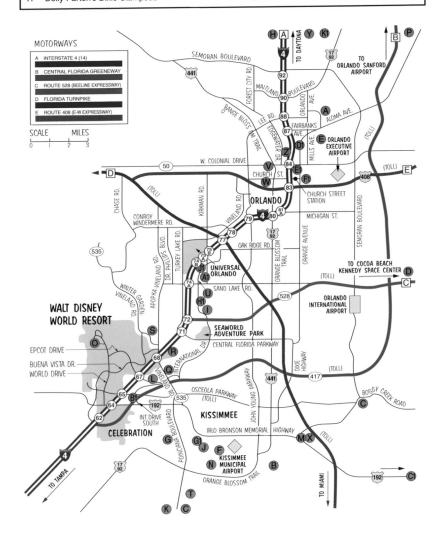

MOTORWAYS

A INTERSTATE 4 (14)
B CENTRAL FLORIDA GREENEWAY
C ROUTE 528 (BEELINE EXPRESSWAY)
D FLORIDA TURNPIKE
E ROUTE 408 (E-W EXPRESSWAY)

SCALE MILES
0 1 2 3

and first moon landing with two deeply impressive theatrical presentations on the risks and triumphs, with an actual 363-ft (111-metre) *Saturn V* rocket and a hands-on gallery that brings the past, present and future of space exploration into sharp focus. It is also quite a humbling experience. You should allow a good 2–3 hours to do the main tour justice.

Equally impressive back at the Visitor Complex are the **IMAX cinemas** – 55-ft (17-metre) screens that give the impression of sitting on top of the action. The 37-minute film **The Dream Is Alive** puts you inside a space shuttle mission, while the new **Space Station 3-D** (narrated by Tom Cruise) is a breathtaking slice of science fact, living with the crew of the International Space Station and affording a heart-stopping look at the construction process. Both films are included in the admission price.

The Complex also has an excellent **Space Shop**, four restaurants, including the full-service **Mila's**, and three snack counters. The Apollo/Saturn V Center has its own café, too.

The newest element, though, is the thrilling **Astronaut Training Experience (ATX)**, a full-day programme into the training and rigours required for a Shuttle mission. You progress through a sequence of simulated and hands-on preparations, with the input of various NASA veterans. The training provides a range of interactive activities, from the multi-axis trainer and ⅙-gravity chair, to operating a full-scale Shuttle mock-up and taking the helm in Mission Control. There is also an exclusive tour of the Space Center, with stops at the Shuttle Launch Pads, the International Space Station Center and NASA's Press Site. The ATX is limited to only a few participants each day and you must be at least 14 (under 18s must be accompanied by a parent). Hard-wearing clothes and athletic shoes are advised, and 'recruits' should be free of neck and back injuries. It costs a hefty $225/person (including lunch and ATX gear), but it guarantees a truly memorable day for all potential space cadets. You need to book in advance on 321 449 4400 or online.

Getting there: take the Beeline Expressway out of Orlando (Route 528, and a toll road, see map on page 188) for about 45 minutes, then bear left on SR 407 (don't follow the signs to Cape Canaveral or Cocoa Beach at this point) and turn right at the T-junction on to SR 405. The Visitor Complex is located 6 miles (10km) along on the right.

Admission to the Space Center is $29 for adults and $19 for children 3–11, including the Bus Tour and IMAX films. The Maximum Access pass ($35 adults, $25 children) adds entry to the Astronaut Hall of Fame. Parking is free. Open 9am–7pm every day (except Christmas Day and launch days; call 321 449 4444 to check), and it is busiest at weekends. The first tours and IMAX presentations start at 10am, while the final tour of the day is 3.45pm (www.KennedySpaceCenter.com). AAAAA.

The Kennedy Space Center

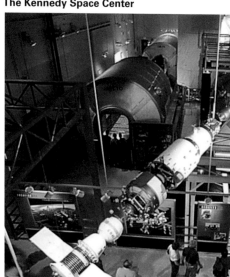

If you want to learn more about the past and present of NASA, **Cape Canaveral: Then and Now** is a 2-hour-plus guided journey into the early days of space exploration around the older part of the facility. Highlights include the Air Force Space Museum, Mercury launch sites and Memorial, original astronaut training facility and several active launch pads, all of which are otherwise off-limits. It costs an extra $22 for adults, $16 for 3–11s.

The 90-minute **NASA Up Close** guided tour takes visitors along the astronaut's launch-day routine and includes a look at both launch pads, the VAB and the gigantic crawler transports, as well as the International Space Station Center ($22 adults, $16 for 3–11s).

> BRIT TIP: Reader Les Watson advises: 'Head to Port Canaveral, and there is a recreation area called Jetty Park. It has a wooden jetty about 100yd (91 metres) long, brilliant for watching Shuttle launches. What an experience.'

The greatest thrill of all is watching an actual **Shuttle launch**, (although following the *Columbia* disaster in February 2003, there are no launches scheduled just yet.). You can call the number above for information and Launch Transportation Tickets to a viewing area just 6 miles (10km) from the launch pad or buy them online via the Center's website. Adult tickets cost $45.50 ($33.50 for children), including admission to the Visitor Complex, or $15 a head for the launch-viewing site only. However, in the event of a launch cancellation, there are NO refunds, and the traffic in the area is usually

horrendous, taking anything up to 3 hours to get here from Orlando. Alternative viewing sites are available along Highway 1 in Titusville and Highway A1A through Cape Canaveral and Cocoa Beach. To be on hand to witness a shuttle launch is certainly an awe-inspiring experience.

Astronaut Hall of Fame

While the Space Center tells you primarily about the machinery of putting men and women in space, the Astronaut Hall of Fame (on SR 405, just before the main entrance to the KSC) gives you the low-down on the people involved and their work. This museum to the space programme houses fascinating memorabilia, exhibits and engaging explanations of the people behind the spacesuits. A chronologically coherent approach divides the Astronaut Hall of Fame into six sections. The **Entry Experience** introduces the visions of space flight, with an 8-minute video of the astronauts as modern explorers, and leads into **Race to the Moon**, the stories of the *Mercury, Gemini* and *Apollo* missions. The **New Frontier** opens the way for Skylab and Shuttle missions, adjacent to the Astronaut Hall of Fame, the museum's heart and soul. **Space Explorers Today and Tomorrow** includes an audio-visual experience aboard a replica Shuttle, before introducing the hands-on **Astronaut Adventure** with its working models, G-force and flight simulators (a cabin that does six 360-degree rolls at once!), space-walk 'chairs', moon exploration, interactive computers and Mars Mission experience.

Admission: part of the Maximum Access pass for the Kennedy Space Center (see page 183), or $16 adults, $12 for 3–11s, purely for the Hall of Fame itself. There is a gift shop and refreshments are provided by the **Cosmic Café**. If you enjoyed the KSC, try to spend a couple of hours here. AÁÁ½.

Cypress Gardens Adventure Park

Central Florida's original theme park (dating back to 1936) closed in 2003 as visitor numbers dropped post-September 11, but a public campaign to save the famous gardens, some state funding and a new private management company (who also owns the Wild Adventures theme park in Georgia) looks to have the answer, with provisional re-opening late in 2004 (see map on page 188). The new owners are planning to add more than 30 rides and a children's water park to the traditional mix of scenic gardens, graceful Southern Belles and water-ski shows in order to give the park more all-round appeal. In the past, Cypress Gardens and its quiet, flower-lined pathways has been more of an interest for the older generation, although it had tried to introduce more child-friendly elements with a handful of rides, slides and animals.

Now, if all the plans are carried through as they were laid out in February 2004, the Gardens will still boast their magnificent array of refreshing and tranquil greenery (plus the world-famous water-ski shows), but will have whole new areas devoted to the young 'uns and other ride fans. This increase in size will also see a new transportation system of trains and trams to assist those who'd rather not walk around all of it. The $42-million redevelopment calls for a new entrance plaza that brings visitors into the **Craftsman's Village** of shops, restaurants and arts and crafts.

From there, you can wander into the pre-existing (but revamped)

Nature Area or take the **Sunshine Sky Adventure** ride (formerly the Island in the Sky, a massive circular arm that raises guests 150ft/46 metres for a bird's eye view of the park). The main **Garden** section, with some of the park's original development, is being carefully brought back to life, and from here you can pass on to the new **Adventure Grove**, with many of the new rides (which include four junior or family coasters, two water rides, seven out-and-out thrill rides – notably a 120-ft/37-metre Super Shot tower – and 11 kiddie rides). The **Paradise Pier** section is more rides and slides, set in the middle of the **Orange Blossom Boardwalk**, a suspended walkway over a new gardens area.

The original **Botanical Gardens** feature a host of exotic plants and trees (including a massive Banyan Tree) and, at the furthest end of the park is the new **Water Park**, complete with lazy river feature and beach area. It is an ambitious and extremely costly venture, and it deserves to succeed to breathe new life back into an area of Florida which has suffered since the park closed. There were no details of opening times or prices as we went to press, but you should get more information on www.cypressgardens.com.

Historic Bok Sanctuary

For those wishing to experience the genuine peace, tranquillity and floral ambience of Florida, there is no better recommendation than this national monument and natural garden centre at Lake Wales, 50 miles (80km) to the south-west of Orlando. With one of the most extraordinary attractions in the state – a majestic 205-ft (62.5-metre) pink-and-grey marble carillon tower – set in 250 acres (101ha) of unique

7

parkland, this is a feast for the eyes and soul. Called the **Singing Tower**, the 1920s-built carillon is the centrepiece of the park and recitals are given every day at 3pm. A carillon is a series of cast bronze bells that are played by a keyboard, or clavier. There are only around 500 in the world, and Bok Sanctuary's version consists of 60 bells (crafted in Loughborough, England) ranging from 16lb (7.2kg) to nearly 12 tons. The park has its own resident player, or carilloneur, and his daily recital is an undoubted highlight. The tower is also a work of art, consisting of a neo-Gothic and art deco mix crafted from coquina stone and marble, with some stunning sculptural elements at various stages. It is wonderfully photogenic and, on a cloudless day, the combination of sight and sound is utterly captivating.

Around the tower is a wide moat, a long pond and a series of semi-formal gardens. At the highest point on peninsular Florida (all of 298ft/90 metres above sea level), the view is both uncluttered and inspiring, and retains an inherent peace and solitude which persuaded founder and philanthropist Edward W Bok to grant the estate to the local people almost 75 years ago.

The **gardens** themselves provide a wildlife observatory (the Window by the Pond, where you can see up to 126 species of birds, plus reptiles, butterflies, local squirrels, turtles, rabbits and armadillos, as well as the endangered gopher tortoise), nature

The Singing Tower

trails, an endangered plant exhibit, butterfly and woodland gardens, and pine forests. The acres of ferns, palms, oaks and pines create a surprisingly lush backdrop for the spectacular seasonal bursts of azaleas, camellias, magnolias and other flowering shrubs.

The award-winning **Education and Visitor Center** illustrates the story of Edward W Bok (don't miss the orientation film about him and his impact on American society), his vision for the gardens, the carillon and tower architecture (with a close-up look at the bells themselves), the landscape design and the ecology of Florida. The **Carillon Café** then adds a pleasant opportunity to grab a light lunch and other refreshments (in the open air when it's not too hot – and there always seems to be a pleasant breeze up here), while the **Tower & Garden Gift Shop** offers some unique gift and souvenir items.

For an additional fee ($5 for adults and $3 for 5–12s; Mon–Sat at 11am and Sun at 1.30pm), you can tour the **Pinewood Estate**, one of the finest examples of Mediterranean revival architecture in Florida. The 20-room mansion was built as a winter retreat for a Pennsylvania steel tycoon in the early 1930s, and has been lovingly maintained to demonstrate a real slice of period opulence.

Historic Bok Sanctuary

Chalet Suzanne

With this genuine sanctuary being situated somewhat off the beaten track yet an easy drive from Orlando (around 45–50 minutes), it makes for a thoroughly worthwhile day out with some of the other attractions of Lake Wales.

Getting there: Historic Bok Sanctuary can be found off US Highway 27 on Burns Avenue (see map on page 12). Take I-4 west to Exit 55, then head south on US 27 for 25 miles (40km), turn left on Mountain Lake Cutoff Road (two traffic lights past Eagle Ridge Mall) and follow the signs.

Admission: $8 for adults, $3 for 5–12s (under 5 free), apart from occasional specially ticketed events (mainly carillon festivals and recitals). Open 8am–6pm daily (last entry at 5pm). This is also an extremely attractive wedding venue (863 676 1408, www.boktower.org). AAAA.

High on the list of other must-see places around here is **Chalet Suzanne**, a wonderfully eclectic yet classy little country inn and restaurant, quietly famous throughout Florida. This family-run delight (since 1931) is a 100-acre (40.5-ha) estate featuring 30 individual and quite striking guest rooms, a tropical sunken wedding garden, a ceramic salon and gift shop, swimming pool and private lake, plus, wait for it, a soup cannery, which sent its produce to the moon! In fact, Chalet Suzanne is such a sought-after hideaway, it now has its own airstrip.

Its other claim to fame is its restaurant – voted one of Florida's Top 20 for more than 30 years, and a truly amazing venue before you even get to the menu. Consisting of various cast-off buildings (a wing of stable here, a chicken house there) that have been lovingly restored and melded together, the restaurant consists of a series of dining rooms with 14 different levels.

Eclectic is something of an understatement. The food is another highlight, gourmet cuisine of the highest order but with a semi-set menu which barely changes year by year. Specialities include broiled grapefruit, baked sugar-cured ham, Chicken Suzanne, and their own signature soup, Romaine Soup – such a favourite of *Apollo 15* lunar module pilot James Irwin, he persuaded NASA to take it on the mission with them, hence it became known as Moon Soup! The traditional set luncheon starts at $19 a head ($14 for under 12s), while dinner varies from $59–79 ($19 for under 12s), depending on your main course (which includes filet mignon,

Pinewood Estate exterior

lobster and crab thermidor). But, even if you don't stop to eat, or stay in one of their remarkable Swiss-style cottage rooms ($169–229 per night, plus tax), it is well worth a visit to experience the unique charm and style, learn the family story of the owning Hinshaws – and have a tour of that truly one-off soup cannery! Apart from anything else, a gift pack here is one of the most original souvenirs you will ever bring back from Florida. Call 863 676 6011 to book (always essential) or visit www.chaletsuzanne.com.

Getting there: Chalet Suzanne can be found just outside Lake Wales, off Highway 27 on Chalet Suzanne Road.

Head into the quaint town of **Lake Wales** and you will discover Spook Hill (where cars mysteriously roll uphill!), Grove House Visitor Center (home of Florida's natural fruit juice products – as fresh as it gets) and the quaint Museum and Cultural Center (set in a restored 1928 Atlantic Coast Line railroad station), as well as the world's sky-diving capital (from Lake Wales Airport – every kind of parachuting known to man). For more info, call Lake Wales Chamber of Commerce on 863 676 3445 or visit www.lakewaleschamber.com.

Silver Springs

Continuing the theme of natural attractions, we have Silver Springs, just under 2 hours' drive to the north of Orlando. This peaceful 350-acre (142-ha) nature park surrounds the headwaters of the crystal-clear Silver River. Glass-bottomed boats take you to watch the artesian springs (the largest in the world) that bubble up here, along with plenty of wildlife.

Expect to have some close encounters with alligators, turtles, raccoons and lots of waterfowl, while the park also contains a collection of more exotic animals such as bears, panthers and giraffes.

BRIT TIP: Silver Springs and Wild Waters are both busy at the weekends, but you shouldn't encounter many queues here during the rest of the week.

Four animal shows, an alligator and crocodile encounter, the world's largest bear exhibit, a petting zoo, a kids' adventure playground, a new tower ride, a white alligator exhibit and a nightly water-fountain finale (peak season only) complete the attractions. To ruin a few more illusions of the film industry, this was the setting for the 1930s' and 1940s' *Tarzan* films starring Johnny Weissmuller. And, once you have absorbed the timeless tropical nature of the landscape, you will understand why they decided to save on the cost of shipping the film crew to Africa.

The park's main attraction (dating back to 1878) is the **Glass-bottomed Boat Ride**, a 20-minute tour which goes down well with all the family and gives a first-class view of the seven different springs and a host of water life. Similarly, the **Lost River Voyage** is another 20-minute boat trip down one of the unspoilt stretches of the Silver River, including a visit to the park's animal hospital. The third boat trip, the new **Fort King River Cruise**, takes you back in time to pioneer Florida, the Seminole wars and a reconstruction of the army Fort King. With sightings of native wildlife, an archaeological dig, movie set and Florida Cracker Farm, it is another gentle 20-minute historical perspective, with some wonderful storytelling from the boat captain as well.

As an alternative to messing about

on the river, the **Jeep Safari** is a 15-minute ride in the back of an open trailer through a natural forest habitat, home to more animals from other corners of the world, such as tapirs, marmosets, antelope and vultures (plus a drive-through alligator pond!). Then there are the three **Ross Allen Island Animal Shows**, each one lasting 15 minutes and featuring an entertaining – and occasionally hair-raising – look at the worlds of reptiles, birds (including comical parrots, macaws and cockatoos) and creepy crawlies. The hair-raising part occurs only if you happen to be the victim chosen to display a large tarantula, giant cockroach or scorpion.

As you exit the animal shows take time to wander round **Big Gator Lagoon** and the **Crocodile Encounter** in a cypress swamp habitat, viewed from a raised boardwalk. See the largest American crocodile in captivity, the 16-ft (5-metre), 2,000-lb (900-kg) Sobek, as well as a collection of alligators, turtles and Galapagos tortoises. The **Florida Natives** attraction features a collection of snakes, turtles, spiders, otters and other denizens of the state. The **Botanical Gardens** then provide a peaceful haven in which to sit and watch the world go by.

Other large-scale exhibits are the **World of Bears**, an educational presentation including conservation information in a 2-acre (0.8-ha) spread devoted to bears of all kinds (including the largest of its type in the world), from grizzly to spectacled and black bears, and the **Panther Prowl**, with a unique look at the endangered Florida panther and Western cougar. Both of these have educational presentations on their welfare several times daily.

Wings of the Springs is a 30-minute bird show in the Silver River Showcase arena, highlighting the strengths, beauty and conservation issues of the park's collection of hawks, eagles, owls, falcons and vultures in a dramatic free-flight demonstration.

Children are not forgotten, either. **The Kids Ahoy!** playland, with its centrepiece riverboat featuring slides, rides, an air bounce, ball crawl, 3-D net maze, carousel, bumper boats and games, and **Doolittle's Petting Zoo**, with deer and goats, are big draws for the young 'uns. Older children will also gravitate to the new **Lighthouse Ride**, a combined carousel and gondola lift rising up almost 100ft (30 metres) above the park (and magnificently lit at night). At peak times, watch out for the **Fantastic Fountains Show**, which adds another novel element to the park's entertainment.

The usual collection of shops and eateries are fairly ordinary here, in contrast to the slick appeal of Orlando's parks, although the **Deli** offers some pleasant sandwich alternatives and the **Springside Restaurant** is above average. In all, you would probably want to spend a good half day here, with the possibility of a few hours in the neighbouring 9-acre (4-ha) water park of **Wild Waters**, which offers slides like the Twin Twister, a pair of 60-ft (18-metre) high flumes, the free-fall Thunderbolt, the twin-tunnelled Tornado, the 220-ft (67-metre) Silver Bullet and the helter-skelter Osceola's Revenge, as well as a 400-ft (122-metre) tube ride on the turbo-charged Hurricane, a huge wave pool, and various kid-sized fun in Cool Kids Cove and Caribbean Sprayground.

Getting there: Silver Springs is located on SR 40 just through the town of Ocala, 72 miles (116km) to the north of Orlando. Take the Florida Turnpike north (it's a toll road, see map on page 12) until it turns into I-75 and, 28 miles (45km) further north, you turn off and head east on SR 40. Another 10 miles

7

Attractions no more

Here is a list of places that have closed in recent years: Trainland Inc (early 2004); Splendid China (December 2003); SoulFire Dinner Experience (September 2003); Guinness World Records Experience (April 2002; now Hard Rock Vault); Disney's River Country water park (October 2001); Masters of Magic show (September 2001); Church Street Station (summer 2001); Mystery Fun House (February 2001); King Henry's Feast and Wild Bill's dinner shows (January 2000); Disney's Discovery Island (July 1999); Terror on Church Street (May 1999).

(16km) brings you to Silver Springs, just past the Wild Waters water park on your right.

Admission: $32.99 for adults, $29.99 for seniors (55+) and $23.99 for children under 4ft (122cm) tall (under 3s free). A joint ticket (Silver Springs and Wild Waters) is $36.99 and $27.99. Parking is $6. Open 10am–5pm daily (352 236 2121, www.silversprings.com). AAAA.

Silver Springs glass-bottomed boat

Gatorland

For another taste of the 'real' Florida wildlife, this is as authentic as it gets and is popular with children of all ages. When the wildlife consists of several thousand menacing alligators and crocodiles in various natural habitats and four fascinating shows, you know you're in for a different experience. 'The Alligator Capital of the World' was founded in 1949 and is still family-owned, hence it possesses a home-spun charm and naturalism which few of its big-money competitors can match. However, it also looks to add new features, hence the novel (and rare) **Blue Gator Display** started in 2004.

> BRIT TIP: If you have an evening flight home from Orlando International Airport, Gatorland is handy to visit on your final day. Conveniently located about 20 minutes' drive away from the airport, it is the ideal place to soak up half a day.

Start by taking the 15-minute **Gatorland Express** railway around the park to get an idea of its 110-acre (45-ha) expanse. This costs an extra $1 but is good for multiple rides, is fully narrated (usually in amusing style) and is especially fun for kids. You also get a good look at

Gatorland Jumparoo

the native Florida animal habitat, which features whitetail deer, wild turkey and quail. Wander through the natural beauty of the 2,000-ft (610-metre) long **Swamp Walk**, as well as the **Alligator Breeding Marsh Walkway**, where there's a 3-storey observation tower, and get a close-up view of these great reptiles, who seem to hang around the walkway in the hope someone might 'drop in' for lunch.

> **BRIT TIP:** If you are at Gatorland first thing, take the Swamp Walk straight away. There will be far more wildlife activity then and the peaceful ambience is quite invigorating.

Breeding pens, baby alligator nurseries and rearing ponds are also situated throughout the park to provide an idea of the growth cycle of the Florida gator and enhance the overall feeling that it is the visitor behind bars here, not the animals. Many of the small-scale attractions have been designed with kids in mind and there is plenty to keep even the youngest amused, notably at **Lilly's Pad**, an imaginative water playground guaranteed to get them good and wet (swimming costumes advisable).

Allie's Barnyard is a petting zoo, while you can feed some friendly lorikeets at the **Very Merry Aviary**, and view the pink inhabitants of **Flamingo Lagoon**. Other animals to see include bats, iguanas, turtles, turkey vultures, tortoises, snakes, emus, a Florida bear and deer.

However, the gators and crocs are the main attraction and it is the three shows which are the real draw (although you will never find yourself on the end of a queue here). The 800-seat **Wrestling Stadium** sets the scene for some real cracker-style feats (a cracker is the local

term for a Florida cowboy) as Gatorland's resident 'wranglers' catch themselves a 7–8-ft (2–3-metre) long gator and proceed to point out the animal's various survival features, with the aid of some daredevil stunts that will have you questioning the cowboys' sanity.

The **Gator Jumparoo** is another eye-opening spectacle as some of the park's biggest creatures use their tails to 'jump' out of the water and be hand-fed tasty morsels, such as whole chickens! Gatorland has been working on different aspects of this show to provide new looks at the animals – and even some audience participation!

Jungle Crocs of the World features some of the deadliest animals of Egypt, Australia and Cuba, with authentic lairs and brilliant presentation, while the show element has its scare-raising moments as the highly knowledgeable guides enter the pens to tell you all about the inhabitants. The revamped **Upclose Animal Encounters** is another entertaining and highly amusing showcase of various creatures, from the obvious snakes to less obvious scorpions and cockroaches. Brave children can provide some great photo opportunities here!

Obviously, face-to-face encounters with the park's living dinosaurs are not everyone's cup of tea, but it's an experience you're

7

Egret at Gatorland

unlikely to repeat anywhere else. In addition, you can dine on smoked alligator ribs and deep-fried gator nuggets (as well as burgers and hot dogs) at **Pearl's Smokehouse**, with excellent kids' meals at $3.99.

The park is also home to hundreds of nesting herons and egrets, providing a fascinating close-up of the nests from March to August. Gatorland is actually central Florida's largest wading-bird sanctuary and it adds an extraordinary ecological and environmental aspect to this very user-friendly park.

A recent venture is Gatorland's **Cypress Glades Adventure Tours** providing more hands-on wildlife opportunities and sightseeing (see page 219 for details).

Getting there: Gatorland is located on the South Orange Blossom Trail, 2 miles (3km) south of its junction with the Central Florida Greeneway and 3 miles (5km) north of Highway 192 (see map on page 12).

Admission: Gatorland also scores on its great value for money, with adult tickets at $19.95 and $9.95 for 3–12s. There is also a highly worthwhile $6 Walkabout Tour several times a day, which includes an encounter with a baby gator. Open 9am–5pm daily and parking is free (www.gatorland.com). AAAA.

Fantasy of Flight

Another wonderful and fresh alternative on the central Florida scene is this aviation museum, which offers a 5-part adventure featuring the world's largest private collection of vintage aircraft. Even those not usually interested in the history of flight or the glamour of the Golden Age of flying will find this a fascinating experience.

You start by entering the **History of Flight**, a series of expertly recreated 'immersion experiences' into memorable moments in aviation history. The entrance alone is eye-opening – you enter the fuselage of a DC-3 Dakota as if for a parachute drop, and step out into a moonlit night. Then you visit set-pieces that include a dogfight over the trenches in World War One and a bomber mission with a Flying Fortress in World War Two. Audio-visual effects and film clips enhance the experience and give everything an awe-inspiring feeling of authenticity.

You exit into the **Vintage Aircraft** displays in two huge hangers, with the exhibits ranging from a replica Wright Flyer, to a Ford Tri-Motor, a Mk-XVI Spitfire and the world's only fully working Short Sunderland flying boat. From the museum's collection of 75 or so vintage planes, one is selected each day as the **Aircraft of the Day**, with a pilot holding a question-and-answer session about that plane before performing an aerial demonstration over Fantasy of Flight.

Two **guided tours** are given each day, one taking visitors into the Backlot and the other visiting the Restoration Shop, highlighting in fascinating detail what it takes to restore and maintain these magnificent machines. Finally, **Fightertown** features eight realistic fighter simulators that take you on a World War Two aerial battle. You get a pre-flight briefing on how to handle your 'plane' (a Vought Corsair), and then climb into the totally enclosed cockpit in order to do battle with the Japanese Air Force. It's difficult, absorbing, fun and totally addictive.

The whole experience is crafted in 1930s' art deco style and includes a full-service diner (the excellent **Compass Rose**) and an original gift shop. There is strong British appeal, too, with the war portrayals and exhibits of both world wars.

Getting there: just 25 minutes

down I-4 towards Tampa (see map on page 12) take Exit 44, Polk City, continue north on SR 559 for half a mile, then turn left into the museum's main entrance.

Admission: $24.95 for adults, $22.95 for seniors (60+) and $13.95 for kids 5–12 (under 5s free). Open 9am–5pm daily and parking is free.

In addition, you can take a vintage **biplane ride** here with Waldo Wright's Flying Service in an open-cockpit 1929 New Standard D-25 for $55/person (up to 4 passengers a time) or try the Fantasy of Flight 3-hour **balloon ride** experience for $165 (up to three passengers). Both operate seasonally and reservations are required.

Fantasy of Flight is the brainchild of American entrepreneur and aviation whiz Kermit Weeks, and I have yet to encounter an attraction put together with more genuine affection. In fact, it is as much a work of art as a tourist attraction, and the masses have yet to discover it (863 984 3500, www.fantasyofflight.com). AAAA.

INTERNATIONAL DRIVE

The long tourist corridor of I-Drive continues to be a fast-developing source of hotels, restaurants, shopping and, more importantly, fun. It now has its own development council to emphasise its attractions. The I-Ride trolley brings it all together in transport terms and the website www.InternationalDriveOrlando.com highlights all the options. There is an Official Visitors Guide with an I-Ride map and valuable money-off coupons (which they will mail to the UK), and a freephone number – 1-866 2437 483 – to steer people in the right direction. New in 2004 was the **Fantasy of Lights Holiday Light Celebration (**Nov 19–Jan 2), a 6-week festival that includes

dazzling Christmas lights, decorations, seasonal activities and special events at various I-Drive businesses. Many events are free and the whole festival is brilliantly showcased by the impressive I-Ride Trolley system.

Here's a look at the top I-Drive attractions (see also Chapters 9 and 11 – Orlando By Night and Shopping – to get a complete picture of the area):

Ripley's Believe It Or Not

You can't miss this particular attraction, next to The Mercado shopping village on I-Drive (see map on page 12), as its extraordinary tilted appearance makes it seem as though it were designed by an architect with an aversion to the horizontal. However, once inside you soon get back on the level and, for an hour or two, you can wander through this museum dedicated to the weird and wonderful.

Robert L Ripley was an eccentric and energetic explorer and collector who, for 40 years, travelled the world in his bid to assemble a collection of the greatest oddities known to man. The Orlando branch of this chain features 8,900sq ft (830sq metres) of displays, including authentic artefacts, video presentations, illusions, interactive exhibits and music. The elaborate re-creation of an Egyptian tomb showcases a mummy and three rare mummified animals, while the Primitive Gallery contains artefacts from tribal societies around the world (some quite gruesome). Human and Animal Oddities, Big and Little galleries, Illusions and Dinosaurs have all received some recent updates and extra interactive elements.

The collection of miniatures includes the world's smallest violin and a single grain of rice hand-painted with a tropical sunset.

BRIT TIP: Ripley's, Hard Rock Vault and WonderWorks are all handy retreats to keep in mind for places to visit on a rainy day.

Larger-scale exhibits include a portion of the Berlin Wall, a two-thirds-scale 1907 Rolls Royce which has been built entirely out of matchsticks and a novel version of the *Mona Lisa* textured completely from toast!

Admission: $15.95 for adults and $10.95 for 4–12s. Open daily 9am–1am (last ticket sold at midnight). AAA.

Titanic

A new attraction in 1999 inside The Mercado was **Titanic – The Exhibition** (see map on page 12), the first permanent exhibit of the great maritime disaster of 1912. With a mixture of genuine artefacts, full-scale re-creations of the ship's interior, several clever scene-setting presentations, film memorabilia from *Titanic* and *A Night to Remember*, plus live interpretations by storytellers in period costume, you will see, hear and feel just about everything there is to know about the *Titanic* and her tragic fate. The full experience takes at least an hour.

Admission: $17.95 for adults and $12.95 for 6–12s (5 and under free). Open 10am–8pm daily (first guided tour at 10.30am). AAAA.

Restoration tour at Fantasy of Flight

Hard Rock Vault

New in December 2002, this is a wonderfully creative interactive rock 'n' roll 'hall of fame' type museum from the worldwide and innovative restaurant chain (see map on page 181). After the success of their Hard Rock Live venue at Universal's CityWalk and the Hard Rock Hotel, this is another exercise in rock chic, with 17,000sq ft (1,580sq metres) of dedicated space paying homage to the past and present of rock 'n' roll. Both guided and self-guided tours are available through a 'living timeline', or chronological review, of music and its effect on society, era by era, from the 1950s on.

The Vault also features some of the most prized pieces from the Hard Rock collection from all over the world (more than 100 HR Cafés in 40-plus countries), as well as material which has never been seen before. The highlight is the guided Total Immersion Tour through five galleries of re-created period history, from The Beatles and Rolling Stones (The Light and the Dark) to Punk Rock (The Back Alley), and Elvis (The King's Chamber) to the Grateful Dead (The Psychedelic Meltdown). The stories unfold through video, artefacts, music and instruments, while the tour guides play a highly individual and distinctive part in bringing it all to life. There is a listening room, with a show of its own (The Sound

Sunderland flying boat at Fantasy of Flight

Back Alley at Hard Rock Vault

Asylum), a snack bar and an eye-catching Hard Rock merchandise shop. Spend time wandering around The Hub and you will come across showcases of such rock luminaries as Eric Clapton (whose guitar, donated to the London Hard Rock, actually began the whole memorabilia phenomenon back in the 1970s), The Beach Boys, Led Zeppelin and Bruce Springsteen, plus the Blues Masters who originated the whole rock idiom. Almost 1,000 original items are on display, including more than 40 stars' guitars, and rock devotees will want to spend at least 2 hours here.

Admission: $14.95 for adults and $8.95 for 5s and over (under 5s free). Open 9am–midnight daily (407 445 7625, www.hardrock.com). AAAA.

Skull Kingdom

The walk-through haunted house idea takes on a new dimension here. Not content with a house, this is a full-blown castle on I-Drive (opposite Wet 'n Wild, see map on page 188) dedicated to frights, horrors and grisly goings-on at every turn. The setting and lavishness of the Kingdom of the Skull Lord marks it out as way

above average, and the combination of elaborate light and sound effects, robotics and the scream-inducingly brilliant live actors (who are kept suitably creepy by full-time make-up artists) provides a hair-raising experience. The shock tactics are state of the art, with the best elements of horror films and haunted houses well maintained over the 2-storey spread of mazes, caverns and other demonic challenges (watch out for the monster spit!).

> **BRIT TIP:** Friday and Saturday evenings are peak periods for Skull Kingdom, with queues of up to 30 minutes.

The Haunted Gift Shop and Ghoulish Arcade Games await you at the end of your 20–30-minute (depending on how much you 'enjoy' the experience!) Skull Kingdom immersion. TTTTT.

While the fully-fledged Evening Show is seriously intense, a new **Day Show** offers less scary guided tours through the castle, geared towards under 12s. Each child is given a torch and guests are never left without their escort. They get to explore every room and ask questions while touring.

Skull Kingdom

Another new element in 2004 was the **Chamber of Magic** dinner show, with magic, laser lighting and special effects. It also has all-you-can-eat pizza, soda, beer and wine.

Admission: Evening Show $14.04 open 6pm–11pm Mon–Thur, noon–midnight Fri–Sun, with extended hours in peak season (not recommended for under 12s); Day Show $8.99, open 10am–5pm daily; Chamber of Magic dinner and show $19.75, $15.95 for under 7s and seniors. Dinner show and Skull Kingdom admission is $28.25, $24.45 for under 7s and seniors (www.skullkingdom.com).

Fun Spot

Here is another choice for full-scale, family-sized fun, just off I-Drive on Del Verde Way (look for the 102-ft/31-metre big wheel past the junction with Kirkman Road). With four different and highly challenging go-kart tracks, bumper cars and boats, four daring fairground-type rides (check out the Spyder and Paratrooper), an impressive 2-storey video arcade (one of the largest in Florida) and food court, plus five Kid Spot rides for the little ones, the 4.7-acre (2-ha) park promises several hours of fun.

Admission and parking are free, but you must buy tickets for the rides, which are $3 each (or $22 for eight). Go-karts require two tickets, while the other rides are a ticket apiece. However, if you are planning on a visit of an hour or longer, their 'armband' tickets are better value. The Adult Armband (for ages 10+) includes all-day privileges on all tracks and rides for $29.95, while the Child Armband (2–9) allows all-day access to the six rides geared towards younger kids, for $9.95. The Rides Armband allows unlimited rides on the 13 Family and Thrill Rides for only $19.95. It

is $6 for an all-day ticket to the Freeplay Arcade, which contains 37 classic arcade games and a spread of more than 100 token-driven games (some of them state-of-the-art). Open 10am–midnight daily (high season), or 2pm–11pm Mon–Fri, 10am–midnight Sat and noon–11pm Sun in low season. Call 407 363 3867 or visit www.fun-spot.com for more info. TTTT.

In a similar vein, **Magical Midway** on I-Drive (just north of Sand Lake Road) offers more go-karts, games and thrill rides (including 0–230ft/70 metres in 3 seconds on the Space Shot Tower!). The two elevated kart tracks, the double uphill corkscrew of *The Avalanche* (you must be at least 12 years old and 4ft 8in/147cm tall to drive, at least 16 to drive a passenger, and at least 3ft/91cm to be a passenger) and the sharply banked *Alpine Jump* (for which you must be at least 12 and 4ft 8in/147cm to drive, 16 to drive a passenger, and at least 3ft/91cm to be a passenger) are their signature rides. New is the *Fast Track*, a flat, concrete track with a 25-degree bank turn (riders must be 12 and 4ft 8in/147cm to drive; single cars only). And then there are bumper cars, a giant slide, bumper boats, four more fairground-type rides and a large arcade.

Admission: $24.95 Play All Day ticket includes unlimited go-karts and unlimited Midway rides; the $19.95 Play Pass is just unlimited go-karts and other rides for 3 hours; the $12.95 Midway Pass gives unlimited rides all day (but not go-karts) and 10 tokens; individual ride tickets are $6 (go-karts), $5 (Space Blast) and $3 (all other rides); must be 4ft/121cm to participate in Space Shot, Tornado, and Bumper Cars, and 3ft 6in/106cm to participate in Bumper Boats, Fun Slide, Kiddie Track. Open 10am–midnight daily (407 370 5353, www.magicalmidway.com). TTT½.

WonderWorks

I-Drive's most unmistakable landmark is the 'interactive entertainment centre' of **WonderWorks**, a 3-storey chamber of real family fun with a host of novel elements (see map on page 188). Unmistakable? You bet – how many buildings do you know that are upside down? That's right, all of the 82-ft (25-metre) edifice is constructed from the roof up! The basic premise (working on the theory that every attraction has to have a story behind it) is that WonderWorks is a secret research facility into unexplained phenomena that got uprooted by a tornado experiment and dumped in topsy-turvy fashion in the heart of this busy tourist district. (Yeah, right!) Well, you have to give them full marks for imagination and, if the interior attractions aren't quite as entertaining as the exterior façade, there is still a lot here, especially for the 6–12s.

You enter through an 'inversion tunnel' that orientates you the same way round as the building (look out of the window to check!) and progress to chambers of entertaining and mildly educational hands-on experiences that demand several hours to explore fully. Without ever using the words 'science' or 'museum', WonderWorks steers you through five 'labs' of interactive activities, including the **Bermuda**

BRIT TIP: WonderWorks, Fun Spot and Magical Midway are open until midnight in high season, long after most theme parks are shut, so you can have a day at the park, then let the kids loose here for a while to tire them out!

Triangle Corridor, the **Mystery Lab** (experience earthquakes and hurricanes and see famous disasters on a bank of computer monitors), **Physical Challenge Lab** (virtual basketball, table tennis, a baseball test, health and lifestyle quizzes and the wonderfully creepy Shocker Chair, a high-voltage simulation that gives you the feeling of 2,000 jolts rather than volts – it's weird!), **Illusions Lab** (with the Bridge of Fire static electricity generator, a computer ageing process and 'elastic surgery', hall of mirrors and bubble table), plus the **WonderWorks Emporium** gift shop, souvenirs and **Wonderworks Café**. A Laser Tag game on the top floor adds even more appeal for youngsters.

On no account miss the two virtual roller-coasters, a pair of amazing enclosed 'pods', which let you design and ride your own coaster. If you have already been to *DisneyQuest*, this may seem tame, while it isn't as educational as the Orlando Science Center.

WonderWorks offers a fun new dinner-show option, *The Outta Control Magic Show* (see Orlando By Night, page 255), with a good value combination ticket.

Admission: $16.95 for adults, $12.95 for seniors (55+) and 4–11s; $4.95 for the Lazer Tag; $19.95 and $14.95 for the Magic Show on its own; $33.95 and $25.95 for the WonderWorks/dinner-show combo; $19.95 and $15.95 for WonderWorks/Lazer Tag; and $34.95 and $26.95 for all three elements. Open 9am–midnight daily (www.wonderworksonline.com). AAA/TTT.

I-Drive Adventure Tour

This is an innovative venture based at Pointe*Orlando on I-Drive (see map on page 285). If you have seen the amazing two-wheeled

7

Segway Human Transporters in *Epcot* you might want to know how you could try them out in the real world. Well, Relay Transport has just started a hands-on Adventure Tour taking guests on a ride to various I-Drive attractions and providing additional time for some video instruction, too.

Admission: $49.95 (16 and over), while there is also a 30-minute kids' clinic for 8–16s for $14.95 each. Other electric vehicle rentals are available, too. Open 10am–5pm daily (407 351 4876, www.RelayToGo.com).

DOWNTOWN ORLANDO

The last couple of years have seen a significant move towards regenerating Orlando's city centre – the 'downtown' area – with new offices, apartments, shops and restaurants. This has also brought significant tourist developments.

Orlando Science Center

Because this is Orlando, there is no such thing as a simple museum or science centre. Everything must be all-singing, all-dancing just to compete. Hence, the Orlando Science Center is more than a mere museum and far more fun than the average science centre. Here, you are given a series of hands-on experiences and habitats that entertain as well as inform, and school-age children in particular will benefit greatly from it.

Orlando Science Center

WonderWorks

The Science Center has nine main components, plus an inviting café, a night sky observatory and an IMAX cinema. **Natureworks** is an immersion-style exhibit creating a number of typical Florida habitats (with several shows like the *Circle of Life Game* and a series of hands-on field stations). **Science City** introduces fun ways to understand and use physical science and maths (including some mind-bending puzzles and challenges, notably in the Power Station), while the **Cosmic Tourist** offers a trip around our solar system with an amusing travel theme.

Bodyzone provides some fascinating insights into the human body, with an interactive element called Measure Me, which explores size, strength, flexibility, agility and sensory abilities. A Healthy Lifestyles exhibit shows how bad habits like smoking affect a healthy body. Next door, **TechWorks** is a four-part adventure into light, imaginary landscapes, showbiz science and a micro-world of microscopic investigation.

For those a bit too young for the educational element, **KidsTown** has plenty of junior-sized fun and games for under 8s. You'll be amazed at how much they learn in the course of having fun. **DinoDigs: Mysteries Unearthed** was a gift from the Walt Disney Company of their former Dinosaur Jubilee exhibit in the DinoLand USA area

> **BRIT TIP:** The CineDome film and laser show can operate until midnight on Friday and Saturday for a show independent of the Orlando Science Center.

of *Disney's Animal Kingdom*. It has been re-created in the OSC as a palaeontological excavation site, complete with eight full dinosaur skeleton replicas and a number of genuine fossils. **Wired Science** is then a series of networked multimedia kiosks introduced by wacky characters illustrating basic scientific principles and supporting other exhibits around the Center. The **Darden Adventure Theater** features science-themed comedy shows and demos, like PreHisto Rock (fun for all would-be palaeontologists) and the audience participating Science Spectrum.

In addition, the Center has two separate programmes in the **Dr Phillips CineDome**, a 310-seat cinema that practically surrounds its audience with large-format films, digital planetarium shows (a virtual tour of the universe, anyone?) and laser shows. It also boasts a 28,000-watt digital sound system that makes the experience unforgettable.

Getting there: the Science Center is on Princeton Street in downtown Orlando, just off Exit 85 of I-4 (go east on Princeton, the Center is on your left but the multi-storey car park is on the RIGHT, see map on page 188).

Admission: $14.95 for adults, $13.95 for seniors (55+) and $9.95 for 3–11s ($9.95, $8.95 and $4.95 after 6pm on Fri and Sat). Parking is $3.50. Open 9am–5pm Tue–Thur, 9am–9pm Fri and Sat, noon–5pm Sun. Closed Mon (except school holidays), Thanksgiving, Christmas Eve and Christmas Day (www.osc.org). AAAA.

Orange County History Center

This relatively recent addition offers an imaginative journey into central Florida history, from the wildlife and Native Americans to today's tourist issues and the space programme. Again, the accent is on the interactive, with hands-on exhibits and audio-visual presentations, and it is very much a journey through time, starting outside in renovated Heritage Square, complete with cypress trees and fountains. The History Center itself is in the former 1927 Orange County Courthouse, with the foyer converted into a dome featuring more than 150 icons unique to central Florida (see how many you can identify before and after your tour).

> **BRIT TIP:** Combine a visit to the History Center with lunch at the wonderfully eclectic Globe restaurant on the corner of the square.

7

The 4-storey adventure starts at the top with the **Orientation Theater's** 14-minute multimedia presentation as you sit in rocking chairs on the 'front porch'. Then you visit the Natural Environment and First Peoples exhibits (12,000 years ago), before First Contact

Orange County History Center

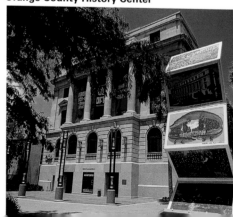

brings in the European element. Jump into the 1800s and you visit a Seminole settlement, a Pioneer Cracker home (the first true 'cowboys'), hear tales of the old cattle-ranching days and learn about the citrus industry.

The early 20th century brings the story of Transportation, Tin Can Tourists, Aviation and the great land boom, Selling Central Florida. Then witness how the region dramatically altered with the development of the Space Programme and the arrival of a certain Walter Elias Disney in The Day We Changed. From there, you move on to the beautifully restored Courtroom B for some more real-life Orlando history.

Finally, you hit the present in the Community exhibit, a spotlight on famous places, people and activities in the area, and a chance to view the dome from the top, testing all your new-found knowledge of the icons. In 2003, a new exhibit on African American history was added, featuring the achievements and tragedies of central Florida's African American community. You will also find periodical travelling exhibits here (the story of World War Two in Florida was on show during summer 2003), as well as the **Historium** gift shop.

Getting there: the Orange County History Center can be found off Central Boulevard and Magnolia Avenue downtown (Exit 82C off I-4, left on to Magnolia, right on to Central Boulevard, see map on page 188). Best parking is Orlando Public Library multi-storey car park on Central Boulevard (History Center admission includes 2 hours free parking if you show your ticket).

Admission: $7 for adults, $3.50 for 3–12s and $6.50 for seniors (60+), and it is open 10am–5pm Mon–Sat and noon–5pm Sun. For more information call 407 836 8500,

(www.thehistorycenter.org. AAA.

Other downtown developments include the free **Lymmo** bus service which connects the central stretch along Magnolia Avenue, from South Street to the **TD Waterhouse Center** (formerly the Orlando Arena for sports and concerts) on Amelia Street, the **Downtown Arts District and Arts Market** (on Wall Street, off Orange Avenue, every Saturday; 11am–9pm Oct–April), seasonal concerts and firework shows, plus new shops and restaurants around **Lake Eola**. The Lake itself is a beautiful area to wander around, with a park, children's play area and an extremely peaceful ambience. Children can feed the birds and fish or take a Swan paddleboat ride, plus regular free open-air events such as concerts and storytelling.

The **Cultural Corridor** links the Downtown Arts District (which includes the Bob Carr Performing Arts Center and the Centroplex), with the Loch Haven area (where you can find the Orlando Museum of Art, Mennello Museum of American Folk Art, Orlando Philharmonic Orchestra and the Orlando-UCF Shakespeare Festival), via the **Dr Phillips Performing Arts Center**, which is home of the Orlando Opera and Orlando Ballet.

The Saturday **Farmers' Market** (7am–1pm) has become a real downtown focal point (in the park area just outside the Orange County History Center), with vendors now including local artisans such as glassblowers and dressmakers, as well as wonderful fresh produce. The **Thornton Park** area is currently the most happening part of Orlando, with the new Thornton Park Central (at the junction of Summerlin Avenue and Central Boulevard, just south-east of Lake Eola) offering a mix of unique small boutiques and trendy restaurants, with the monthly Third Thursday street party (5–10pm) attracting a crowd. For the latest information visit www.downtownorlando.com.

The Holy Land Experience

Not so much a conventional attraction but right in the heart of the tourist mainstream is this 15-acre (6-ha) 'living Biblical museum', which sets out to re-create in detail the city of Jerusalem and its religious significance from 1450BC to AD66. Its aim is also to provide an explanation and celebration of the Christian faith.

The staff are all in period costume, the architecture and landscaping are impressive and the background music in both the indoor and outdoor areas is all original and suitably atmospheric. From the **Jerusalem Street Market** entrance to the **Qumran Dead Sea Caves**, **Calvary's Garden Tomb** and on to the highly impressive **Temple of the Great King** (destroyed by the Romans in AD70), everything is portrayed in literal Biblical terms. **The Theater of Life** shows a 25-minute film of Bible landmarks, from Adam and Eve to the Crucifixion, while the **Wilderness Tabernacle** is a 25-minute theatrical portrayal of Old Testament worship, featuring the Holy Ark with lasers and some impressive pyrotechnics.

A huge model of Jerusalem – which took more than a year to build – is explained in great detail several times a day in the form of a guided tour. Live performances include the *Garden Tomb Music & Drama* celebrating the Resurrection and an original musical drama *Today's The Day*, which plays out in the Plaza of Nations. There is even a Middle Eastern-style café where you can eat a Goliath Burger.

BRIT TIP: Reader Peter Crumpler suggests: 'The Holy Land is an unusual cross between a theme park and an educational tour, but I'd say British Christians would find it fascinating – both for learning more about the Bible and for seeing their livelier American cousins in action.'

Recently opened is the **Scriptorium** centre for Biblical antiquities, another themed environment showcasing various rare artefacts. It is a thoroughly unusual 'attraction' (although they don't call it that), and sits rather awkwardly among the main tourist offerings, but it may well pique the interest of some.

Getting there: The Holy Land Experience can be found immediately off Exit 78 on I-4, on the junction of Conroy and Vineland Roads (just north of Universal Orlando, see map on page 12).

Admission: $29.99 for adults and $19.99 for children 4–12. Parking is free. Open 10am–6pm Mon–Fri, 9am–6pm Sat, noon–6pm Sun. For more information call 407 367 2065 (www.theholylandexperience.com). AAA.

THE WATER PARKS

If anyone has been down the slides and flumes at the local leisure centre, they will have an inkling of what Orlando's four big water parks are all about. Predictably, Disney has the two most elaborate ones, but the Universal-owned Wet 'n Wild and Water Mania are equally adept at providing hours of fun in a variety

7

BRIT TIP: While water parks are a great way of cooling down, it is easy to pick up a 5-star case of sunburn. So don't forget the high-factor, waterproof suntan lotion.

of styles that owe much to the flair of the theme park creators.

All four require at least half a day of splashing, sliding and riding to get full value from their rather high prices. Lockers are provided for valuables and you can hire towels.

Disney's Typhoon Lagoon Water Park

Until *Disney's Blizzard Beach* water park opened in 1995, *Disney's Typhoon Lagoon* was the biggest and finest example of Florida's water parks. In high season, it is also the busiest, so be prepared to run into more queues. The park's 56 acres (23-ha) are spread out around the 2½-acre (1-ha) lagoon fringed with palm trees and white-sand beaches. If it weren't for the high-season crowds, you could easily feel you had been washed up on some tropical island paradise. *Disney's Typhoon Lagoon* is extravagantly landscaped introducing some clever detail. The walk up Mount Mayday,

for instance, provides a terrific overview as well as adding scenic touches such as rope bridges and tropical flowers. Sun loungers, chairs, picnic tables and even hammocks are provided to add to the comfort and convenience of restful areas like Getaway Glen. However, you need to arrive early to bag a decent spot.

The park is overlooked by the 90-ft (27-metre) Mount Mayday, on top of which is perched the luckless *Miss Tilly*, a shrimp boat that legend has it landed here during the typhoon that gave the park its name. Watch for the water fountains that shoot from Miss Tilly's funnel at regular intervals, accompanied by the ship's hooter, which signal another round of 6-ft (1.8-metre) high waves in the **Surf Pool** (you can hire inner-tubes to bob around on or just try body-surfing). Circling the lagoon is **Castaway Creek**, a 3ft (1 metre) deep, lazy flowing river that offers the opportunity to float happily along on rubber tyres.

BRIT TIP: As the busiest of the water parks, *Disney's Typhoon Lagoon* can hit capacity quite early in the day in summer. Call 407 824 4321 in advance to check on the crowds.

The series of slides and rides are all clustered around Mount Mayday and vary from the breathtaking body slides of **Humunga Kowabunga**, which drop you 214ft (65 metres) at up to 30mph (48kph) down some of the steepest inclines in waterdom (make sure your swimming costume is SECURELY fastened!), to **Ketchakiddee Creek**, which offers a selection of slides and pools for all youngsters under 4ft (122cm) tall. In between, you have the three **Storm Slides**, which twist and turn

Disney's Typhoon Lagoon

© Disney

through caves, tunnels and waterfalls, **Mayday Falls**, a 460-ft (140-metre) inner-tube ride down a series of banked drops, **Keel Haul Falls**, an alternative tube ride that takes slightly longer, and **Gangplank Falls**, a ride on tubes that take up to four people down 300ft (90 metres) of mock rapids. The hugely imaginative (but chilly) **Shark Reef** is an upturned wreck and coral reef, which you can snorkel around among 4,000 tropical fish and a number of real, but quite harmless, nurse sharks. Like all the areas, this is carefully supervised, and those who aren't quite brave enough to dive in can still get a close-up of the fish through the underwater portholes of the sunken ship (the Reef is closed during the coldest winter months).

BRIT TIP: 'Buy a disposable waterproof camera to tie around your wrist when you visit the water parks. We bought one cheap at Wal-Mart and have some lovely photos from *Typhoon Lagoon*,' says Judith Bingham.

There are height and health restrictions on Humunga Kowabunga (it's not suitable for anyone with a bad back or neck, or for pregnant women), while the queues for this slide, plus the Storm Slides and Shark Reef, can touch an hour at times, which can take a lot of the fun out of it. Keeping out of the sun can also be a problem as there's not much shade, but a quick plunge into Castaway Creek usually prevents overheating.

For snacks and meals, **Lowtide Lou's** and **Let's Go Slurpin'** both offer a bite to eat and drinks while **Typhoon Tilly's** and **Leaning**

BRIT TIP: Ladies, please remember, down some of the whizziest slides it is advisable to wear a one-piece swimsuit rather than a bikini. Your modesty could be at stake here!

Palms serve a mixture of burgers, sandwiches, salads and ice cream. It is essential to avoid main mealtimes here if you want to eat in relative comfort. You can, however, bring your own picnic (unlike the main theme parks) which you can eat in special scenic areas (but no alcohol or glass containers are allowed). You CAN'T bring your own snorkels, inner-tubes or rafts, but snorkels are provided at Shark Reef and you can hire inner-tubes only for the lagoon. If you have forgotten to bring a sunhat or bucket and spade for the kids, or even your swimsuit, they are all available (along with gifts and souvenirs) at **Singapore Sal's**.

To avoid the worst of the summer crowds (when the park's 7,200 capacity is often reached), Monday morning is the best time to visit (steer clear of weekends at all costs), and, on other days, arrive either 30 minutes before opening or in mid-afternoon, when many decide to dodge the daily rainstorm. Early evening is also extremely pleasant when the park lights up.

Disney's Blizzard Beach

Getting there: on Buena Vista Drive, just half a mile from the *Downtown Disney* area (see map on page 12).

Admission: $33.02 and $26.63 for 3–9s (under 3s free), or it is one of the options with the Park Hopper Plus Tickets. Parking is free. Open from 9am to dusk every day. TTTT/AAAAA.

Disney's Blizzard Beach Water Park

Ever imagined a skiing resort in the middle of Florida? Well, Disney has, and this is the wonderful result. *Disney's Blizzard Beach* water park puts the rest in the shade for size as well as extravagant settings, with the whole park arranged as if it were in the Rocky Mountains rather than the sub-tropics. That means snow-effect scenery, Christmas trees and water-slides cunningly converted to look like skiing pistes and toboggan runs. It delivers a real feast for water lovers and Disney admirers in general, and the basic premise of snow-surfin' USA is an unarguable 5-star knockout.

Main features are **Mount Gushmore**, a 90-ft (27-metre) mountain down which all the main slides run, (including the world's tallest free-fall speed slide, the terrifying 120-ft (37-metre) **Summit Plummet**, which rockets you down a 'ski jump' at up to 60mph (97kph),

BRIT TIP: You can save money on your day at the Disney water parks by buying refillable drinks mugs – $11.95 each – when you arrive and using them all day. Return another day and get a $5 sticker to use them again!

Tike's Peak, a kiddie-sized version of the park's slides and a mock snow-beach, and **Ski-Patrol Training Camp**, a series of slides and challenges for pre-teens. **Melt-Away Bay** is a 1-acre (0.4-ha) pool fed by 'melting snow' waterfalls (actually blissfully warm), and **Cross Country Creek** is a lazy-flowing half-mile river around the whole park which also floats guests through a chilly 'ice cave' (watch out for the mini-waterfalls of ice-cold water!).

A ski chair-lift operates to the top of Mount Gushmore, providing a magnificent view of the whole park and surrounding areas. Don't miss the outstanding rides – **Teamboat Springs**, a wild, family inner-tube adventure, Runoff Rapids, a 1-, 2- or 3-person tube plunge, and the **Snow Stormers**, a daring head-first 'toboggan' run. **Toboggan Racers** gives you the chance to speed down the 'slopes' against seven other head-first daredevils. All four go to new heights of water park imagination and provide good-sized thrills without overdoing the scare factor.

The **Downhill Double Dipper** is two side-by-side slides that send you down 230-ft (70-metre) tubes in a race that is timed on a big clock at the bottom, and which gives you a real jolt halfway down! For those not quite up to Summit Plummet lunacy, the wonderfully named **Slush Gusher** is a slightly less terrifying speed slide. There is a 'village' area with a **Beach Haus** shop and **Lottawatta Lodge** fast-food restaurant, offering diners a grandstand view of Mount Gushmore and Melt-Away Bay beach. Snacks are also available at **Avalunch** (ouch!), the **Warming Hut** and **Polar Pub and Frostbite Freddie's Frozen Refreshments**. Avoid the weekends and from mid-morning onwards on Wednesday to Friday when the crowds are massive.

Getting there: just north of *Disney's All-Star Resorts* off Buena

Vista Drive (see map on page 12).

Admission: $33.02 for adults and $26.63 for 3–9s; or one of the free optional extras with the Disney Hopper Plus Tickets; open daily from 9am to early evening. TTTTT/AAAAA.

Adjacent to *Disney's Blizzard Beach* is the amazing **Winter Summerland Miniature Golf Courses** (where Santa's elves hang out!), with two wonderfully elaborate courses that provide children with a great diversion. Watch out for a riot of visual gags and puns, as well as some tricky mini-golf.

Wet 'n Wild

If Disney scores highest marks for scenic content, Wet 'n Wild, the world's first water park back in 1977, goes full tilt for thrills and spills of the highest quality. This park will test the material of your swimsuit to the limit!

Wet 'n Wild is one of the best-attended water parks in the country, and its location in the heart of I-Drive makes it a major draw. Consequently, you will encounter some crowds here, although the 15 slides and rides, **Lazy River** attraction, an elaborate kids' park (with mini versions of many of the slides), **Surf Lagoon** and restaurant and picnic areas manage to absorb a lot of punters before queues develop. Amazingly, waits of more than half an hour at peak times are rare, but it is busiest at weekends,

BRIT TIP: The Children's Playground at Wet 'n Wild was built especially for those under 4ft (122cm) tall – right down to having the only junior wave pool in the world.

BRIT TIP: For all the water parks, it is a good idea to bring a pair of deck shoes or sandals that can be worn in water.

with July attracting most crowds.

You are almost spoilt for choice with main rides, from the highly popular group inner-tube rides of the **Surge** and **Bubba Tub**, through the more demanding rides of **The Blast** to the high-thrill factor of the 2-person **Black Hole** (like the *Magic Kingdom's* Space Mountain, but in water!), **Blue Niagara** (also enclosed, but this one's a body slide) and **Mach 5**, to the ultimate terror of **Der Stuka** and the **Bomb Bay**. The latter duo are definitely not for the faint-hearted. Basically, they are two 76-ft (23-metre) high body slides with drops as near vertical as makes no difference. Der Stuka is the straightforward slide, while the Bomb Bay adds the extra terror of being allowed to free-fall on to the top of the slide. And they call it fun! Suffice it to say, your author has not put himself at risk on these particular contraptions, and has no intention of doing so! For some reason, only 15–25 per cent of the park's visitors pluck up the courage to try it. Height restrictions of 4ft/122cm are in force on the Bomb Bay, Der Stuka and Blue Niagara, while older kids can get their own excitement on the huge, inflatable **Bubble Up**, which bounces them into 3ft (1 metre) of water.

The thrilling toboggan-like **Flyer** takes four passengers in 8-ft (2-metre) in-line tubes which whoosh down more than 450ft (137 metres) of banked curves and speed-enhancing straights, and the bungee-like **Hydra Fighter** is a 2-person swing equipped with a large fire-type hose that sends the

7

contraption into mad gyrations as you increase the water pressure!

New in 2003 was **The Blast**, a 1- or 2-passenger thrill ride which surprises you with sudden twists and turns, explosive pipe bursts and drenching waterspouts that lead up to a final waterfall plunge. And don't miss **The Storm**, a pair of identical circular slides billed as 'body coasters'! The enclosed tubes – complete with storm sound and light effects – send the rider plunging into a circular bowl, around which they spin at high speed before landing in the splash-pool below. Huge fun.

For those under 4ft (122cm) tall, the recently renovated **Kids Park** area has a full range of junior-sized slides, plus a new sandcastle structure with two semi-circular water-slides and a giant bucket that fills and tips up at regular intervals. Uniquely, the children can use speciality tubes, beach chairs and tables that have been designed specifically for their height.

The neighbouring lake is also part of the fun (although not in winter when it's more than chilly), adding the opportunities to try the cable-operated **Knee Ski, Wakeboarding** and (for a nominal fee) ride the **Wild One** (large inner-tubes tied behind a speedboat). Alternatively, take a breather in the slow-flowing, newly renovated **Lazy River** as you float leisurely through reaching palms and soothing waterfalls or abandon the water altogether for one of several shaded picnic areas, although they are popular. The energetic can also play beach volleyball. Lockers, showers, tube and towel rentals are all available but, if you bring your own floating equipment, you must have it checked by one of the lifeguards.

For food, **Bubba's Bar-B-Q** serves chicken, ribs, fries and drinks, the **Surf Grill** features burgers, hot dogs, chicken and sandwiches and another seven snack bars offer similar fast-food fare, including a pizza bar. Picnics can also be brought in, provided that you don't include any alcohol or glass containers.

Getting there: Wet 'n Wild is half a mile north of I-Drive's junction with Sand Lake Road at the intersection with Universal Boulevard (see map on page 12).

Admission: $32.95 for adults, $26.95 for 3–9s and free for under 3s; alternatively, it is included with the Orlando FlexTicket. Tube rentals are $4 ($2 deposit), towels $2 and lockers $5 ($2 deposit), or $9 for all three ($4 deposit). Parking is $5. Open year-round (with heated pools in the cooler months) from 9am in peak periods (10am at other times) until variously 5, 6, 7, 9 or 11pm (www.wetnwildorlando.com). TTTTT/AAA.

Water Mania

If Wet 'n Wild attracts the serious thrill seekers, Kissimmee's version, Water Mania, is more family-orientated and laid back, with the crowds greatest at weekends when the locals flock in. That's not to say this park doesn't have its fair share of scary slides (or Wet 'n Wild doesn't cater for families), it's just that their emphasis is slightly different and those looking to avoid the crowds often end up here. Where this 36-acre (15-ha) park scores a minor victory over its rivals is in the provision of 3 acres (1ha) of wooded picnic area where you can enjoy your own picnic (although no

The Abyss at Water Mania

BRIT TIP: Kids are again extremely well catered for, and Water Mania can even host birthday parties in Mr Kool's Party Land. Call 407 396 2626 for details.

glass items are allowed).

Eight different slides, including a patented non-stop surfing challenge called **Wipe-Out**, the usual **Cruisin' Creek**, a 720,000-gallon (3,276,000-litre) **Wave Pool** (waves every 15 minutes, up to 4ft/122cm high) and three separate kids' areas provide the main attractions – plenty to keep you occupied for at least half a day. Top of the list for those daring enough to throw themselves down things like Der Stuka is the **Screamer**, an aptly named 72-ft (22-metre) free-fall speed slide, and the **Abyss**, 380ft (116 metres) of enclosed-tube scary darkness.

The **Anaconda** and **Banana Peel** both feature family-sized inner-tubes down long, twisting slides, while the **Double Berzerker** offers two different ways to be whooshed along and spat out into a foaming pool at the bottom.

However, the outstanding feature, for both trying and watching, is the **Wipe-Out**, one of only two such attractions in the world. The challenge is to grab a body board and try to ride the continuous wave, risking going over the edge into another pool if you stray too wide, or being sent flying backwards if you lose your balance. A real blast!

When it comes to pint-sized fun for the children, Water Mania is one of the best. The **Rain Forest** is designed for the 2–10s, with a 5,000-sq-ft (464-sq-metre) pool ranging from 3in (7cm) to 2ft (60cm) deep and featuring a selection of mini-slides, fountains and water guns, all arranged around a wonderful large-scale pirate ship, with more chances to climb, jump and generally swashbuckle.

Other innovative recent additions are the **Rain Train**, a near life-size locomotive that sprays water out of its stack in the centre of a shallow pool, with other interactive play features and more slides; and **Tot's Town** for the toddlers (and their parents who want to relax a little), which is a partly fenced playground with sand beach and paddling area, added shade and refreshment hut.

In addition to the cooling picnic areas, there are several snack bars, a mini-golf course, volleyball and basketball courts and a large shop.

Getting there: Water Mania is located on Highway 192, just a mile (1.6km) east of the I-4 intersection (see map on page 12).

Admission: $26.95 and $21.35 for 3–9s; parking is $6. Open 10am–5pm daily from early March to the end of September, 11am–5pm Thur–Sun only in October (hours subject to change) (407 396 2626, www.watermania-florida.com). TTTT/AAA.

So that sums up the main large-scale attractions, but many people are now looking for the 'something different' factor, so let's explore some alternatives to the mass-market experience…

7

Rain Forest at Water Mania

Off the Beaten Track
(or, When you're All Theme-Parked Out)

After several days in the midst of the hectic tourist whirl of mainstream Orlando, you may be in need of a break from the non-stop theme park activities. Or you may be a repeat visitor looking for a different experience. If either is the case, this chapter is for you.

Hopefully, you will already have noted the relatively tranquil offerings of Silver Springs and Historic Bok Sanctuary in the previous chapter but, to get away from it all more completely and to enhance your view of the area further, the following are guaranteed to take you well off the beaten tourist track. This chapter should really be subtitled 'A Taste of the Real Florida', as it introduces the areas of Winter Park and Seminole County, nature boat rides, eco-tours and journeys by airboat, balloon, ship, train and plane (for the best maps, see page 58).

Winter Park

Foremost among the 'secret' hideaways is this elegant northern suburb of Orlando, little more than 20 minutes' drive from the hurly-burly of I-Drive yet a million miles from the relentless commercialism. It offers renowned museums and art galleries, fabulous shopping, numerous restaurants, pleasant walking tours, a delightful 50-minute boat ride around the lakes and, above all, a chance to slow down.

The central area is **Park Avenue**, a classy street of fine shops, boutiques, two museums and a wonderfully shaded park. At one end of the avenue is Rollins College, a small but highly respected arts education centre which houses the **Cornell Fine Arts Museum**, with the oldest collection of paintings, sculpture and decorative arts in Florida (open 10am–5pm Tue–Fri, 1pm–5pm Sat–Sun, closed Mon and main holidays, admission free) and the **Annie Russell Theater** (www.Rollins.edu).

The **Morse Museum of American Art** is a must for admirers of American art pottery, American and European glass, furniture and other decorative arts of the late 19th and early 20th centuries, as it includes one of the world's foremost collections of works by Louis Comfort Tiffany. The dazzling chapel restoration from the 1893 Chicago World Expo is now on display in its original form for the first time since the late 19th century and is worth the entrance fee alone. The museum is open 9.30am–4pm Tues–Sat and 1–4pm Sun, admission $4, under 12s free (www.morsemuseum.org).

The **Albin Polasek Museum and Sculpture Gardens** are also worth a look for culture buffs and for the serene setting devoted to this Czech-American artist. Open 10am–4pm Tue–Sat, 1–4pm Sun (closed July and August), admission is free and it is a superb setting for weddings.

The **Scenic Boat Tour** is located at the east end of Morse Avenue and offers a charming, narrated 12-mile (19-km) tour of the 'Venice of America' around the lakes and canals for a fascinating glimpse of some of the most beautiful houses, boat houses and lakeside gardens (properties in the area start at $800,000 and several top $4 million!). Tours run 10am–4pm daily and cost $8 for adults and $4 for children 2–11, and it is one of the most relaxing hours you will spend in Orlando (www.scenicboattours.com).

Alternatively, a trip with **Home Town Bicycle Tours** gives a gentle but unique overview of this picturesque neighbourhood, including several parks and Rollins College, with full guide narration ($30 per hour/per ride group with four riders or more, up to 10; $10 per hour/per person for up to three riders; plus $20 bike hire; call 407 332 8703 or e-mail hometownbicycletours@hotmail.com) You can also take the **Park Avenue Walking Tour**, with useful free maps provided by the Chamber of Commerce on New York Avenue.

The shops of Park Avenue are a cut above most you will encounter and, while you may find the prices equally distinctive, just browsing is an enjoyable experience with the charm of the area highlighted by the friendliness hereabouts. For shops that are both unique and fun, look out for **Panache** (jewellery), **Park Avenue Gallery** (art), **Kendyl's Kloset** (children's clothes and toys) and **The Doggie Door** (for pets). Recent additions are **Winter Park Teddy Bear Co.** (make and stuff your own soft toys), **Olive This Relish That** (a wonderful gourmet food store with Mediterranean specialities) and **Peter Brook Chocolatier**. Regular pavement craft fairs and art festivals add splashes of colour to an already inviting scenario, plus live jazz in Central Park once a month on Sundays in summer.

In addition to **Park Plaza Gardens**, which specialises in Continental cuisine (see Chapter 10, page 281), you can sample French, Italian and Thai cuisines, among others. The new **Zak's on Park Avenue** receives rave reviews from the locals for its sparkling New Orleans-flavoured menu. **Allegria Café and Cucina** is another fine romantic, Italian-flavoured choice, while **310 Park South** offers the epitome of elegant, European-style café culture. Watch out, too, for Dress Up Thursdays, where the best-dressed diner in each of six restaurants receives a goody bag from Park Avenue merchants. Street parking usually allows 2 hours free, but the SunTrust Building on the corner of Comstock and Park Avenue is a better bet. And keep an eye out for the **Sidewalk Art Festival** every March and the Autumn Art Festival in October.

The **Central Park** area alongside Park Avenue, notable for its fountains and flowers, is due to be expanded in the near future, which should enhance things still further. Check out www.wpfl.org and www.parkave-winterpark.com for more info.

Another high point of a visit to Winter Park is the **Kraft Azalea Gardens** on Alabama Drive (off Palmer Avenue at the north end of Park Avenue), 11 acres (5ha) of shaded lakeside walkways, gardens and hundreds of magnificent azaleas. The main focal point, the mock Grecian temple, is a beautiful setting for weddings. **Mead Botanical Gardens**, on Garden Drive (just off Highway 17/92) offers more trails through a sub-tropical forest, with native birds and plants from around the world. There is no admission charge for either.

To get to Winter Park, take Exit 87 from I-4, Fairbanks Avenue. Turn right on to Fairbanks and head east for 2 miles (3km) until it intersects with Park Avenue and turn left.

8

Midway between Winter Park and downtown Orlando is another botanical gem, **Leu Gardens**, a 50-acre (20-ha) retreat featuring formal gardens, peaceful walks and a boardwalk overlooking Lake Rowena. **The Leu House Museum** is open 10am–3.30pm (closed in July) with tours every 30 minutes (last tour at 3.30pm). The gardens are open daily from 9am–5pm (9am–8pm in summer) and cost $4 for adults and $1 for under 13s. You will find them on the corner of Forest and Nebraska Avenues, via Mills Avenue and Princeton St from Exit 85 on I-4.

Sailing school

Aquatic Wonders Boat Tours

To go further into the real world of Florida nature and its wildlife, **Aquatic Wonders** operates a delightful break from the theme park business on Lake Tohopekaliga in Kissimmee (the bigger of the two lakes; NOT East Lake Toho). Operated by Captain Ray Robida and limited to a maximum of six per trip, the choice of eight cruises offers a series of gentle adventures that are entertaining, educational and relaxing. Every cruise on the 30-ft (9-metre) covered pontoon boat is different depending on local conditions and Captain Ray's individual style, which is wonderfully laid back yet informative. His knowledge of the waterways and wildlife is outstanding and children with enquiring minds will benefit. His boat is wheelchair accessible and there is a loo!

The 3-hour **Aquatic Wonders cruise** studies the local lakes and rivers, water ecology and the fish, insects and other animals of the area ($35 for adults and children). The **Eagle Watch Tour** is an ornithologist's delight as it goes out for 2 hours to look at the nesting bald eagles on the lake (and this is an area renowned for them), rare ospreys and many other birds ($21 for adults, $14 for 3–12s). The rather romantic **Sunset Sounds** is another 2-hour trip aboard *Eagle Ray* to enjoy the sights and sounds of dusk over the lake as the birds come home to roost ($24 and $17). **Starlight Wonders** is a 2-hour tour for a spot of star-gazing, gentle music and Native American stories surrounding the origins of the constellations ($30 and $24). **Rivers in Time** is a 2-hour journey back in time to the days of the river boat and the Seminole Indian War, a fascinating live history lesson with

> **BRIT TIP:** Amazingly, the waterways feeding Lake Toho stretch all the way to Miami in the south. Captain Ray of Aquatic Wonders is a mine of fascinating geographical and historical information.

Mead Botanical Gardens

Fishing at Clearwater

all the sights and sounds of the lake for good measure ($21 and $14).

The **Gator Watch Tour** is a 2-hour night-time journey to view some of the locals hunting, nesting and just hanging out and there are plenty of them out there! ($30 and $24). **Family Fishing Adventures** offers 4–5 hours of fishing fun with all bait and tackle (but not fishing licence) provided, especially for beginners ($200 for up to six). A new 2-hour tour of unspoilt **Makinson Island** is also available, providing an interpretive guided tour of this 132-acre (54-ha) nature preserve ($21). There is even a **Maritime Wedding Chapel** cruise, with the ceremony performed by the Captain himself, starting at $200 for a party of six.

Games and videos are provided on all trips for the kids in case their attention wanders! All tours supply non-alcoholic drinks and snacks (but you can also take your own) and Captain Ray is fully licensed by the US Coast Guard, so you are guaranteed a high level of safety as well as entertainment. The *Eagle Ray* departs daily from 101 Lakeshore Boulevard in downtown Kissimmee (via Main Street and Broadway, turn left into Ruby and

right at the end, Lakeshore Boulevard). Call 407 846 2814 to make reservations (recommended), or visit www.florida-nature.com.

Airboat rides

The thrill of airboat rides can be experienced on many of Florida's lakes, rivers and marshes. An airboat is a totally different experience to any boat ride you will have had before, as it is more like flying at ground level. As much a thrill as a scenic adventure, it has the advantage of exploring areas otherwise inaccessible to boats.

Airboats simply skim over and through the marshes, to give you an alternative, close-up and very personal view. Travelling at up to 50mph (80kph) means it can be loud (hence you will be provided with headphones) and sunglasses are also a good idea to keep stray flies out of your eyes. However, it is NOT the trip for you if you are spooked by crickets, dragonflies and similar insects that occasionally land in the boat! In summer months, a good insect repellant is also advisable.

Several operations offer airboat rides in the area, from 'you-drive' boats that do barely 5mph (8kph) to much bigger ones, but for the most quality-conscious operation my tip goes to **Boggy Creek Airboat Rides**. Their airboats can be found at their main site on Lake Toho at peaceful Southport Park (all the way down Poinciana Boulevard, off Highway 192 between Markers 10 and 11, and across into Southport

8

Airboat ride

BRIT TIP: Look out for discount coupons in tourist literature offering up to $3 off airboat rides.

Road – about a 30-minute drive) and at a secondary location on East Lake Toho. For the latter, you either take Exit 17 off the Central Florida Greeneway (417) and go south on Boggy Creek Road, then right into East Lake Fish Camp; better still, take Osceola Parkway all the way east until it hits Boggy Creek Road. Go left and then turn right at the Boggy Creek T-junction, then right into East Lake Fish Camp after 2 miles (3km).

The **East Lake Fish Camp** is itself a little gem, offering a variety of boating and angling opportunities (call 407 348 2040 for details) as well as the wonderfully authentic rural Florida charm of the **restaurant and gift shop** (open 8am–9pm every day). If you are heading for a morning airboat ride, consider arriving early for a huge all-day breakfast at the fish camp first, where the more adventurous will want to try the local delicacies – catfish, frogs' legs and gator tail. For another great slice of local eating, try the Friday buffet and Saturday night seafood buffet, fabulous value at $10.95 and $12.95 each on an all-you-can-eat basis.

Boggy Creek's **half-hour ride** features the most modern 18-passenger airboats in Florida, skimming over the local wetlands for a close-up view of the majestic cypress trees and wildlife that can

BRIT TIP: Best time for an airboat ride is first thing on a weekday morning when the wildlife is not hiding from the weekend boaters.

include eagles, ospreys, snakes and turtles, as well as the ever-present gators. The Southport Park site tends to be the quieter of the two, with more wildlife – especially in the spring – but involves a longer drive than East Lake Fish Camp.

You do not need to book, just turn up as boats go every half-hour (9am–5.30pm daily), and rides cost $18.95 for adults and $14.95 for children 3–12 (don't forget the sunscreen as you can really burn out on the water). They also do a 1-hour **Night Tour** ($29.95 for adults, $24.95 for 3–12s, Mar–Oct only) for a completely different and exhilarating experience (gator eyes glow red in the dark!), but you must book at least 3 days in advance. In addition, they run a night-time **Gator Safari**, with dinner, on Tue and Sun (May–Oct only) in conjunction with Gator Tours (www.gatortours.com). (See page 257 for more details.)

Finally, they offer a 45-minute **private tour** in their 6-passenger boat ($45/person), which provides an even more personal view of this amazing area. Call 407 344 9550 or visit www.bcairboats.com for more info and a money-off coupon.

Boggy Creek Parasail

Complementary to the airboat rides, this is an opportunity to float over East Lake Toho for some breathtaking views. You rise up with the greatest of ease from the back of a 16-passenger boat and reach heights of up to 400ft (122 metres), 600ft (183 metres) or 800ft (244 metres) depending on how much you pay, descending again after about 15 relaxing minutes to land gently, standing up – and completely dry. The sit-down harness used requires no skill or effort on your part and makes it accessible to everyone (even me!). The system is also deft enough to allow the operators to dip you in the water – upon request! Single flyers cost $45 (up to 400ft/122 metres), $55 (600ft/183 metres) and $65 (800ft/244 metres), while double flyers are $75, $85 and $95. There is also a romantic Sunset Cruise package, with drinks and hors d'oeuvres, at $180 per couple. Observers may ride free if there is space in the boat. Open 10am–5.30pm daily, reservations are not usually required but it is wise to check by calling 407 348 2700 or visit www.boggycreekparasail.com.

Cypress Glades Adventure Tours

Brand new in 2003 and in conjunction with Gatorland, this is an adventurous series of offerings into the Florida countryside and waterways. Based either in Gatorland itself or out on some of the many unspoiled lakes of the area, the genuine feel of real Florida nature here is all encompassing. The local wildlife includes whitetail deer, Osceola turkeys, bald eagles and wild hogs, as well as the inevitable gators, and birdlife, such as ospreys, cranes, white pelicans, owls, Coopers hawks, cardinals, storks and ivies.

Their four main options are a fully-guided **half-day airboat excursion** including picnic lunch and some real local insight ($55 and $45); a **night-time airboat ride** on its own ($38 and $28), with the chance to see how amazing Florida's

BRIT TIP: If you are staying in or visiting Seminole County, visit Black Hammock Fish Camp for their version of the wonderful airboat adventure (see page 226).

oldest inhabitants are by torchlight (don't forget the bug repellant here); the 1-hour **gator egg collection** out in the 10-acre (4-ha) breeding marsh at Gatorland itself, a fairly labour-intensive tour for the true adventure seeker (12 and up only, $49.95; Jun–Jul); and the exclusive **Trainer for a Day** programme, also at Gatorland, with the opportunity to work behind the scenes at the park, finding out what it takes to handle such dangerous animals, behavioural training and a go at gator wrangling ($100 for 2 hours for 12s and up). You can also visit Bass Pro Shops Outdoor World at Festival Bay (see page 288) for their Adventure Center.

For more details, call 407 855 5496 or visit www.gatorland.com.

Balloon trips

Florida is one of the most popular areas for ballooning and, if you are up early enough in the morning, you will often see several. The experience is a majestic one. If Orlando represents the holiday of a lifetime, then a balloon flight is the ride of a lifetime. The utterly smooth way in which you lift off into the early morning sky is breathtaking in itself, but the peace and quiet of the ride, not to mention the stunning views from 2,000ft (600 metres) above ground, are quite awesome. It is not a cheap experience, but it is equally appealing to all but the youngest children or those who have vertigo or a fear of heights. It is a highly personalised ride, taking up to six people. Some baskets take up to 12, but it's a squeeze!

Orange Blossom Balloons is one of the premier companies in central Florida, with more than 18 years' experience and a wonderful laid-back style that stems from their British-owned operation. You meet

8

in the restaurant at **La Quinta Inn** on Highway 192 (five traffic lights WEST of the main entry to Disney) at 6am – the best winds for flying are nearly always first thing in the morning – and then transfer to the take-off site, where you help the crew members set up one of their three balloons.

Owner-operator Richard Ornstein and his team (Jonathan, Jeff, Bill, Bob and Pat) are a real hoot, and you are soon up, up and away in awe-inspiring style, floating serenely up into the sky or sinking down to skim the surface of one of the many lakes (disturbing the occasional gator or deer). After about an hour you come back to earth for a traditional champagne landing ceremony and return to La Quinta for a full breakfast and your special balloonist's certificate. The full experience lasts 3–4 hours and costs $175 per adult (inclusive of tax) and $95 for 10–15s (under 10s go free with their parents). Hotel pick-up is also available at $10/person round trip, or you can pay $20 to be part of the chase crew and just enjoy the champagne landing and breakfast. Call 407 239 7677 for reservations (they do book up well in advance, even though they fly every day, weather permitting) or go to www.orangeblossomballoons.com.

Kayaking in Wekiva Springs State Park

> **BRIT TIP:** Dresses are not advisable for balloon trips and wearing sensible shoes is essential.

Alternatively, check out **Blue Water Balloons** for a more small-scale experience, finishing with a breakfast and champagne picnic out in the peaceful wilds of Florida where you land. Owner-operator Don Edwards and his team are also a pleasure to fly with and have thousands of hours' flying experience plus a wealth of stories to pass on (they have flown in more than 30 US states and piloted the Energizer Bunny – the largest shaped balloon in America!). The picnic includes fresh fruit, cheeses, pastries and nachos and salsa, plus champagne and fresh orange juice. Don says: 'We have asked our passengers over the years if they would prefer a restaurant breakfast or our traditional picnic, and the answer is usually "We can eat in a restaurant anytime, this is much more personal and intimate".' Each passenger receives a Flight of Ascension certificate and a souvenir balloon-etched champagne glass. The price is $165 for adults and $85 for children under 90lb (41kg), while you can also book a private flight for two for $425 or $200/single, and buy gift certificates at $150. Wedding flights are available on request. Visit www.bluewaterballoons.com for a $10 discount voucher. Call 407 894 5040 or 1-800 586 1884 to book.

Everglades and the Bahamas

Day trips are increasingly common from Orlando to the Everglades, Miami, the Florida Keys and the Bahamas and, if you are prepared to

Blue Water Balloons

optional excursions on the amazing Sea Screamer giant speedboat ($66 for adults, $34 for 3–12s), dolphin encounter cruise ($58 and $34), Captain Memo's Pirate Cruise ($76 and $62) and deep-sea fishing ($85 and $69). The trip itself costs $69 for adults and $19 for 3–9s (plus $12/person hotel tax). Alternatively, a 1-day **Clearwater Beach** trip ($50 and $29) provides ample time on the beach, with lunch included and optional speedboat, dolphin cruise, pirate cruise and fishing excursions.

Real Florida's **Naples-Everglades Adventure** trip provides a taste of Florida in just a day (although a greater proportion of time is spent on the coach), with a 30-minute airboat ride through the Everglades, lunch in beautiful Naples and an afternoon cruise along the coastal waterways. This costs $109 (adults) and $70 (3–12s).

A relatively new offering is their limo evening out to Universal's CityWalk, with dinner and a pass for the clubs. Called **Be A Star in a Great Big Car**, it involves a return trip from your hotel to CityWalk in a stretch limo, and is proving highly popular at $74 for adults and $59 for 3–12s. A **Kennedy Space Center** day trip costs $64 and $52 (including admission,) and there is a **Kennedy Eco Tour** and an airboat ride ($75 and $63). The **Shopping Bonanza** (including an all-you-can-eat buffet breakfast and visits to Wal-Mart, Premium Outlets and Mall at Millenia) will set you back $31 for adults and $19 for 3–9s. Call Real Florida Excursions on 1-866 266 5733 or visit www.realfloridaexcursions.com.

International Divers offers several memorable excursions, chiefly a **Florida Adventure Tour**, a personal, all-day experience in real Florida. It includes a breakfast buffet stop, a 2-hour boat trip and snorkel on the picturesque Crystal River (where you often encounter

put up with a long day out (up to 16 hours) you can see a lot of the state this way. However, it's a long journey for kids for a half-hour airboat ride, in the case of the Everglades.

Real Florida Excursions and **International Divers** are two companies worth recommending.

Real Florida has a variety of tours, from an Orlando Shopping Bonanza excursion to a new 2-day **Grand Bahama Tour**. For the latter, you make an early start by coach down to Palm Beach (3 hours), with breakfast en route, and catch the high-tech, high-speed catamaran Cloud-X for the 2-hour transit to Grand Bahama Island, where you check in at the Royal Oasis Casino Resort, with shopping, dining and beautiful white-sand beaches. The following day can be spent back on the beach, at the resort or with the optional **Dolphin Encounter**, before the return at 6.30pm and the (rather long) coach ride back to Orlando. This good-value package (every Wednesday) costs $249 for adults, $119 for first child and $159 each child thereafter, plus $14/person hotel tax.

Another Real Florida 2-day trip is the new **Clearwater Getaway**, which provides luxury coach transport to the Gulf coast, overnight accommodation at a 3-star hotel with beach access, plus

8

the harmless manatee), a relaxing picnic lunch, 45-minute airboat tour on the Withlacoochee River, plus a 20-minute, narrated boat tour on Pepper Creek and a visit to Homosassa State Wildlife park to see panthers, bobcats, bears, eagles, alligators and flamingos. It costs $109 for adults and $79 for 3–9s (under 3s not permitted). Alternatively, their 2-day Miami and Florida Keys **Swim with the Dolphins** is an excellent, action-packed proposition, visiting the Everglades en route, seeing an alligator-wrestling and snake-handling show and taking an airboat ride before arriving at the Keys for a beach barbecue. Part two of the adventure, after an overnight stay and breakfast at your beach resort, is the **dolphin encounter**, a 2-hour programme of instruction, observation and interaction with the Keys' tame resident dolphins (including one-to-one swims, dorsal tows and foot pushes). Finally, you have half a day in Miami to explore the Bayside Shopping plaza or take the Star Island tour of the homes of the rich and famous. Prices are $199 for adults and $179 for 3–9s, with a $135 supplement for the dolphin swim (not for under 7s).

Two recent additions are **Sun, Sand and Scales** (an all-day trip to Cocoa Beach leaving at 9am, with time to enjoy the beach, pier, Ron Jon's Surf Shop before heading off to the Airboat Outpost for an animal show and barbecue with unlimited food and drink, followed by a fascinating night-time airboat ride in search of gators; $89 and $59) and **The Fast & The Furious** (an all-day adventure to Daytona, including either the morning at the USA Raceway, or a Trolley Duck Amphibious Ride and beach time, packed lunch, an afternoon trip to New Smyrna Beach to include either bike hire, beach chair/ umbrella hire or boogie board for

the kids. Leaves between 7 and 8am; $99 and $79). There are also a number of tempting Florida sea-dive expeditions every Saturday, from $36/person. Call International Divers on 407 352 5151 or visit www.swimdolphins.com.

Flying Tigers Warbird Air Museum

Vintage aeroplane and nostalgia buffs will want to make a note of this offbeat museum adjacent to Kissimmee Airport, which builds and restores World War Two fighters and bombers. Kids who like building Airfix kits will especially enjoy the 1-hour tour of the facilities, which basically represent a couple of large hangars with aircraft in various stages of restoration and repair. It is one of the most fascinating programmes of its kind, with the exhibits ranging from a fully restored B-25 Mitchell bomber and a P-51 Mustang to scraps of fuselages and engines that will gradually be incorporated into the latest rebuilding project. It's a place where you see, smell and touch the history of the 1940s' newsreels, and the guides have a detailed knowledge of everything they show you.

You could be forgiven for thinking you have walked into a scrap yard, but the main hangars reveal the full scale of the operation, with the wholesale restoration of a B-17 Flying Fortress being their pride and joy. In fact, owner Tom Reilly insists: 'All those clean, tidy sterile museums you have seen in the past, well, this isn't one of them. We have oil on the floor we refer to as bomber blood and, if you are lucky, you might get some on you to take home as a souvenir.'

Restoration projects include a Vought Corsair and a Lockheed Lightning, while a Lockheed Starfighter and MIG 21 are among around 13 planes on static display. Another 18 or so are airworthy, including a Focke-Wolf 190 and a B-25 bomber. The site includes a charming gift shop that houses some more museum pieces, uniforms and memorabilia from World War Two. It is open 9am–5pm every day, and there's always some reconstruction work in progress. Charges are $9 for adults and $8 for 60+ and under 12s (under 8s free). This 'living museum' can be found off Highway 192, half a mile (1km) down Hoagland Boulevard on the left.

A new **Flight of Four Passport** includes entry to the Flying Tigers Warbird Museum, Fantasy of Flight in Polk County (see page 198), the Florida Air Museum at Sun 'n Fun in Lakeland, central Florida (www.sun-n-fun.org), and Valiant Air Command's Warbird Air Museum in Titusville, near the Kennedy Space Center (www.vacwarbirds.com), for only $44. It is good for a year from activation and includes gift shop discounts and a pin from each museum. Purchase Passports at www.fantasyofflight.com.

Warbird Adventures

Once you have seen the displays, you should consider neighbouring Warbird Adventures. *This is the best ride in town, bar none, guaranteed.* Not only do you get to fly in one of their three 1945 T-6 Harvard fighter-trainers, but also, after a period of getting used to the front seat of this vintage two-seater… you get to fly it! And you don't just handle the controls, your instructor will get you doing loops, barrel rolls and all manner of aerobatics. This is simply the most exhilarating ride I have ever done, enhanced by in-flight video and wingtip camera to record every moment. It is the only place where you can walk in off the

street and, 20 minutes later, be flying a plane with no previous experience at all.

My instructor was the excellent Thom Richard and, despite my initial reluctance, he eventually had me doing the full aerobatic business before long. Roller-coasters? They're for wimps! Mind you, this is not cheap – a 15-minute flight costs $160, a 30-minute trip is $270 and an hour $490. Aerobatics (on 30- or 60-minute flights only) cost $30, while the PAL video is $40 (or DVD for $50) and the stills $20 (or all three 'extras' for $85). Nevertheless, this is a memory to last a lifetime, and the thought of it still thrills me to bits. They also operate a 1966 Bell 47-G M*A*S*H helicopter for flights and instruction (407 870 7366, www.warbirdadventures.com).

Green Meadows Petting Farm

From one extreme to another, here is guaranteed fun for kids aged 2 up to about 11 and their parents (don't forget your cameras). It's the ultimate hands-on experience as, on the 2-hour guided tour, kids get to milk a cow, pet a pig, cuddle a chick or duckling, feed goats and sheep, meet a buffalo, chickens, peacocks and donkeys and learn what makes a farm

BRIT TIP: Reader Lynda Letchford says: 'Wear enclosed shoes to Green Meadows, which my 2-year-old really enjoyed. When you are in the pens with the animals, they nibble your toes and you step in all sorts! Also take some hand wipes for extra hygiene.'

tick. There are pony rides and a play area for the young ones and tractor-drawn hay rides for all, plus the Green Meadows Express steam train which takes you on a a scenic chug around the farm.

The shaded areas, free-roaming animals and peaceful aspect all contribute to another pleasant change of pace, especially as Green Meadows is barely 10 minutes from the tourist hurly-burly of Highway 192 (south on Poinciana Boulevard). It is open 9.30am–5.30pm daily (last admission at 4pm) and costs $18 ($14 for seniors, under 2s free); allow 3–4 hours for your visit. Drinks, snacks and gifts are available, but it is also the ideal place to bring a picnic (407 846 0770, www.greenmeadowsfarm.com).

Osceola County Pioneer Museum

Only just off the beaten track in Kissimmee but a delightful discovery is this small-scale homage to 19th-century Florida life, with a preserved cracker (cowboy) homestead portraying how the original settlers lived in the 1890s. The fascinating little museum traces the history of Osceola County, and includes a cattle camp, nature walk, country store and information centre with library. But the real highlight is provided by the volunteers who take you round, providing a fascinating view of life here more than 100 years ago. Situated on N Bass Road (turn off Highway 192 right by the big Wal-Mart Supercenter next to Medieval Times), it is open 10am–4pm Tue–Fri and noon–4pm Sat and Sun and admission is by $2 donation per adult and $1 per child (407 396 8644).

Reptile World Serpentarium

Another throwback to an earlier time in Florida (albeit only BD – Before Disney) is this wonderfully kitsch roadside attraction in St Cloud. Florida is actually home to a wide variety of snakes, both venomous and non-venomous, and all of them can be seen here. In all, there are more than 60 species of worldwide reptile featured in the clean, indoor exhibits (including the Australian Taipan – rated the world's deadliest snake), but the standout feature is the twice-daily (at midday and 3pm) 'milking' of venom from some of the more hazardous residents – cobras and vipers – for snake research. Snakes are their stock-in-trade, but you will also meet turtles, gators and iguanas. Out on the eastern stretch of Highway 192, just past St Cloud, it is open 9am–5.30pm Tue–Sun and costs $5.50 for adults, $4.50 for 6–17s and $3.50 for 3–5s (407 892 6905).

> **BRIT TIP:** If you are brave enough to volunteer during the venom show, you won't actually be asked to help in this genuinely dangerous activity, but you will get the chance to stroke a boa constrictor afterwards.

Warbird Adventures

Disney and cruising

Taking a cruise is fast becoming a regular option with an Orlando stay and, with the introduction of *Disney Cruise Line* in 1998, you will now see a lot of publicity for these competitively priced 2-, 3-, 4- and 7-day sailings out of fast-developing Port Canaveral.

Although a newcomer to cruising, Disney has a couple of breathtaking ships, the 83,000-ton *Disney Magic* (1998) and *Disney Wonder* (1999), with their own dedicated cruise terminal. Classic design plus the usual Disney Imagineering have produced these two huge vessels, incorporating special features for kids, teenagers AND couples without children. Both ships are a destination experience in their own right, each with four restaurants, a 1,040-seat theatre, cinema, nightclub complex, sports club and a full health spa, while they sail to the Bahamas, Caribbean and Disney's stunning private island. It is not a cheap option and the 3- and 4-night cruises can feel a little frenzied, but the 7-night Caribbean cruises – either to St Maarten and St Thomas or Key West, Grand Cayman and Cozumel in Mexico – offer a genuinely relaxing style that is hard to beat. They boast some novel touches with superb on-board entertainment, Disney character interaction and wonderful features like the adults-only champagne brunch. Many tour operators offer *Disney Cruise Line* packages but you can also book cruise-only at great rates with Dreams Unlimited Travel (see page 29).

The ships are identical in practical terms, and the week-long cruises allow you to enjoy fully the wide range of facilities. The impact of the four-restaurant set-up (where you dine in a different one each night, including the amazing black-and-white *Animator's Palate* which

comes to life all around you), the fabulous entertainment 'district', the vast array of kids' facilities (including Buzz Lightyear's Cyberspace Command Post) and the picturesque beaches of Disney's Castaway Cay island is just superb. NB: In summer 2005, the *Disney Magic* will sail out of Los Angeles as part of Disneyland's 50th Anniversary, offering 7-night voyages to the Mexican Riviera.

Other Port Canaveral options (www.portcanaveral.org) include the glitzy **Carnival Cruise Lines** (all-modern hardware, party atmosphere; call 1-888 2276 4825 in the US or 020 7940 4466 in the UK) with 3- and 4-day Bahamas voyages on the *Fantasy*, and alternating 7-day cruises to the east and west Caribbean on one of their newest and biggest ships, the *Carnival Glory*; **Royal Caribbean International** (more modern, glamorous ships, call 1-800 327 6700 in the US or 01932 834231 in the UK) with similar trips to Nassau and RCI's private island of Coco Cay, plus new 1-week Caribbean cruises on their amazing new mega-ship *Mariner of the Seas*; **Holland America Line** (more traditional cruise elegance, call 1-877 932 4259 in the US, 020 7940 4477 in the UK) offering 1-week cruises (Oct–April) to the Eastern Caribbean and their private Bahamian island of Half Moon Cay; and a unique 1-week cruise with **NCL**, one of the brightest and most quality-conscious brands, (call 1-800 327 7030 in the US or 08705 906060 in the UK), who takes their magnificent new *Norwegian Dawn* on a round trip from Port Canaveral to Miami, the Bahamas and New York (yes, the Big Apple itself). For more advice, consult my book *Choosing A Cruise* (Foulsham) or specialist UK travel agent, **The Cruise Line Ltd**, on 0870 112 1102. In Orlando, try Cruise

8

Planners on 1-877 772 7847 or www.gocruiseplanner.com.

For a smaller and more low-key approach, the **Rivership Romance** (daily out of downtown Sanford) is a great choice, especially for the lunch cruises on the wildlife-rich St John's River. The old-fashioned steamer can take up to 200 in comfort and adds a fine meal, live entertainment and a river narration, as well as providing a relaxing alternative to the usual tourist rush. Choose from the 3-hour lunch cruise (11am–2pm Wed, Sat and Sun) at $36.75 a head, the 4-hour cruise (11am–3pm Mon, Tue, Thur and Fri) at $47.25 or an evening dinner-dance voyage (7.30–11pm Sat) at $52.50. New in 2004 was the **Wedding Comedy Dinner Show**, featuring Tina and Tony and their slightly deranged relations in a madcap wedding 'reception' that involves everyone aboard (7–9.30pm Fri; $45). To book, call 407 321 5091 or visit www.rivershipromance.com. Their dock can be found off Exit 101A of I-4, east into Sanford, then left on Palmetto Avenue.

Seminole County

Having arrived in the historic town of Sanford, the heart of Seminole County, it is worth pointing out the possible diversions of a day or two in this area that will get you well off the beaten track. The **Central Florida Zoological Park** is a private, non-profit-making organisation that puts a pleasant, natural accent on the zoo theme and is set in 116 wooded acres (47 ha) of unspoilt Florida countryside with boardwalks and trails around all the attractions. These include more than 100 species of animals, weekend feeding demonstrations, educational programmes, a picnic area, pony rides and a butterfly garden, plus the Zoofari Outpost

gift shop. It's good value, too, at $8.75 for adults, $6.75 for seniors (60+) and $4.75 for 3–12s (half-price admission 9–10am Thur), and the park (off Exit 104 of I-4) is open every day (except Thanksgiving Day and Christmas Day) 9am–5pm. They were in the process of adding new attractions and enlarging several exhibits in 2004 – notably their vulture, cougar and siamang habitats – making it even better value (www.centralfloridazoo.org).

St John's River Cruise, at Blue Spring State Park, features a 2-hour nature tour of this historic waterway, with interactive narration of the history, flora and fauna (which includes manatees in winter months). This immensely personable, family-run tour costs $16 for adults, $14 for seniors (60+) and $10 for 3–12s and leaves from Orange City marina several times a day (take Highway 17/92 north from Sanford to French Avenue and head west for 1 mile/ 1.6km). Call 407 330 1612 to check times and book.

One of the most fun and entertaining of the area's airboat rides is to be found at the **Black Hammock Fish Camp and Restaurant** (off Exit 44 of the Central Florida Greeneway, take SR 434 east, turn left on Deleon St and left on to Black Hammock Road). This peaceful backwater on beautiful Lake Jesup is home to Captain Joel Martin, a Frenchman who enjoys his Florida boating, and his **1-hour tours** will take you into every nook and cranny of either the east or west lake (and this really is a great lake to explore, positively crammed with gators, including some of the biggest I've seen in the wilds). It is an eye-opening adventure, and Captain Martin even keeps his own gators, large and small, back at the Fish Camp. Rides are $30 and $25 for under 10s, (30-minute rides available for $19.94 and $15.95) and you

BRIT TIP: Visit Central Florida Zoo at the weekend and you will be offered a series of educational Animal Encounters (ranging from gators and snakes to hedgehogs).

should book in advance on 407 365 1244.

Afterwards you can grab lunch or dinner at the **Black Hammock Restaurant** (fine local delicacies, especially the catfish and gator tail, plus other dishes and a kids' menu; 11am–10pm Sun and Tue–Thur, 11am–midnight Fri and Sat, with Happy Hour 4–6.30pm; call 407 365 2201) or visit the **Lazy Gator Bar** (open 3.30pm Tue–Fri, 2pm Sat and Sun) for karaoke (Sat) and live music (Fri–Sun), with Happy Hour all night on Wed. You can even rent canoes or fishing boats and enjoy another view of this unspoilt corner (www.theblackhammock.com).

Alternatively, **Bill's Airboat Adventures**, on the St John's River east of Sanford, offers 90-minute tours in the company of conservationist and river historian Captain Bill Daniel for $35 ($20 for under 14s) on his 6-person boat, subject to a $90 minimum (407 977 3214, www.airboating.com).

Dana's Fishing and Scenic Tours can take you out on to Seminole County's lakes and waterways for some brilliant bass fishing or guided scenic tours (by appointment only, call 407 645 5462 or check out www.fishingincentralflorida.cc).

Of course, you can just head for one of the splendid **State Parks** in this area and take your own tour of the well-marked trails. **Wekiva Springs State Park** offers hiking, canoeing and swimming, plus picnic areas and shelters and most recently started offering bike rentals, while

Little Big Econ state forest has 5,048 acres (2,045ha) of scenic woodlands and wetlands.

Sanford itself is a fascinating city (more of a town by UK standards) on the south shore of Lake Monroe and a designated historic centre, full of brick-paved streets and rather faded antique shops. It is very much small-town America, having lost the growth battle with Orlando many years ago, but it makes a peaceful diversion with some lovely walks, notably the new **Riverwalk** project and First Street renovations.

Head for the **Sanford Museum** (520 East First Street) to get the full historic overview of the city's growth from its incorporation in 1877, under the patronage of pioneering lawyer and diplomat Henry Sanford, as a hub destination on the St John's River, the 'Nile of America'. The museum (open 11am–4pm Tue–Fri, 1–4pm Sat; admission free) beautifully illustrates the life and times of the city's founder, its growth into the 'celery capital of the world' and its modern history as a US Naval Air Force base.

From there, head on to **First Street** and check out the turn-of-the-19th century buildings, stop for a bite at Morgan's Gourmet Café and finish up by wandering down to the river.

Sanford also harbours **The Rose Cottage Inn**, a wonderful tea room, restaurant and quaint B & B. It is one of the prettiest settings for lunch, tea or dinner in Florida, serving a mouth-watering array of soups, sandwiches, pastas, salads and quiches, as well as fabulous fruit teas. This little treasure (open 11am–3pm and 5–9pm Wed–Sat) can be found on Park Avenue, 13 blocks out of Sanford city centre (dinner reservations are advisable on 407 323 9448). Their B & B features a full English breakfast and five completely individual rooms, all with a real turn-of-the-last-century

8

country cottage style.

Or you could try the equally stylish and Victorian **Higgins House** (on South Oak Avenue and 5th Street; 407 324 9238, www.higginshouse.com).

For more info on things to do and see in Seminole County visit www.visitseminole.com or call in at one of their **Visitor Centers** at Orlando Sanford Airport (in the Welcome Center as you exit the main building) and at 1230 Douglas Avenue in Longwood (one block west of Exit 94 on I-4; 407 665 2900).

Out on the Gulf Coast, just north of Homossasa Springs, the **Crystal River** offers another wildlife fiesta as it is home, seasonally, to the endangered manatee, and it is possible to go swimming with these wonderful creatures. **Orlando Dive and Snorkel Tours** (407 239 3573, www.diveorlando.com) offers magical opportunities to see them (Manatee Dive $65, Manatee Snorkel Encounter $40).

Finally, if you enjoy hiking, biking or in-line skating – literally getting off the beaten track – then Seminole County boasts miles of trails and other recreational pursuits. **Spring Hammock Preserve** offers 1,500 acres (607ha) of wilderness to explore, while the **Lake Proctor** wilderness area is home to 6 miles (10km) of hiking, biking and equestrian adventures. There are more trails to explore in the **Econ River Wilderness Area**, along the Econlockhatchee River, while Chuluota boasts 625 acres (253ha) and the **Geneva**

Wilderness Area 180 acres (73ha) including the **Ed Yarborough Nature Center** (407 665 7352, www.co.seminole.fl.us/trails).

> BRIT TIP: Need a hotel in Seminole County for a night or several? Look up www.NorthOrlandoHotels.com for a great selection of short-term accommodation at good prices.

Eco-tourism

Genuine eco-tourism is still in its infancy, in general terms, in central Florida, but there are two major exceptions worth knowing about.

Florida Eco-Safaris at Forever Florida is, for my money, one of the most outstanding, non-theme park attractions. It is both a 4,700-acre (1,900-ha) wilderness preserve and a working ranch. As well as a close-up of Florida's flora and fauna and its conservation issues, you get a taste of the original cowboy life, cracker style (crackers were the original cowboys, pre-dating their Western counterparts by 50 years), which is a fascinating slice of history. Eco-safaris, covered wagon tours, horse rides, bike trails, nature walks and, for the kids, pony rides and a free petting zoo, are the highlights, as well as the magnificent **Cypress Restaurant** and **Visitor Center**, which offers an essential 30-minute orientation programme into the conservancy's creation.

Beginning as a dream of gifted young biologist and ecologist Allen Broussard, Forever Florida was completed after his death (from complications of Hodgkin's disease) by his parents, Dr William and Margaret Broussard. They continue to give their time and energy to developing the wilderness as a non-

Extreme games in St Pete

profit-making memorial to their son. The education element alone is awesome, and tours feature a strong conservation message in this tranquil, untouched corner of Florida. The **Swamp Buggy Tours** (2 hours, including lunch, at $28/person) are their stock-in-trade, a tranquil trundle around much of the woods, swamp and prairie that make up the ranch and conservancy in a large-wheeled, open-sided buggy. An education coordinator provides the low-down on the history and environmental issues of the ecosystems. You are likely to encounter alligators (at a safe distance), whitetail deer, armadillos and a host of bird life – including bald eagles – and leave with a good understanding of the real Florida. They also have a new **Swamp Buggy Heritage Safari** (at $35) that involves taking part in a cattle round-up, while the **Rawhide Roundtrip** is a full half-day ranch experience, again including lunch ($89.50). Their 1-, 2- and 3-hour **Horseback Trailrides** ($35, $55 and $69.50) require a minimum of two people per ride, and the **City Slickers Round-up** is the full Florida ranch experience ($150). **Pony rides** are available, too, at $5.

Forever Florida is a good 80-minute drive out of Orlando, 40 miles (64km) east on Highway 192, through St Cloud as far as Holopaw, then 7½ miles (12km) south on Highway 441, but it is well worth the journey.

Call 1-866 854 3837 at least a day in advance as each tour requires a minimum number to go out (www.floridaeco-safaris.com).

> BRIT TIP: The **Kissimmee Convention and Visitors Bureau** (see page 47) publishes an excellent eco-guide.

On an equally authentic scale is **Disney's Wilderness Preserve**, run by the Nature Conservancy (the world's leading private international conservancy group) in Poinciana, south of Kissimmee. This restoration of a 12,000-acre (4,860-ha) preserve is a work in progress and allows visitors in for various (well-marked) hiking trails, a 1-hour guided tour on Saturdays (at 9.30am) and 2-hour buggy tours on Sundays (1.30pm).

The preserve's pine and scrubby flatwoods, dry and wet prairies, freshwater marshes and forested wetlands are home to more than 300 wildlife species, including bald eagles, Florida scrub-jays and sandhill cranes, Sherman's fox squirrels, eastern indigo snakes and gopher tortoises, plus more than 50 butterfly species. Come here for a chance to unwind and enjoy the peace and quiet of the real Florida countryside – just a few miles from the tourist hubbub. Admission is $3 for adults and $2 for children, while the buggy tours are an extra $7 and $5. Located at the end of Pleasant Hill Road (follow Hoagland Boulevard south off Highway 192), the preserve is open daily 9am–5pm Oct–May, Mon–Fri Jun–Sept (407 935 0002, http://nature.org/wherewework/northamerica/states/florida/).

Beach escapes

When it comes to beaches – another key component of a Florida holiday – you are again spoiled for choice. The sea, sand and surf of **Cocoa**

Riding in the Florida countryside
© Disney

8

Beach is only an hour's drive from Orlando (east on the Beeline Expressway – 528 – then south on Highway A1A) and offers some good shopping (including the unmissable **Ron Jon's Surf Shop**, a massive neon emporium of all things water related) in addition to the two main public beaches. As it's the Atlantic, the sea can be pretty chilly from November to March, but Cocoa Beach is rapidly developing into a major coastal resort, so the facilities are excellent.

Its more famous neighbour, just to the north, is **Daytona Beach**, which is still only an hour away from Orlando if you take I-4 all the way east. This is the prime site of the Atlantic coast scene, with an array of good beaches (some of which you can even drive on – for a $5 toll, speed limit 10mph/16kph), boating and fishing trips, sightseeing – including the **Ponce de Leon Inlet Lighthouse**, a formidable 203 spiralling steps to the top of this magnificently preserved monument, but well worth it for the view (10am–5pm daily, $5 for adults, $1.50 for children), and surprisingly smart shopping and dining at the redeveloped **Ocean Walk Village**, next door to the main beach, pier and boardwalk area. New in 2003 were **RC Theatres' Ocean Walk** 10 cineplex, the serious film-themed fun of **Bubba Gump's Shrimp Company**, the **Mai Tai** bar and **Adobe Gila's Margarita Fajita Cantina** (check out their near-lethal range of cocktails!). Then there is the lively **Riverfront Marketplace** along historic Beach Street.

New in 2002 was the **Marine Science Center** (just around the corner from the lighthouse at Ponce Inlet), which showcases whale, mangrove, mosquito and sea turtle exhibits, along with turtle rehabilitation facilities and a 5,000-gallon (22,750-litre) artificial reef aquarium, as well as static and interactive educational displays. A boardwalk and nature trail system extends throughout the park, which naturally has a gift shop. Open 10am–4pm Tue–Sat and noon–4pm Sun (closed Mon) and costs $1 for 5– 12s and $3 for 13 and older, under 5s free (www.echotourism.com/msc).

The **beaches** themselves are a lively affair around Spring Break (pre-Easter college holiday) but fairly quiet otherwise. Other highlights include cruising the intra-coastal waterway to see the dolphins at play – check out **A Tiny Cruise Line** (386 226 2343, www.visit daytona.com/tinycruise/) for details of their four cruises, $11.03–18.85 with tax, which offers a lovely Sunset/City Lights tour from April to October.

The **Riverfront Marketplace** is the heart of downtown Daytona Beach, with a museum of local history, restaurants, nightclubs, coffee bars and a performing arts theatre, all in a quaint riverside setting. Dining opportunities are many and inviting along the beaches, with **Inlet Harbor** and **Lighthouse Landing** among the best. The tide can retreat by up to 500ft (150 metres) and the beaches are open to the public year-round.

> BRIT TIP: Check out the **Lighthouse Landing** in Lighthouse Point Park for lunch or dinner for a truly eclectic piece of Floridian restaurant life.

Lighthouse Point Park is especially worthy of note, a 52-acre (21-ha) stretch of nature trails, fishing, observation deck, swimming and picnicking (open 8am–9pm, $3.50/vehicle).

For the latest on all Daytona Beach has to offer, call 020 7935

Florida's Beach: St Pete/Clearwater

The huge stretch of beaches and 'cities' from St Pete Beach to Clearwater (collectively known as Florida's Beach) represent the heart of the Florida Beach experience, with a wonderful array of attractions as well as 35 miles (56km) of lovely white sands and an average 361 days of sunshine a year. **St Petersburg** (or St Pete as it's known) itself, just across the Howard Frankland Bridge from Tampa, is a bright, attractive and 'happening' city, with a range of developments, both recent and historical, which makes a visit worthwhile. Take time here for the wonderful **Dali Museum** (open 9.30am–5.30pm Mon–Sat, 12 noon–5.30pm Sun; $13 for adults ($11 for seniors, $7 for 5–9s), and the new **Bay Walk** complex of shops, restaurants and a 20-screen cinema. An additional assortment of museums, pedestrian-friendly streets and the Pier all provide plenty of interest, while fan-friendly **Tropicana Field** hosts the Tampa Bay Devil Rays baseball team – April to September – for another slice of highly recommended local fun (tickets from $5; www.devilrays.com).

Out in the **Beaches**, from the 800-acre (324-ha) Fort De Soto Park in the south to stunning **Caladesi Island** in the north, there is plenty to do, too, with the likes of Treasure Island, Sand Key and St Pete Beach all receiving the Blue Wave Award for cleanliness and safety. **Fort De Soto Park** offers free walking tours of its Spanish-American War era fort and wilderness areas and has one of the prettiest beaches (rated No 1 on mainland USA in 2004).

John's Pass Village and Boardwalk is an unusual shopping district full of art galleries and restaurants (and home to the fun Pirate Cruise daily – a replica sailing ship that offers a 2-hour party cruise around the waters of Treasure Island; $30 for adults and $20 for children, inclusive of beer, wine and soft drinks; 727 423 7824), while **Dolphin Landings** in St Pete Beach is another big draw for its dolphin-watch cruises, Shell Island day trips and sunset sailings (the dolphin cruise is a real highlight for its guaranteed close-up encounters along the calm inland waterway; the 2-hour yacht voyage costs $30 for adults and $20 for children – 727 367 4488, www.dolphinlandings.com).

Along at Indian Shores, you must not miss America's largest wild bird hospital, the **Suncoast Seabird Sanctuary**, usually caring for more than 500 injured patients. **Clearwater Beach** boasts the Marine Aquarium and Pier 60, where the daily sunset celebration, complete with craft stalls and music, is held. Reaching **Caladesi Island** brings you to one of the world's most picturesque beach spots and another Blue Wave award-winner.

For those wishing to take it easy, rather than drive, the **Suncoast Beach Trolley** is the perfect transport link both along the beaches and into St Petersburg ($1.23/ride or $3 for an all-day pass; 727 530 9911, www.psta.net).

A suitably wide choice of accommodation is available, too. A range of **Superior Small Lodgings** combines desirable beachfront locations with small-scale, personalised service (check out the Seahorse Cottages and Apartments on Treasure Island Beach as the perfect example – with weekly rates from $450 for a 1-bedroom cottage; 727 367 2291, www.beachdirectory.com). Of course, there are upmarket hotels, too, witness the superbly equipped **Tradewinds Beach Resorts** (a 1,100-room complex of three resorts that combine their wide range of facilities; 727 562 1221, www.tradewindsresort.com) on St Pete Beach and the huge (and hugely impressive) **Sheraton Sand Key Resort** at Clearwater Beach, a 10-storey edifice with 10 acres (4ha) of private beach and facilities ranging from floodlit tennis courts to a fitness centre, children's pool and playground (with supervised programmes in summer). Rates $149–299 (727 595 1611, www.beachsand.com). The area also boasts some 2,000 restaurants. For general info, visit www.floridasbeach.com.

8

Riverfront Marketplace, Daytona Beach

7756 in the UK or visit www.daytonabeach.com. And of course, one of the biggest attractions is the Daytona USA racetrack (see page 242).

To the west you have the **Gulf Coast**, which is a good 90 minutes' drive down I-4 from Orlando and through Tampa on I-275 south to **St Petersburg Beach** (105 miles/169km) or **Clearwater Beach** (110 miles/177km) or 2 hours-plus down I-4 and then I-75 to **Bradenton** (130 miles/209km), **Sarasota** (140 miles/225km) and **Venice** (160 miles/257km), plus the beautiful islands of **Captiva** and **Sanibel** (175 miles/282km) and **Fort Myers Beach**, part of the fabulous Lee Island Coast scene, a mini tropical paradise (www.leeislandcoast.com). The sea is a touch warmer and much calmer, so it's more suitable for small children and less crowded.

Naples is further south still on I-75 and is rated one of the most welcoming beach destinations in Florida.

BRIT TIP: Be warned, during the summer the locals all get the urge to head for the beach at weekends, so unless you leave EARLY (i.e. before 9am) and come back late (i.e. after 8pm) you will encounter serious traffic.

SPORT

In addition to virtually every form of entertainment known to man, central Florida is one of the world's biggest sporting playgrounds, with a huge range of opportunities either to watch or play your favourite sport, whether it's on the water, up in the air or on good old terra firma.

Golf

Without doubt, the number one activity in Florida is golf, with almost 150 courses within an hour's drive of Orlando. The weather, of course, makes it such a popular pastime, but some spectacular courses – many of them designed by world-famous names like Greg Norman, Tom Watson, Arnold Palmer and Jack Nicklaus – add to the attraction, and there are numerous holiday packages geared towards keen golfers of all abilities. With an 18-hole round, including cart hire and taxes, from as little as $40 on some courses (and they average around $75), it is an attractive proposition and quite different for those used to British courses.

If you go in for 36-hole days, it is possible to save up to $30 by replaying the same course, while it is cheaper to play Monday to Thursday than Friday to Sunday.

Sculpted landscapes, manicured fairways and abundant use of spectacular water features and white-sand bunkers add up to some memorable golfing. The winter months are the high season, hence the most expensive, but many courses are busy year-round. Be aware also that some courses pair up golfers with little thought for age, handicap, etc. So, if two of you turn up, the chances are that you will play with two complete strangers ('A little frustrating when you get paired with two middle-aged ladies from Switzerland who have only just taken up golf,' says *Brit's Guide* reader John Cartlidge).

Virtually every course will offer a driving range to get you started, plus lockers, changing rooms and showers, while the use of golf carts is universal (and many include the amazing GPS positioning system which gives the yardage for every shot, plus the ability to order drinks or even lunch while you're on the course!). They all feature comforts like iced water stations and drinks carts that circulate the course (don't forget to tip the trolley drivers). Some have swimming pools, and all offer a decent bar and restaurant for that all-important 19th hole.

Your best starting point is to visit one of the five **Edwin Watts** golf shops around Orlando to pick up a free copy of the *Golfer's Guide* or the *Guide To Golf* for a handy introduction to most of the courses available (and even pick up a new set of clubs at the Watts National Clearance Center just south of Wet 'n Wild on I-Drive; 407 352 2535, www.edwinwatts.com). Alternatively, Tee-Times USA (1-888 465 3356) offers an excellent advice and reservation service. The Visit Florida organisation publishes an *Official Golf Guide* (850 488 8374, www.flasports.com, as does Daytona Beach (1-800 881 7065, www.golfdaytonabeach.com).

For a unique and personable touch, you can't beat the all-in-one golf instruction service of **Professional Golf Guides of Orlando**, led by owner/operator and PGA member Phillip Jaffe, who

> **BRIT TIP:** An early-morning tee-off in the summer can provide some of the most peaceful and scenic golf you will find.

is a mine of golfing lore and knowledge, as well as great company. They take up to three golfers at a time around some of the area's finest courses, and can supply transport and high-tech (graphite and titanium) clubs if required. The playing lesson is of the highest quality and includes full on-course instruction, course management strategies, full game analysis, game improvement suggestions, shot-making demos and a wrap-up lesson that will leave you with the knowledge and skills to take your game to the next level. It is an eye-opening experience to play alongside Phillip and his staff of PGA professionals (hey, he even managed to get me hitting the green from some way off, which is no mean feat!) and well worth it for the keen golfer who wishes to improve their game in one round. (Call 407 227 9869 for rates or visit www.progolfguides.com.)

Alternatively, the **Nick Faldo Golf Institute** on the lower portion of I-Drive (1-888 463 2536) is a great place to visit if you just want to hit a few golf balls.

Walt Disney World Resort in Florida has been quick to attract the golf fanatic, with five championship-quality courses, including the 7,000-yd (6,400-metre) **Palm**, rated as one of *Golf Digest's* top 25 (and reputedly the 18th here is one of the toughest

Congo River mini-golf

holes in America), plus a 9-hole par-36 course, **Oak Trail**. Fees vary from $99–174 for Disney resort guests and $119–179 for visitors, with half-price reductions after 3pm. Call 407 939 4653 for tee-times. Private and group lessons are available under PGA professional guidance, with video analysis and a great range of club rentals. The rolling **Osprey Ridge** (up to 7,101yd/6,493 metres) and the visually intimidating **Eagle Pines** (up to 6,772yd/6,192 metres) are the two newest – introduced in 1992 – designed by master architects Tom Fazio and Pete Dye respectively.

Another luxury experience is available at the nearby **Hyatt Grand Cypress** on Vineland Road (407 239 1904, rates from $130–170 depending on season). It has three elegant 9-hole courses and a superb 18-hole links-style offering (all designed by golf legend Jack Nicklaus), which present a truly magnificent challenge.

MetroWest Country Club, on South Hiawassee Road to the north of Universal Studios (407 299 1099; $89–129), is a 7,051-yd (6,447-metre) masterpiece designed by Robert Trent Jones Snr and features elevated tees and greens, with pleasant rolling fairways and expansive bunkers.

The superb **Keene's Pointe** in Windermere to the north of *Walt Disney World Resort in Florida* is Nicklaus's newest and most exciting course, measuring 7,173yd (6,559 metres) if played off the pro Bear tees (there are always five tees for the various handicaps, ladies and seniors). Surrounded by lakes, it has a truly impeccable look and outstanding facilities, including a pool (407 876 1461; $80–125).

The **Legacy Club at Alaqua Lakes** is a masterpiece of conservation and tranquillity (it is part of the Audubon preservation and restoration scheme) as well as a tour de force of lush fairways and weird and wonderful greens (a signature feature of Tom Fazio). Winding through some spectacular forest in the suburb of Longwood in Seminole County, it is a serious challenge for serious golfers (407 444 9995; $45–79).

Also in Seminole, **Magnolia Plantation** is another wonderful contrast, a heavily wooded and peaceful haven that feels miles from the theme park world and yet is less than half an hour away up I-4. Woven among the lakes and ponds of the Wekiva River basin, Phillip Jaffe rates it a 'must play' course (407 833 0818; $31–57).

Falcon's Fire in Kissimmee is an outstanding course, too, featuring the 'ProShot' digital caddy system and water coolers on all golf carts. Plenty of water around the course assures a testing 18 holes, but it is very picturesque (407 239 5445; $75–135).

> BRIT TIP: Some of the best tee times at the *Walt Disney World Resort in Florida* golf courses are reserved for Disney resort guests.

The **Orange Lake Country Club** is a huge vacation resort in Orlando (just 4 miles/6km from Disney) with two 18-hole courses, a 9-hole course and a par-3, floodlit 9 holes. The new **Legends at Orange Lake** course (designed by Arnold Palmer) is their top-of-the-range offering (407 239 1050; $70–90). **Kissimmee Oaks** features some majestic moss-draped oaks and local wildlife as well as 18 holes of memorable lakeside golf, all just 3½ miles (6km) south of Highway 192 in Kissimmee in the Oaks Community off John Young Parkway (407 933 4055; $50–80).

BRIT TIP: Reader John Cartlidge, a keen golfer, advises: 'Take your waterproofs with you. I was looking to buy some in Florida but could only find lightweight slipovers – no use in the UK.'

Down on I-Drive, the former International Golf Club opposite the Faldo Golf Institute has been redesigned and renamed **Marriott's Grande Pines**, with new greens that run fast and true. However, its strategic location close to the Convention Center means it books up early. You can get cheaper for similar quality further out and rates vary quite widely with the season, but its 7,012-yd (6,412-metre), par-72 style is hard to beat this close to the centre of things (407 239 6909; $60–130).

No less than four new courses were built in 2003, with pride of place going to **Grande Lakes Orlando**, the amazing hotel/resort complex just off John Young Parkway. This Greg Norman-designed masterpiece offers 18 holes of genuine Florida nature with the added benefit of a Caddie-Concierge service for every twosome and foursome (call for rates, 407 206 2400). The monstrous **Harmony Golf Preserve** in the town of Harmony in Osceola County (out on the east stretch of Highway 192, past St Cloud) is an incredible 7,428yd (6,792 metres) at its longest, designed by Johnny Miller and with terrific club and associated recreation facilities (407 891 8525; $40–100).

The rolling and aptly named **Victoria Hills** in DeLand (mid-way between Orlando and Daytona Beach, Exit 116 off I-4) gets a big thumbs up from Phillip Jaffe ('A

great track – very challenging!'), with a par-72 course designed by Ron Garl and a superb practice facility (386 738 6000; $39–75).

The extravagant **Reunion Resort and Club** (in Davenport, just to the south of Disney, Exit 54 off I-4) is still being developed as they complete the massive resort around the three courses – a Watson, Palmer, Nicklaus collaboration, with 18 holes designed by each. Watson's 7,257-yd (6,636-metre) Independence Course is possibly the most challenging, with a style not dissimilar to the famous Augusta National (1-888 300 2434; $50–85). However, golf here is restricted to those who own property in the resort or are staying here (highly recommended; see page 85). The main clubhouse is positively 5-star in its design and facilities and each course is quite superb just to look at, never mind play. It certainly gets the Jaffe seal of approval ('great conditions, great layout').

Seminole County itself is another golf haven, with 18 public or semi-private courses, and offers golf-and-hotel packages from $65 (1-800 555 9589, www.visitseminole.com).

When you book, check on the club's dress code, as there are a few differences from course to course. There are also dozens of other choices, this is only a small (if representative) sample.

Mini-golf

Not exactly a sport, but definitely for holiday fun, are the many quite extravagant mini-golf centres around Orlando. They are a big hit with kids and good fun for all the family (if you have the legs left for it after a day at a theme park!). Several attractions and parks offer mini-golf as an extra, but for the best, try out the self-contained centres, of which there are six main ones.

8

Predictably, Disney has come up with some terrific courses of their own. **Disney's Fantasia Gardens Miniature Golf Courses**, next to the Swan Hotel just off Buena Vista Drive, is a 2-course challenge over 36 of the most varied holes of mini-golf you will find. Hippos dance, fountains leap and broomsticks march on the 18-hole crazy, golf-themed **Fantasia Gardens** – its style is taken from the Disney classic *Fantasia*, meaning lots of cartoon fun as the park's Imagineers challenge you with a riot of visual gags as well as some diabolically difficult mini-golf. Watch out for *Toccata and Fugue in D Minor* where good shots are rewarded with musical tones, and *The Nutcracker Suite*, where obstacles include dancing mushrooms!

Fantasia Fairways is a cunning putting course, complete with rough, water hazards and bunkers to test even the best golfers. The 18 holes range from 40ft (12 metres) to 75ft (23 metres), and it can take more than an hour to play a full round. Each course costs $10.65 (adult) and $8.52 (child), and they are open 10am–11pm every day.

The 36-hole **Winter-Summerland Miniature Golf Courses** is located at the entrance to *Disney's Blizzard Beach* water park. Divided into two 18-hole courses, these mini works of art feature a 'summer' setting of surf and beach tests (watch out for squirting fish), and a 'winter' variety of snow and ice-crafted holes, all with a welter of visual puns as befits the vacation resort of Santa's elves (yes, that's the theme, and kids love it – you can even see the marks where Santa landed his sleigh!). An adult round is $10.65 (3–9s $8.50), a double round is half price. Open 10am–11pm.

Elsewhere, **Pirate's Cove** has a twin-course set-up at Lake Buena Vista (by the Crossroads shopping plaza) and at I-Drive (just south of The Mercado), with mountain caves, waterfalls and rope bridges to test your skill and please the eye. The twin-course I-Drive location is one of the premier sites around here; the **Captain's Course** costs $7.99 for adults and $6.99 for children, while **Blackbeard's Challenge** is $8.49 and $7.49, with a 36-hole adventure at $12.49 and $11.49. Open 9am–11.30pm daily year-round (407 352 7378).

Tiki Island Golf is the newest thing on I-Drive, another 36-hole set-up with enthusiasts able to putt through a 4-storey volcano and among tiki statues, caves, paddleboats and waterfalls. **River Adventure Golf** (on Highway 192, almost opposite Medieval Times) offers a Mississippi River adventure with rolling rapids, waterfalls and an authentic water wheel. **Bonanza Miniature Golf and Gifts** (next door to the Magic Mining Co restaurant on west Highway 192) has an imaginative – and tricky – 36 holes with a gold mining theme. **Pirate's Island** (further along Highway 192 to the east) is another spectacular 36-hole spread, while arguably the most impressive of the lot is the **Congo River Golf and Exploration Co.**, which has courses on Highway 192, I-Drive and Highway 436 in Altamonte Springs. They could almost be Disney-inspired, they are so artificially scenic. The Kissimmee location also has paddleboats, while I-Drive has the option of go-karts, and all three have games and video arcades.

Golf at Reunion Resort

Charges are $6.95 for a single round and $11.95 for a double (look out for money-off coupons on www.congoriver.com which give a couple of dollars off each one). Open 10am–11pm Mon–Thur, 10am–midnight Fri and Sat (weather permitting).

Million Dollar Mulligan is worthy of mention here, although it is neither mini-golf nor the real McCoy. Instead, Million Dollar Mulligan, just off Highway 192 on Florida Plaza Boulevard (next to Old Town – look for the giant golf ball), is a 9-hole, floodlit pitch-and-putt course that looks spectacular at night when the lake and fountains are illuminated. It costs $11.75 for adults and $7.50 for children and seniors and is open daily from 10am–midnight (407 396 8180).

Freshwater fishing

Freshwater fishing on Central Florida's abundant rivers and lakes (St John's River, Kissimmee Chain of Lakes, and Lake Tohopekaliga, for example) attracts enthusiasts worldwide. In addition, many visitors find a quiet day of fishing provides a highly enjoyable and welcome change of pace. The primary draw for most out-of-towners is the opportunity to catch giant Florida bass – which often grow to record-breaking size in the area's grassy waters – and to view some of the local and plentiful wildlife in its natural environment.

To fish in a freshwater lake, river, or stream you need a Florida Freshwater Fishing License, which you can buy online from the Florida Fish and Wildlife Commission (http://myfwc.com/license/index.html – have your credit card handy). You will be issued a temporary licence number within minutes, which enables you to fish right away. A permanent licence will be mailed to you within 48 hours. The cost of a 7-day licence is $17.

It is also advisable to book a reservation for a guided trip two or more weeks in advance, especially in holiday periods. **Cutting Loose Expeditions** is operated by A Neville Cutting, one of America's leading fishing adventurers. Cutting, who maintains high standards with his guides, can organise fresh or seawater expeditions and arrange hotel pick-up if necessary. Rates start at $200 for a half-day's bass fishing (two fishermen per boat with a licensed guide). Bait and licence are included. Other trips, including offshore fishing for marlin, can be arranged. Call 407 629 4700, or write to Cutting Loose Expeditions, PO Box 447, Winter Park, Florida 32790-0447.

AJ's Freelancer Bass Guide Service is the oldest continuously operating guide service in central Florida. Freelancer specialises in trophy bass fishing on Lake Tohopekaliga, just minutes from Disney. Toho is rated the best big bass lake in Florida. Saltwater guide trips are also offered. The Freelancer Bass Guide Service is owned and operated by Captain A James Jackson, one of the top professional fishing guides in the country. Jackson is featured in fishing magazines and a new book on fishing around the world (*Adventure Fishing* by H Gilbey, Dorling Kindersley). Those in-the-know rate Freelancer guide trips as one of the greatest fishing experiences anywhere, providing a highly personable service to both experienced and novice fishermen. All guides are experienced, full-time professionals and run trips of 4, 6

Deep sea fishing

and 8 hours. For rates, services, photos, testimonials and seasonal fish reports, check out Jackson's excellent website at www.orlandobass.com. For reservations call 407 348-8764 or e-mail capjackson@aol.com.

Seminole County has its share of fishing action, too. Check out **Spotted Tail** for a good range of angling adventures with fly and light tackle (407 977 5207, www.spottedtail.com).

Water sports

Florida is mad keen on water sports of all types. So, on any area of water bigger than your average pond, don't be surprised to find the locals water-skiing, jet-skiing, knee-boarding, canoeing, paddling, windsurfing, boating or indulging in any other watery pursuits.

Walt Disney World Resort in Florida offers all manner of boats, from catamarans to canoes and pedaloes, and activities, from water-skiing to parasailing, on the main **Bay Lake**, as well as the smaller **Seven Seas Lagoon Crescent Lake** and **Lake Buena Vista**. Parasailing (from *Disney's Contemporary Resort* – see page 61) comes in two price categories, a Regular flight which goes up to 450ft (137 metres) for 8–10 minutes, and a Premium flight up to 600ft (183 metres) for 10–12 minutes. It costs $85–105 solo or $135–155 tandem, while boat rentals (from a range of resorts) vary from $8/hour (14-ft/4-metre sailboats and catamarans) to $66.04/hour (21-ft/6-metre pontoon boats). For reservations, call 407 939 7529.

Several operators serve the lakes around Orlando and Kissimmee, but some leave much to be desired safety-wise. **Dave's Ski School** on Lake Bryan at Lake Buena Vista (right next to the Holiday Inn Sunspree Resort on SR 535) gets our recommendation for their safety-conscious approach and virtual guarantee to get beginners up and water-skiing. Their **Watersports Adventure** includes an hour's water-ski lesson and ride, a tube ride and a wave-runner ride ($55 adult, $48 child), and lasts up to 3 hours; an hour's water-ski school costs $75. You can also rent wave-runners at $45 for half an hour. Many tour operators endorse this ski school (407 239 6939, www.bvwatersports.com).

Horse riding

Orlando is home to one of the foremost equestrian centres in America – the **Grand Cypress Equestrian Center**, which is part of the 1,500-acre (608-ha) Grand Cypress Resort, and all its rides and facilities are open to non-residents. This stunningly equipped equine haven offers a dazzling array of opportunities for horse enthusiasts of all abilities.

A full range of clinics, lessons and other instructional programmes are available, from half-hour kids' sessions to all-summer academies, plus a variety of trail rides. Serious horse riders will note this was the first American equestrian centre to be approved by the British Horse Society, and it operates the BHS test programme. Inevitably, this 5-star facility does not come cheap but it is a worthwhile experience, especially for children. Private lessons are $55/half hour or $100/hour, while a week's package of eight 1-hour group lessons is $280. Young Junior Lessons (15-minute supervised rides for under 12s) are $25, while the Western Trail Ride (a 50-minute excursion for novice riders) is $45 per person and the Advanced Trail Ride $100.

The Center is open 8.30am–6pm Mon–Fri, 8.30am–5pm Sat and Sun, and can be found by taking Exit 68 on I-4 on to Route 535 north, turning left after half a mile (1km) at the traffic lights and then following the road north for a mile (1.6km) past the entrance to the Grand Cypress Hotel, and it's on the right (407 239 1938, www.grandcypress. com/equestriancenter).

On a smaller scale and none the less charming is the **Horse World Riding Stables** on Poinciana Boulevard, just 12 miles (19km) south of Highway 192. This gets you more out into the wilds and you can spend anything from an hour to a full day enjoying the rides and lessons on offer. The three main rides are the Nature Trail ($35), a walking-only tour of 45–50 minutes, for beginners aged 6 and up, through 750 acres (304ha) of untouched Florida countryside, the Intermediate Trail (10 years and up) for nearly 1 hour ($42), and the Advanced Private Trail, a 75- to 90-minute trip for advanced riders with private guide ($59). There is also a picnic area with fishing pond, playing fields, pony rides for under 7s ($6) and farm animals to pet. Riding lessons are $45/hour for group or private lessons. A 3-hour Children's Horse Camp (for 8–14-year-olds) is available on Saturdays at 9am (call for prices). There is no charge for just looking, and the stables are open 9am–5pm daily (407 847 4343, www.horseworldstables.com).

Spectator events

When it comes to spectator events, Orlando is not quite as well furnished as other big American cities, but there is always something for the discerning sports fan who would like to see a local big match. There are no top-flight American football or baseball teams here, but there is an indoor version of gridiron (American football), called Arena Football, plus Spring Training (pre-season) for several baseball teams (notably Cleveland in Winter Haven).

The main sport is **basketball** and the team is Orlando Magic of the National Basketball Association (NBA). The season runs from November to May (with exhibition games in October), and the only drawback is the 16,000-seat **TD Waterhouse Center** where they play (on Amelia Street, Exit 83B off I-4, turn left, then left again) is occasionally fully booked. Contact the Center's box office (407 649 3245) to see if there are any tickets left, although you will need to call in person to buy them (from $10 up in the gods to $100 courtside), or you can call TicketMaster on 407 839 3900 for credit card bookings.

The Orlando Predators, one of America's top **Arena Football** teams, is also popular at the same venue (from February to June, $10–50; call several days in advance to see one of their lively home games that feature some great entertainment as well as their fast, hard-hitting version of indoor gridiron).

For the Real Thing in gridiron terms, the nearest teams in the **National Football League** are the Tampa Bay Buccaneers, 75 miles (120km) to the west, the Miami Dolphins, some 3–4 hours' drive to the south, down the Florida Turnpike, or the Jacksonville Jaguars way up the east coast past Daytona, a 3-hour drive up I-4 and I-95. Again, TicketMaster can give you ticket prices ($30–60) and availability (Sep–Dec; and the Buccaneers sell out early these days).

A Spring Training **baseball** opportunity can be seen at Osceola County Stadium in Kissimmee, where the Houston Astros take up home for the month of March. Being part of the audience here is to experience a genuine slice of Americana. Call 321 697 3201 for

8

more details, or TicketMaster to book tickets on 407 839 3900.

Disney's Wide World of Sports Complex™

The newest sports facility in the area is inevitably a Disney project to bring in some world-class events and competitors. *Disney's Wide World of Sports Complex™* is a 200-acre (81-ha), state-of-the-art complex, featuring 30 sports and is quite awesome to wander round even when no one is playing. The complex's main features are a 7,500-seater baseball stadium, a softball quadraplex, an 11-court tennis complex, sports field and the **Official All Star Café®** with a massive array of sports memorabilia and even themed food. The Cracker Jack Stadium is home for spring training of baseball's mighty **Atlanta Braves**, and the crowds flock in for pre-season games in March (recommended).

Sadly, there is no longer a Minor League team based here, and you would need to head to Tampa for the nearest Major League team (the Tampa Bay Devil Rays; highly recommended, see Florida's Beach section on page 231). The complex is also home from mid July for a month to the NFL's **Tampa Bay Buccaneers** as they begin their pre-season training, and it is an eye-opening experience to watch these amazing athletes in action, even if it is only in practice. A 20-acre (8-ha) expansion in 2004 is adding more fields for soccer, lacrosse and American football, plus four extra baseball and softball fields.

Other high-class events here include athletics, in-line hockey and even cricket. Standard admission is $10.50 for adults and $7.75 for 3–9s, but it is also an optional extra with a Park Hopper Plus Ticket (excluding special events). *Disney's Wide World of Sports Complex™* can be found off Osceola Parkway, on Victory Way. Call 407 939 4263 for details of events and prices.

The **Walt Disney World Marathon** is a major annual sporting event and its 11th running will be on January 9, 2005. Some 13,500 runners take part – including some of the world's leading athletes – drawing some huge crowds, as the route takes in all four theme parks. Be aware the parks face some serious disruption but, as with the London Marathon, the Disney version also serves up a great spectacle. The annual **Half-Marathon** takes place on the same day (www.disneyworldsports.com).

Fitness centres

You may decide you can't spend a full 2 weeks here and not go to the gym at least once (as if walking all round the parks won't keep you in trim!). So here, especially for the health-conscious, is a quick guide to your fitness centre choice: **Ritz-Carlton Spa**, 4012 Central Florida Parkway (407 206 2400; Guest Pass $25; Spa and Fitness Center included in daily guest pass); **The Orlando Fitness and Racquet Club**, 825 Courtland St (407 645 3550; 6am–9pm Mon–Fri; 7am–8pm Sat and Sun; guest fee $10; full service fitness centre with childcare); **World Gym**, 5600 West Colonial Dr (407 447 5800; 8am–10pm Mon–Fri, 8am–6pm Sat and Sun; guest fee $15; childcare); **Paramount Health Clubs**, 2317 North Orange Ave (407 898 4884; 6am–9.30pm

Baseball

Disney's Wide World of Sports®

Mon–Thur, 6am–8pm Fri, 9am–5pm Sat, noon–5pm Sun; guest fee $5; childcare); **Ladies Workout Express**, 12086 Collegiate Way (407 243 9835; 8am–8pm Mon–Fri, 10am–5pm Sat; guest fee $10; women only); **Creative Health and Fitness**, 1218 South John Young Parkway (407 933 1300; 6am–10pm Mon–Fri, 8am–7pm Sat, 9am–2pm Sun; guest fee $10; childcare).

Rodeo

An all-American pursuit straight out of the Old West, the **Silver Spurs Rodeo** is staged twice a year at the brand new, 8,300-seat Silver Spurs Arena. The biggest event of its kind in the south-east, it is held in mid-October and the last week in February. However, it sells out fast so book well in advance on 407 677 6336 or www.silverspursrodeo.com. The event features classic bronco and bull riding and attracts top competitors from as far away as Canada. The new arena is part of the $84-million **Osceola Heritage Park**, which includes Osceola County Stadium (for baseball) and the Kissimmee Valley Livestock Show and Fair Pavilion. The **Silver Spurs Arena** is a state-of-the-art facility which can also be used for concerts, and there is not a bad seat in the house. The ease with which they convert it from the rodeo venue and back again, with truckloads of dirt, is quite amazing.

On a slightly smaller scale, the **Kissimmee Rodeo** is held every Friday at 8pm (except when the Silver Spurs is on) at the Kissimmee Sports Arena, on Hoagland Boulevard 2 miles (3km) south of Highway 192. Events include calf roping, steer wrestling and bull riding, and admission is $18 for adults and $9 for children 12 and under. Kids love the live action, which can be surprisingly rugged (if not dangerous), and there is even a kids' contest – grab the ribbon from the calf's tail! The **Catch Pen Saloon** lounge is open 8pm–2am Fri and Sat, and 6pm–2am Sun, with line dancing 6pm–8pm and $1 drinks (407 933 0020, www.ksarodeo.com).

Motor sport

For the guaranteed ultimate in high-speed thrills, *Walt Disney World Resort in Florida* has its own speedway oval where **Richard Petty Driving Experience** is based (in the car park for the *Magic Kingdom*, NOT at the *Wide World of Sports*). Here you can experience one of their 650-bhp stock cars as either driver or passenger at up to 145mph (233kph). The programmes have been devised by top NASCAR driver Richard Petty and offer the three-lap **Ride-Along Experience**; a 3-hour **Rookie Experience** (with tuition and eight laps of the speedway); the **Kings Experience** (tuition plus 18 laps); and the **Experience of a Lifetime** (an intense 30-lap programme).

The Ride-Along Experience will probably appeal to most (16 and over only) – three laps of the 1.1-mile (1.8-km) circuit with an experienced, race-proven driver lasting just 37 seconds a lap but an unbelievable blast all the way. Your initial take-off from the pit-lane takes you 0–60mph (97kph) in a couple of seconds and you are

8

straight into Turn One with your brain some distance behind. It is a bit like flying at ground level, it is hot and noisy and you must wear sensible clothes (you have to climb in through the window), but it is definitely the Real Thing in ride terms and a huge thrill.

You don't need to book for the Ride-Along Experience, which is available from mid-February to the end of September and there is no admission fee, so you can come along just to watch. The three driving programmes all require reservations, while the track is occasionally closed for race testing from October to February. However, before you get carried away, wait for the prices: $99 for the Ride-Along Experience; $379 for the Rookie Experience; $749 for the Kings and $1,249 for the Lifetime Experience – you must be 18 or over for the last three (407 939 0130, www.1800bepetty.com).

Race fans will also want to check out **Daytona International Speedway** just up the road in Daytona (take I-4 east, then I-95 and Highway 92) for lots more big-league car and motorcycle thrills. It hosts more than a dozen race weekends a year, including stock cars, sports cars, motorcycles, go-karts and trucks, and highlights are the Daytona 500 (February 20, 2005), and Pepsi 400 (first Sunday in July). The big events attract more than 200,000 devotees and provide some of the most colourful sport anywhere in the world (386 253 7223, www.daytonainternational speedway.com).

Daytona USA, an interactive motor sport-themed attraction, is here as well, offering a series of hands-on exhibits, rides and films to give you a taste of all the high-speed action. Change tyres in a timed pit stop, design and video test a racing car, commentate on a race and

BRIT TIP: Race fan Alan Rogers, of Chester, rates Daytona USA highly: 'Try the hands-on Pit Stop Live, the excellent Daytona 500 movie and the 30-minute tour of the track. It's a real thrill.'

experience the Daytona 500 film. Other elements include Acceleration Alley (for an additional fee), with full-size NASCAR simulators combining motion, video and sound to capture the thrills of head-to-head racing at more than 200mph (322kph), and Daytona Dream Laps, another elaborate motion simulator to put riders inside the Daytona 500 itself. The history and great moments of speedway are well detailed and there is a good gift shop. A half-hour, open-sided tram tour of the speedway stops in Pit Road, giving a real close-up of this amazing arena. New in 2004 was *NASCAR 3-D: The IMAX Experience* and *Daytona 500: The Movie* at the **Pepsi IMAX Theater**.

Open 9am–7pm daily (not Christmas) and costs $20 for adults, $16 for seniors (60+) and $14 for 6–12s (under 6s free with adult). The Combo ticket with the Speedway tour is $21.50, $18.50 and $15.50, while the tour on its own is $7/person (386 947 6800, www.daytonausa.com).

The Richard Petty Driving Experience is available here too (for those aged 16 and over) and the $134 fee for three laps of the world-famous, steeply banked 2½-mile (4-km) tri-oval also includes entrance to Daytona USA.

Okay, that's the full daytime scene, now let's check out everything there is to know about the night-time entertainment…

Orlando by Night

(or, Burning the Candle at Both Ends)

Hands up those who still have plenty of energy left! Right, this chapter is especially for you. If we can't wear you out at the theme parks and Florida's other attractions, we'll just have to resort to a full-frontal assault on your sleep time.

For, when it comes to night-time fun and frolics, Orlando again has a dazzling collection of possibilities, from its purpose-built entertainment complexes, through its range of evening dinner shows and on to a full array of bars and nightclubs. The choice is suitably widespread and almost always high in quality.

Unfortunately, the development that started the evening entertainment ball rolling has now closed down. **Church Street Station**, in the heart of the downtown area, shut in 2001 and there is still no firm news of what will take its place. The site formerly occupied by Rosie O'Grady's, the Cheyenne Saloon, the Orchid Room, Apple Annie's Courtyard, Phineas Fogg's and Lili Marlene's is now home to a comedy club – **Orlando Improv**, a mini (non-smoking) theatre with a separate bar/dining area – and **GameTime** sports bar and grill (open 4pm until midnight Wed–Sun; 321 281 8181). Orlando Improv features stand-up comedians from various American TV shows (DEF JAM, BET and Comic Review) but plays to a largely adult audience, i.e. 21 and over only, except for Friday nights, when it's 18 and up. (Shows run at 7 and 8pm Wed–Sun – smoke-free on Thur and Sat – with a 9:30 and 10.30 performance on Fri and Sat. Admission price varies but is usually around $22; (321 281 8000, www.orlandoimprov.com). What used to be Crackers Restaurant is now **Louis'**, an equally upscale fine dining experience. There are plans afoot to redevelop the Station for offices, retail and more restaurants, but they still seem a year or more away from doing so.

Disney joined the big evening entertainment concept in 1987 with **Pleasure Island**, an imaginative range of clubs, discos and restaurants, and it is continuing to refine the formula to keep it fresh and appealing. **Disney's BoardWalk Resort**, which opened its doors in 1996, has added more to their night-time options.

International Drive (I-Drive) caught up with this process in 1997 when **Pointe*Orlando** opened. Although its prime focus is shopping and restaurants, it has a strong evening entertainment component with the big Muvico 21-screen cinema centre, its lively bars and two recent nightclubs.

Finally, Universal Orlando got with the beat in late 1998 with the opening of **CityWalk**, possibly the most elaborate and sophisticated centre of the lot. They all represent yet another slick opportunity for you to be dazzled and relieved of your cash in the name of holiday fun. However, you should try to experience at least one.

DOWNTOWN DISNEY

The large-scale development of what is now *Downtown Disney* (the old Village Marketplace and *Pleasure Island*) has evolved into a 3-part complex (*Downtown Disney* Marketplace, *Pleasure Island* and West Side) doubling the size of the old site and providing two key evening entertainment sources.

Pleasure Island

This is the traditional nightclub zone which packs in the locals as well as the tourists and where every night is New Year's Eve. You must be 18 or over to enter (unless accompanied by a parent), while you must be at least 21 to enter two of the clubs (see below). *Pleasure Island* (which forms the centrepiece, or linking part, of *Downtown Disney*) consists of eight original club venues and just about every music type you can think of, plus several novel twists. The **Rock 'n Roll Beach Club** is a multi-level live music venue featuring 40 years of classic rock (mainly the 1980s and 1990s) with a resident cover band and DJs. It also boasts pool tables, arcade games and several bars. The **Pleasure Island Jazz Company** offers some excellent modern jazz and blues in a 1930s-style 'warehouse' nightspot. You can grab a snack here and listen to some of the coolest sounds in town. Serious clubbers head for **Mannequins Dance Palace** (21 and over), a

huge, popular disco, with a revolving dance floor, mirrored walls, dry ice and lasers, plus a pounding sound system and superb lighting. At the **Comedy Warehouse**, the highly talented and quick-witted Improv Co. gives periodical shows with guest 'volunteers' (beware sitting near a phone – you WILL end up in the show!). Queuing can begin up to half an hour before a performance, which lasts for around 45 minutes and is guaranteed to be different every time. For a touch of retro groovin', **8Trax** is a homage to 1970s' music, dance and styles (right down to the lava lamps) and usually draws a lively crowd of all ages.

The unmissable **Adventurers' Club** is a personal favourite, a 2-storey entertainment lounge, in 1920s' Gentleman's Club style, which comes to life around you (watch the animal heads and masks!) and the stars of the shows mix with the guests. Again an element of comedy improvisation is mixed in with the scripted action and, if the cast happens to pick on you, don't try to win a battle of wits – they have the microphone, remember!

The BET Soundstage Club™ (21 and over) is a totally modern offering, with an interactive VJ/DJ and featuring the best of R & B, soul and hip-hop sounds. Finally, the newest venue **Motion** (formerly the Wildhorse Saloon) is a cavernous dance club, featuring Top 40 to Alternative music, animated DJs and a giant TV screen. This is another

Downtown Disney

© Disney

> BRIT TIP: Taking a form of photo ID is essential for *Pleasure Island*, even if you happen to be the 'wrong' side of 30. No ID equals no alcohol, and there are no exceptions.

happening club, and is especially popular with the locals at weekends. In addition, the outdoor **West End Stage**, which hosts *Pleasure Island*'s resident band and occasional big-name acts, is the focus for the street party and fireworks at midnight, because, of course, every night is New Year's Eve...

As well as the clubs, *Pleasure Island* has a range of six shops, including **Reel Finds** for film memorabilia, **DTV**, an up-scale Disney fashion store and **Changing Attitudes**, offering some stylish men's and women's clothing. You can grab a snack at the **Missing Link Sausage Co.** (hot dogs, burgers, sandwiches and fries) and stop for coffee, ice cream or frozen yoghurt at the splendid **D-Zertz**.

For a full-scale meal, the neighbouring **Portobello Yacht Club** offers excellent northern Italian cuisine in smart, lively surroundings. Of course, you can also visit the many eating outlets elsewhere around *Downtown Disney*, including **Planet Hollywood**® (the largest of this world-wide movie-themed chain, and the busiest restaurant of the lot), **Cap'n Jack's Restaurant** (for great chowder, crabcakes, shrimp or the trademark 'fishbowl' margaritas), and **Fulton's Crab House** (for some of the best seafood in Orlando – see page 275). Lunch is served from 11am–4pm and dinner from 5–11pm.

As ever, to make a **Priority Seating** booking for a Disney restaurant, call 407 939 3463 (see page 61). *Pleasure Island*'s shops and cafés used to be open free of charge during the day, but now the hours are purely 7pm–2am each night, with the entry charge $19.95 and strict age restrictions. Admission is also one of the options on a Park Hopper Plus Ticket. However, in summer 2004, Disney were testing a new system whereby there was general free admission to *Pleasure Island*, but a fee to enter each nightclub (with Hopper Plus passes still being valid).

West Side

This is the newest element of the Downtown Disney expansion and incorporates the AMC® Pleasure Island 24 Theaters Complex with 24 screens and 6,000 seats in state-of-the-art surroundings, as well as the...

Cirque du Soleil®

The most eye-catching part of West Side is home to the greatest show on earth (or at least, the greatest I've seen anywhere in the world), the Cirque du Soleil® production *La Nouba*™. Twice a day, five times a week, the company's purpose-built, 1,671-seater theatre stages the most stupendous combination of dance, circus, acrobatics, comedy and live music in a 90-minute show that involves more than 60 performers. Anyone familiar with the unique styling, outrageous costumes and captivating sounds of the world-famous Cirque company will know what to expect, but even they will be left in awe by this multi-dimensional assault on the senses. It features trampolines, trapezes, balancing acts and even mountain bikes, woven with innovative dance routines, comedy (watch out for the inspired clowns) and spell-binding music, all with the most magnificent staging.

9

La Nouba at Cirque du Soleil®

© Disney

BRIT TIP: If you need to escape the *Downtown Disney* hurly-burly, head upstairs in the Virgin™ Megastore, where their great coffee/sandwich shop is a relative oasis of calm offering a good range of snacks and drinks, usually queue-free.

Words alone do not do it justice – go and see it. It is not cheap, but I believe it is worth every cent. Booking is vital and can be done up to 6 months in advance on 407 939 7600. Shows are at 6pm and 9pm Tue–Sat but try to be early for some excellent pre-show fun. There are two pricing categories: Cat. 1 (front centre seats), $86.92 adults, $51.94 children; Cat. 2: $76.70 and $46.87 (but no seat has a bad view).

More venues

The other *Downtown Disney* elements are a fantastic mix of live music, fine dining, unique shopping and *DisneyQuest*, the ultimate in interactive game arcades.

The cavernous **House of Blues**®, a combination live music venue and restaurant in backwoods Mississippi style, is a must for anyone even vaguely interested in blues, rock 'n' roll, R & B, gospel and jazz and some top-name bands play here (407 934 2583, www.hob.com), while their trademark **Gospel Brunch** on Sundays serves up some fabulous food with a full gospel show (10.30am and 1pm; $30 for adults, $15 for 3–9s). 'Praise the Lord and pass the biscuits', is their slogan, and it is a lot of fun.

The 500-seat restaurant next door to the concert hall also offers some fine fare, including catfish, jambalaya and a host of other delicious Cajun dishes, with more good, footstompin' live music, free, in the **Blues Kitchen** (Thur–Sat). The inevitable gift shop also stocks some quality merchandise.

Bongos Cuban Café™ (co-owned by Gloria and Emilio Estefan) brings the sights, sounds and tastes of Old Havana to another imaginative setting, with red-hot Latin music and some excellent Cuban fare. **The Wolfgang Puck**® **Café** offers a rich experience from the renowned Californian chef, with no less than four dining options: the Café, gourmet food in a casual setting; Wolfgang Puck Express, the fast-food version; B's Bar for sushi, seafood, pizzas and micro-brew beers; and the Dining Room, an upscale restaurant featuring the best of the group's international cuisine (407 938 9653).

The West Side shopping is also original and engaging, from the basic sweet shop **Candy Cauldron**, which resembles a fairytale dungeon, through the one-off outlets like **Sosa Family Cigars**, **Celebrity Eyeworks** and the wonderfully stylish glass and ceramics of **Hoypoloi Gallery**, to the predictable souvenir stores and the truly mega **Virgin**™ **Megastore**, the largest music store in Florida, with more than 100 listening stations, a full-service café, hydraulic outdoor stage and a mean sound system!

DisneyQuest

The most unusual element to *Downtown Disney*, *DisneyQuest* opened in June 1998 and brought yet another novel idea to life. It is described variously as 'an immersive, interactive entertainment environment', the latest in arcade games, a series of state-of-the-art adventure rides or, as one Cast Member told me, 'a theme park in a box'. It houses 11 major adventures, such as CyberSpace Mountain (design and ride your own roller-coaster), Invasion – An Alien Encounter (a fun virtual-reality rescue mission), Virtual Jungle Cruise (shooting the rapids, prehistoric style) and Aladdin's Magic Carpet (more virtual-reality riding in best cartoon fashion), a host of old-fashioned video games in the Replay Zone, the latest sports games, a test of your imagination in Animation Academy and two futuristic cafés, one with computers and internet tables, the other, Food Quest, straight out of a space-age comic book.

Two additional highlights are Radio Disney SongMaker (a computer-generated professional audio system that creates a CD with you as the star!) and Pirates of the Caribbean: Battle for Buccaneer Gold (an amazing 3-D immersion in a swashbuckling, cannon-shooting adventure for pirate treasure). The newest attraction, Ride the Comix! is another virtual-reality battle, this time with super-villains.

DisneyQuest is open 11.30am–11pm Sun–Thur, 11.30am–midnight Fri and Sat but, if you want to avoid the queues (the building admits only 1,500), go during the day. A 1-day ticket costs $32.02 ($26.63 for 3–9s, although it is a bit too elaborate for most youngsters) and teenagers love it. Finally, the whole of *Downtown Disney* West Side is characterised at night by outstanding lighting effects and a vibrant, thrilling, almost intoxicating atmosphere.

> BRIT TIP: You can buy a combined annual pass for *DisneyQuest* and Disney's water parks at $137.39 for adults and $105.44 for 3–9s that can work out better value for multiple visits.

Disney's BoardWalk

Disney's other big evening entertainment offering is part of their impressive **Disney's BoardWalk Resort**, where the waterfront entertainment district contains several notable venues (not counting the excellent micro-brewery and restaurant of the Big River Grille and Brewing Works, the thrilling ESPN Club for sports fans and the 5-star Flying Fish Café). **Jellyrolls** is a variation on the duelling piano bar, with the lively pianists conjuring up a humorous and often raucous evening of audience participation songs ($7 cover charge; 21 and over only; 7pm–2am).

The **Atlantic Dance** club features mainly modern dance music (it started life as a classic 1930s' dance club and also moved through a Latin phase) with both house and guest DJs, plus occasional live music, all with a huge dance floor and a great bar service and ambience. It is especially popular on Friday and Saturday nights (perhaps because there is no cover charge any more; 9pm–2am; closed Mon). It is strictly 21 and over, so remember your ID (no ID, no entry here). *Disney's Boardwalk Resort* also features some amusing stalls and live entertainers, which add to the carnival atmosphere.

UNIVERSAL'S CITYWALK

As part of the big Universal Orlando development – and in direct competition with *Downtown Disney* – this 30-acre (12-ha) spread has just about everything in the world of entertainment. The resort's hub is a busy, bustling expanse of shops, restaurants, snack bars, open-air events and nightclubs. It offers a huge variety of cuisines, from fast food to fine dining, an unusual mix of speciality shops and a truly

9

BRIT TIP: Park in Universal's multi-storey car park where there is no charge after 6pm for all the CityWalk venues. For more info on the complex, call 407 363 8000 or visit www.citywalkorlando.com.

eclectic nightclub mix, from reggae to rock 'n' roll to salsa to jazz and high-energy disco. Unlike *Pleasure Island*, there is no overall entry fee, but you do pay a cover charge ($5–7) at the seven clubs. You can also buy a **CityWalk Party Pass** ($9.95 plus tax) or **Party Pass with Movie** (one free film at the 20-screen Universal Cineplex; $13) for entry to all seven (except one-off concerts at Hard Rock Live), while the FlexTicket includes a Party Pass.

The area splits into three, with the main plaza featuring shopping and restaurants. Among the most original (and amusing) of the 13 shops are **Endangered Species**, with products designed to raise eco-awareness; **Quiet Flight**, for radical surf and beachwear; the retro-American decor of **Fossil** for leather goods, watches and sunglasses; the **Universal Studios Store** for park merchandise; and **All Star Collectibles** for (American) sports fans.

For eating, you have the **NASCAR Café** (a must for motor-racing fans, 10am–late) with full-size stock cars and racing memorabilia, videos and interactive games while you dine on burgers, ribs, steaks and popcorn shrimp. **Pastamore** is a delightful indoor/outdoor Italian diner, with the choice of full-service dining (5pm–midnight) for pizza, pasta, grilled chicken and steaks or the **Pastamore Café** (8am–2am) for sandwiches, pastries and ice cream. **Emeril's** restaurant is at the 5-star end of the range, a sophisticated and vibrant journey into the cuisine of New Orleans master chef Emeril Lagasse. Fine wines and a cigar bar both add to Emeril's Creole-based gourmet creations, and if you don't try the Louisiana oyster stew here, you have missed a real treat (lunch 11.30am–2pm; dinner 5.30–10pm Sun–Thur, 5.30–11pm Fri and Sat). It also books up well in advance at weekends, so try weekdays (call 407 224 2424 to book). **Jimmy Buffet's Margaritaville** (11am–2am) is an island homage to Florida's laid-back musical hero, with 'Floribbean' cuisine (a mixture of Key West and Caribbean), live music and three bars, including the Volcano Bar which 'erupts' margarita mix (!) when the blender needs filling. There is a cover charge ($5) after 10pm when their live band hits the stage.

Pirates of the Caribbean: Battle for Buccaneer Gold at DisneyQuest®

CityWalk

excellent gift shop friendlier here than the UK.

Finally, you come to the **Promenade** area, which offers a choice of nightclubs and some more fine dining (notably in the case of Latin Quarter), plus the ubiquitous Starbucks coffee house. **Motown Café** is the one disappointment as it has been downgraded from a performance venue to just a Motown memorabilia restaurant and bar, with a big video arcade downstairs. It is worth perusing for its homage to the performers of the renowned record label, from the Four Tops and Jackson Five to modern artists, but there is better food elsewhere (open 11.30am–11pm Sun–Thur, 11.30–2am Fri and Sat). $5 cover after 9pm.

Across the CityWalk waterway is the **Lagoon Front** location of another huge dining experience, the 2-storey **NBA City**, which is sure to thrill basketball fans with its Cage dining room, interactive playground area and Club lounge where you can watch live and classic games (11am–10.30pm Sun–Thur; 11am–11.30 pm Fri and Sat). Next door is the massive mock-Coliseum architecture of **Hard Rock Live**, a 2,500-seat concert venue with state-of-the-art staging and sound. Big-name bands and performers are on stage several times a week (Robbie Williams and Oasis have both played here) in this slightly retro rock 'n' roll theatre (407-351-LIVE, www.hardrocklive.com). Of course, you can't miss dining at the **Hard Rock Café** here, the world's largest example of this international chain, with its collection of rock 'n' roll memorabilia (including a pink 1959 Cadillac). It remains hugely popular, so try to get in early for lunch or dinner (11am–2am) to sample their classic diner fare (notably the Pig Sandwich). Collectors of Hard Rock souvenirs will also find prices in the

> BRIT TIP: CityWalk too crowded? Can't get in any of the restaurants? Jump on one of the boats to the Hard Rock Hotel or Portofino Bay Hotel and you can usually dine without a wait at The Kitchen (Hard Rock) or Trattoria del Porto or Mama Della's (Portofino Bay).

9

Bob Marley – A Tribute to Freedom is a clever re-creation of Marley's Jamaica home, turned into a courtyard live music venue, restaurant and bars. The bands are excellent, the atmosphere authentic and the place really comes alive at

Hard Rock Café

night (4pm–2am, 21 and over after 10pm; cover charge $5 after 8pm).

Next up is **Pat O'Brien's**, a faithful reproduction of the famous New Orleans bar and restaurant (4pm–1am), with its Flaming Fountain courtyard, main bar and special duelling piano bar (6pm–2am, cover charge $5 after 9pm, 21 and over with passport ID). Excellent Cajun food and world-famous Hurricane cocktails are the order of the day, but don't drink too many and expect to walk home!

CityJazz is a real contrast, a hip, upmarket centre combining history, education and live music from a series of local and international musicians, with tapas-style food. Visually it is stunning, with good sound quality and, if you're keen on the live music, which varies from swing and R & B to pure jazz (8pm–1am Sun–Thur, 7pm–2am Fri and Sat, cover charge $5), you can easily spend all night here. From Thur–Sat, CityJazz becomes Bonkerz Comedy Club, with some outstanding stand-up comedy acts at 8pm (cover charge $7, but still included with CityWalk PartyPass).

For younger, club-minded visitors, **the groove** is the next generation in disco entertainment, a vivid, pounding, high-energy dance venue designed like a Victorian theatre but with the latest in club music, lighting and special effects (9pm–2am, cover charge $5; 21 and over only).

Finally, completing the Promenade tour is the **Latin Quarter**, a wonderful venue/restaurant that serves up a genuine slice of Latin American style in its atmosphere, music, dance, decor and cuisine. The food is outstanding – a combination of beef, fresh fish and poultry with tangy fruit sauces, spicy salsas and mouth-watering marinades (don't miss their version of rack of lamb) – the ambience is mesmerising and the sounds are so wonderfully vibrant and alive, you can't help dancing, even in your seat. From Cuba to Chile, here is a great experience, with the live bands whipping up a samba and salsa storm. Drop in for a meal or just check out who's playing the music on Fri and Sat (5pm–2am Mon–Fri, midday–2am Sat and Sun; cover charge $6 after 10pm).

Breathless yet? Well, there's still the **Universal Cineplex**, a 20-screen cinema complex with a 5,000 capacity and the latest in stadium seating, curved-screen visuals and high-tech sound systems.

Pointe*Orlando

This eye-catching development on I-Drive, almost opposite the Convention Center, is a mix of unique shops, cinemas, restaurants, the WonderWorks science centre (with its magic-themed dinner show), an arcade-style entertainment centre and two nightclubs. It is open all day but has plenty of evening appeal, too.

The big-name stores (open 10am–11pm) are all upscale and include some imaginative touches that make them stand out from the crowd (see page 287). The collection of bars and restaurants strive to be different too. On the main ground level you have **Johnny Rockets**, a highly entertaining 1950s-style diner with an indulgent burger-and-milkshake menu (and waiters and waitresses who perform dance routines if the right song comes on the jukebox!). **Dan Marino's Town Tavern** is a surprisingly elegant sports-themed diner (check out the football-shaped bar), with a mix of lively and intimate areas and a well-balanced menu from this former American football star. Head upstairs to the second level and you find **Lulu's Bait Shack** leading the way for New

Orleans-style cuisine and entertainment (it looks like an old shack blown in from Bourbon Street). Then there is **Adobe Gila's**, a fine Mexican *cantina* featuring more than 70 tequilas (!) and some south-of-the-border dining delicacies (try the Gila Wraps), and the 'soon to be relatively famous' wings, burgers and seafood of **Hooters** (with its equally famous 'Hooter Girl' waitresses). Lulu's and Adobe Gila's are especially popular with locals and are often packed at weekends, as they stay open until 2am, while they feature live outdoor music and DJs several days a week. On a Friday or Saturday, the atmosphere should be kicking from 6.30pm, while on weekdays it is more likely to be from 8.30pm.

New in 2004 were **Origami Seafood and Grill** (international-flavoured seafood and sushi bar), with a lovely outdoor patio and private rooms (407 352 2788) and **Wise Guy's** Italian restaurant (pizza, pasta; 407 226 2399).

The 21-screen **Muvico** cinema, with its wonderfully vast and cleverly themed entrance foyer, boasts state-of-the-art stadium seating and sound systems, and you can often see a newly released film here several months before it gets to the UK. By the way, American cinema popcorn is almost invariably of the SALTED variety!

Entertainment venue **XS Orlando** (motto: Too much is not enough) offers three floors of fun and games where you can 'dine, dance and defend the world'. An appealing restaurant (try their excellent steaks, salads or brick oven pizzas) occupies the ground floor, and you ride the escalator up to the entertainment levels. Here, you will find more than 110 interactive games and attractions (including a virtual-reality roller-coaster, rock-climbing challenge, several state-of-the-art shoot 'em up games, a new role-playing horse-race game, some arcade-style prize games and high-speed internet access), fully stocked bars, live music with resident DJs and two roof terraces that enjoy views over I-Drive. For the games, you can get Time cards for 1 or 2 hours ($20 or $25) or buy a Cash card for any amount. It is open noon–midnight Sun–Thur, and noon–2am Fri and Sat, and is also an ideal place for lunch (www.xsorlando.com).

The Pointe also boasts two popular recent additions to the nightclub scene: **Matrix** (open 9pm–2am, Wed–Sun), a high-tech, high-energy, high-volume club, pulses to the techno beat for much of the time and has a kind of future-surreal decor that appeals to the younger (18–25) crowd. Age restrictions are strictly 18 and up (apart from Tue, when it's over 21). The dance floor is huge and is ringed by two video walls, 16 TV screens and a multi-million dollar light show, while the lounge features art deco loungers, chairs and loveseats. Thursday is College Night (with $2 beers, and no cover until 11pm), Saturday is Inferno (top DJs, BreakBeats and Hip-Hop) and Sunday is Latin Night.

Metropolis (open 9pm–2am Thur–Sun) offers a more sophisticated atmosphere, with retro Top 40 music in a plush disco environment. It has seven Victorian billiards tables in the lounge area, various TV and video screens, and another large dance floor, and it tends to attract a slightly older crowd (25–35). It is 21 and over here only for men (18 and up for ladies; 25 and over only on Fridays), except for college night on Thursdays. At both clubs, the cover charge (after 10pm) varies per night (from $5–15, free for ladies over 21 on Fridays). Stylish dress is required (no jeans, baseball caps or trainers). Every Monday is Teens Night for

9

14–18s during the summer (8pm–1am). With a no-alcohol bar, it offers a safe environment to let your teenagers have some space of their own on holiday (407 370 3700, www.metropolismatrix.com).

For more on The Pointe, call 407 248 2838 or visit www.pointeorlando.com.

DINNER SHOWS

Another source of evening entertainment comes in the many and varied dinner shows that are a major Orlando phenomenon. From murder mysteries to full-scale medieval battles, it's all wonderful imaginative fun, even if the food is usually quite ordinary. As the name suggests, it is live entertainment coupled with dinner and unlimited free wine, beer and soft drinks in a fantasy-type environment, where even the waiters and waitresses are in costume and taking part.

They always have a strong family appeal and you are usually seated at large tables where you can get to know other folks, too, but, at $35–45 for adults, they are not cheap (especially with taxes and tips). Beware, too, the attempts to extract more dollars from you with photos, souvenirs, etc.

Hoop-Dee-Doo Musical Revue

© Disney

Disney shows

Walt Disney World Resort in Florida's offerings here are often overlooked by visitors unless they are staying at one of the hotel resorts. For an excellent night of South Sea entertainment, try **Disney's Spirit of Aloha** (at the Luau Cove at *Disney's Polynesian Resort*). It's a bit expensive at $49.01 for adults (including tax and tip), and $24.81 for under 12s, but it is still good value as the 2-hour show features some splendid entertainment, varying from the fun to the thrilling (Hawaiian sounds, singers, dancers and other Polynesian acts, including the amazing Samoan fire juggler, all with a strong family story). You need to come hungry for this show, too, as the food is plentiful, with salad, roast chicken, ribs, rice and vegetables, plus a fresh fruit dessert (or peanut butter and jam sandwiches, macaroni cheese, chicken fingers and hot dogs for the kids). Beer, wine and soft drinks are all included. For reservations (usually necessary), call 407 939 3463, and shows are 5.15pm and 8pm Tue–Sat.

The **Hoop-Dee-Doo Musical Revue** at *Disney's Fort Wilderness Resort & Campground* is an ever-popular nightly dinner show that maintains the resort's impressive cowboy theme, and has great food (all-you-can-eat ribs, fried chicken, corn on the cob, baked beans and strawberry shortcake, plus unlimited beer, sangria and soft drinks). Especially loved by children, it features the amusing song and dance of the Pioneer Hall Players in a merry American hoedown-style show. Okay, it's corny and a tad embarrassing to find yourself singing along with the hammy action, but it is performed with great gusto, and you're on holiday, remember! The Revue plays nightly at 5pm, 7.15pm and 9.30pm at the

Pioneer Hall, $49.01 for adults (inclusive of tax and tip), $24.81 for under 12s, and lasts almost 2 hours. Reservations are ALWAYS necessary but can be made up to 2 years in advance on 407 939 3463.

An alternative is the nightly (and free!) **Electrical Water Pageant** which circles Bay Lake and the Seven Seas Lagoon, passing by each of the *Magic Kingdom* Park resorts in turn from 9pm. It lasts just 10 minutes so it is easy to miss, but it is almost a waterborne version of the SpectroMagic parade, with thousands of twinkling lights on a floating cavalcade of boats and mock sea creatures. The usual schedule is 9pm at *Disney's Polynesian Resort*, 9.15pm at *Disney's Grand Floridian Resort and Spa* (and you get a grandstand view in Narcoossee's restaurant), 9.35pm at *Disney's Wilderness Lodge* , 9.45pm on the shores of *Disney's Fort Wilderness Resort & Campground*, and 10.05 at *Disney's Contemporary Resort*. It can also be seen from the boat jetties outside the *Magic Kingdom* Park.

Arabian Nights

This lovingly maintained, family-owned attraction is a real large-scale production and one of the most popular with locals as well as tourists. It's a treat for horse lovers, but you don't need to be an equestrian expert to appreciate the spectacular stunts, horsemanship and marvellous costumes as some 70 horses, including Lipizzaners and Walter Farley's black stallion, perform a 20-act show. Loosely based on the celebration of Princess Scheherazade's engagement to Prince Khalid, the show is staged in the huge indoor Moorish-themed arena at the centre of this 1,200-seater palace. The magnificent close-quarter drill of the Lipizzaner stallions, the daring riding and the

> BRIT TIP: Most dinner shows can feel quite cool, especially those involving animals such as Arabian Nights, Medieval Times and Dixie Stampede, so bring a jacket or sweater to beat the air-conditioning.

thrilling chariot race all add up to a memorable show that kids, especially, adore. The recent addition of new characters (notably the comic Gaylord Maynard and his horse Chief Bear Paw), costumes and special effects, plus the incorporation of a bumbling genie, have given Arabian Nights a real boost and helped to keep its appeal fresh. A special Christmas Holiday show takes over for the winter season, while more new elements are promised in 2005. The food (green salad, roasted prime rib with new potatoes, and a dessert; vegetarian lasagne on request) is above average, too. Located just half a mile east of I-4 on Highway 192 (on the left, just to the side of the Parkway shopping plaza, or just past Water Mania if you are coming from the eastern end of 192), Arabian Nights runs every evening

9

Arabian Nights

at 7.30pm or 8.30pm, with occasional matinees. It lasts almost 2 hours, and tickets ($47 for adults and $29 for 3–11s) may be purchased at the box office between 10am and 6pm or by credit card on 407 239 9223 (visit www.arabian-nights.com for a saving offer or free upgrade). A 'VIP' upgrade ($15 for adults, $10 for children) adds a stable tour, reserved priority seating (in the first three rows) and the chance to meet the stars.

Pirate's Dinner Adventure

This show (which has been revamped several times since it opened in 1997) features one of the most spectacular settings, with the Spanish galleon pirate ship centrepiece being 150ft (46 metres) long, 60ft (18 metres) wide, 70ft (21 metres) tall and 'anchored' in a 300,000-gallon (1,365,000-litre) lagoon. It also delivers good value with its pre-show elements, plentiful (if ordinary) food and drink, and the imaginative after-show Buccaneer Bash disco (until 10.30pm), plus the Pirate's Maritime Museum, which guests are free to wander around. The basic premise of the audience being 'hi-jacked' by the wicked 18th-century pirates is a clever one,

BRIT TIP: When there are two shows of The Pirate's Dinner Adventure in one night, opt for the second one if you want the disco bash afterwards. A new Pirate's Preferred seating upgrade provides front row priority and guaranteed cast interaction for a small extra cost (407 248 0590, www.orlandopirates.com).

even if the actual storyline is occasionally hard to follow. Chaos and mayhem ensue, with the local princess being abducted by the villainous crew of Captain Sebastian (boo! hiss!), and swashbuckling abounds, with sword fights, acrobatics, trapeze artists and boat races. There are plenty of stunts and special effects (plus audience participation, which the kids love) and tickets are $46.90 for adults and $28.12 for 3–11s (look out for discount coupons). The show is located on Carrier Drive between I-Drive and Universal Boulevard, and runs daily from 6, 7.45, 8 or 8.30pm, with appetisers served for 45 minutes until seating begins.

Medieval Times

Eleventh-century Spain is the entertaining setting for this 2-hour extravaganza of medieval pageantry, sorcery and robust horseback jousts that culminate in furious hand-to-hand combat between six knights. It is worth arriving early to appreciate the clever mock castle design and the staff's costumes as you are ushered into the pre-show hall before being taken into the arena itself. The weapons used are all quite real and used with skill, and there are some neat touches with indoor pyrotechnics and other special effects. You need to be in full audience participation mode as you cheer on your knight and boo the others, but kids (not to mention a few adults) get a huge kick out of it and they'll also love eating without cutlery – don't worry, the soup bowls have handles! The elaborate staging takes your mind off the unexciting chicken dinner, but there is positively heaps of it and the serfs and wenches who serve you make it a fun experience. Prices, which include the Medieval Life exhibition (see next page), are $46.95 for adults and $30.95 for 3–11s (again, check their website for discounts). A Royalty Package upgrade for $7.99 per person includes preferred seating, Knight's cheering banner and commemorative programme member. Doors open 90 minutes prior to showtime. Times vary with the season, so call 1-800 229 8300 or visit www.medievaltimes.com for more details.

For those who have been before, the **Knights of the Realm** show made its debut in January 2003, with a new storyline and characters (although much of the fast-paced action is the same), plus a musical score by the Prague Symphony Orchestra and the addition of a superb black Friesian stallion, which contrasts with the snowy Andalusian horses ridden by most of the cast.

The castle is on Highway 192, 5 miles (8km) east of the junction with I-4. If you have 45 minutes to spare pre-show, the **Medieval Life** exhibition makes an interesting diversion. This mock village portrays the life and times of 900 years ago, with artisans demonstrating pottery and tool-making, glassblowing, spinning and weaving, plus a gruesome Chamber of Horrors that is definitely not for young children.

Sleuth's Mystery Dinner Shows

This is a real live version of Cluedo acted out before your eyes in hilarious fashion while you enjoy a substantial meal (with a main course choice of honey-glazed Cornish hen, prime rib or lasagne) and unlimited beer, wine and soft drinks. You can choose between three theatres and no less than 11 different plot settings (several of which have amusing British settings), including *Joshua's Demise*, *Roast 'Em, Toast 'Em* and *WKZY TV* (a clever skit on trash television),

that add up to some elaborate murder mysteries. The action takes place all around you and members of the audience can take part in some cameo roles. The quick-witted cast keeps things moving and you guessing during the 35-minute show, then during the main part of dinner you can think up some questions for interrogation (but be warned, the real murderer is allowed to lie!). If you solve the crime you win a prize, but that is pretty secondary to the overall enjoyment – this is a show I enjoy a lot. Prices are $43.95 for adults and $23 for 3–11s and again show times vary, so call 407 363 1985 for details or visit www.sleuths.com.

Purely for children is **Sleuth's Merry Mystery Dinner Adventure**, with a special kids' dinner, dessert and unlimited soft drinks. Designed primarily for 6–12-year-olds (mainly on Saturday afternoon), it features one of two adventures, *The Faire of the Shire* and *The Magical Journey of Juniper Junior* costing $28 for adults and $16 for 3–12s.

Sleuth's Mystery Dinner Shows can be found in Republic Square Plaza, on Universal Boulevard (half a mile north of its Sand Lake Road junction).

WonderWorks: The Outta Control Magic Show

On a smaller scale but no less fun, this show is offered at WonderWorks on I-Drive (on one corner of Pointe*Orlando). A novel mixture of improvised comedy and clever, close-up magic, the show is accompanied by all-you-can-eat pizza, beer, wine and coke. Set in the intimate Shazam Theater, it features live music, special lighting effects and some slick magic tricks from illusionist Tony Brent and sidekick Danny Devaney. The tricks

9

are all fairly routine, but the show is served up in style and involves plenty of audience participation. Performed twice nightly at 6pm and 8pm, it costs a reasonable $19.95 for adults and $14.95 for children and seniors. Alternatively, a Magic Combo ticket for the show and unlimited access to WonderWorks afterwards (open till midnight, see page 203) costs $33.95 and $25.95 (407 351 8800, www.wonderworks online.com).

Dolly Parton's Dixie Stampede

The biggest development in Orlando dinner shows for many a year opened in June 2003, when Country and Western queen Dolly Parton unveiled the fourth venue for her Dixieland extravaganza of music, comedy, horsemanship and ostrich races(!). The show features a high-energy cowboy competition (with lots of audience participation) between north and south, with various contests, speciality acts,

Sleuth's Mystery Dinner Show

BRIT TIP: You can visit the stars of Dolly Parton's Dixie Stampede – the horses – for free from 10am till showtime. You'll find them along the horsewalk outside the venue.

song, dance and a huge southern-style feast. Indeed, the food is a major part of the experience – which has been a big hit elsewhere in America – as you chow down on vegetable soup, whole rotisserie chicken, corn on the cob, home-made biscuit (that's a savoury scone to us), barbecue pork loin, jacket potato and apple pastry. Your unlimited drinks are Pepsi, tea and coffee (with some excellent non-alcoholic cocktails available pre-show). Alcohol is limited to two glasses of beer or wine per meal.

The quality of the entertainment is high and the $28 million development provides a spectacular venue, with an elaborate pre-show (featuring the trick riding and cowboy rope and whip tricks of Greg Anderson – beware being one of his chosen audience 'victims' as you'll be in for a real test of nerve!) in the Carriage Room before the audience moves into the 1,000-seat, 35,000-sq-ft (3,255-sq-metre) main arena. Here the headlining abilities of the 32 horses and 30 riders are demonstrated over a series of tests and races, from Roman-style riding to trick riding and fast-paced barrel racing. Spectacular costumes, ostrich races, pig races and a feature buffalo 'stampede', plus a rousing, patriotic finale, American-style, with doves, flags and Dolly's closing anthem (penned after September 11) complete the picture.

Sadly, Dolly herself does not make an appearance, apart from on screen, but it all adds up to 5-star family fun. A separate **Christmas show** is staged from November 1 to January 1, featuring a live Nativity scene, snow and other seasonal festivities (the show contest pits the North Pole v South Pole instead!).

Dixie Stampede operates once or twice a night, depending on the season, at either 5.40pm or 7.40pm (with the main show at 6.30pm or 8.30pm), and lasts almost 2½ hours, including the pre-show, plus browsing time in the inevitable gift shop. It's billed as Orlando's 'Most Fun Place To Eat', and it is hard to argue. Tickets are a well-priced $43.99 for adults and $18.99 for 3–11s and it is located right next to Orlando Premium Outlets, just off I-4 at Exit 68, or via I-Drive (407 238 4455, www.dixiestampede.com).

Gator Safari by Night

Brand new in 2003, this is a joint venture by Boggy Creek Airboats and Gator Tours (see page 218), serving up an evening of Floridian food, fun and Native American activities out in beautiful Southport Park, Kissimmee, with a night-time airboat ride thrown in (Tue and Sun, May–Oct only). The basic idea is to host a family barbecue under the moss-covered grandfather oaks of the park, with plenty of food and drink and the transport laid on, too. Torchlight and Native American dancers provide a wonderfully rustic yet authentic ambience, and the whole thing is enhanced with organised games for the children, with face painting, treasure hunts (with metal detectors) and native stories in the specially constructed tepee. You also get to roast marshmallows on the bonfire and meet a live alligator, while the 45-minute night-time airboat ride is a real highlight.

With the coach transport (round-trip from your hotel) and airboat ride, however, this adds up to a pricey evening at $75 for adults and $55 for 3–12s, but it is one of the most unusual dinner 'show' offerings, and it is an extremely enjoyable experience (prices without transport are $54 and $34). To book, call 1-800 537 0917 (in Florida) or 407 522 5911 (outside) or visit www.gatortours.com.

THEATRE

If the dinner shows are only playing at theatrical entertainment, there is still some genuine theatre to be enjoyed in Orlando. The **Bob Carr Performing Arts Center** is the premier venue, hosting a variety of acts from ballet to opera (it is home to the Orlando Opera and Southern Ballet companies) as well as the Broadway in Orlando series which, in 2004, featured *Phantom of the Opera*, *Lord of the Dance*, *Mamma Mia* and *The Producers* plus productions by local theatre groups. The Center is located in the Orlando Centroplex (407 849 2001, www.orlandocentroplex.com).

The **Orlando-UCF Shakespeare Festival** is a purely classical offering, year-round at the **John & Rita Lowndes Shakespeare Center** in Loch Haven just off Princeton Street (Exit 85 off I-4).

The more eclectic (as the name suggests) **Mad Cow Theatre** has

9

Arabian Nights dinner show

grown from very humble roots to mainstream theatre in a new downtown location, with educational shows, workshops and cabaret performances (Fri and Sat). Recent productions have included *My Fair Lady*, *Les Liaisons Dangereuses* and *Yellowman* and performances are usually Thur–Sun (with matinées Sun). Tickets vary from $14–22 (407 297 8788, www.madcowtheatre.com).

The **Theatre Downtown** company has its own individual style, its non-profit ethos giving rise to some challenging theatre, bordering on the experimental. The venue, an old citrus-packing plant on the corner of Orange and Princeton Avenues, provides a wonderful setting for their stagecraft. Tickets are $15 or $12 for students and seniors (407 841 0083, www.theatre downtown.net).

THE NIGHTCLUB SCENE

Orlando is blessed with a huge variety of nightlife, from regular discos to elaborate live music clubs and no less then three 'duelling piano' bars. The majority are situated in the downtown area, away from the main tourist centres. The *Orlando Sentinel* has a Friday supplement, *Calendar*, which has all the local entertainment listings, while www.orlandocitybeat.com details the nightspots, events, happy hours and other essential info. The free *Orlando Weekly* (available from supermarkets and tourist centres) is also a valuable guide, or visit www.orlandoweekly.com.

Bars and discos come and go at an amazing rate, so don't be surprised if you go to a nightclub you have visited before to find it has had a complete change of name and personality. The basic distinctions tend to be **Live Music Clubs**, **Mainstream Nightclubs**, with the occasional live band, and **Bars** with evening entertainment.

Live music clubs

The following should give you a representative taste of the most popular venues (in most cases for those aged 21 and over only).

The rock 'n' roll piano bar idea was pioneered here in Orlando by the wonderfully named **Howl at the Moon Saloon** on West Church Street and is still going strong (7pm–2am Wed–Thur, 7pm–2am Sun and 5pm–2am Fri and Sat). Classic rock 'n' roll, show tunes, current hits, the saloon's duelling pianists play them all, with full audience involvement and non-stop banter. No cover charge Sun–Tue, while Wed–Thur it is $5 after 7.30pm, on Fri it's $7 after 6pm and Sat $7 after 5.30pm. The live piano action begins at 8pm (it gets rowdy and even bawdy later, so remember your sense of humour).

Then, of course, you have **Jellyrolls** (see page 247) at *Disney's BoardWalk Resort* and **Pat O'Brien's** (the original New Orleans version, see page 250) at Universal's CityWalk, which are both popular with locals and tourists alike.

Country music fans (and others in search of the 'in' crowd) will definitely need to check out **:08 Seconds**, a huge, multi-level entertainment centre. It earns its 'unique' tag by hosting live bull riding (!) and monster truck wars as well as having a huge dance hall with live bands, line dancing lessons, 12 bars ($2 for all alcoholic drinks on Saturday, a real bargain), a pool hall, games room and classic country barbecue. The atmosphere is both authentic and infectious, right down to the well-priced gift shop. This is one of my favourite clubs in town. On West Livingston Street in the heart of downtown, it has bags of style, but call 407 839 4800 for the latest details (usually, ladies' night Thur – ladies get in free all night and drink free until 11pm – monster trucks Fri, and bull riding Sat; $7 ages 18–20, $5 for 21 and up; Fri $20 admission, drinks are free all night). By the way, the :08 seconds refers to the average time a bull-rider stays on his bull! Check out www.8-seconds.com for more.

Blues, rock and jazz are the staples of **The Social** (formerly Sapphire) at 54 North Orange Avenue, where resident DJs, a wide range of bands and special guest acts vary from week to week. With San Francisco-inspired decor, this has the reputation for being one of the 'hippest' places to be seen in (407 246 1419, www.orlandosocial.com). You'll catch some seriously up-and-coming acts here and enjoy being part of a really busy music scene, while their website also offers the chance to hear some of the bands in advance.

For pure, relaxed jazz and other live music, check out the Bosendorfer Lounge at the **Westin Grand Bohemian hotel** (see page 78), also on South Orange Avenue. Usually from 6–10pm every evening (plus Saturday Jazz Brunch 10.30am–2.30pm), the sounds of their $250,000 Bosendorfer piano are well worth travelling to hear.

As a complete alternative to the music scene, **Sak Comedy Lab** (on West Amelia Avenue in the Theater Garage) is like a live version of the TV show *Whose Line Is It Anyway?* Fast-paced and funny (and with a 'no obscenity' rule for concerned parents), the Sak performers do a mix of competitive ad lib comedy, with every show offering something different and the young performers living on their wits. Consistently voted Florida's best live comedy, see for yourself Tue–Sat (with two different shows Fri and Sat), admission $5–13. Their Lab Rats show (Tue) features Sak's 'students' and costs just $5. Booking is advisable on Fri and Sat (407 648 0001, www.sak.com).

Mainstream nightclubs

In addition to the mainstream DJ dance centres at *Downtown Disney's Pleasure Island* and Universal's CityWalk, **Tabu** (formerly the Zuma Beach Club on North Orange Avenue, just up from Church Street) appeals widely to the young, disco crowd with regular nightly line-ups, guest DJs and special events, usually of a fairly raucous nature! $7–12 (21 and over) Wed–Sun (407 648 8363).

Bar Orlando, on South Orange Avenue, is another high-energy offering, with modern techno styles jostling with retro sounds from the 1980s and 1990s. **Cairo** has quickly become a haunt of the younger set on South Magnolia Avenue, with three rooms featuring dance music, reggae and out-and-out disco – high energy, disco and reggae every Fri and Sat; alternative sounds from the 1980s and 1990s Sun; old school and house Wed; ladies don't pay $5–10 cover charge and drink free until 11.30pm on Fri (407 422 595).

The **Independent** (formerly Barbarella) on Orange Avenue on the corner of Washington Street, offers alternative and new wave music 9pm–3am Wed–Sat. Again, it offers more of a techno-dance sound, but features various retro-progressive, old wave and Video Go-Go nights. Friday is ladies' night, and the club has three contrasting levels, including an area with pool tables. Cover charge $5–10 (407 839 0457).

The Club at Firestone is also hard to categorise but scores well with the alternative/progressive crowd. It occasionally hosts rock and pop acts too big for The Social but otherwise ranges from mainstream disco to acid jazz lounge, with something different each night Wed–Sat (gay night on Wed). Two venues inside the club– the Den and the Glass Chamber – feature dance, house, jungle and

9

hip-hop, with their Latin night, El Club Caliente, usually on Fri. About half a mile north of Church Street on the corner of Orange Avenue and Concord Street, The Club is open 9pm–3am with cover charge $6–12 (407 872 0066, www.theclub-online.com).

The **Blue Room** (West Pine Street) is another lively offering, although more intimate, drawing a more diverse crowd with its mixture of art, music and style. With DJs Thur–Sat (closed Sun–Wed) and live music (occasionally) on Thur, it successfully mixes hip-hop, dance and R & B in a highly successful style. Open 10pm until late with a $7–10 cover charge (407 423 2588, www.blueroomorlando.com).

For the gay scene, **Parliament House** (on North Orange Avenue) and **Southern Nights** (Bumby Avenue and Anderson Street) remain the most happening venues, while the **Cactus Club** (on North Mills Avenue), **Faces** and **Studz Bar** (both on Edgewater Drive) and **Wylde's** (out at 3535 South Orange Blossom Trail) are also popular.

BARS

With live entertainment, extrovert barmen, sports-themed bars and raw bars (offering seafood, often by the bucket!), the choice is, as ever, wide-ranging. Bars of all types simply abound in Orlando. The area

around Church Street is the core of this development (even since much of Church Street Station closed), with a terrific range of restaurants and bars. Look out in particular for the raucous **Mako's** and **Antigua** (DJ house music). Upstairs from the latter is **Ybor's Martini Bar**, an upscale cigar and cocktail emporium. Also on this floor (and easy to overlook next to Antigua) is the highly recommended **Big Belly Brewery** with a micro-brewery and an impressive range of other beers (as well as an outrageous collection of wall art), and above that is roof-top bar **Latitudes**.

Travel out past Church Street into Orange Avenue and Pine Street and you are into real locals' territory with the likes of **One-Eyed Jack's**, which has a party pop atmosphere and live music singalongs, and is connected to the **Loaded Hog** and **Wall Street Cantina**, which are packed at weekends (there is often a queue to get in, but, once in, you can roam between all three). Turn left on to West Central Boulevard and you find **Kate O'Brien's Irish Pub** for more lively bar entertainment (and a great beer garden), the similarly Irish-themed **Scruffy Murphy's** is a block further north on Washington Street. There is no cover charge and it has a real good-time atmosphere. South on Orange, the underground **Tanqueray's Bar and Grille** offers live music (Fri and Sat).

On Pine Street you have the **Pine Street Bar and Grill** (11am–2am Mon–Fri, 8pm–2am Sat and Sun) for one of the best bar-restaurants in the area, ideal for a late-night snack, with pool and billiards, and the fun Hawaiian style of **Maui Jack's Draft House and Raw Bar**.

The eclectic duo of **Slingapour's** and **The Globe** (the latter an off-the-wall 24-hour diner) are also worth seeking out for a lively drink or three on Wall Street, just off

Pirates Dinner Adventure

American radio

American radio stations come in a vast number of types and styles that conform to fairly narrow musical tastes. Here is a quick guide to finding the main ones in your car.

CONTEMPORARY	NEWS/TALK	COUNTRY
98.9 FM (WMMO)	90.7 FM (WMFE)	92.3 FM (WWKA
99.3 FM (WLRQ)	104.1 FM (WTKS)	97.5 FM (WPCV)
105.1 FM (WOMX)	**SPORT**	98.1 FM (WGNE)
107.7 FM (WMGF)	540 AM (WQTM)	102.7 FM (WHKR)
POP	740 AM (THE TEAM)	**ROCK**
99.9 FM (WFKS)	**CLASSICAL**	91.5 FM (WPRK)
106.7 FM (WXXL)	90.7 FM (WMFE)	93.1 FM (WKRO)
OLDIES	91.5 FM (WPRK)	96.5 FM (WHTQ)
100.3 FM (WSHE)	**JAZZ**	101.1 FM (WJRR)
790 AM (WLBE)	89.9 FM (WUCF)	105.9 FM (O-ROCK)
	103.1 FM (WLOQ)	

(I recommend WJRR and O-ROCK as the best rock radio anywhere!)

Orange, boasting a range of bars, a pool hall and live music, as well as The Globe's fun eating style.

Sports bars

Finally, with the multitude of sports bars that are another particularly American speciality, **Friday's Front Row Sports Grill** on I-Drive (just south of the Sand Lake Road junction) really sticks out as a major tourist trap that even the locals enjoy. Here you can catch ALL the action (and, yes, they do show soccer) on 84 TV screens, plus enjoy some 100 beers from around the world – the bar features $1 domestic 12oz drafts! – as well as try out their basketball nets, pool tables and shuffleboard, and rub shoulders with local sports stars from time to time. The food is standard American diner fare and there is plenty to keep the kids amused, too (paper tablecloths to colour and video games). The atmosphere varies according to the time of day and which sports event it is (pretty rowdy for Orlando Magic basketball games), so call 407 363 1414 for up-to-the-minute info. Open 11am–2am daily.

Other choices for the sports bar experience include the massive **Players Sports Pub** on Curry Ford Road; 87 TV screens, with 12 big-screens, open 11am–2am every day (407 273 7363) and **Headlightz Sports Bar** on East Colonial Drive, which also offers live music (407 273 9600). My favourite is the **Orlando Ale House** on Kirkman Road, just opposite Universal Studios (407 248 0000). With more than 30 TVs, a raw bar and great seafood, it also has an above-average range of beers.

Walt Disney World Resort in Florida can boast the excellent **ESPN Club** at *Disney's BoardWalk Resort*, a full-service restaurant with sports broadcast facilities, video games, more than 70 TV monitors, giant scoreboards and even a Little League menu for kids. No sports fan should miss it. Equally, **NBA City** (for basketball fans) at Universal's CityWalk, and the **Cricketers' Arms** (for British sport) in The Mercado should not be overlooked, especially for TV addicts (www.cricketersarmspub.com).

Now, you will also want to know a lot more about where, when and how to tackle that other holiday dilemma – where to eat. Read on…

9

10 Dining Out

(or, Man, these portions are HUGE!)

Eating is a big deal in America. Consequently, dining out is a vital component of their entertainment business. Whether it be breakfast, lunch or dinner, the experience needs to be well-organised, filling and good value. To say Americans take mealtimes seriously would be the understatement of the year.

It is sometimes hard to dispel the notion that food is the 'be all and end all' of some Americans' holiday experience, as the options for dining are seemingly omnipresent and large scale. However, this is all good news for us Joe Tourists.

Variety

The variety, quantity and quality of restaurants, cafés, fast-food chains, snack bars and hot-dog stalls is in keeping with the American tradition of eating as much as possible, as often as possible.

At first glance, the full selection of food is rather overwhelming. Cruising along either I-Drive or Highway 192 will quickly reveal a dazzling array of eateries, the choice of which can be quite bewildering.

As a general rule, food is plentiful, relatively cheap, available 24 hours a day and nearly always appetising and filling. You will encounter an increasing number of fine-dining possibilities, but the basic premise remains that you will get good value for money and are unlikely to need more than two meals a day. Put simply, portions tend to be large, and of a steak, chicken or pizza-based variety, with service of an efficient, friendly character. It is actually hard to come by a BAD meal. The one real exception (as pointed out by several readers) is if you like fresh veg. The US diet often overlooks this staple, but if you look up the vegetarian options lower down or check out one of the outlets of **Chamberlin's**, notably at the Market Place on Dr Phillips Boulevard and in the new Winter Park Village, you will find a healthy, balanced choice.

Exceptional deals

In keeping with the climate, most restaurants tend towards the informal (T-shirts and shorts are usually acceptable) and cater readily for families. This also leads to two exceptional deals for budget-conscious tourists, especially those with a large tribe. Many hotels and restaurants offer 'kids eat free' deals, provided they eat with their parents. The age restrictions can vary from under 10s to under 14s, but it obviously represents good value for money. The second item of interest is the 'all-you-can-eat' buffet, another common feature of the large chain restaurants. This means you can have a hearty meal for not too much and probably eat enough at, say, breakfast, to keep you going until dinner. A few establishments also offer 'early bird' specials, a dinner discount if you dine before 6pm (quite often, you may have to wait for a table if you want dinner between 6 and 8pm; you need to arrive by 5 or after 8.30pm to beat the typical dinner rush).

Don't be afraid to ask for a doggy bag if you have leftovers (even if you haven't brought the dog). It is common practice to take away the half of that pizza you couldn't finish, or those chicken legs or salad. The locals do it all the time and, again, it is highly wallet-friendly. Just ask for the leftovers 'to go'. And don't hesitate to tell your waiter or waitress if something isn't right with your meal. Americans will readily complain if they are not happy, so restaurants are keen to make sure everything is to your satisfaction.

BRIT TIP: As portions are so large, you can save money by sharing an entrée, or main course, between two. Your waiter or waitress will be happy to oblige (provided you keep their tip up to the full rate).

And, please, don't forget to tip. The basic wage for waiters and waitresses is low, so they rely heavily on tips to supplement their income – and they are taxed on the tips, whether they receive them or not. Unless service really is shoddy, in which case you should mention it, the usual rate for tips is 10 per cent of your bill at buffet-style restaurants and 15 per cent at full-service restaurants. It is worth checking to see if service is already added to your bill, although this is not common in the US.

With Orlando being the world's favourite holiday destination, and with the city springing up from such eclectic roots, you will encounter a monumental array of food types. Florida is renowned for its seafood, which comes at a much more reasonable price than in the

BRIT TIP: Don't worry about eating 'dolphin', it's not a mammal related to Flipper but a different species called dolphin-fish or mahi-mahi.

Mediterranean. Crab, lobster, shrimp (what we call king prawns), clams and oysters can all be had without fear of breaking the bank, as well as several dozen varieties of fish, many of which you won't have come across before.

Cuban, Cajun/Creole and Mexican are other more local types of cooking which are well represented here, and there is plenty of Asian fare from Chinese and Indian to Japanese, Thai and Vietnamese.

The big shopping malls offer a good choice in their food courts, which are often particularly good value. Cracker (cowboy) cooking is original Floridian fare, and the more adventurous will want to try the local speciality – alligator meat. This can be stewed, barbecued, smoked, sautéed or braised. Fried gator tail 'nuggets' are an Orlando favourite. Of course, you must try the traditional Key Lime Pie, a truly decadent dessert. Look for the stall in *Pleasure Island* selling it at $1 a slice – true heaven!

10

How to order

Ordering food can be an adventure in itself. The choice for each item is often the cue for an inquisition of exam-type proportions from your waiter or waitress. You can never order just 'toast' – it has to be white, brown, wholegrain, rye, muffin or bagel; eggs and bacon come in a baffling variety of ways; an order for tea or coffee usually provokes the response 'Regular or decaf? Iced,

BRIT TIP: American bacon is always streaky and crisp-fried and sausages are chipolata-like.

lemon or English?' and salads have more dressings than the National Health Service. Whenever I've finished ordering, I'm tempted to ask, 'Have I passed?' Ask to see a restaurant's menu if it isn't displayed. It is no big deal to Americans and they won't feel insulted if you decide to look for somewhere else.

Vegetarian options

In a country where beef is culinary king, vegetarians often find themselves hard done by, and Orlando is no different. However, there are a couple of bright spots, plus a handy hint when all seems lost.

Firstly, there are two speciality vegetarian restaurants in Orlando, the Indian cuisine of **Woodlands** on the South Orange Blossom Trail (407 854 3330) and the Chinese **Garden Café** on West Colonial Drive downtown (407 999 9799), while the tapas-style **Café Tu Tu Tango** on I-Drive serves a good variety of veggie dishes.

However, most of the upscale restaurants should be able to offer a vegetarian option and will be happy for you to ask in advance. *Walt Disney World Resort in Florida* is slightly more enlightened in that the **California Grill** (in *Disney's Contemporary Resort*), **Citricos**

(Disney's Grand Floridian Resort and Spa), **Le Cellier** (Canada pavilion in *Epcot* park) and **Spoodles** (*Disney's BoardWalk*) feature vegetarian dishes, while the seafood-orientated **Flying Fish** (*Disney's Boardwalk*) and **'Ohana** (*Polynesian Resort*) can also serve up decent veggie fare if asked (thanks to Kaylee Robbins for that tip via www.wdwinfo.com). Most full-service restaurants (notably **Bongos Cuban Café™ and Wolfgang Puck's® Café** in *Downtown Disney*) and even some of the counter-service ones are usually keen to try to cater for non-menu requests. It is always worth asking.

BRIT TIP: An excellent section of the *Unofficial Walt Disney World Information Guide* website lists places that cater for special dietary needs, including veggie, at www.wdwig.com/special.htm.

Sweet Tomatoes is a salad buffet restaurant (distinctly vegetarian-friendly) with possibly the best meal deals in central Florida. On I-Drive (by Kirkman Road junction), it offers an astonishing all-you-can-eat choice for just $7.50 at lunch ($8.99 at dinner, after 4pm) that includes a vast salad spread, a choice of soups, pizza, pasta, bread and pastries, plus fruit and frozen yoghurt. Drinks are $1.59 (with free refills) and kids' meals are $1.59 for under 6s and $4.99 for 6–12s. Open 10.30am–9pm Sun–Thur, 10.30am–10pm Fri and Sat, the restaurant should be sought out by all value- and health-conscious eaters. **Chamberlin's Market and Café** (with eight Orlando locations) is another more enlightened choice, with homemade soups, vegetarian chilli, sandwiches, salads and blissful fresh fruit smoothies (www.chamberlins.com).

Dining at Disney's Pop Century Resort

© Disney

Eating 24/7

It is not unusual to find restaurants that never close – you can eat around the clock, or 24/7 as the Americans say. So especially for those who can't sleep on their first few nights in the USA (plus those who just like to eat!), here is a guide to where you can go for a snack or even tuck into a full-scale meal at 4 in the morning:

Chain restaurants: Denny's, Waffle House, Steak & Shake.

Individuals: B-Line Diner (Peabody Hotel, I-Drive), Mickey D's (world's largest McDonald's, Sand Lake Road; high season only), The Globe (downtown Orlando), Planet Java (Gaylord Palms Resort), Baskervilles (Grosvenor Resort), Tubbi's Buffeteria (Disney's Dolphin Hotel), and the Village Inn (in St Cloud).

Drinking

The biggest complaint of Brits on holiday in the USA is about the beer. With the exception of a handful of English-style pubs (see pages 268–69), American beer is always lager, either bottled or on draught, and ice cold. It goes down great when it's hot, but it is generally weaker and fizzier than we're used to.

Of course, there are exceptions and they are worth seeking out (try Killian's Red, Michelob Amber Bock or Dos Equis for a fuller flavour), but if you are expecting a good, old-fashioned British pint, forget it (although **The Cricketers Arms** in The Mercado and the **Rose & Crown** at *Epcot's* UK pavilion come

> **BRIT TIP:** If there are several of you, ordering a pitcher of beer will work out cheaper than buying it by the glass.

> **BRIT TIP:** Tourist brochures often include money-off coupons for many restaurants so you can make useful savings. See www.floridacoupon.com.

close if you don't mind paying more than $6 a pint. You are better off trying **The Big River Grille** at *Disney's Boardwalk Resort*, **Big Belly Brewery** in downtown Orlando or any of the excellent new **Hops Bar & Grill** chain, which are all micro-breweries. Spirits (always called 'liquor' by Americans) come in a typically huge variety, but beware ordering just 'whisky' as you'll get bourbon. Specify if you want Scotch or Irish whiskey and demand it 'straight up' if you don't want it with a mountain of ice. If you fancy a cocktail, there is a massive choice and most bars and restaurants have lengthy Happy Hours where prices are very consumer-friendly. Good-quality Californian wines also work out better value than European.

If you are sticking to soft drinks (sodas) or coffee, most bars and restaurants give free refills. You can also run a tab in the majority of bars and pay when you leave.

Another few words of warning. Florida licensing laws are stricter than ours and you need to be **21 or over** to enjoy an alcoholic drink in a bar or lounge. You will often be

10

The Nine Dragons Restaurant at Epcot
© Disney

asked for proof of your age before you are served (or allowed into entertainment complexes like *Downtown Disney Pleasure Island*), and this means your passport or new-style driving licence with a photo. It's no good arguing with a reluctant barman. Licensing laws are strict and they take no chances. No photo ID, no beer! Anyone under the age of 21 may not sit or stand near a bar either.

Right, that gives you the inside track on HOW to eat and drink like the locals, now you want to know WHERE to do it, so here's a guide to that veritable profusion of culinary variety. At the last count there were more than 4,000 restaurants in the metro Orlando area, with new ones being added and some biting the dust all the time and, while it would be a tall order to list every one, the following section covers the main tourist areas and chain groups.

Fast food

If you are a **McDonald's** fan you are coming to the right place as there are no less than 65 outlets in the greater Orlando area, varying from small drive-in types to the mega, 24-hour-a-day establishment on Sand Lake Road, Mickey D's (near the junction with I-Drive), that also has the biggest play area for kids of any McDonald's in the world and a number of differently themed eating areas. **Burger King** is also well represented, with 45 outlets, as is another familiar American franchise, **Wendy's**, which has 23 restaurants. If you're a burger freak and want to sample a variation on the theme, give **Checkers** (eight outlets) or **Hardees** (four) a try.

KFC has 25 restaurants around the area, but for something different on the chicken theme, try **Popeye's Famous Fried Chicken & Biscuits** (ten). If it's pizza you're after, **Pizza Hut** has 40 restaurants and **Domino's** has 21, and both deliver locally, even to your hotel room.

A particularly American form of take-away is the 'sub', or torpedo-roll sandwich. This is what you will find at any one of the 49 local branches of **Subway**, or the 14 of **Sobik's** or eight of **Miami Subs**. They're a rather healthier option than yet another burger, and offer some imaginative fillings. Two other variations on the fast-food theme are **Arby's** (with eight outlets), which offers a particularly appetising roast beef sandwich and other beefy delicacies, and **Taco Bell** (30 outlets), which does for Mexican food what McDonald's does for the hamburger. If you've never had Mexican food, this is probably not the place to start but, for anyone familiar with their tacos, nachos and tortillas, it's a quick and cheap meal.

A much better bet is the more health-conscious chain **Tijuana Flats**, which started in central Florida and now has some 20 outlets, most notably on E Central Boulevard downtown near Lake Eola. Their Tex-Mex style is geared around fresh, hand-made products in a lively, convivial atmosphere. (McDonald's eat your heart out!) Check out their burritos, quesadillas, enchiladas, tacos and salads, and you will struggle to spend more than $9 a head (www.tijuanaflats.com).

Most of these establishments will have a drive-through part, which will be fun to try at least once on your visit. Simply drive around the side of the building where indicated and you will find their take-away menu with a voice box to take your order. Carry on around the building and your food will be served from a side window where you pay. You will probably find your car has a slide-out tray from the central dashboard area that will take a cup.

Family restaurants

This section may, at first, seem similar to the American Diner type (on page 269), but there are two major differences. First, these are restaurants *only*. You usually won't find a bar here as with a diner. And second, they make a big effort for family groups in terms of kids' menus, activities (in many cases the kids' menu doubles up as a colouring and puzzle book) and budget-conscious prices. They also serve breakfasts and you will find the best of the all-you-can-eat buffet deals here. Nearly all are chain groups in the same way that you find Little Chef all over Britain, but there are one or two worthy individuals, too.

The most popular are the **Ponderosa Steakhouse** and **Sizzler** restaurants. Whether it's breakfast, lunch or dinner, you'll find great value and good, reliable food. You order and pay for your meal as you enter and are then seated, before being unleashed on some of the biggest buffet and salad bars you will have seen. Ponderosa has the rather flashier style (and the better reputation in town) but you'd be hard pushed to tell whose food was whose. Expect to pay about $4–5 for their breakfast buffets and $6–9 for lunch and dinner (there IS a difference in price depending on location, with the I-Drive area tending to be a dollar or two more expensive).

Standard fare includes chicken wings, meatballs, chilli, ribs, steaks and fresh seafood, while their

> **BRIT TIP:** A buffet breakfast at Ponderosa or a similar establishment should keep you going until tea-time and is a good way to start a theme-park day.

> **BRIT TIP:** Reader Alastair Gillies says: 'We took your advice with Ponderosa (good-value buffet breakfasts and dinners), but we also liked Shoney's for a slightly dearer but definitely superior buffet.'

immense salad bars in particular represent major value for money. Both are open from 7am until late evening and can be found in all the main tourist spots.

A more homely touch can be found at the following selection, with equally good if not better value for money. For a hearty breakfast at any time of day, **International House of Pancakes** (aka IHOP) and the **Waffle House** are both a good bet. You will struggle to spend more than $6 on a full meal, whether it be one of their huge breakfast platters or a hot sandwich with fries. The Waffle Houses are also open 24 hours a day, while IHOP's open 6am–midnight. Another traditional American 24-hour family restaurant is **Denny's Diner**, the nearest thing to our Little Chef. Again, they make a traditional bacon-and-egg breakfast seem ordinary with their wide selection, and they do an excellent range of hot, toasted sandwiches and imaginative dinner meals, such as grilled catfish, as well as a Senior Selections menu, featuring smaller portions at reduced prices for the over 55s.

Perkins Family Restaurant has a lookalike menu (eight in central Florida, with some open around the clock). For a really hearty breakfast try Perkins Eggs Benedict (two eggs and bacon on a toasted muffin with hash browns and fresh fruit), while their bread-bowl salads are equally satisfying. Another that impresses

10

for its clean, fresh style is **Golden Corral** (48 in Florida; 7.30am–10pm) which has already chalked up a number of reader recommendations, and offers a delicious Carver's Choice of hand-carved meats plus the usual buffet deals, an excellent vegetable selection and a terrific dessert bar.

If you are travelling on the major highways of Florida and you see one of the 50 branches of **Cracker Barrel**, stop and check out their delightful Old Country Store style, with mountainous breakfasts, well-balanced lunch and dinner menus, Kid's Stuff choices and a real old-fashioned charm that is a nice change from the usual tourist frenzy (6am–10pm Sun–Thur, 6am–11pm Fri and Sat). The **Bob Evans** chain (three in Kissimmee, eight in central Florida) is another personal favourite for their friendly, country style, hearty menus (plus a range of low-carb options) and truly mouth-watering desserts (6 or 7am–10pm). They also offer a take-away and country store selection which is well worth trying.

Two recent additions worthy of note for any time, but especially breakfast, are the mushrooming chains of **Panera Bread** (wonderful pastries and fresh breads, salads and sandwiches, with some good vegetarian selections; 7am–10pm) and **First Watch**, specialising in breakfast, brunch and lunch (all manner of egg dishes, plus great coffee and pastries, served double-quick; 7am–2.30pm).

One of the most popular one-off restaurants that appeals to families is **Captain Nemo's** on Highway 192 opposite Fort Liberty. It serves breakfast 8am–noon, lunch until 3pm and dinner until 11pm, and its seafood and steak menu means Mum and Dad can try oysters, lobster, salmon, swordfish or grouper while the kids still get their burger fix. Prices are budget-

Orlando has more than 4,000 restaurants

orientated, with daily specials, and Happy Hour 3–7pm.

Home from home

To complete this section it is appropriate to mention the handful of British pubs and diners that seek to attract the UK visitor. All offer a fairly predictable array of pub grub and a few imported British beers. You'll find the odd Brit or two working behind the bars, and you can happily take the kids into all of them, providing they don't sit at the bar. First and foremost is the **Cricketers' Arms** in The Mercado on I-Drive (midday–2am). This has become a favourite haunt of British visitors due to the large selection of beers, appetising food, live evening entertainment and (soccer fans take note) live Premiership matches on their giant TV screen on a Saturday morning (from 10am – remember the time difference). It gets busy in the evenings, their live music is usually good, and many of the staff are Chelsea fans, but we won't hold that against them! NB: There is usually a cover charge for soccer matches.

Highway 192 in Kissimmee sports a number of fairly derivative pubs all keen to appeal to the home market. The best are **Harry Ramsbottom's** at Fort Liberty (between Markers 10 and 11), which also has its own fish 'n' chippie, and the wonderfully kept

Stage Door, 6 miles (10km) west of the junction with I-4 (and west of Marker 4, just past Lindfields Boulevard). This bar/restaurant gets full marks from the locals, too. *Coronation Street* fans should make a beeline for **The Rovers Return** on the Vine Street stretch of 192, then there is the **Fox and Hounds**, **Queen Victoria Tavern** and **The Albert**, all of which are British owned and run.

Up in Winter Park, **Fiddlers Green** (on Fairbanks Avenue) is possibly the best Irish pub version in central Florida. With Happy Hour from 4–7pm, live jazz every Sunday evening, more than 20 beers on tap and a suitably authentic Irish-tinged menu, it's a winning formula (11.30am–2am Mon–Sat, 11.30am–midnight Sun; www.fiddlersgreenorlando.com).

American diners

Not surprisingly, there are so many American-style restaurants, it would be a full-time job just to keep track of them all. Therefore, I will limit this particular survey to the main tourist areas, plus a couple off the beaten track that are well worth tracking down. The $ price listings are intended only as a rough guide for a 3-course meal per person:

$	=	$10–15
$$	=	$15–20
$$$	=	$20–25
$$$$	=	$25–30
$$$$$	=	$30-plus

Steak and Ale is a popular diner and can be found at four locations around Orlando (11.30am–10pm Mon–Thur, 11.30am–11pm Fri, noon–11.30pm Sat, noon–10pm Sun; $$). They do some great steaks and ribs, plus tempting seafood and chicken dishes, with early bird specials of a 3-course set meal 4–7pm (4–6pm Nov–Mar), and two-

for-one drink specials at the same time. The nationwide chain **Bennigan's** has 11 outlets in Orlando and is a particular personal favourite for their friendly, efficient service, smart decor and tempting menu, especially at lunchtime. They make the ordinary seem appetising and have a bar atmosphere straight out of the TV programme *Cheers!* Their Irish flavour really comes into its own on St Patrick's Day (March 17), and they have Happy Hour(s!) 2–7pm and 11pm–midnight (11am–2am; $$).

Another enjoyable dining experience can be found at the two branches of **Darryl's** (one on I-Drive, the other at Fort Liberty on Highway 192). Their weird and wonderful decor is totally original; they also have a great bar area and a nicely varied menu with interesting choices such as Cajun-fried shrimp. Thick, wood-fired steaks, delicious burgers and southern-style dishes are the main fare, but they also offer tasty soups and quiches (11am–1am; $$).

Hooters makes no bones about its style. 'Delightfully tacky yet unrefined' declares the menu proudly, and sure enough here is a relatively simple, lively establishment, especially popular with the younger crowd for its beach-party atmosphere – and the famous Hooter Girl waitresses (eight Orlando locations; 11am–midnight Mon–Thur, 11am–1am Fri–Sat, noon–11pm Sun; $). Their 10 restaurants have a truly entertaining menu featuring great value seafood, salads and burgers, plus Hooters Nearly World

10

Kids enjoy a character breakfast

© Disney

Famous Chicken Wings in five strengths: mild, medium, hot, 3 Mile Island or Wild Wing. You have been warned!

Uno Chicago Pizzeria is the place to go if you're bored with Pizza Hut. Their four outlets offer great deep-dish pizzas plus pastas, chicken dishes, steaks and salads. They also have the novelty value of charging kids by their *weight* off the children's menu – if they only weigh 60lb (27kg), they pay 60c! (11am–midnight; $$).

The **Olive Garden** restaurants (12 of them) are one of America's big success stories as they have brought Italian food into the budget, mass-market range (11am–10pm Sun–Thur, 11am–11pm Fri–Sat; $$). Their light, airy restaurants create a relaxing environment and, while they don't offer a huge choice, what they do they do well and in generous portions. Pastas are their speciality, but they also offer chicken, veal, steak and seafood and some great salads, and unlimited refills of salad, garlic breadsticks and non-alcoholic drinks add to their good value. Their large, new property next to Race Rock on I-Drive is also a distinct cut above their others for quality and style.

Similarly, the **Macaroni Grill** chain (five in Orlando) offers a wonderful slice of family dining Italian style. Their spacious restaurants are stylish, comfortable and well served, with an excellent à la carte menu as well as a family-style menu (serving 8–10), which is great value for large groups. Their pasta is first class, as are their wood-oven pizzas, and the wine list is impressive, too. Don't be put off by the downbeat name – this place is well above average and good enough for special occasions (11.30am–10pm Sun–Thur, 11.30am–11pm Fri and Sat; $$–$$$).

The two **Bahama Breeze** restaurants (one on I-Drive, the other on SR 535 at Lake Buena Vista, next to the Holiday Inn Sunspree) are appealing for their striking Caribbean styling – but are very popular (the I-Drive one features an hour's wait at peak periods!). The food is also well above average for a typical diner. Try West Indies Patties or Creole Baked Goat Cheese as a starter, while the main courses (primarily pastas, seafood, chicken, beef or pizza) feature outstanding items like Black Pepper Seared Tuna or the Cuban beef stew Ropa Vieja, with every dish coming up immaculately fresh. Service is in keeping with their lively, personable style and there is a pleasing individual touch to all they do. The plantation-room decor, delightful outside wooden deck for a pre- or post-dinner drink and live music most nights fully endorse their own slogan: 'At Bahama Breeze there are no worries, just happy, friendly people and island hospitality!' (4pm–2am Mon–Sat, 4pm–midnight Sun; $$$).

Hard to categorise but well worth visiting is the **Cheesecake Factory** in Winter Park Village and the new Mall at Millenia. While they make a feature of their desserts, the rest of the menu (menu? – more like a book!) is pretty impressive, too, not to mention the eclectic, high-tech setting. Mexican dishes jostle with pizza, pasta, seafood, burgers, steaks and salads, and they also offer a great brunch selection, as well as plenty of everything (you really need to come hungry here). If you do nothing else in this selection, visit the Cheesecake Factory for dessert (as many do) and sample one of their 30 varieties of cheesecake (11am–11pm; $$$$).

Ribs

When it comes to steaks, ribs and barbecue food, Orlando has a magnificent array of restaurants that all proudly proclaim some kind of 'world famous' variety. In many instances they are right, and here's a selection of the best.

Cattleman's Steak House (on Vineland Road, at the intersection of SR 535 and Highway 192, and on I-Drive south of The Mercado) goes for the cowboy approach once again, with a neat saloon bar, early bird specials (4–6pm) and the Little Rustlers' Round-up menu for the kids. Steaks are again the order of the day, but you can also order chicken and seafood, and their Heavenly Duck is worth trying for something different (4–11pm, saloon open until 2am; $$$).

The upmarket version of this type of establishment is **Wild Jack's** (on I-Drive, just north of Sand Lake Road) where the most magnificent wood-smoked barbecue aroma hits you as you walk in the door. The huge, Western-themed interior features a big, open-pit barbecue where you can watch your food being cooked (11.30am–11pm; $$$). Steaks, ribs, chicken and turkey represent the main choices and they are all served with bags of panache and a big helpin' of Wild West style. Happy Hour is 4–7pm, kids eat free with a full-paying adult and you can even buy a Wild Jack's souvenir boot-shaped beer mug.

Another good choice which also pulls in a lot of positive reader feedback is **Key W Kool's Open Pit Grill** on Highway 192 (just opposite the now-closed Splendid

BRIT TIP: Don't miss Wild Jack's Jalapeño Mashed Potatoes, Dynamite Chicken Wings, Cowboy Baked Beans and the Jack Daniels Chocolate Cake for dessert!

China). Choice cuts of meat, mouth-watering steaks – check out the eye-popping 32-oz (900-g) porterhouse! – prime rib, daily specials and a succulent, inviting aroma add up to an outstanding dining choice (4–11pm; $$$).

I can also recommend any of the six **Tony Roma's**, which rightly pronounce themselves 'famous for ribs'. The airy but relaxing decor and ambience, clever kids' menu (the Roma Rangers Round-up, full of puzzles and games), junior meals, and their melt-in-the-mouth ribs (try their Original Baby Backs) make a winning combination. You can still get chicken, burgers and steaks, but why ignore a dish when it's done this well? The Rib Sampler is a great platter, with delicious chicken-rib and shrimp-rib combos, while the 'unlimited rib' option is a real stomach-enlarger (11am–midnight Sun–Thur, 11am–1am Fri and Sat; $$).

Going local again, **Sonny's Real Pit Bar-B-Q** (four in Orlando, two in Kissimmee) is a national chain with no great pretensions, just masses of food of the barbecue persuasion. Ideal for families, with a good kids' menu, try their ribs and their own recipe coleslaw (11am–10pm; $$).

Out of the same log-built mould is **JT's Prime Time**, just past Orange Lake Country Club on West Highway 192, with another heavily barbecue-orientated menu, good kids' choice (plus a games room), and a slice of original old pioneer style. It is also popular with the locals at weekends (noon to 11pm; $$).

Tex-Mex

What the Olive Garden does for Italian cuisine, **Chili's** (with 10 outlets) does for Mexican. Actually, it's an Americanised version of

10

Mexican cooking that originated in Texas (hence Tex-Mex), with the emphasis more on steak and ribs and less on tortillas and spices (11am–1am Mon–Sat, 11am–11pm Sun; $$). Service is frighteningly efficient and, if you are looking for a quick meal, you'll be hard-pushed to find a quicker turnaround. The atmosphere is lively and bustling and they provide a good kids' menu that doubles up as a colouring and puzzle book.

Similarly, the rather identikit **Chevy's** chain has three restaurants in the area and offers a healthy slice of Mexicana, while still providing some reassuring American selections (4–11pm Mon–Thur, 4–midnight Fri, 11am–midnight Sat, 11am–11pm Sun; $$).

The most elaborate Mexican offering is the cavernous **Don Pablo's**, next to the Visitor Center on I-Drive. Clever theming, lively atmosphere (especially around the Cantina bar!) and a classic, well-explained menu add up to a fun experience (11.30am–10pm Sun–Thur, 11.30am–11pm Fri–Sat; $$).

Another one-off restaurant that has a lot of Brit appeal is **Café Tu-Tu Tango** on I-Drive, next to Vito's. The accent is artist-colony Spanish (whatever that means), with a really original menu, live entertainment and artwork all over the walls that changes daily. Vegetarians will find themselves well catered for here, and you can try some particularly succulent pizzas, seafood, salads and paella. Mexican and Chinese dishes are also on offer along with a thoughtful kids' menu (11.30am–midnight; $$). The style is based more on a tapas bar, so you order several different dishes at once rather than a starter and main course. Ultimately, it is as much an artistic experience as a meal, and the fun atmosphere complements the rich array of dishes perfectly.

Steakhouses

Serious steak-lovers will have to pay a visit to **Ruth's Chris Steak House** (with new restaurants in the Winter Park Village and on West Sand Lake Road) where prime beef in a mouth-watering variety of choices is the order of the day. It isn't cheap, but you'll be hard-pushed to get a better steak (5–11pm Mon–Sat, 5–10pm Sun; $$$$$). 'Only the best', proclaims their slogan. 'Come judge for yourself, but come hungry'.

Similarly, the **Butcher Shop** (in The Mercado on I-Drive) offers steaks, steaks and more steaks. Hugely impressive is the cold counter, where you can select your own piece of meat and cook it on the hickory charcoal grill along with the chef (5–10pm Sun–Thur, 5–11pm Fri–Sat; $$$$).

Charley's Steak Houses (three branches, the biggest being on I-Drive just north of The Mercado) continue the theme of excellent steaks cooked over a specially built pit woodfire. Highly rated in American steakhouse reviews, they are not cheap (although the one at Orange Blossom Trail, 2 miles (3km) north of the Florida Mall, is the least expensive of the three), but the bar area is splendidly furnished, and if you don't fancy steak, which you can watch being grilled on a large, hardwood grill, there is seafood (5–11pm; $$$$$).

Another imaginative option is **Vito's Chop House** in front of the

Bahama Breeze

Castle Hotel on I-Drive. Their choice beef cuts – check out the Tuscan T-Bone – are aged for 4–6 weeks and cooked over wood fires. Pork chops, seafood and pasta are also available, as well as an extensive wine list (5pm–10.30pm Sun–Thur, 5pm–11pm Fri–Sat; $$$$).

Morton's of Chicago (on the Market Place on Dr Phillips Boulevard) has a more upmarket (sometimes pretty smoky) style, offset by a lively ambience that adds to the enjoyment of its trademark steaks, which are cooked on their open range. You are provided with a fully exhibited menu (they bring examples to the table) and invited to enjoy some of the biggest, most succulent steaks it has been my pleasure to sample. The porterhouse is inspired, as is one of the principal alternatives, Shrimp Alexander. It does not come cheap, especially as vegetables are extra, but it is a memorable experience (5pm– midnight Mon–Sat, 5pm–11pm Sun; $$$$$).

Similarly, **Shula's Steak House** in the *Walt Disney World Dolphin Hotel* is both expansive (on your waistline) and expensive. The porterhouse and prime rib are outstanding, and this restaurant (the latest in a chain owned by famous former American football coach Don Shula) is extremely popular with locals (5–11pm; $$$$$).

Also in expensive territory, and one that frequently gets the locals' vote for Best Steakhouse, is **Del Frisco's** at 729 Lee Road just north of Winter Park. Here in a fairly down-to-earth atmosphere (although a jacket is advisable attire), they concentrate on prime cuts of US beef, generous portions and reliable, friendly service (5–10pm Mon–Thur, 5–11pm Fri and Sat; $$$$$).

The **Outback Steakhouse** chain (ten in Orlando) has an Australian slant with thick, juicy well-seasoned steaks, ribs and a small seafood selection. Appetisers include the Bloomin' Onion, a large fried onion accompanied by special dipping sauce. Queues build up in the evening, so try to avoid the usual dinner time or you can just visit the bar. They also feature a good kids' menu (4–10.30pm Mon–Thur, 3.30–11pm Fri and Sat, 3.30–10.30pm Sun; $$$$).

Perhaps more fun is **Logan's Roadhouse** (with five in central Florida, notably on Highway 192 at its junction with I-Drive South) where the funky, rustic atmosphere is enlivened with masses of peanuts in their shells, which end up all over the wooden floor. Burgers, chicken, steaks and ribs are their stock in trade, while they also offer an Express lunch selection (11am–10.30pm Sun–Thur, 11am–11.30pm Fri and Sat; $$$).

Black Angus and **Western Steer**, along more budget lines, complete the line-up of steakhouses. They also serve breakfasts and aim for the family market. Black Angus (two outlets on Highway 192) offers an all-you-can-eat breakfast buffet as well as a typical range of steaks, and has a nightly karaoke session (7am–11.30pm; $$). Western Steer (on I-Drive, opposite Wet 'n Wild) has breakfast and dinner buffets. Steaks are the main fare, and with a large tribe to feed, it's great value (7am–11.30pm; $$).

10

Seafood

You won't be surprised to learn that the choice of seafood eateries is

Olive Garden

equally wide. **The Crab House** (at Goodings Plaza on I-Drive and Palm Parkway) should be self-explanatory. Garlic crabs, steamed crabs, snow crabs, Alaskan king crabs, etc. Yes, this is THE place for crab. You can always try their prime rib, pasta or other seafood, but it would be a shame to ignore the house speciality when it's this good (11.30am–11pm Mon–Sat, noon–11pm Sun; $$$).

Red Lobster (four restaurants) is part of the same company that owns the successful Olive Garden chain. This is seafood for the family market, with a varied menu, lively atmosphere and one of the best kids' menu/activity books. While lobster is the speciality, their steaks, chicken, salads and other seafood are equally appetising, and they do a great variety of combination platters (11am–10pm Sun–Thur, 11am–11pm Fri–Sat; $$$).

Charlie's Lobster House (on I-Drive at The Mercado) has a similar menu, with nightly fresh fish specials and reservations recommended. The bar areas are immaculately furnished and the service adds that extra charm (4–10pm Sun–Thur, 4–11pm Fri–Sat; $$$$).

Completing the chain restaurants

BRIT TIP: *Brit's Guide* reader John Cartlidge says: 'While we agree with the recommendation for Ponderosa, one morning we found a huge line for their breakfast buffet, so we drove 200yd (180 metres) down the road to the Black Angus – and the biggest buffet we saw all the time we were there. And no queue!'

here are the three outlets of the **Boston Lobster Feast**, with elaborate nautical decor and an unlimited lobster and seafood buffet (hence the 'Feast'). They have early-bird specials from 4.30–6pm Mon–Fri, 2–4.30pm Sat–Sun, which are excellent value, while their 40-item Lobster Feasts are guaranteed to stretch the stomach (4.30–10pm Mon–Fri, 2–10pm Sat–Sun; $$$$).

Of the one-off restaurants, **Ocean Grill** (on I-Drive, just north of the Sand Lake Road junction) offers great seafood at moderate prices. Daily specials, including the early-bird variety from 4–6pm, jostle with the likes of fried clams, south-western swordfish, fried catfish, shrimp Creole and seafood lasagne. Their fish and chips would put most British chippies to shame and, for the really hearty appetite, their surf 'n' turf is superb (lobster or shrimp and steak), although at a hearty price (4–11pm; $$$) .

The **Atlantic Bay Seafood Grill** (on Highway 192, just east of I-4) surprisingly offers a breakfast buffet on top of its well-priced seafood dishes, early-bird specials (4.30–6.30pm) and steaks, ribs and pasta. It's not gourmet but it is hearty and good value, especially the all-you-can-eat seafood bar (4–11pm; $$).

Inside the new Omni Rosen hotel on I-Drive is the **Everglades Restaurant**, an upmarket seafood and steak choice, which again combines unusual decor (an environmental look at the Everglades, complete with manatee, swamp scenery, tropical music and a 12-ft/3.5-metre aquarium) with fine cuisine. Daily seafood specials jostle with wild boar, venison and buffalo steak, while the Gator Chowder is a must-try starter. There is a relaxing adjacent bar area in this cavernous hotel, and diners at the Everglades also enjoy complimentary valet parking (5.30–11pm daily; $$$$).

My vote for the most memorable seafood dining experience in town is a split decision, however. **Fulton's Crab House** in *Downtown Disney's* Marketplace is a wonderful choice. This mock riverboat has six differently themed dining rooms (albeit with the same menu), plus the Stone Crab Lounge which features a complete raw bar (and always seems to be busy). Nautical props, photos and lithographs fill the interior, giving it a wonderfully eclectic, period atmosphere, but the real attraction is the food – some of the freshest and most tempting fish, crab and lobster dishes in Florida. The Alaskan king crab is a rare treat, as is tuna filet mignon, but there are fresh specials every day (the air shipping bills for which are posted in the main hall), as well as a children's menu. Fulton's features an extensive wine list, micro-brewed beers and its own specialities, but the dining rooms often have a queue as early as 6pm, so it is advisable to book (407 394 2628). The Stone Crab Lounge serves lunch and dinner 11.30am–midnight, while the restaurant is open for dinner (5–11pm; $$$$).

The **Flying Fish**, at *Disney's Boardwalk Resort*, is also a 5-star seafood experience. The menu is not overburdened with choice, but what they do they do with great panache and wonderful presentation. Their 'Peeky Toe' Crab Cake starter melts in the mouth, while the Oak-Grilled Wahoo and Coriander Rubbed Yellowfin Tuna are both outstanding. Steak and pork, plus a vegetarian option are also available (4–11pm Mon–Sat, 4–10pm Sun; $$$$$).

Another great place for seafood (in a group of fine restaurants on West Sand Lake Road) is the splashy **Moonfish**, a true individual in both decor and menu terms. You could make a feast of their appetisers alone, while their sushi is inspired. Many restaurants that go for the avant garde look often fail to deliver the goods, but Moonfish does not fall into that trap. It also makes a good romantic excursion for two (but not at the tables nearest the bar). Dare to be different could be the motto here (407 363 7262; 11.30am–10pm; $$$$$).

Another contender for this crown is **McCormick and Schmick's Seafood Restaurant** at the Mall at Millenia, where the ambience, decor and service are all suitably upscale. This is the latest in a quality-conscious US chain, but there is nothing mass-produced or identikit about their style. The chef creates a daily menu based on product, price and availability from local waters, as well as the Pacific Northwest and the Atlantic (with a prominent listing of what's fresh). Oysters are a speciality, along with their soups and salads (not to mention their stellar wine list), and it is hard to believe anyone offers better shrimp, scallops and Atlantic salmon. However, there is little other choice, apart from a couple of steaks (11am–11pm Mon–Thur, 11am– midnight Fri and Sat, 11am–10pm Sun; $$$$$).

All under one roof

Arguably the greatest restaurant selection in one place is in the new Mall at Millenia, just off Exit 78 of I-4. Here you will find the Cheesecake Factory and McCormick and Schmick's along with **Brio Tuscan Grill** (wood-grilled and oven-roasted steaks, chops and fresh fish, all with a highly pleasing American–Italian ambience), **PF Chang's** (see page 278), **California Pizza Kitchen** (for a more notably health-conscious selection, with vegetarian options such as Japanese eggplant and Caramelised pear and gorgonzola, plus great salads and pastas), **Panera Bread** (sandwiches will never be the

The Red Lobster

same again!) and **Johnny Rockets** (the latest outlet of the popular 1950s-style diner chain). The Food Court takes the choice still further (and maintains the sophisticated style) with 12 outlets, including several new to Orlando, such as **Bistro Sensations** (salads, fresh pastas, pittas and wraps), **Cajun Grill** (a real taste of exquisite New Orleans), **Chinatown** (fast food Mandarin-style) and **Nori Sushi & Grill** (authentic Japanese chicken and beef Teriyaki). Not keen on shopping? The Mall at Millenia (see page 293) will convert you!

Novel dining

Four other restaurants could be categorised as diners but are really delightful, individually styled restaurants. All provide an exciting dining experience in novel settings that will linger long in the memory and not cost a fortune.

Planet Hollywood®, the largest restaurant in the worldwide chain of this glitzy, showbiz-style venture, is next door to *Downtown Disney*

BRIT TIP: Want great quality snacks at bargain prices? Visit McCormick and Schmick's during daily Happy Hour (5–7pm) and all their appetisers are $1.95 if served as bar snacks.

Pleasure Island and is a pure fun entertainment venue. The food is fairly predictable, although everything is served with pizzazz, but the cavernous interior lends itself to a party atmosphere, complete with film clips and a stunning array of movie memorabilia. Some memorable house cocktails, too, but visit either mid-morning or mid-afternoon to avoid the serious queues (11am–2am; $$$).

B-Line Diner, inside the Orlando Peabody Hotel on I-Drive, is an amazing art deco homage to the traditional 1950s-style diner, faithful in every detail, including the outfits of the staff. You sit at a magnificent long counter or in one of several booths, with a good view of the chefs at work and with a rolling menu that changes four times a day (which isn't bad when it is open around the clock). The food is way above usual diner standards, but the prices aren't, so you can munch away on chicken marsala with egg noodles, crispy-fried red snapper or even their trademark Ostrich Burger, as well as more traditional burgers, steaks and ribs, happy in the knowledge you won't break the bank. Their desserts are displayed in a huge glass counter and I dare you to ignore them.

The two versions of **Rainforest Café**, an eco-aware, jungle-themed restaurant chain, are adjacent to *Disney's Animal Kingdom Theme Park* and in the heart of *Downtown Disney* Marketplace, one with a huge waterfall exterior and the other topped with an 'active', smoking volcano, and they have to be seen to be believed. You don't dine, you go on a 'safari adventure' in a rainforest setting amid audio-animatronic animals (including elephants and gorillas), thunderstorms, tropical birds, waterfalls, aquariums and some of the cleverest lighting effects I have seen. It is an amazing experience, especially for children, and the food is well above average. Try the Rasta Pasta or Mojo Bones ribs, but the menu alone will take a while to negotiate. Unless you arrive before midday, you'll have a wait, but that's no hardship given their locations. Beware the huge gift shop! (11am–11pm; $$$).

Another unmistakable landmark on I-Drive is the super-charged, super-large restaurant of **Race Rock**, packed with rare motor-racing memorabilia and eye-catching machines of all kinds. This does for motor sport what the Hard Rock does for music, and how! Two giant car transporters line the entrance, which also boasts a giant-wheeled buggy, two dragsters and a hydroplane speedboat, welcoming you into the circular, 20,000-sq-ft (1,860-sq-metre) restaurant itself. Giant TV screens and a host of regular TVs, video games, virtual reality racing machines and loud, loud music, plus chequered flag tables complete the atmosphere, while the central bar sports an upside-down racing car circulating as the world's biggest ceiling fan! The food is traditional diner fare given a few tweaks like Start Your Engines (the starter selections), Circle Tracks (pizza), Stock and Modified (burgers and sandwiches), Pole Position Pastas and The Main Event (ribs, chops, chicken and salmon). I rate the Road Runner chicken, marinated in lime juice, olive oil and garlic and chargrilled, very highly. A Quarter Midget menu costs $4.99 for children 12 and under (11.30am–midnight; $$).

Chinese

Chinese food is well established in America and well represented in Orlando, although many outlets are pretty uninspired, not to mention downright insipid.

Ming Court on I-Drive, just south of King Henry's Feast, is the Rolls-Royce of local Chinese restaurants. With such a magnificent setting and live entertainment you can easily convince yourself you have been transported to China itself. The menu is extensive and many dishes can be had as a side order rather than a full main course (they specialise in *dim sum*) to give you the chance to try more (11am–2.30pm and 4.30pm–midnight; $$$).

Bill Wong's Famous Super Buffet (yes, they really do call it that) on I-Drive offers a cross between Chinese and diner-type fare. Their all-you-can-eat buffet features jumbo shrimp (and they mean JUMBO!), as well as crab, prime rib, fresh fruit and salad. Think cheap and cheerful and that's Bill Wong's (11am–10pm; $$).

A rather classier version is the **China Garden Buffet** at The Mercado. The elegant surroundings are the perfect complement to the extraordinary buffet choice, with more than 50 items – from spring rolls to chilled crab claws – on offer at any time. There is also a full à la carte selection, but the buffet price of $15.95 for adults and $6.95 for 3–10s ($8.59 and $4.95 at lunch) make this one of the best deals going (10am–11pm; $$).

Similarly, the **Sizzling Wok**, on Sand Lake Road, just across from the Florida Mall, offers an opportunity to get stuck into a massive Chinese buffet at a very

10

Emeril's at CityWalk

reasonable price (11am–10pm Sun–Thur, 11am–10.30pm Fri–Sat; $$).

The **China Café** on I-Drive (at the corner of Kirkman Road) is also above average, with a lunch buffet from 11am–3pm and a well presented array of dishes (the crispy duck is outstanding). Daily specials also feature (11am–11pm; $$).

Arguably the best of the bunch, though, is the latest 'chain' offering, **PF Chang's China Bistro** (at Winter Park's Village Shops and Mall at Millenia), which mixes classic Chinese fare with an American bistro style that makes fans of virtually all who sample it. Seek out their Spicy ground chicken and eggplant, the Cantonese roasted duck or Oolong marinated sea bass for dishes with real distinction. There is also a good vegetarian selection (5–11pm; $$$).

Japanese

The more adventurous (and those already familiar with their cuisine) will want to try one of the fine Japanese restaurants that Orlando is blessed with. **Shogun Steakhouse**, on I-Drive under the Rodeway Inn, is ideal for those who don't like the idea of sushi (basically, raw fish). If you decide to 'chicken' out, you can still order a no-nonsense steak or chicken, but their full Japanese menu is well explained and vividly demonstrated by their chefs in front of you at long, bench-like tables (6–10pm Mon–Thur, 6–10.30pm Fri–Sun; $$).

Kobe brings a touch of Americana to its dining content. With four locations in the area, Kobe goes for the mass market but still achieves individuality with the chef preparing your food at your table in a style that is as much showmanship as culinary expertise (11.30am–11pm; $$).

Ran-Getsu, on I-Drive opposite The Mercado, does for Japanese cuisine what the Ming Court does for Chinese – it's stylish, authentic and as much an experience as a meal, and still reasonably priced. The setting is simple and efficient, and you can choose to sit at conventional tables or at the long, S-shaped sushi bar as many Americans do (5pm–midnight; $$$).

Benihana completes a formidable quartet of restaurants in the Hilton Hotel at Lake Buena Vista. Again, it's a memorable experience, with everything cooked in front of you by expert chefs, and their steaks are among the most tender you will experience (5–10.30pm; $$$).

Indian

If you have come all this way and still fancy a curry, believe it or not you will be able to get one as good as any you have enjoyed back home (albeit more expensive than in your local High Street). Already more than a dozen Indian restaurants have sprung up in the Orlando area and they all maintain a pretty fair standard, from the upmarket **Far Pavilion**, at the intersection of I-Drive and Kirkman Road, to the budget-price **New Punjab** at the upper end of I-Drive and on West Vine Street, Kissimmee, which has excellent lunch and dinner specials.

For a medium-range restaurant, **Passage to India** (also on I-Drive) gets the locals' top vote and is a cut above the average, with unusual and exotic chicken dishes and vegetarian Sabzi Dal Bahar. It is a particular personal favourite for its attentive service and relaxed atmosphere, and you'll probably find yourself dining with a few fellow Brits. (11.30am–midnight; $$$).

The newest Indian game in town is **Essence of India** on West Sand Lake Road (on the junction with

Universal Boulevard). Their style again aims to be traditional rather than avant garde (you won't find that curious Indian–English hybrid the Balti dish here) and they offer a superb value lunch buffet ($7.99 a head) in addition to the à la carte choice (a touch pricey), which features some tasty vegetarian dishes (11.30am–2.30pm Mon–Fri, noon–3pm Sat and Sun; 6–11pm nightly; $$$).

Thai and more

For other types of Oriental cooking, the **Siam Orchid** (on Universal Boulevard, round the corner from Wet 'n Wild) offers exceptional Thai food in a picturesque setting overlooking Sandy Lake (5–11pm; $$$). **Little Saigon** (on East Colonial Drive) will introduce you to Vietnamese cuisine and a whole new array of soups, barbecue dishes, fried rice variations and other interesting treats (10am–9pm; $$).

The new **Red Bamboo** (on South Kirkman Road just north of I-Drive) is a wonderful mix of authentic Thai and beautiful contemporary, clean decor. Their soups and curries are to die for, while the house speciality Smokey Pot is a heavenly stew of marinated shrimp, vegetables, and glass noodles in chilli (11am–2.30pm Tue–Fri, 5–10pm Sat, noon–10pm Sun, closed Mon; $$$).

Cuban

Cuban food is a Floridian speciality and you'll find some of the best examples at **Rolando's** (on Semoran Boulevard, in the suburb of Casselberry; head east from I-4 Exit 92). Try the red snapper or pork chunks and find out why the *Orlando Sentinel* rates this the best Cuban food north of Havana (11am–9pm Tue–Thur, 11am–10pm Fri–Sat, 1–8pm Sun; $).

However, the new **Samba Room** on West Sand Lake Road is the 5-star experience, an elegant lakefront restaurant full of Latin verve and ambience. The menu exhibits a wonderfully exotic touch, with the likes of Mango-barbecued ribs, Cachaca-smoked boneless chicken and Sugar cane beef tenderloin (with Chipotle mashed potatoes and mushroom sofrito), and their range of cocktails is suitably Cuban-laced (with lots of rum and martini). Extremely popular, so reservations are advised (407 266 0550; 11am–midnight Mon–Sat, noon–10pm Sun; $$$$$).

Italian

No survey of Orlando's restaurants would be complete without mention of its fine tradition of Italian cooking. **Pacino's** on Highway 192, opposite Old Town, has a friendly atmosphere and Sicilian style, plus clever animated puppet operettas, a fountain that occasionally spouts flame and a relaxing open-air feel that is enhanced by the clever use of the differently arranged seating areas. Targeting the family market, it is great value (4pm–midnight; $$$).

Bergamo's, in The Mercado, is actually German-owned but nonetheless authentically Italian. Don't be surprised if your waiter suddenly bursts into song – it's all part of the unique charm of this extremely tempting and highly entertaining restaurant (5–10pm Sun–Thur, 5–11pm Fri–Sat; $$$$).

The 5-star version of Italian cuisine here belongs to three contrasting restaurants, Christini's on Dr Phillips Boulevard, Antonio's on Sand Lake Road and Michaelangelo on Kirkman Road. Strolling musicians, elegant surroundings and a 40-year history of award-winning cuisine characterise **Christini's**, where the homemade pasta and filet mignon are as good as anything you will find

10

in Italy (5–11pm; $$$$$). The new **Antonio's**, up on the second floor in the Fountains Plaza on West Sand Lake Road, is another haven of quality (albeit at a price) in an area fast becoming synonymous with fine dining. This is the biggest and fanciest of three local outlets and has an exclusive style as well as outstanding cuisine – sensational risottos are a signature dish while veal and New York strip steak are an equally wise choice (5–10pm Mon–Sat; $$$$$).

Michaelangelo, just north of Universal Studios in Turkey Lake Village, promotes a candlelit atmosphere with live music in the cocktail lounge, formal, dinner-jacketed staff and a northern Italian cuisine that features veal, snapper and pasta delicacies. The pasta, bread and desserts are homemade, and it is all presented in an old-world style that is a million miles from the tourist hurly-burly of the parks (meals 6–11pm, 6pm–2am in the bar; $$$$$).

Continental

A somewhat unlikely but highly worthwhile discovery is **Gain's German Restaurant**, on the South Orange Blossom Trail (just past Oakridge Road going north), both for food and an excellent selection of bottled and draught beers. The friendly welcome, authentic Bavarian decor and tempting menu come as a real surprise in the heart of tourist Orlando, but owners Hans and Kessy Gain have lavished much care and attention on building up

Emeril's Tchoup Chop

their trade here. A tasty ragout is an ideal appetiser, while there are sausage specialities (naturally), wiener schnitzel (of course), and rotisserie chicken and pan-fried rainbow trout (for something different). Apple strudel and Black Forest cake are the ideal desserts, while the Diebels amber ale is a fine choice for beer connoisseurs (407 438 8997 for reservations; 11.30am–2.30pm and 4.30–10pm Tue–Thur, 4.30–11pm Fri and Sat, 4.30–10pm Sun; $$–$$$).

Another surprise but welcome choice is **The Melting Pot** (a national chain with three outlets in central Florida, including their newest in the Fountains Plaza on West Sand Lake Road). As the name suggests, this is fondue territory and an extremely quality-conscious version of the genre. Their Fondues for Two feature a cheese fondue, salad course and entree (a main fondue with one of three meat selections in a choice of four cooking styles). You can still order from a standard entree list (including chicken, shrimp and steak), but that would be to miss the point (5.30–9.45pm Sun–Fri, 5.30–10.45pm Sat; $$$$).

Splashing out

Finally, if you fancy really splashing out, here are some notable suggestions where both the food and ambience are way above average with prices to match. Fine dining is really on the increase in Orlando and long may it continue. Most notably, the area of Sand Lake Road immediately to the west of I-4 (the Fountains Plaza area and the opposite side of the street) has become a gourmet's delight. These top restaurants are so popular it's advisable to book well in advance.

The wonderfully trendy **Seasons 52** is the most upmarket offering of the Darden group (Bahama Breeze, Olive Garden, Red Lobster). The restaurant's name refers to the fact every week, all year long, different products come into season, which is reflected in the menu. New items feature weekly, with some seriously creative choices from the culinary team. It is also designed to be more healthy than the average restaurant, with a balanced approach to carbohydrate/fat content. All appetisers, side salads and soups range from 100 to 250 calories, the vast majority being either grilled or oven-roasted, and all entrees are in the 300–475 calorie range. Your server will be able to offer bags of advice – not least with an extensive wine list – and the whole contemporary, bustling atmosphere makes for a thoroughly refreshing experience (407 354 5212; 4.30–11pm; $$$$).

The **Park Plaza Gardens** is part of the Park Plaza Hotel on Park Avenue, Winter Park, and this beautiful courtyard restaurant gives you the feel of outdoor dining with the air-conditioned comfort of being indoors. Attentive service is coupled with an elegant, versatile menu that offers the choice of a relatively inexpensive lunch or a 3-course adventure featuring escargots, pasta with salmon, medallions of beef or one of several tempting fish dishes. Cuisine is distinctly 'nouvelle' rather than American, but nonetheless satisfying for all that. Its setting becomes even more intimate and charming in the evening with lights scattered among the foliage. Enjoy Happy Hour in the lounge (5–7pm, with complimentary buffet Thur and Fri), while their popular 3-course Sunday brunch features unlimited champagne and live jazz (407 645 2475; 11.30am–3pm Mon–Sat and 11am–3pm for Sunday brunch, 6–10pm Mon–Thur, 6–11pm Fri–Sat; 6–9pm Sun; $$$$).

A highlight of the Renaissance Orlando Resort is the **Atlantis** seafood signature restaurant. This wonderfully elegant and quite intimate corner of an equally smart hotel not only offers fine dining in the normal course of events, but also a scintillating range of daily fresh Floridian seafood specials that just demand to be sampled. A fine wine list complements the full à la carte dinner menu (5–10.30pm; $$$$$).

For another meal with a difference check out the **Renaissance's Sunday Brunch**, which is something of an Orlando tradition. Not so much a buffet as a 100-item banquet, it costs $32.95 for adults, $16.50 for 4–12s. Try this and for you brunch will never be the same again (407 351 5555; 10.30am–2.30pm).

A pleasant addition to The Mercado's upscale style is **DiVino's**, a rural-themed Italian restaurant with the full essence of Tuscany. Relatively simple pastas jostle with wood-grilled swordfish, braised chicken and the trademark osso buco (roast veal shank), plus some excellent daily specials (seafood in particular). It is not a cheap exercise (main courses run from $20–30) but the deep flavours, allied with excellent service, create a memorable meal. Reservations are not always necessary but it does get busy around 8pm most evenings (407 345 0883; 5–11pm daily; $$$$$).

The opening of Universal's Hard Rock Hotel brought with it the **Palm Restaurant**, the latest in an

bluezoo at the Dolphin

10

© Disney

upscale nationwide chain that has a big celebrity following. Founded in New York in 1926, it is famous for prime-aged steaks and jumbo lobsters, served in spacious, elegant surroundings and with personable, knowledgeable service. The house speciality, Jumbo Nova Scotia lobster, is spectacular. Their steaks are a bit special, too (check out the Double steak, a 36-oz/1kg+ New York strip for two at $60), plus you can choose swordfish, crab, salmon, pork, veal and pasta. All this decadence is reflected in the prices, and vegetables are extra, but the lunch menu shows a more modest touch while maintaining the quality (407 503 7256; 11am–11pm Mon–Sat; noon–10pm Sun; $$$$$).

Jiko in *Disney's Animal Kingdom Lodge* is possibly their most imaginative and impressive culinary offering to date. Maintaining the hotel's African theming with its decor and lighting, Jiko ('The Cooking Place') features twin wood-burning ovens, a masterful menu and an exclusive selection of South African wines that's sure to please any connoisseur.

The menu reflects influences from India and Asia as well as Africa, with dishes like Banana-leaf steamed sea bass, Whole roast papaya stuffed with spicy minced beef and Oven-baked garlic chicken tagine with grapefruit, olives and herbs. The personal service and ethnic ambience underline the adventure of eating here and make it a real highlight (407 939 3463; 5–11pm; $$$$$).

Old Hickory Steakhouse is another hotel-based offering in the new Gaylord Palms on I-Drive South. Its elaborate Everglades theming gives it an extra dimension, but the steak needs few gimmicks as the house speciality certified Black Angus beef is aged for 21–35 days and cooked to perfection. Side dishes are extra, hence it is an expensive option, but the attentive service and alternatives such as oven-roasted swordfish and Maine lobster provide a memorable experience. Watch out, too, for their artisanal cheese course, imported by trendy New York chef Terrance Brennan. If you are fortunate enough to be staying at this amazing hotel, Old Hickory should definitely be on your to-do list. Otherwise, it is a great excuse to pay the Gaylord Palms a visit (5–10.30pm Mon–Fri, 5–11pm Sat, 5–10pm Sun; $$$$$).

Find a good hotel and there will be an outstanding restaurant, and that is true of the Wyndham Palace Resort & Spa at *Downtown Disney*, where **Arthur's 27** is a magnificent discovery. With its setting high atop the hotel (27th floor, of course), it commands an amazing view of the area, and of the *Epcot* fireworks each night. Superb continental cuisine is offered with some of the best presentation and service I've enjoyed anywhere. There is a prix fixe menu as well as à la carte (the former is usually better value), while the wine list is truly stellar (for choice AND price). Don't miss their trademark Lobster bisque or the soufflé for dessert, while the Herb-crusted rack of lamb and Pineapple-soy glazed duck are outstanding entrees (but the menu is changed regularly). There is no set dress style but you may feel out of place without a jacket (407 827 3450; 6–10pm daily; $$$$$+).

When it comes to one of the hippest new places in town, **bluezoo** (at the *Walt Disney World Dolphin Hotel*) not only looks the part, it easily serves up some of the finest food in the Disney realm. Celebrity chef Todd English has made a name for himself in America by creating individual and contrasting restaurant experiences in places as diverse as Seattle and the new *Queen Mary 2* cruise ship – and bluezoo is another gem. With an under-the-sea themed

BRIT TIP: For a special occasion (particularly a romantic one), bluezoo, Arthur's 27 and Tchoup Chop (see below) are the pick of a rich crop.

decor that benefits from superb lighting (dine here later rather than earlier for the full effect), it has a wonderfully soothing effect, whether you are just at the bar or in one of the three main areas of the restaurant. Both the service and the waiting staff's knowledge of the cuisine and wine list (which is extensive) are impeccable, so feel free to let them steer you around a truly mouth-watering menu. For starters choose between Steamed mussels in a red curry broth, Teppan seared sea scallops and crab gnocchi, or individual pieces from their raw bar. Fish is their signature dish naturally enough (although they still offer rotisserie chicken, beef filet and slow-roasted pork chop) and seafood lovers will struggle to narrow down the choice here: Miso-glazed Chilean sea bass, Spit-roasted swordfish, Rare yellowfin tuna, Cantonese lobster, Barbeque pan-roasted prawns and more, or you could just opt for bluezoo's Dancing fish – your choice of freshly caught fish, whole-roasted over their special rotisserie. With so much quality on offer you will want to linger over every morsel as you admire the creativity that has gone into both the restaurant and the food (3.30–11pm daily; $$$$$).

Finally, I have saved the best for last with what I consider to be the most amazing and enjoyable restaurant experience currently in central Florida. **Tchoup Chop** (pronounced 'chop chop'), at Universal's Royal Pacific Resort, is the latest establishment in the gourmet stable of New Orleans master chef Emeril Lagasse, and it offers Asian–Pacific fusion cuisine in the most eye-catching setting.

The huge central pond is a tribute to feng shui, and you can easily sit and study the interior for much of the meal and still be noticing new things at the end. Service is a team effort at every table (which can be a touch off-putting), but the superb menu is well presented and explained. And oh, that menu! Taking some of the most aromatic and flavoursome elements of Thai, Chinese, Japanese, South Seas and other Pacific Rim cultures, Lagasse has conjured up a mouth-watering array of dishes, all immensely tempting and tasting as good as their promise. Start off with Homemade dumpling box (with a fresh port and ginger filling, hand-rolled, steamed and served with sake soy dipping sauce) or the Polynesian crabcake (with ginger scallion aioli and papaya-serrano salsa), then graduate to superb entrees like Macadamia-nut crusted Atlantic salmon (served with ginger soy butter sauce, steamed rice and stir-fried vegetables), Tchoup Chop's Clay pot of the day (served with steamed rice and seasonal vegetables) or the Hawaiian-style dinner plate including kiawe-smoked ribs, kahlua pork, teriyaki-grilled chicken, chorizo potato hash and baked macaroni. If that doesn't set your tastebuds trembling, nothing will!

Dinner here is exceptionally busy, so try lunch if they cannot squeeze you in (407 503 2467; 11.30am–2pm; 5.30–10pm Sun–Thur, 5.30–11pm Fri and Sat; $$$$$).

Now on to another of my favourite topics. The other main way in which Orlando will seek to separate you from your hard-earned money is shopping…

10

11 Shopping
(or, How to Send Your Credit Card into Meltdown)

As well as being a theme park wonderland, the vast area that constitutes metropolitan Orlando is a shopper's paradise, with a dazzling array of specialist outlets, malls, flea markets and discount retailers. It is also a vigorous growth market, with new centres springing up seemingly all the time, from the smartest of malls to the cheapest of gift shop plazas – and you can hardly go a few yards in the main tourist areas without a shop insisting it has the best tourist bargains of one sort or another.

In fact, in many ways the shopping centres have become as much of a tourist trap as the theme parks, and you will be bombarded by shopping opportunities every way you turn. The only hard part is avoiding the temptation to fill an extra suitcase or two with goods that cost twice as much back home.

As a general rule, you can expect to pay in dollars what you would pay in pounds for items like clothes, books and CDs, and real bargains are to be had in jeans, trainers, shoes, sports equipment and cosmetics.

But beware! Your duty-free allowance in the catch-all duty category of 'gifts and souvenirs' is still only £145 per person, and it is easy to exceed that sum by a distance. Paying the duty and VAT is still often cheaper than buying the same items at home, however, so it is worth splashing out, but remember to keep all your receipts and go back through the red 'goods to declare' channel on your return. You will pay duty (which varies depending on the item) on the total purchase price (i.e. inclusive of Florida sales tax) once you have exceeded your £145 allowance, plus VAT at 17.5 per cent. Unfortunately, you cannot pool your allowances to cover one item that exceeds a single allowance. Hence, if you buy a camera, say, that costs £200, you have to pay the duty on the full £200, taking the total to £213.20, and then the VAT on that figure. However, if you have a number of items that add up to £145, and then another which exceeds that, you pay the duty and VAT only on the excess (and the customs officers will usually give you the benefit of the lowest rate on what you pay for). Duty rates are updated regularly and vary from 2.7 per cent (golf clubs) to 15 per cent (mountain bikes). For more info, contact the Customs and Excise National Advice Service on 0845 010 9000 or visit www.hmce.gov.uk.

Your ordinary duty-free allowances from America include 200 cigarettes and 1 litre of spirits or 2 litres of sparkling wine and 2 litres of still wine. Alligator products, which constitute an endangered species, require a special import licence, and you should consult the Department of the Environment first.

Be aware, also, of the 'hidden extras' of shopping costs. Unlike our VAT, the local version in Orlando, the Florida State sales tax, is NOT added to the displayed

ORLANDO'S SHOPPING CENTRES

A Downtown Disney Marketplace
B The Mercado
C Pointe*Orlando
D Old Town
E Festival Bay
F Belz Factory Outlet World
G Quality Outlet Center
H Belz Designer Outlet Center
I Kissimmee Manufacturers' Outlet Mall
J Lake Buena Vista Factory Stores
K Orlando Premium Outlets
L Flea World
M Osceola Flea And Farmers' Market

N Florida Mall
O Colonial Plaza Mall
P Altamonte Mall
Q Seminole Towne Center
R Osceola Square Mall
S Orlando Fashion Square Mall
T Mall At Millenia
U Park Avenue
V Winter Park Village
W Kissimmee Historic District
X Goodings International Plaza
Y Crossroads Plaza
Z Fountains Plaza

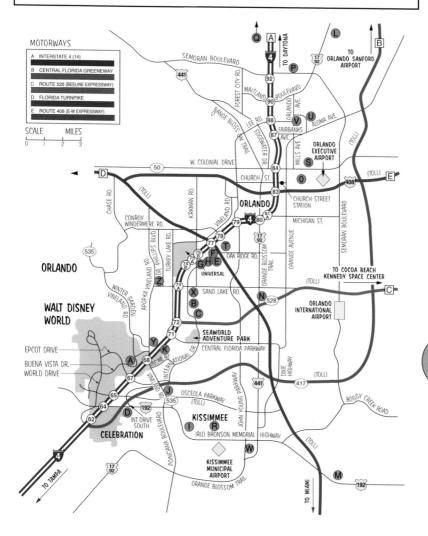

purchase price, so you must add 6 or 7 per cent (depending on which county you are in) to arrive at the 'real' price when paying. This frequently catches visitors out.

If those are the mechanics of shopping, here is a rundown of the main attractions and the sort of fun and bargains to be had.

Downtown Disney

The heart of *Walt Disney World Resort in Florida* in many ways is its *Downtown Disney* development. And the **Downtown Disney Marketplace** is typical Disney, a beautiful location, imaginative building and landscaping and a host of one-off elements that make shopping here a pleasure, along with 24 outstanding shops and dining opportunities. Don't miss the awesome **World of Disney** store, the largest of its kind in the world, the **Lego Imagination Center** (an interactive playground and shop), the amazing **Art of Disney** and **Team Mickey's Athletic Club**. New in 2002 was **Once Upon A Toy**, a gigantic toy emporium complete with a host of classic games, many with a novel Disney theme, for kids to try out. Other recent additions are the wonderfully scented **Basin** (for hand-carved soaps, bubble baths and shampoo bars) and **Disney's Wonderful World of Memories** (for all

> BRIT TIP: Don't buy electrical goods in the US – they will not work back home without a special adapter. Beware also, some games systems (notably the Nintendo Gamecube) are NOT compatible with UK players.

scrapbook fans, plus the only place to get a Disney postmark for your postcards home!).

Dancing fountains and squirt pools (where kids tend to get seriously wet), the lakeside setting and boating opportunities all add to the appeal here. Restaurants include the superbly themed **Rainforest Café** and a **McDonald's**, plus the excellent **Cap'n Jack's Restaurant**, while ice cream and chocolate fans should check out **Ghirardelli's** for some cool sundaes and super shakes. For a typically British touch, you can opt for a bite (speciality hot sandwiches) at the **Earl of Sandwich**, a new restaurant which is a joint venture between Planet Hollywood and Lord John Montagu, the 11th Earl of Sandwich himself. Those keen on the Disney hobby of pin trading should check out **Pin Traders**, while **Summer Sands** offers an excellent range of swimwear and casual clothing.

Then you can stroll over to **Downtown Disney West Side**, see a film at the superb **AMC 24** cinema complex and visit the world's largest **Virgin Megastore** or another of the 17 retail and dining outlets. The **Hoypoloi Gallery** is one of my favourites for a wonderfully eclectic range of artwork, from metal to glass, while **Magic Masters** (all kinds of magic tricks and souvenirs, with demonstrations) and **Wetzel's Pretzel's** are both new.

The whole *Downtown Disney* complex is open 9.30am–11pm every day (7pm–2am in *Pleasure Island*, separate admission required; Disney was experimenting with a new entry system for *Pleasure Island* in summer 2004, with admission only charged to go into the clubs, leaving the shops and restaurants open to all-comers). It is off Exits 67 and 68 on I-4 and is well signposted (Exit 68 can be congested at peak periods).

I-Drive

This core tourist area has three cleverly built developments which offer some unique shopping attractions, starting with **The Mercado**, the original speciality complex, in the heart of the I-Drive corridor just south of Sand Lake Road. Although it is looking a bit tired compared to the newer developments, this Mediterranean-style 'village' includes 25 speciality shops, five high-quality restaurants (Italian duo **Bergamo's** and **DiVino's**, **Charlie's Lobster House**, the new seafood-orientated **Mahi Mahi Bistro**, the **China Garden Supper Buffet** and the **Butcher Shop**), the **Cricketers' Arms** (see page 268) and an impressive food court (especially for the budget-conscious).

The Mercado is open 10am–10pm daily (from 8am in the food court and until 11pm at the restaurants), and will amuse you and your wallet for an hour or two.

Shops like **The Looking Glass**, **Andean Manna**, **One For The Road**, **Del Sol** and **Crystal Nature** sell a variety of unusual gifts, while hand-carts piled up with goodies to buy and artists also enliven the scene (www.themercado.com).

The second shopping complex to stand out on I-Drive is the 17-acre (3-ha) **Pointe*Orlando** (see also Orlando by Night, page 250), which is as much an evening adventure as mere shopping. The 60-plus stores here are all more upmarket than usual tourist fare, and you can indulge your passion for fashion at places like **Victoria's Secret**, **Armani Exchange**, **Image Leather**, **Tommy Hilfiger**, **Chico's**, **Gray Fifth Avenue**, **Abercrombie & Fitch** and the **Everything But Water** swimwear store, or stock up on gifts and souvenirs at **Disney Worldport**, **Bath & Body Works**, **Yankee**

> BRIT TIP: Need a proper British breakfast? Head for The Mercado food court and check out **Best of British** for the full Monty in brekkie terms, plus lunch and dinner specialities. Run by Brits Paul and Lorna Hunjan, it is a rare gem.

Candle (highly recommended), **Glow** and **Sunglass Hut**.

Sadly, the feature toy shop FAO Schwarz here has closed, but you can still visit the state-of-the-art, 21-screen **Muvico** cinema complex, and finish up with a meal at lively **Johnny Rockets** American diner, where the staff all join in with various jukebox favourites. The landscaping and 2-level design are also extremely eye-catching, and the new **XS Orlando** arcade-and-restaurant offers the chance to let the kids play for a while on a vast array of video games and simulators while Mum and Dad take some time to do the shops in peace. Visit www.pointeorlando.com for more information.

The newest centre is **Festival Bay**, right at the top of I-Drive and with a lot to recommend it. It has been under construction for almost four years, and the second phase finally opened in 2003, with more following in 2004. The mix of shops and entertainment is quite unusual, and many of the stores will be unfamiliar to Brits – but don't let

11

> BRIT TIP: Coffee shop Café Grande in The Mercado is the place to go if you need to log on to the internet and check your e-mail while in town.

The Mercado

that put you off as there is much to discover here.

The main entrance sees **Ron Jon's Surf Shop** battling for prominence with **Fuddrucker's** diner (superb burgers), while inside the covered mall area is a huge water feature and another 38 stores and restaurants, plus **Vans Skate Park** and the superb **Cinemark 20-screen Movie Complex**, arguably the fanciest cinema in Orlando. The massive **Bass Pro Shops Outdoor World** is worth checking out for its range of outdoor clothing and equipment (fishing, boating, hunting, hiking) as well as the amazing themed decor, while **Shepler's Western Wear**'s range of apparel, boots and other footwear has to be seen to be believed (all at great prices, too). **Steve & Barry's University Sportswear** is another unusual clothing store (especially for the value-conscious), while **Hilo Hattie's** is a wonderful emporium of all things Hawaiian. Other standouts include **Candle Time, Charlotte Russe** (trendy women's clothing); and **Swim Smart**, plus a unique, glow-in-the-dark mini-golf course, the **Putting Edge**, which is a great place to occupy the kids for a while.

Of course, **Vans Skate Park** is the perfect opportunity to unleash anyone with a skateboard obsession (look up www.vans.com, then Skateparks, then Orlando) and offers six 2-hour sessions a day (10am–midnight) as well as a full range of safety equipment and board rentals, plus a chill-out lounge.

The whole emphasis of Festival Bay, though, is on entertainment as much as shopping, and the relaxing, village street style of the mall is aimed squarely at (and rewards) the casual wanderer. There is no food court as such, but there are small dining outlets dotted around, notably **Long John Silver's, Auntie Annie's, Villa Pizza Cuccina** and **Mrs Fields**, as well as the full-service **Fuddrucker's**. Open 10am–9pm Mon–Sat and noon–7pm Sun (www.belz.com/realestate/retail/festival). Due in May 2005 is the **Murray Bros Caddyshack**, a wacky golf-themed diner created by actor Bill Murray and his brothers.

Kissimmee's version of the purpose-built tourist shopping centre is **Old Town**, an antique-style offering in the heart of Highway 192, with a tourist-friendly mix of shops, restaurants, bars and fairground attractions, all set out along brick-built streets. The shops – some 75 of them – range from standard souvenirs, novel T-shirt outlets and Disney merchandise to sportswear, motorbike fashions and other collectibles (check out the **General Store** for a step back in time, too, or the **Old Town Portrait Gallery** for period style).

The **International Space Station** is new, with a host of NASA-inspired

BRIT TIP: Visit Charlotte Russe's clothes shop for a free Advantage card offering $200 in savings throughout Festival Bay.

gifts and games, as is the fascinating **Petrified Rock Forest**. In addition, you will find 12 restaurants or snack bars, the 5-storey **Haunted House of Old Town** ($7 for adults, $5 for children), and a host of rides, including the 60-ft (18-metre) tall Century Wheel, the Windstorm roller-coaster, go-karts, a **Kids' Town** area of junior rides and the 365-ft (111-metre) **Slingshot** mega-ride – 0–100mph (60kph) in 2 stunning seconds! Tickets are sold separately for most rides (at $1 each), but if you plan to do several, go for the Valuepak at $20 for 22 tickets or $30 for 35.

New in 2004 was the **Hollywood Wax Museum and Tower of London Experience**, a novel and well-constructed diversion that offers both a waxworks and a fairly grisly torture chamber replica (probably too graphic for young children). It costs $5 per person (under 5 free) or $15 for a family of five (two adults, three children). Those in need of some pampering or a massage should head for the new **Sothy's Paris Day Spa** (open 10am–11pm daily).

Allow up to 4 hours here and try at all costs to take in the weekly **Saturday Nite Cruise** at 8.30pm, a drive-past of 300-plus vintage and collector cars (the biggest in America) which has become a real trademark here and celebrated its 14th anniversary in June 2004. A **Friday Nite Cruise** features cars built from 1973–85, plus live music and prizes. Every Thursday is **Motorcycle Nite** from 6pm, and the place can get fairly raucous later on, with plenty of alcoholic libations (witness the cavernous new **Sun on the Beach** bar). Parking is free and Old Town is open 10am–11pm daily (rides open from noon–11pm).

Damon's Clubhouse restaurant is an excellent dining choice, with great ribs, burgers and salads (plus various Trivia games and sport on their big screens) but the **Blue Max Tavern** is a fun alternative. Check out more on www.old-town.com.

Discount outlets

Belz Factory Outlet World is easily the biggest in this category of shops – the 'factory' or discount outlet – and is a big draw for British shoppers on I-Drive (although it is starting to look a bit tired these days in the face of all the new malls). A combination of mall and outlet centre, it's spread over a huge area at the top of I-Drive at the junction with West Oak Ridge Road. It consists of more than 170 shops arranged in two indoor malls (both with lively food courts and one with a vintage carousel to amuse the kids), plus four separate annexes that all require a separate journey by car (unless you want to wear out a lot of shoe leather). Avoid Belz at weekends when the locals come here in force.

The aim is to sell name brands at factory-direct prices and, while you may have to wade through a fair amount of worthless stuff, you will find shoes, clothes, books, jewellery, electronics, sporting goods, crockery and more at bargain rates. Check out the Nike superstore (Annex 1), Calvin Klein outlet (Annex 2), Reebok footwear (Annex 4), the Van Heusen

11

BRIT TIP: Fans of ice cream should make a beeline to Festival Bay and the Cold Stone Creamery for some truly magnificent concoctions.

Shops for the boys in Old Town

factory store (Malls 1 & 2), OshKosh B'Gosh kidswear, the Levis/Docker store, adidas and Guess Jeans (all Mall 2). Belz Factory Outlet World is open 10am–9pm Mon–Sat and 10am–6pm Sun.

Quality Outlet Center further down I-Drive offers much of the same, although not in the same quantity, but Disney Gifts for heavily discounted Disney items is worth a look (9.30am–9pm Mon–Sat, 11am–6pm Sun).

For a classier version, the **Belz Designer Outlet Center**, just south of Belz on I-Drive has a more upmarket range of 45 shops, including DKNY, Bose, Fossil, Fila, Liz Claiborne Shoes and Polo Ralph Lauren, plus the new Texas de Brazil restaurant (10am–9pm Mon–Sat, 11am–6pm Sun).

Kissimmee's version of the discount outlet is the **Kissimmee Manufacturers' Outlet Mall** on Old Vineland Road (just off the central drag of Highway 192, between Markers 13 and 14). With 30 shops again featuring brands like Nike, Levis and Van Heusen, plus Publishers Outlet for a wide range of discounted books, it is open 10am–9pm Mon–Sat, 11am–5pm Sun.

The recently expanded **Lake Buena Vista Factory Stores** offer another range of big-name products at discount prices, from Fossil, Sony, Reebok and Calvin Klein to a budget-priced Disney Character Corner, OshKosh B'Gosh Superstore and (the better-priced) Carter's Childrenswear, plus a lively food court (now serving

BRIT TIP: For the best-value genuine Disney merchandise, try the Character Warehouse in Mall 2 and Character Premiere in Mall 1 of Belz Factory Outlet World.

beer) and a kids' playground. A 1999 expansion added Gap and Liz Claiborne stores and, in 2002, Old Navy, Perfume Outlet, SAS Shoes, Welcome Home, Rack Room Shoes and Danskin appeared. **Borders** books is due soon, while the **World of Coffee** is both an internet café and one of the most pleasant places you will find to sip a speciality coffee and enjoy a Turkish pastry, with its outdoor terrace and bird cages.

New in 2004 was **Soccer & More** for some great value sportswear. Other services include an office of Florida Leisure vacation home management, their Cruise Planners agency and the quirky **Notable & Notorious** for some excellent film and rock music memorabilia.

The Factory Stores can be found on SR 535 (2 miles/3km south off Exit 68 on I-4) and are open 10am– 9pm Mon–Sat, 10am–6pm Sun. Their daily shuttle service picks up at various hotels and timeshare units in a 10-mile (16-km) radius (407 238 9301, www.lbvfs.com).

Possibly the best of the lot (especially if you can get hold of their Discount Voucher booklet) are the **Orlando Premium Outlets**, which were an instant hit with UK shopping devotees when they opened in 2000. Offering a fresh look and style, and with a legion of big-name designers (from Burberry and Ralph Lauren to Hugo Boss, Versace and Ermenegildo Zegna) they can be found on Vineland Avenue between I-Drive and I-4 (just south of SeaWorld; Exit 68 on I-4). In all, they offer 110 stores of well-known brand names (like Timberland, adidas, Reebok, Banana Republic, Nike and Calvin Klein) over four Mediterranean-themed plazas, with easy parking and the convenience of being at the southern end of the I-Ride Trolley (Main Line). New in 2003 were Travel 2000 (luggage and travel accessories), Ecco Unltd (upscale T-shirts, jeans and sportswear), Fendi (stylish women's clothing and signature handbags), Little Me (baby/toddler clothes), Rack Room Shoes (a mini-warehouse of footwear fashion) and KB Toys (a huge discount choice for kids of all ages).

Watch out also for big Disney bargains at the Character Premiere store and Universal items at Universal Studios Outlet Store. Even the food court is above average. Open 10am–10pm Mon–Sat, 10am–9pm Sun (407 238 7787, www.premiumoutlets.com).

For those without a car, there is a daily shuttle bus service at $6/person round trip from hotels in the Lake Buena Vista area and $9/person from Highway 192 in Kissimmee. Call 407 390 0000 for schedule and reservations. The Lynx bus service also stops here (407 841 2279) or you can try Star Taxi (407 857 9999).

Flea markets

Flea World is America's largest covered market, with 1,700 stalls spread out over 104 acres (42ha), including three massive, themed buildings, plus a 7-acre (2.8-ha) amusement park, **Fun World**, to keep the kids amused (rides cost about $2 each). It is open Fri, Sat and Sun only, 9am–6pm, and can be found a 20- to 30-minute drive away on Highway 17/92 (best picked up from Exit 90 on I-4) between Orlando and Sanford (to the north). The stalls include all manner of market goods (nearly all new or slight seconds), from fresh produce to antiques and jewellery, while there is a full-scale food court and a 300-seat pizza and burger eatery, the **Carousel Restaurant**, plus free entertainment on the Fun World Pavilion stage. Call 407 330 1792 or look up www.fleaworld.com.

On a slightly smaller scale is the **Osceola Flea and Farmers' Market** at the eastern end of the

> BRIT TIP: Ladies, if the tourist hustle-bustle has become too much for you, head to the Lake Buena Vista Factory Stores for the **Salon Central** salon and spa for some reviving treatments, a hair do or just a manicure. Same-day appointments are often possible (407 239 0518).

tourist area of Highway 192 in Kissimmee (8am–5pm Fri–Sun), offering food, clothing, household and kitchen supplies, electronics, sporting goods, collectibles and handicrafts (call 407 846 2811 for more details).

In downtown Kissimmee, Toho Square is home to a small-scale **Farmers' Market** every Thursday (7am–1pm) with everything from fresh produce to jewellery and candles for sale. Hot dogs and sausages are available at lunch carts, but you would be better off trying the nearby **Susan's Courtside Café** for a delicious array of sandwiches, pizzas, salad, smoothies and coffees (7am–8pm Mon–Fri). Prices for lunch range from $3.99–5.95.

Malls

The area's big indoor malls tend to run a touch more expensive than the outlets already mentioned, but they do have a huge range of pretty stylish shops and their periodic sales usually make things great value. The outstanding **Florida Mall,** the largest in central Florida, features 264 shops, with seven large department stores and an excellent food court offering a choice of 17 outlets, plus the lively bar-restaurant **Ruby Tuesday** and the excellent **California Pizza Kitchen.** Located

11

on the South Orange Blossom Trail, on the corner of Sand Lake Road, this spacious and extremely smart mall is open 10am–9.30pm Mon–Sat, 11am–6pm Sun. Highlights are the department stores, led by the upmarket (but expensive) Saks Fifth Avenue and Burdines-Macy's (Florida's oldest – and biggest – department store), plus JC Penney, Sears and Dillard's. New in October 2002 were Nordstrom, another upscale department store, and Lord & Taylor, renowned in the US for high-quality clothing (men's, women's and children's).

You can also benefit here from a discount coupon packet (from Guest Services) and the regular sales at many stores, which can make the Florida Mall as competitive price-wise as the discount outlets. Additional services include free wheelchair use, pushchair rental and video arcade (for the kids) in the food court. There are even spa and beauty treatments available in the Lancôme Institut de Beauté in Dillard's, the JC Penney styling salon and day spa, and the Elizabeth Arden salon at Saks Fifth Avenue.

It is also worth knowing you can visit the smart Adam's Mark hotel (now renamed the Florida Mall Hotel for a year) here for their **Le Jardin** restaurant and bar. For more info, visit www.shopsimon.com.

The huge 2-storey **Altamonte Mall**, on Altamonte Avenue in the suburb of Altamonte Springs (take Exit 92 on I-4 and head east for half a mile on Route 436 and it is on the left), is also above average and slightly off the beaten tourist track. It is one of the largest in Florida, featuring 175 speciality shops, four major department stores – Burdines, Dillard's, JC Penney and Sears – 15 outlets in the food court, plus four more restaurants, including Ruby Tuesday and the **Orlando Ale House**, and an elegant design with

Kids Town in Old Town

marble floors that makes shopping a pleasure. A major refurbishment in 2003 added an 18-screen cinema, a remodelled food court and children's soft-play area. You can do some serious shopping here from 10am–9pm Mon–Sat and from 11am–6pm Sun (weekdays are best), and they offer a VIP savings book to visitors at the Customer Service Center (www.altamontemall.com).

One of the most extensive mall developments is **Seminole Towne Center** just off I-4 to the north of Orlando on the outskirts of Sanford. This vast complex offers a 2-storey wonderland of 100 designer shops and boutiques and five department stores (such as Burdines and JC Penney) as well as craft stalls, food court and six full-service restaurants (including **Orlando Ale House**, **Olive Garden** and **Red Lobster**). Turn right off Exit 101C on I-4 and you are there, and it makes a handy place to while away your last few hours if you have an afternoon flight from the nearby Orlando Sanford Airport. The Towne Center is open 10am–9pm Mon–Sat, and noon–6pm Sun.

The spacious **Osceola Square Mall** (where Highway 192 mysteriously becomes Vine Street along its central stretch) is the only enclosed mall in Kissimmee, with 54 shops and a 12-screen cinema complex (open 10am–9pm Mon–Sat, noon–6pm Sun), including the local outlet of the retail store Ross, which deals in end-of-line items from big-names like Calvin Klein, Gap and

Tommy Hilfiger. If you are prepared for a good rummage through their packed racks, you can collect some real bargains. 'Ross should be on every Brit's shopping list,' advises reader Mrs B Mair of Stockport.

Orlando Fashion Square Mall, just out of the city centre (on East Colonial Drive (Route 50), take Exit 83B off I-4 and head east 3 miles (5km) to Maguire Boulevard), has undergone a major redevelopment and now offers a 165-shop spread, including four department stores, four restaurants, a 14-counter food court and an eight-screen cinema complex. Open 10am–9pm Mon–Sat and noon–6pm Sun.

The big mall news, though, was the opening in October 2002 of the **Mall at Millenia**, just off I-4 to the north of Universal Orlando (Exit 78). It features the most upmarket, dramatic and technologically advanced shopping complex in Florida, with New York's most famous department stores – Bloomingdale's, Neiman Marcus and Macy's – among a select number of other top-name boutiques such as Tiffany and Louis Vuitton. You need only walk in the main entrance to realise that this is a modern marvel of the retail world and worth investigating whether you enjoy shopping or not.

The principal entrance (of six) features a 60-ft (18-metre) glass rotunda with a flowing water garden theme and a helpful concierge desk

BRIT TIP: Need a good book? Make a beeline for Barnes & Noble on West Sand Lake Road by the Florida Mall or opposite Colonial Plaza (on Route 50) for a magnificent array of titles (especially travel) and a great coffee shop.

(valet parking is also available). Then you can head out in one of four directions over the marble and terrazzo floors or go upstairs to the refreshing high-quality 12-outlet food court, the Orangerie Cafés, where the only difficulty is deciding which of the tempting (and decidedly health-conscious) eateries to choose.

BRIT TIP: For great deals on CDs, DVDs and video games, head to Best Buys on the Orange Blossom Trail going south past the Florida Mall.

Look out in particular for **Bistro Sensations** (wonderful salads, pastas, pittas and wraps), the authentic Mandarin-style cuisine of **Chinatown**, the fresh taste of **Nori Sushi** (beef and chicken teriyaki and excellent sushi, all prepared on the spot) and the **Southwest Grill** (succulent chicken, barbecue beef and salads), as well as the **Tango Grill**, an Argentinean-style café (steaks, chicken and signature crêpes).

The grand architecture is also focused on five separate courts along a flattened, serpentine 'S' shape, which is topped with a flowing, arched glass roof like some gigantic conservatory. On two airy levels (three in Burdines-Macy's and Bloomingdale's) and with eight 'Juliet' balconies connecting the two sides, the mall consists of a colossal amount of glass, plus a stunning

11

The Mall at Millenia

central Grand Court, featuring a dozen 20-ft (6-metre) columns capped by curved plasma screens showing various images to support the theme of Man, Time and the Environment.

And, while around 20 per cent of the 150 outlets are upscale and exclusive (Cartier, Chanel, Lacoste, Jimmy Choo, Bang & Olufsen, etc, plus the ultimate luxury of Neiman Marcus, for brands like Gucci and Prada), the other 80 per cent comprise more mainstream shops like Gap, Banana Republic and Victoria's Secret. Several outlets provide a truly distinctive shopping experience – Metropolitan Museum of Art, Blunauta and Rocks Fine Jewellery – without necessarily the price tag to go with it.

The four main restaurants are also an attraction in themselves as they are the heavenly **Cheesecake Factory**, gourmet seafood offering **McCormick & Schmick**, **PF Chang's China Bistro** and **Brio Tuscan Grille**. On top of that little lot (AND the Orangerie Cafés), you have the excellent fresh bread and sandwich style of **Panera Bread**, the **California Pizza Kitchen** and a **Johnny Rockets** 1950s-style diner (see Dining Out, page 275) .The MaM is also the only mall to have a US Post Office inside (NB: standard postcards back to the UK cost 70c, 80c for large ones).

All in all, it takes the shopping experience to a new level in Florida and is open from 10am–9.30pm Mon–Sat, 11am–7pm Sun (www.mallatmillenia.com).

Traditional shopping

The attractions and possibilities of Winter Park's **Park Avenue** have already been detailed in Chapter 8 (see page 215), but the area also has the new **Winter Park Village**, a small, upscale, open-plan development of boutique shops,

larger speciality stores like Borders Books, and some fine restaurants. The Village replaced the old Winter Park Mall and is on North Orlando Avenue – Exit 87 on I-4, head east on Fairbanks Avenue and then north on Highway 17/92, North Orange Avenue, for 2 miles (3km), and it is on the right. It has proved immensely popular with the locals and offers a nice change from the usual malls and plazas – as well as some excellent dining. Check out **PF Chang's China Bistro** (their spicy Szechuan chicken is delicious), **Brio Tuscan Grille** (fine Italian fare) and the amazing (not to mention cavernous) **Cheesecake Factory** (www.shopwinterpark village.com).

More traditional shopping can also be found in the revamped **Historic District of Kissimmee** on Broadway, two blocks south of Highway 192 on Route 17/92, along Main Street and Broadway. These are a number of restored turn-of-the-century buildings featuring craft and gift shops, a children's boutique, country store and seven restaurants (including **Azteca's** for fine Mexican fare), plus antiques, Western and sportswear. Every Thursday, the Downtown Farmers' Market sells its produce here, too. The Historic District shops are open 10am–5pm weekdays, 10am–3pm Sat.

Another recent development (and off the beaten tourist path) is the shops and restaurants of Disney's town of **Celebration**, a unique collection of speciality stores, an ice cream and candy shop, restaurants, cinemas, lakeside dining and a Saturday Farmers' Market, plus boat and bike rentals and the superb Celebration Hotel (see page 71). Follow the signs to downtown Celebration along Celebration Avenue, just off Highway 192, a quarter of a mile east of its junction with I-4. The shops are open 10am–9pm Mon–Sat, noon–6pm

Sun. This is a re-creation of the 'ideal' 1950s-style town, complete with white picket fences, and there are some lovely walks around the main lake. The dining opportunities – notably the stylish Spanish–Cuban ambience of the **Columbia Restaurant**, the Italian offering of **Café D'Antonio** and the New England seafood accent of the **Celebration Town Tavern** all on Market Street – are quite superb.

Supermarkets

Apart from the big chemist chain stores, **Eckerd** and **Walgreens**, there are a few more typical large-group stores. The main supermarkets you will find are **Publix** and **Goodings**, which are comparable with Asda, Morrison or (in the case of Goodings) Marks and Spencer. **Albertson's** supermarket, on Dr Phillips Boulevard, is another well-priced choice, as is the **Winn-Dixie** chain.

For clothes, DIY, home furnishings, souvenirs, toys, electrical goods and other household items as well as groceries, the big discount stores are **Kmart**, **Wal-Mart** (owners of Asda and open 24 hours for serious shopaholics!) and **Target** (like a big version of Tesco's, but without the food). If there is anything you've forgotten (heaven forbid!), the chances are you can get it at one of the seven **Wal-Mart Supercenters** (notably on Highway 192 next to Medieval Times, another at the junction of Sand Lake Road and John Young Parkway, on Kirkman Road north of Universal,

> BRIT TIP: To save money on your holiday snaps (especially if you want them put on CD), Wal-Mart offers 1-hour processing at great savings on UK prices.

> BRIT TIP: Visit the Concierge office at Mall at Millenia, fill out their marketing questionnaire and receive a free gift.

and a new one towards the east end of Osceola Parkway in the Buenaventura Lakes area). The Wal-Mart near Medieval Times also has a bank inside with a fast-track counter for visitors.

For photographic supplies and film processing, try one of the many branches of **Eckerd Express Photo** (although they are dearer in the main tourist areas).

Specialist shops

Finally, a few shops worth making a note of for specific items are the various outlets of **World of Denim** (no explanation necessary), **The Sports Authority** and **Sports Dominator**, the former on Sand Lake Road and the latter north of Sand Lake Road, on I-Drive, which both offer all manner of sporting goods and apparel, while serious sportsmen and women will also want to visit the magnificent range of the five **Edwin Watts Golf** shops, including their national clearance centre on I-Drive, or any of the five **Special Tee Golf & Tennis** shops. On golf clubs in particular you can pick up some great deals and save a lot on the same equipment back home. By the same token, keen anglers can stock up on the latest fishing gear at bargain prices at **Bass Pro Shops Outdoor World** (Festival Bay). Last but by no means least, **Greg's Western Wear** (on Highway 192 opposite Medieval Times) offers the chance to get yourself fully kitted out in the latest cowboy gear.

Now the shopping's done, it is time to think about the journey home.

11

12 Going Home
(or, Where Did The Last Two Weeks Go?)

And so, dog-tired, financially stressed but (hopefully) blissfully happy and with enough memories to last a lifetime, it is time to deal with that bane of all holidays – the journey home.

If you have come through the last week or two relatively unscathed in terms of the calamities that can befall the uninformed, here's how to avoid any last-minute pitfalls.

The car

Returning the hire car can take time if you had to use an off-airport car depot so allow half an hour. The process is much slicker with the firms who operate directly from the airports. Most airlines also require you to arrive 2–3 hours before an international flight because of enhanced security processes, so don't be tempted to leave your check-in until the last minute. Virgin Atlantic's morning check-in facility at *Downtown Disney* is a major bonus in this respect for their passengers.

> BRIT TIP: You are advised to leave all luggage unlocked (no combination locks or padlocks) when you check in for your return flight as the TSA security open a LOT of bags at their screening process and they have the right to open any case, locked or unlocked.

Now you probably have some time to kill, so here is a detailed guide to the two main airports.

Orlando International Airport

Orlando International is 46 miles (74km) from Cocoa Beach and 54 miles (87km) from Daytona Beach on the east coast, 84 miles (135km) from Tampa and 110 (177km) from Clearwater and St Petersburg to the west, 25 miles (40km) from *Walt Disney World* and 10 miles (16km) from Universal Studios; so always allow enough time for the return journey, plus check-in.

This modern airport is the 24th largest in the world, one of the fastest-growing and one of the most widely acclaimed for passenger satisfaction values (regularly No 1 in America). It topped 30 million passengers in 2000 for the first time (some 80,000 a day on average), putting it level with Gatwick and Hong Kong, and with half the traffic of Heathrow (which has four terminals to Orlando's one). It can, therefore, get busy at peak times, but its 854-acre (345-ha) terminal complex usually handles the crowds with ease, and this is one of the most comfortable airports you will find. It boasts a great range of facilities, and its wide, airy concourses feel more like an elegant hotel (one end of the terminal is taken up by the airport-run Hyatt Regency Hotel).

Ramps, restrooms, wide lifts and large open areas ensure easy wheelchair access, and features like TDD and amplified telephones, wheelchair-height drinking fountains, Braille lift controls and companion-care restrooms are there to assist travellers with disabilities.

Should you have more than 2 hours to spare, it is worth leaving your hand luggage at the Baggage Checkroom and taking the 15-minute taxi ride to the Florida Mall, or checking in early, keeping the car and going somewhere like Gatorland about 20 minutes away (see page 196).

In keeping with the Orlando area, the International Airport is always engaged in staying a step ahead, and a major renovation completed in 2004 added a host of new elements, including a major food court, other restaurant options and some superb shopping opportunities.

Construction of a second major terminal building is going on beyond the Hyatt Hotel end of the terminal.

Landside

As with all international airports, you have a division between LANDSIDE (for all visitors to the airport) and AIRSIDE (where you need to have a ticket). Orlando's Landside is divided into three levels: **One** is the recently enhanced area for ground transportation, tour operator desks, parking, buses and car rental agencies; **Two** is for Baggage Claim (which you negotiated on your arrival) and for private vehicles meeting passengers; **Three** is where you should enter on your return journey as it holds all the check-in desks, shops, restaurants, lockers, bank and information desks. Level Three is effectively subdivided into five inter-connected sections: **Landside 'A'** is the check-in section for **Gates 1–29** and **100–129**. Here you will find Spirit, American Airlines, ATA (American TransAir), Continental, Southwest, JetBlue and

AirTran. **Landside 'B'** has check-in desks for **Gates 30–99** and airlines such as Northwest, United, USAirways, BA, Delta and Virgin.

Once you have checked in, you can choose to explore the **east** and **west** sections of the main concourse in the centre of Level Three.

The **west end** houses the **Great Hall**, with some more shopping and dining, a currency exchange and ATM (cash dispenser). Inevitably, Disney & Co make one last attempt to part you from what's left of your money, so you will find some more impressive gift shops for *Walt Disney World* (The Magic of Disney), SeaWorld and Universal (with no airport mark-up). Other outlets include Sunglass International, Orlando Harley-Davidson, the eclectic pet shop Bow Wow Meow, jewellers Erwin Pearl, the clothing and gifts of Spirit of the Red Horse, Keys Gift Shop and Global Cellular & Electronics. Then there are two newsagents and the new duo of Fox Sports Bar and Macaroni Grill (highly recommended). The Barnes & Noble bookshop here also has a Seattle's Best Coffee outlet. Up the escalators in the centre of the hall is Chili's, a Tex-Mex diner and bar.

Travelling (along moving walkways) between the two ends of the terminal, you pass through the newest and smartest area of the airport, with more shops on the **North Walk** and **South Walk** (Swatch, The Discovery Channel Store, Gem Collection, GNC Nutrition, Flag World, music store Altitunes, L'Occitane, and the Power Play Arcade). The new, circular **Food Court** here is one of the most upscale you will find, with plenty of seating and different cuisines, including Sbarro pizza, Zyng's Noodlery, Chick-Fil-A, Krispy Kreme Donuts, McDonald's and Carvel ice cream. The central aquarium feature is a draw to the children and there is a SunTrust

12

Bank, a wonderful massage spa and hair salon (D-parture), a post office and cash machine.

The east end of Level Three is quieter and more picturesque as it is dominated by the 8-storey Hyatt Hotel atrium, featuring palm trees and a large fountain. There are fewer shops but they include: Universal Orlando, Anheuser-Busch, Disney's The Earport (!) and the new Kennedy Space Center shop. There's a Hudson's newsagent, a Starbucks and WH Smith's, more ATMs, a currency exchange and two business centres. Both west and east halls have an information kiosk.

Up the escalator (or lift) is the entrance to the **Hyatt Regency Airport Hotel** if you fancy seeing out your visit in style (see page 80). **McCoy's Bar and Grill** (up and turn right) is a smart bar-restaurant with a grandstand view of the airport runways (good for kids). All flight timings are shown on TV monitors.

To go really upmarket, take the hotel lift to the ninth-floor **Hemisphere Restaurant** (dinner only). Not only do you have an even more impressive view of the runways, its superb continental cuisine and wine tasting evenings offer some of the best fare in the city. It's pricey, but the service and food are 5-star (from 5–10.30pm daily).

Airside

Once it is time to move on to your departure gate, you have to be aware of the four satellite arms that make up the airport's AIRSIDE. Also note they have installed Advanced Technology Checkpoint screening here, and you may have to queue.

The 'arms' are divided into **Gates 1–29** and **30–59** at the west end of the terminal, and **60–99** and **100–129** (American domestic flights) at the east. ALL the departure gates are here, plus duty-free shops, more restaurants and lockers.

The airport's four satellites are each connected to the main building by a shuttle service, so you need to be alert when it comes to finding your departure gate. There are no tannoy announcements for flights, so it's wise to check your departure gate and time when you check in. However, there are large monitors in the terminal that display all the departure information. As a rule, British Airways, Virgin and Delta use Gates 60–99. Northwest, United and USAirways usually use Gates 30–59, while ATA, American and Continental depart from Gates 1–29. Airlines using Gates 100–129 include Spirit and low-cost carriers Southwest, JetBlue and AirTran.

In most airports, once you have moved Airside it is not possible to return to the Landside area again. However, that is not the case here, and, if you find the crowds milling around your departure gate too much, you can return to one of the main terminal hostelries **(bear in mind you will need to go through the security check again)**.

However, you should find the Airside areas just as clean and efficient as the main terminal, with the bonus of three duty-free shops.

As you pass through the ticket and baggage check at the west end of the terminal, you will find the **Alpha Retail Duty Free** on your right. This is the biggest of their four shops and is open only to departing international passengers, so you will need your boarding card. Your purchases will be delivered to the departure gate for you to collect as

> BRIT TIP: Save some film for a couple of excellent photo opportunities at the airport shops – outside the Disney stores and the Harley-Davidson shop.

you board.

At **Gates 1–29**, you will find another duty-free shop, plus a newsagents (the Keys Group News and Gifts), two Café Azalea lounge bars, a kids' play area and a mini food court, featuring **Burger King, Cinnabon** and **TCBY** (which stands for The Country's Best Yogurt). **Gates 30–59** also have their own duty-free shop, plus a **Café Azalea** lounge bar, **Pepito's Cuban Café**, the Floribbean Court (with **Miami Subs, Villa Pizza** and **Freshens Yogurt**) and Hudson News.

Gates 60–99 (the main satellite terminal for UK return flights) offer another duty-free shop, a currency exchange, newsagents, the speciality Mindworks shop, The Grove gifts, a play area and WH Smith. A food court contains **Burger King, Nathan's Famous Hot Dogs**, the table service **Shipyard Brewport** and a bar..

Gates 100–129 offer two **Johnny Rivers Smokehouse Express** outlets, a food court with **The Coco Oasis Bar & Lounge, McDonald's** and **Sbarro Pizza**, plus four shops.

For more details on Orlando International Airport, visit www.fcn.state.fl.us/goaa, which features 'live' departure and arrival information.

Orlando Sanford International Airport

Returning to what is now the main Orlando gateway for British charter flights should be a relatively simple experience, providing you retrace your route on the Central Florida Greeneway (following signs for Orlando *Sanford* Airport, NOT Orlando International) and come off at Exit 49. Go across one set of lights, turn right at the second set on to Lake Mary Boulevard and follow the signs to the airport. The efficiency of Alamo and Dollar's car rental return adds to the simplicity.

Orlando Sanford was created as a full international airport in 1996, as an initiative between the airport authorities and several British tour operators. And so MyTravel (Airtours), Thomson (Britannia), Monarch, Thomas Cook, the burgeoning Travel City Direct and First Choice (Air 2000) all now go for this simpler option. With its small, uncomplicated design (straight off the plane into Immigration, one baggage carousel and then a walk across the road to the Dollar or Alamo offices), it can get you mobile much quicker. Of course, you are further north, so your journey time is 30–35 minutes longer and you have to pay an extra $2–3 in tolls compared with the journey to and from Orlando International but, providing you follow the simple directions to the main tourist areas, you can save time overall.

And, while this charter gateway is smaller than Orlando International, it boasts a spacious check-in area and works hard to make the departure as painless as the arrival process, especially with their Guest House facility. **Terminal B**, opened in 2001

Duty-free delight

For those who can't resist a bargain, it is worth saving some shopping time for the Duty Free stores at both airports. Prices are up to 60 per cent cheaper than in the UK, better even than the local malls. Here is a guide to some of the guaranteed savings on offer (based on exchange rate of £1=$1.75):

Perfumes – Calvin Klein 45%, Chanel 25%
Cosmetics – Clinique 40%
Alcohol – 45%
Tobacco – 60%
Watches – Gucci 25%, Tag Heuer 35%

12

ORLANDO INTERNATIONAL

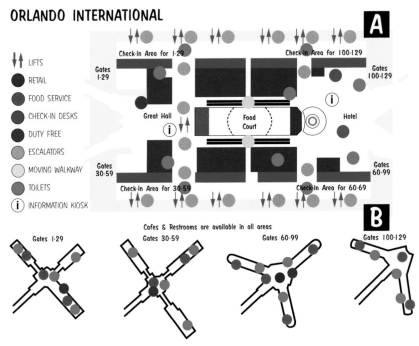

Cafes & Restrooms are available in all areas

ORLANDO SANFORD INTERNATIONAL AIRPORT

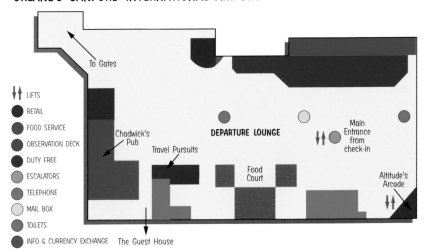

and both Thomas Cook and Monarch now use it for check-in, right next door to the Alamo Rent A Car return; all other UK airlines still check in at **Terminal A**. All passengers still use the same international departure lounge. Its facilities have been dramatically upgraded in recent years and are now more than adequate for a comfortable stay. **Chadwick's Pub** serves a decent range of food as well

Get the Spirit

To really make the most of your American adventure, the *Brit's Guide* can heartily recommend exploring some other vital destinations direct from Orlando with Florida-based **Spirit** Airlines, one of the most go-ahead and reliable operators in the US. With low fares – especially if you book well in advance – and a specialist route network that includes New York (La Guardia), Chicago, Atlantic City (the Vegas of the East Coast), Detroit and San Juan (on the Caribbean island of Puerto Rico) direct from Orlando, and Las Vegas and Los Angeles with a stopover, Spirit can extend your holiday in the best possible way.

The airline is in the process of introducing a new fleet of Airbus A-320 aircraft, they have one of the best reliability records in the US and only alcoholic drinks and snack packs cost extra on board. For a low-cost carrier they are rare in offering a comfortable business class upgrade at less than business class prices. In fact, they put many scheduled services to shame and we at the *Brit's Guide* have enjoyed numerous hassle-free flights in their company. Book online (www.spiritair.com) for the best bargains, or call 1-800 772 7117 (in the USA) or 954 447 7965 (from the UK). If you are holidaying on the Gulf Coast, they also fly direct to Chicago, Detroit and New York from Tampa.

---

as British beers, and there is a completely revamped (in 2003) food court, an **Information** and **Currency Exchange** kiosk, **Altitudes Arcade** (neatly located in one corner), a **Reel Stuff** film memorabilia shop and a new entertainment shop, **Travel Pursuits**, which features travel games, electronic toys, soft toys, Lego and Knex sets, mood jewellery and novelty sweets, as well as **News World** for books and magazines. The **Duty-Free** store has been dramatically enhanced and extended during the 2003 makeover and will now seriously test your wallet. The excellent new four-part **Food Court** offers American Grill (burgers and fries), Daily Specials (shepherd's pie, chicken pot pie, lasagne and more), Sweet Endings (baked goods and pastries) and the aptly named Grab-N-Go (soft drinks, snacks and bottled water). There is also an outdoor smoking deck (smoking is severely restricted inside).

The big extra here, though, is the **Guest House**, a premium lounge

available to all passengers for a modest fee. It is located in a separate annexe from the main departure lounge and is an oasis of comfort and quiet, more reminiscent of an upscale hotel. There is a lovely conservatory-style café, where you can take advantage of the unlimited tea, coffee, soft drinks and snacks (plus two drinks of beer or wine per over-21), or opt for something from their exclusive lunch menu. It also provides a home theatre set-up, with widescreen TV and surround-sound, for recently released films, a reading lounge, internet access, youth entertainment centre, with eight Sony Playstation 2 consoles, and, for the young 'uns, a separate playroom with soft toys and games.

The Guest House is billed as an airport lounge with the comforts of home and, to my mind, it is well worth the $20 each extra ($15 for children) to while away the last few hours here. Most tour operators offer it in advance at a discount, but you can still book on arrival (it's popular though) and there are plans for expansion. See the Guest House

12

Fly Transmeridian Airlines

For a *Brit's Guide* recommendation from Orlando Sanford International Airport, look no further than **TransMeridian Airlines**. This archetypal low-cost carrier is one of Sanford's busiest operators, taking in Syracuse (New York State), Toledo (for Ohio and Michigan), Rockford (for Chicago), Harrisburg (in Pennsylvania) and San Juan (for Puerto Rico and the Caribbean). They use smaller regional airports, hence getting in and out is usually much easier. If you have flown EasyJet or Ryanair in Europe, you will already know the TransMeridian style and ease of use, and their simplicity of flight procedures makes for hassle-free travelling. Their in-flight service is also above average (with a full meal where appropriate). No Saturday overnights are required with any flight, there are no advance purchase requirements, advance seat selection is available and all seats are pre-assigned. For more information and to make reservations online, visit www.IFLYTMA.com or call toll-free on 1-866 435 9862.

(and airport facilities) on www.OrlandoSanfordAirport.com.

Whether you are travelling from Orlando International or Orlando Sanford, you can expect your return flight to be about an hour shorter than the journey out, thanks to the Atlantic jetstreams that provide tail-winds to high-level flights.

Nevertheless, you will land back at Heathrow, Manchester, Glasgow, etc, rather more jet-lagged than on the trip out. This is because the time difference is more noticeable on eastward flights, and it may take a good day or two to get your body clock back on to local time. It is even more important not to indulge in alcohol on the flight if you are driving when you get home.

And, much as it may seem like a good idea, the best way to beat Florida jet-lag is NOT to go straight out to the travel agency and book another holiday to Orlando!

But, believe me, the lure of this theme park wonderland is almost impossible to resist once sampled – you WILL return!

Your chance to give something back

After hopefully having the holiday of a lifetime, you might like to know about two charities helping children with serious and terminal illnesses to have a memorable time here, too. **Give Kids The World** is an amazing organisation in Kissimmee providing a week's holiday for terminally ill children who wish to visit central Florida. GKTW works with other wish-granting foundations worldwide to provide all the local facilities for children – and their families – to have a great holiday. It is set up as a village resort and includes meals, accommodation, transport, attractions, tickets and many other thoughtful touches in a magical setting. It is a charity I am happy to support myself, and I hope you will, too. You can make a donation through the website – www.gktw.org – or send to: Give Kids The World, 210 South Bass Road, Kissimmee, Florida 34746, USA. Equally, **Dreamflight** is a registered UK charity taking seriously ill children (aged between 8 and 14) to Florida annually, often with the help of British Airways. It costs around £1,400 per child and, while many generously donate their time to help, cash donations are also essential. You can contribute by writing to: Dreamflight, 3 Saxeway, Chartridge, Bucks HP5 2SH (tel: 01494 792991) or by e-mail to office@dreamflight.org. Thanks for any contributions to these two wholly worthwhile organisations.

Your Holiday Planner

Example: with 5-day Park Hopper Plus Ticket

DAY	ATTRACTION	NOTES
SUN DAY		
EVE		
MON DAY		
EVE		
TUE DAY		
EVE		
WED DAY		
EVE		
THUR DAY	Arrive 2.40pm local time Orlando Sanford Airport	*NB: 55 mins to drive to hotel*
EVE	Check out local shops and restaurants	
FRI DAY	Welcome meeting/UNIVERSAL STUDIOS	
EVE		
SAT DAY	DISNEY'S ANIMAL KINGDOM THEME PARK	*(8am start)*
EVE	Medieval Times Dinner Show	
SUN DAY	DISNEY–MGM STUDIOS	
EVE		
MON DAY	SEAWORLD	
EVE		
TUE DAY	BUSCH GARDENS	
EVE		
WED DAY	KENNEDY SPACE CENTER	
EVE	Skull Kingdom/WonderWorks/Pointe*Orlando	

Disney's 5-Day Park Hopper Plus Ticket gives 5 days at the main theme parks, plus TWO of Blizzard Beach, Typhoon Lagoon, Pleasure Island and Disney's Wide World of Sports™; there may be a separate charge for big events at Wide World of Sports.

DAY	ATTRACTION		NOTES
THUR	DAY	Blizzard Beach/EPCOT	*(Arrive late)*
	EVE		
FRI	DAY	ISLANDS OF ADVENTURE	
	EVE	Universal Orlando's CityWalk	*(until late!)*
SAT	DAY	Winter Park Lakes/shopping/museums	
	EVE		
SUN	DAY	EPCOT	*(early start – 9am)*
	EVE		
MON	DAY	Fantasy of Flight and Cypress Gardens Adventure Park	
	EVE	Pleasure Island	
TUE	DAY	Aquatic Wonders Tours/Warbird Air Museum	
	EVE	Arabian Nights	
WED	DAY	THE MAGIC KINGDOM Park	
	EVE		
THUR	DAY	Gatorland/Back to airport	
	EVE		*Flight 6pm; return car at 3pm*
FRI	DAY	Return Gatwick 7am	
	EVE		
SAT	DAY		
	EVE		
SUN	DAY		
	EVE		

Busy Day Guide

Day	Busiest	Average	Lightest
Mon	Disney's Animal Kingdom Magic Kingdom	Epcot	Disney-MGM Studios Universal Studios Islands of Adventure Busch Gardens Kennedy Space Center SeaWorld Water Parks
Tues	Epcot Disney-MGM Studios Universal Studios	Islands of Adventure Magic Kingdom	Disney's Animal Kingdom Busch Gardens Kennedy Space Center SeaWorld Water Parks
Wed	Epcot Islands of Adventure	Disney's Animal Kingdom SeaWorld Water Parks	Magic Kingdom Disney-MGM Studios Busch Gardens Kennedy Space Center Universal Studios
Thurs	Magic Kingdom Universal Studios	Busch Gardens Disney-MGM Studios SeaWorld Water Parks	Epcot Disney's Animal Kingdom Islands of Adventure Kennedy Space Center
Fri	Disney's Animal Kingdom Epcot SeaWorld Water Parks	Disney-MGM-Studios Islands of Adventure Busch Gardens Kennedy Space Center	Magic Kingdom Universal Studios
Sat	Disney-MGM Studios Busch Gardens Islands of Adventure Kennedy Space Center SeaWorld Universal Studios Water Parks	Epcot Magic Kingdom	Disney's Animal Kingdom
Sun	Magic Kingdom Islands of Adventure Kennedy Space Center SeaWorld Water Parks	Disney's Animal Kingdom Busch Gardens Universal Studios	Disney-MGM Studios Epcot

13

Index

Wyndham Palace
1900 Buena Vista Drive
PO BOX 22206
Lake Buena Vista
Florida
32830
Tel. 407 827 2727

COPYRIGHT NOTICES 311

The author and publisher gratefully acknowledge the provision of the following photographs.

Cover: Mickey Mouse and Cinderella's Castle © Disney; Cinderella's Suprise Celebration © Disney; Speed Racer at Epcot © Disney; Orlando Convention and Visitor's Bureau; Minnie Mouse and Guest © Disney.

Advantage Homes 88; Arabian Nights 253, 257; Bahama Breeze 272; Bok Tower 192; Busch Gardens 45, 176, 180, 181, 184, 185; Chalet Suzanne 193; CityWalk 249; Daytona Beach 232; Doubletree Club Hotel 25; Emeril's 277, 280; Fantasy of Flight 200; Gatorland 196, 197; Gaylord Palms 40; Hard Rock Café 249; Hard Rock Hotel 80; Hard Rock Vault 201; I-Drive 52. 57; International Divers 16; I-Ride Trolley Bus 49; Kennedy Space Center 189; Kissimmee Visitors' Bureau 16, 17, 32, 48, 53, 216, 217, 220, 221, 228, 223, 236, 237, 240, 268, 289, 292; Mercado 288; Nikelodeon Family Suites 85; Olive Garden 273; Orange Blossom Balloons; Orlando/Orange County Convention and Visitors' Bureau, Inc.® 13, 21, 28, 29, 37, 80, 205, 293; Orlando Science Center 204; Pinewood Estate 193; Pirate's Dinner Adventure 260; Portofino Bay 76; Red Lobster 276; SeaWorld and Discovery Cove 165, 168, 169, 172, 173; Silver Springs 44, 196; Skull Kingdom 201; Sleuth's Mystery Dinner Show 256; Summer Bay Resort 13; Travel City 24; Universal Orlando 17, 141, 145, 148, 149, 152, 153, 157, 160, 161; Virgin 25; Warbird Adventures 224; Water Mania 9, 212, 213; WonderWorks 204.

Page 9   Sleeping Beauty signing autograph © 2001 Disney
Page 20   Disney's All-Star Sports Resort © Disney
Page 24   Disney Cruise Line® ship at dock © Disney
Page 33   Disney characters at the Magic Kingdom © Disney
Page 41   Bride and groom with Cinderella carriage © Disney
Page 56   Guests riding bicycles © Disney
Page 60   Disney's Caribbean Beach Resort © Disney
Page 61   Disney's Pop Century Resort © Disney
Page 64   Wilderness Cabin at Disney's Fort Wilderness Resort & Campground © Disney
Page 65   Disney's BoardWalk Inn and Villas Resort © Disney
Page 68   Horse-drawn carriage at Fort Wilderness © Disney; Old Man Island in Disney's Port Orleans Resort French Quarter © Disney
Page 69   Disney's Contemporary Resort © Disney
Page 72   Victoria & Albert's at Disney's Grand Floridian Resort & Spa © Disney
Page 92   Wishes Fireworks Show © Disney
Page 97   Cinderella Castle © Disney
Page 97   Main Street, USA
Page 100   Cinderella's Golden Carousel © Disney; The Jungle Cruise © Disney
Page 101   The Mad Tea Party © Disney; Magic Carpets of Aladdin © Disney
Page 104   Barnstomer at Goofy's Wiseacre Farm © Disney; Disney's Agrabah Bazaar
Page 105   Buzz Lightyear's Space Ranger Spin © Disney; SpectroMagic Parade © Disney
Page 108   Mission Space at Epcot © Disney
Page 112   Katouba Minaret at World Showcase © Disney
Page 113   Soaring Over California © Disney
Page 116   China Pavilion © Disney
Page 121   Lights, Motors, Action! Stunt Show © Disney
Page 125   Twilight Zone™ Tower of Terror © Disney; Rock 'n Roller Coaster ® starring Aerosmith
Page 133   The Tree of Life © Disney; Disney's Animal Kingdom Theme Park © Disney
Page 136   TriceraTop Spin © Disney; Maharajah Jungle Trek® © Disney
Page 137   Festival of the Lion King © Disney; Kali River Rapids © Disney
Page 140   Mickey's Jammin' Jungle Parade © Disney
Page 208   Disney's Typhoon Lagoon © Disney
Page 209   Disney's Blizzard Beach © Disney
Paage 229   Riders at Disney's Fort Wilderness Resort & Campground © Disney
Page 241   Disney's Wide World of Sports® © Disney
Page 244   Downtown Disney © Disney;
Page 245   La Nouba at Cirque du Soleil © Disney
Page 248   Pirates of the Caribbean Battle for Buccaneeer Gold at DisneyQuest® © Disney
Page 252   Hoop-Dee-Doo Musical Revue © Disney
Page 264   Dining at Disney's Pop Century Resort © Disney
Page 265   The Nine Dragons Restaurant at Epcot © Disney
Page 269   Kids enjoy a character breakfast © Disney
Page 281   Bluezoo at the Swan and Dolphin © Disney

The author wishes to acknowledge the help of the following in the production of this book: The Orlando Tourism Bureau in London, The Orlando/Orange County Convention & Visitors' Bureau, Visit Florida, The Kissimmee/St Cloud Convention & Visitors' Bureau, Walt Disney Attractions Inc., Universal Orlando, The British–American Chamber of Commerce, The Greater Orlando Aviation Authority, Orlando Sanford International Airport, The Busch Entertainment Corporation, The Orange County Sheriff's Office, Seminole County Convention & Visitors' Bureau, Central Florida Visitors' & Convention Bureau, Visit USA Association, St Petersburg/Clearwater Area Convention & Visitors' Bureau, Daytona Beach Area Convention & Visitors' Bureau, Winter Park Chamber of Commerce, Alamo Rent A Car, The Kessler Collection Hotels Group, HM Customs and Excise Office.

In person, Margaret Melia (Orlando Tourism Bureau) and Zoe Ward (Icas PR), Nicole Walsh, Louisa French, Jason Lasecki (Walt Disney), Danielle Courtenay, Rick Gregory (Orlando CVB), Larry White, Abby Montpelier and Oonagh McCullagh (Kissimmee CVB), Wit Tuttell (St Petersburg/Clearwater CVB), Susan McLain (Daytona Beach CVB), Carol Williams (Travel City Direct), Michael McLane, Susan Storey, Chris Bielecki (Universal), Kate Burgess (Visit Florida), Sally Hinds (Alamo Rent A Car), Carolyn Fennell (Orlando Aviation Authority), Lynne Koreman (Spirit Airlines), Ron Menke (TransMeridian), David Leake (Quick Transportation), Craig Dorris (Orange County Sheriff's Office), Susan Flower (Discovery Cove), Cara Allen and Jacquelyn Wilson (SeaWorld), Honoria Nadeau and Courtney Ellis (Busch Gardens), Anthea Yabsley (Synergy PR), Suzan Bunn (Seminole County CVB), Laura Richeson (Bennett & Company), Mary Kenny (The Kessler Collection), Treva Marshall (TJM Communications), John Kelman (International Divers), Andrea Farmer (Kennedy Space Center), Steve Specht (Silver Springs), Michael Caires, Greg Dull (Orlando Sanford International Airport), Allan Oakley (Alexander & Associates), Nigel Worrall (Florida Leisure), Bob Mandell (Greater Homes), Christen Svendsen and Bill Cowie (BACC), Wrenda Goodwyn (International Drive/I-Ride), Keith Salwoski (Gaylord Palms Resort), Lori Babb (Renaissance Orlando Resort), Shanon Larimer (Orange County History Center), Jeff Stanford (Orlando Science Center), Michelle Harris (Gatorland), Terry Lynn Morris (Lake Buena Vista Factory Stores), Cindy Turner (Historic Bok Sanctuary), John Stine (Dixie Stampede), Jean Briggs (Arabian Nights), Michelle Valle (Grande Lakes Orlando), Sarah Wilson (Fantasy of Flight), Marcus Lund (Reunion Resort), Fred Zorayq (ResortQuest Orlando), Stormy Washington (Disney's Wide World of Sports), Phillip Jaffe (Pro Golf Guides of Orlando), KT Budde Jones (Warbird Museum), Thom Richard (Warbird Adventures), Rocell Melohn and Sally March (Mall at Millenia), Leigh Jones (Orlando Premium Outlets), Jean Guinup (Chelsea Shopping Group), Margie Long (Boggy Creek Airboats), Rod Wiltshire (Alpha Retail Services), and Naomi Lewis (Virgin Holidays), plus my research team of Susan Haass, Michele Carpenter, Marcia Harris, Michele Plant and travel writer Karen Marchbank.

Big thanks to Pete Werner and all at the DIS – you know who you are!

Got a red-hot Brit Tip to pass on? The latest info on how to beat the queues or the best new restaurant in town? We want to hear from YOU to keep improving the guide each year. Drop us a line at: Brit's Guide (Orlando), W. Foulsham & Co. Ltd, The Publishing House, Bennetts Close, Cippenham, Slough, Berkshire SL1 5AP. Or e-mail simonveness@yahoo.co.uk.

Reader tips from: Kaylee Robbins, Brian Elliott, the Anderson family (Lancashire), Dave and Rita Partridge, Stuart Ainsworth, the Corbet family, Lynda Letchford, Sharone Brown, Mike Webster, Darren Chilcott, John Watt, Mike Lovell and Rose Mason.